Law, Order and the Authoritarian State.

and thanks for
So much support,

Phil xo

1988

Law, Order and the Authoritarian State

Readings in critical criminology

EDITED BY PHIL SCRATON

Open University Press

Milton Keynes· Philadelphia

Open University Press
Open University Educational Enterprises Limited
12 Cofferidge Close
Stony Stratford
Milton Keynes MK11 1BY

and
242 Cherry Street
Philadelphia, PA 19106, USA

First published 1987

Copyright © 1987 The editor and the contributors

All rights reserved. No part of this publication may be reproduced, stored in a
retrieval system or transmitted in any form or by any means, without written
permission from the publisher.

British Library Cataloguing in Publication Data
Law, order and the authoritarian state:
    readings in critical criminology.
    1. Crime and criminals—Great Britain
    I. Scraton, Phil
    364'.941   HV6947

    ISBN 0-335-15511-1
    ISBN 0-335-15510-3 Pbk

Library of Congress Cataloging in Publication Data
Main entry under title:
Law, order and the authoritarian state
    Bibliography: p.
    Includes index
    1. Criminal justice, administration of —Great Britain.
2. Law enforcement—Great Britain.
I. Scraton, Phil.
HV9960.G7L385   1988   364'.941   87-22055

ISBN 0-335-15511-1
ISBN 0-335-15510-3 (pbk.)

Typeset by G.C.S., Leighton Buzzard, Beds.
Printed in Great Britain by St. Edmundsbury Press, Bury St. Edmunds, Suffolk.

Contents

Editor's Preface

In May 1979 a Conservative government was elected in the U.K. which was to have a major impact on the political economy and social conditions throughout the 1980s. For some 'Thatcherism' offered an immediate solution to the disruption of the so-called 'winter of discontent' which preceded the general election. Its roots, however, were well established in the shift towards a free-market economy and greater intervention via the law which had been key characteristics of the Heath government of the early 1970s. The spirit of Thatcherism was born of a conviction that Heath's brand of Conservatism had not been sufficiently tough in dealing with the nation's problems: the 'power of the unions', the 'workshy' and the 'welfare scroungers', the 'immoral', the 'lawless'. These were each products of a post-war welfarism coupled with a decline in moral values. The 'New Right', as it became known, argued that for the entrepreneurial ambition to be released from its strait-jacket the legacy of consensus – both social and economic – had to be laid to rest. Consequently the range of New Right organizations which developed in the mid-1970s and their champion, Margaret Thatcher, successfully hi-jacked the concept of 'freedom', so long the clarion call of parliamentary socialism. The programme adopted by parliamentary conservatism, then, was constructed from a neat dovetail of economic libertarianism, popularly portrayed as monetarism, and social authoritarianism.

Social authoritarianism, as the phrase suggests, relied heavily on regulation via the rule of law. Also it required other pragmatic changes in order to carry through an authoritarian programme. These included massive pay rises for the police and the military; a much-publicized clampdown on welfare fraud and the development of Special Claims Control Units to investigate the 'scroungers'; the introduction of the openly punitive 'short sharp, shock', regime for young offenders; and, eventually, the expansion of British prisons, longer sentences and restricted parole. Together with the attack on welfarism at all levels and the introduction of work-schemes for the unemployed ('long, dull, thud') these initiatives represented collectively a major structural change. Three Employment Acts, the 1983 Prevention of Terrorism Act, the 1984 Police and Criminal Evidence Act and the 1986 Public Order Act consolidated and embodied the Thatcherite programme within the law.

By the mid-1980s the criminalization process was clearly evident from the intense pressure on the courts and the use of prison cells to hold prisoners on remand. In 1985–86 for the first time Britain imprisoned more people per head of population than any other West European country. Political opposition as diverse as the inner-city uprisings of 1980–81 and 1985 and the coal dispute of 1984–5 were portrayed by a predominantly right-wing media and by Tory politicians, with reluctant formal opposition, as proof of the rising tide of crime, violence and lawlessness. Thatcher's military victory in the South Atlantic in 1982, a precursor to the 'Falklands election', was used by Conservative Party Central Office as a clear commitment to a hard line against enemies of the British State. Attention was turned from the 'enemy without' to the 'enemies within'.

The militarization of the police, not only the growth in the use of firearms and consequently in fatal accidents, turned specialist groups such as the Special Patrol Group of the Metropolitan Police from targeting 'high crime' areas to the containment of civil disorder and industrial conflict. Post-Scarman community policing initiatives were run together with paramilitary, hard-line strategies in fulfilment of Commissioner Newman's vision of 'total policing'. Nowhere was this more evident than in the police response to the coal dispute with Police Support Units deployed across force boundaries in a national police operation under a well-prepared and centrally co-ordinated programme of 'mutual aid'. These events were the last act of a long-term battle between chief constables and local police authorities over the political accountability of the police. It was a resounding defeat for local democracy.

In 1979 Stuart Hall gave the Cobden Trust Human Rights Day lecture 'Drifting into a Law and Order Society' in which he mapped the shift towards authoritarianism described above. Despite this significant contribution, a postscript to the theoretical debates of the 1970s, the expansion in the 1980s of critical texts on the state has tended to overlook or underplay the significance of the rule of law and the criminal justice process. The notable exception to this has been the work on Northern Ireland which has concentrated on the relationship between civil rights and civil war within the overall framework of British state interventionism. While not as clear-cut as the Republican–Loyalist conflict the divisions within Britain have become sharpened by a decade of Thatcherite rule. The gap between the unemployed and those in paid work has widened with poverty being both localized within neighbourhoods of larger conurbations and regionally concentrated.

Inevitably black communities have been over-represented in the unemployed population. Racism has not been restricted to work opportunities as there has been a marked increase in racist attacks and a reluctance on the part of the police and government to take seriously the ferocity of racism. Alongside this has been a continual rise in cases of racial harassment and abuse of black people by the police, DHSS officials, prison officers and other state officials which has demonstrated the extent to which racism has become institutionalized within the British state.

During the 1970s significant advances were made in establishing rights of women in Western societies but the Thatcher years have proved to be a backlash period at both institutional and personal levels. There has been a marked increase in violence against women and a clear reluctance on the part of the criminal justice process to take seriously women's suffering. Women who have fought back against their oppression have found little sympathy in the media, from the police or in the courts. The message from successive Conservative governments has been to instruct women back into the family as wives, mothers and carers of the sick and the disabled.

The 1980s, then, have been a period of division and polarization in which the poor, the unemployed, the young, the old, women and black people have become increasingly economically and politically marginalized. Pushed to the edges of mainstream class locations their subjugated positions have been justified by appeals to ideologies of classism, racism and sexism. It has been within this framework that the state has operated to regulate the conflict inherent within the social relations of production and reproduction through the rule of law and the processes of criminal justice.

This collection of papers expands and develops these issues. Some of the contributions have appeared elsewhere in an earlier form while others have been written for *Law, Order and the Authoritarian State*. They have developed out of a collective commitment to critical analysis within criminology which deals with the structural contexts of social interaction and personal experience. By developing research which is rooted in the experiences and struggles of individuals, neighbourhoods and identifiable communities there is an emphasis on establishing the 'view from below'. By dealing with cases and closely monitoring their processing it is possible to arrive at conclusions concerning the operational policies and practices of state institutions. It has been this commitment to the processes by which people have been criminalized and their actions stripped of political meaning which has hall-marked the development and interventionism of critical criminology.

Doing critical research into state institutions which are obsessive over secrecy and obstructive over accountability is a difficult and occasionally threatening project. This book demonstrates that the critical developments within and against academic criminology of the 1970s have persisted and have involved alliances between researchers, academics, campaigners, civil rights workers and victims. While there has been a conscious attempt to integrate the work and reflect our collective concerns there are substantive issues, such as the role of the media, the secret services, welfare policing, and so on, which are not covered here.

The introductory chapter is a collective statement which enlarges on the isues mentioned above, particularly overviewing the interventions of critical criminology since the mid-1970s. Also it provides a thorough critique of the misplaced ideals and realities of the self-styled 'new realist' approach on the left within criminology. Paul Gilroy and Joe Sim provide an extensive historical and contemporary account of the left's response to law and order and Paul Gilroy's short piece on the myth of black criminality raises the issue of the assumptions behind official responses to the inner-city uprisings in the early 1980s. The papers by Paul Gordon and Phil Scraton are complementary analyses of the realities of community-policing strategies and hard-line police responses respectively. Joe Sim provides a critical analysis of the realities of imprisonment in contemporary Britain and the impact of recent changes in sentencing, parole and the prison-building programme. Phil Scraton and Kathryn Chadwick consider one aspect of these developments in terms of deaths in prison and police custody and their handling at inquests.

There are two papers which deal specifically with the relationship between women, the law and the criminal justice process. Kathryn Chadwick and Catherine Little examine the ways in which women's actions and protest have become criminalized. Liz Kelly and Jill Radford analyse the experiences of women who suffer male violence within the structural context of male power. These papers, along with discussions in other papers, stress our collective commitment to the centrality of the feminist critiques of patriarchy, and its institutionalized expression, within critical analysis. Finally, Paddy Hillyard's updated paper emphasizes the significance of Northern Ireland to a critical understanding of the role and function of the British state at its most coercive. For as the inherent structural conflicts within Britain have surfaced and been met with increasing authoritarianism so special powers have been normalized. The parallel with the British state's response to conflict within Ireland is essential. It is also important to consider that conflict as more than a mere footnote to a critical analysis of Britain.

In the preparation, writing and editing of this book I have received support and comment from many people. I have worked closely with the contributors and most of them have visited the Centre for Studies in Crime and Social Policy at Edge Hill to teach on their work. We have all benefited from supportive discussions in those workshops. At the Open University

Press John Skelton has been an informed and active editor who has encouraged and developed a project first commissioned by Stephen Barr. In reading the papers, providing supportive criticism and comradeship Sheila Scraton has been ever-present. Finally, each of the contributors have worked with the people whose cases and experiences form the substance of the analysis within the book. I hope that our work has been a positive contribution to their struggles and serves as a reminder to those who occupy positions of power and authority that interventionist, critical criminology will continue to monitor their policies and practices, their 'administration' of justice and their excesses.

Phil Scraton
April 1987, Merseyside

Notes on Contributors

Kathryn Chadwick is Lecturer in Criminology at Edge Hill College of Higher Education. She coordinates the course 'Sexuality and Gender in State Policy and the Law' on the M.A. in Crime, Deviance and Social Policy. Her research areas include deaths in custody and the imprisonment of women and she is founder member of the North West Women in Prison Group. She has written for *New Socialist* and *The Abolitionist* and is co-author, with Phil Scraton, of *In the Arms of the Law: Coroner's Inquests and Deaths in Custody*, Pluto, 1987.

Paul Gilroy is Senior Lecturer in Sociology at the Polytechnic of the South Bank. He is co-author of *The Empire Strikes Back*, Hutchinson, 1982, and author of *There Ain't No Black in the Union Jack*, Hutchinson, 1987. He has written extensively on racism, particularly in relation to the race-crime debate.

Paul Gordon is Research Officer at the Runnymede Trust. He was a member of the *State Research Group* until its demise in 1982 and he is a Former Research Officer with the Scottish Council for Civil Liberties. He is author of many articles and publications on race and the criminal justice process. His main publications include: *Policing Scotland*, S.C.C.L., 1980; *White Law: Racism in the Police, Courts and Prison*, Pluto, 1983; *Policing Immigration*, Pluto 1985; *Causes for Concern* [co-editor with Phil Scraton] Penguin, 1984; *New Right, New Racism* [co-author with Francesca Klug] Searchlight, 1986.

Paddy Hillyard is Senior Lecturer in Social Administration at the University at Bristol. He has researched and written exclusively on Northern Ireland and on the policing of the 1984–85 Coal Dispute. He is co-author (with Kevin

Boyle and Tom Hadden) of *Law and the State: The Case of Northern Ireland*, Martin Robertson, 1975 and *Ten Years On In Northern Ireland*, Cobden Trust, 1980 and (with Janie Percy-Smith) *The Coercive State*, Fontana (forthcoming).

Liz Kelly lectures in Sociology at the University of Essex and also teaches Adult Education Women's Studies classes. She is a feminist researcher and activist and a founder member of her local refuge for battered women, rape crisis group and women's centre and has been active in a number of national campaigns and networks around sexual violence in Britain. She is still practically involved at the refuge and is working with the Norwich City Council Equal Opportunities Committee on the issue of violence against women. Her current concerns are how to effect policy changes which reflect all women's needs and experience and developing a prevention curriculum for schools which covers all forms of sexual violence. A book based on her doctoral research *Surviving Sexual Violence* will be published by Polity Press, 1987.

Catherine Little teaches sociology and socio-legal studies at Liverpool and Manchester Polytechnics. Her recent research has focused on women and policing which was completed for her M.A. thesis in 1987. She is a feminist activist who works closely with the women's collective at the Manchester Council's Police Monitoring Unit.

Jill Radford has taught Sociology and Criminology at the Open University, the Polytechnic of the South Bank and the University of Keele. She is a feminist and criminologist who is active in the Women's Liberation Movement campaigning and researching around the issue of male sexual violence. Her most recent research is into women and policing in the early twentieth century. She has published widely.

Phil Scraton is Principal Lecturer in Criminology at Edge Hill College of Higher Education where he co-ordinates and teaches on the M.A. in Crime, Deviance and Social Policy. His main research includes: the state's response to Irish Travellers; police accountability; the regulation of welfare claimants; deaths in custody. Formerly a member of the *State Research Group* his publications include: *Causes for Concern* [co-editor with Paul Gordon], Penguin, 1984; *The State v. The People: Lessons from the Coal Dispute* [co-editor with Phil Thomas] Blackwell, 1985; *The State of the Police*, Pluto, 1985 and *In the Arms of the Law* [co-author with Kathryn Chadwick], Pluto, 1987. He lives near Liverpool with Sheila Scraton and their two sons, Paul and Sean.

Joe Sim is Senior Lecturer in Sociology at Liverpool Polytechnic where he has responsibility for teaching Criminology. He is a former member of the *State Research Group* and is a member of the editorial collective of *The Abolitionist*. He is co-author of *Scottish Prisons and the Special Unit* (with Dave McDonald) S.C.C.L., 1978 and of *British Prisons* (with Mike Fitzgerald) Blackwell, 1982. His current research is into medicalization and imprisonment and he is a member of the Independent Inquiry into Peterhead Prison.

1

Introduction: Crime, the State and Critical Analysis

Joe Sim, Phil Scraton and Paul Gordon

1. The Emergence of Contemporary Critical Analysis

> The intellectual's error consists in believing that it is possible to know
> without understanding and especially without feeling and passion...
> that the intellectual can be an intellectual... if he is distinct and detached
> from the people-nation (popolo-nazione) without feeling the elemental
> passions of the people, understanding them and thus explaining and
> justifying them in a particular historical situation, connecting them
> dialectically to the laws of history, to a superior conception of the
> world... History and politics cannot be made without passion, without
> this emotional bond between intellectuals and the people-nation. In the
> absence of such a bond the relations between intellectuals and people-
> nation are reduced to contacts of a purely bureaucratic, formal kind; the
> intellectuals become a caste or a priesthood.[1]

The advancement of western capitalism in the twentieth century, realizing
the inherent, structured logic of capital accumulation and technological
development, presided over the rise of the giant corporation and the
expansion of professional managerialism. The complexity of the corporate
structure of advanced capitalist industry has been matched by the
complexity of the model of corporatism adopted by state institutions. The
political infrastructure provided by advanced capitalist state institutions has
become essential to the management of the structural contradictions and
inequalities inherent in the capitalist mode of production. Just as the state
has required its own corporate managerialist form in order for its fast-

developing agencies to function both at a local and a national level so it has needed specific forms of knowledge. Just as Taylor had provided American industry with programmes of 'Scientific Management' and Henry Ford employed an entire 'Sociological Department' to investigate and regulate his workers so state-monopoly capitalism of the mid-twentieth century has required the application of knowledge to engender stability. For that it turned to 'applied' social sciences.

Within the social sciences there was a measure of opposition to the role played by academics in the postwar industrial-military complex. In the United States the anti-communist fervour engendered by McCarthyism seemingly purged the universities and colleges of radical analysis. C. Wright Mills, whose career undoubtedly suffered by the reaction of 'establishment', sociology to his critical position, argued that 'sociology has lost its reforming push; its tendencies towards fragmentary problems and scattered causation have been conservatively turned to the use of the corporation, army and the state'.[2] With the techniques and resources made available to the social sciences effectively harnessed by the powerful political-economic institutions of advanced capitalism the critical potential of disciplines which 'managed' social problems and political conflict – such as criminology – was muted. The challenge to this silence came gradually from the frustration of students eager to seek answers to the growing conflicts around poverty, racism, sexism, Vietnam, South Africa and the 'imperialism' of multinational economies. It also came from within the social sciences typified by Alvin Gouldner's extensive and diverse critique of the sociological tradition.[3] As with Becker,[4] Lemert,[5] Matza[6] and others involved in the mid-1960s challenge to the criminological traditions, Gouldner directed his attack against the conservatism inherent in the dominant structural–functionalist paradigm. Further, he was impatient with the reduction of social action to the micro-world by the newly established and intellectually fashionable advances of phenomenology and ethnomethodology. Against these positions he pursued the 'rational and liberative' potential that had been central to much of the work in early social sciences.

The general response to Gouldner's work was fierce and bitter on a personal level,[7] but some authors attempted to respond to and develop his critique. Becker and Horowitz argued that social scientists 'have undertaken research designed to further the interests of the powerful at the expense of the powerless'.[8] Their vision was of the social scientist paid by the problem-solving agencies of the state or industry to make oppression 'more efficient' and to legitimate the dynamics and realities of inequality to a 'wider constituency' through theoretical justifications. As Blackburn[9] had argued earlier, the academic tradition within the social sciences, 'constructs theories of the family, of bureaucracy, of social revolution, of "pluralist" democracy, all of which imply that existing social institutions cannot be transcended'. For him the social sciences were concerned with either the 'consecration' of the social order or the running of it. This was a line picked up and developed by Shaw[10] in his claim that there existed 'indissoluble practical [and theoretical] bonds between the social sciences and the very material structure of modern society'.

Shaw's work traced the historical connections between industry, the military and the state and the construction of 'useful' knowledge within social sciences. He argued that the basic functions of physical repression and military organization were extended by the social regulation and control contained within the reformism of applied social research. The role of the state primarily was the creation of stable social and political conditions in which a compliant and organized workforce could be formed, developed and, inevitably, controlled. The connection to academic work was clear for Shaw:

> The state develops a host of agencies concerned with mass education, welfare, social security, broadcasting, etc. – and with the growth of such agencies grows the need for research to assist such functioning.[11]

While much of this analysis trod the thin line of instrumentalism (that is, that state agencies and their interventions were reducible solely to the demands of capitalism) its contribution was to challenge the assertions of value – freedom, neutrality and objectivity – behind which the politics of applied social sciences had been hidden. In a speech to the American Sociological Association Nicolaus[12] hammered this point. For him the professional organization of sociology was a 'branch' of established political power: 'grafted seamlessly, with contractual cement, to the civil, economic, and military sovereignty which constitutes the trunk'. From this central position it transmitted 'authoritative views on matters of social reality' throughout institutions of mass education and to the aid of the industrial, civil and military authorities. The social sciences had become a 'source of legitimation' for repression providing advanced states within western capitalism with a 'laboratory of refinements'. Nicolaus's analysis was a contemptuous, burning indictment of the American Sociological Association (he referred to its members as the 'house-servants of civil, military and economic sovereignty'). It was a professional organization servile to the demands of US imperialism abroad and US welfare and criminal justice strategy in the policing or class, race and gender confrontations at home.

The significance of these critiques of academic social sciences was that they turned attention to the work and utility of applied social research. Much of this work was based on the structural–functionalist assumption that 'crime', 'deviance' and 'conflict' were aberrations in an otherwise efficient, fair and just social system. In that scenario the 'corrective' or rehabilitative function of applied social sciences, particularly criminological or deviancy analyses, was a perfectly legitimate academic, interventionist function. What the critics of academic social sciences argued, however, was that the social and political conflicts which had emerged with such force throughout Western Europe, the USA and Japan were not aberrations but were structural features inherent within the contradictions of advanced capitalist economies. Further they argued, along with Poulantzas,[13] that once the 'soft-cop' policing and regulation provided by social research and social welfare programmes failed to contain passive social unrest and its occasional outbreaks of 'militancy', the criminologists, researchers,welfare and social workers would be replaced by more direct, physical forms of state control. While it is important to recognize that the institutionalization of social sciences 'has not been accompanied by the emergence of consensus within the disciplines', the structural forces and constraints imposed by career hierarchies, research awards and professional bodies have limited significantly the effectiveness of radical progressive developments within the social sciences. Undoubtedly there has been some negotiable space within academic institutions for the development of critical analysis but Gouldner's later work reminded his critics of his original intention in his critique of western sociology:

> that modern academic sociology, directly implicated as it is in the Welfare–Warfare state as consultants, contractors and client–recipients and indirectly through the university as a training/channelling system, and saturated by theories stressing the importance of social order and morality, that this sociology's dominant ideological character is predominantly conservative.

For Gouldner the social scientist was forced to seek reformist solutions to structural contradictions within the parameters of welfare capitalism. At the same time he recognized that the researcher remains 'exposed' to the failures of the state, its agencies and reformist policies in coping with 'social problems' and this process conscientizes the researcher to the 'suffering engendered by such failures'. Gouldner was committed to rescuing the 'rational and liberative kernel' of applied social science from the total rejection of others who had 'over-ideologized academic sociology' and 'under-ideologized marxism'. In his introduction to *The New Criminology* in 1973 he pursued this line:

> What becomes increasingly necessary is a theoretical position that accepts the reality or deviance, that has the capacity to explore the Lebenswelt, without becoming the technician of the welfare State and its zoo keepers of deviance... that can rescue the liberative dimension in both Marxism and Meadianism... [that] work toward a larger theoretical construction without patronizing the concrete and smaller worlds, without using them simply as 'examples' or 'points of departure'.[15]

It was in this academic debate, rooted in the wider political, economic and social conflicts of advanced capitalist expansion and growth, that the radical challenge within criminology emerged and consolidated.

This move towards critical analysis within the social sciences recognized implicitly a set of related propositions. First, that the claims of social scientists to have established value-free, 'objective' and 'scientific' disciplines independent of each other and of the constraints of the structural relations of the political economy were based on theoretical and political assumptions which were seriously flawed. Second, that applied social sciences by the very contexts of their application were part of, rather than apart from, historical, political and social developments. Third, that the emphases and methodologies of applied work must be interpreted and understood within the context of the economic, political and social conflicts of the time. Thus criminology, with its high-profile interventions around crime, social problems and deviance, could no longer be understood as an enterprise with 'the human condition' but had to be located within the structural and social processes which so defined 'crime' or created poverty and deprivation. The emphasis of the critical approach was to analyse the contexts of social action and reaction rather than to persist with the traditional obsession of causation. This objective, balancing the lived experiences of people and the immediate social contexts of daily interaction with the often less visible structural arrangements – the political, economic and ideological managements of daily life – set the radical agenda for the development of critical analysis within criminology.

It was an agenda which was to be extended in the 1970s as the feminist critique exposed the patriarchal assumptions not only in traditional criminology but also in its radical or progressive critiques. For it was Gouldner who had commented that 'like other men sociologists also have sex lives'.[16] The work of women such as Dorothy Smith and Dale Spender demonstrated sharply that the social relations of reproduction and the political economy of patriarchy had produced not only the material dependency of women on men but also had legitimized and enshrined 'male knowledge' as '*the* knowledge'. If the new version of criminology was to read any differently than its predecessors then it had to consider all structural forms of oppression within western societies: capitalism, patriarchy and neo-colonialism.

In 1981, *Crime and Society Readings in History and Theory* was published[17] to accompany the new Open University course, '*Issues in Crimes and Society*'. In this reader there were two articles especially written for the course which attempted to contextualize and evaluate the state of contemporary criminology in Britain. The first, written by Stan Cohen,[18] provided an insightful and insider's overview of the discipline until the end of the 1970s. Cohen reflecting and pursuing the critical analysis discussed above, argued that social scientific theory, the knowledge generated and its development and 'utility' take place not solely within the heads and minds of individual social scientists 'but within particular institutional domains'.[19] He sought to identify what he described as 'the delicate question of the relationship between knowledge and power' by pointing out that the institutional domains within which criminologists work are shaped by their surroundings. In the following statement there is much in common with the critiques of sociology mounted by Gouldner, Nicolaus, Shaw and others:

how academic institutions are organized, how disciplines are divided and sub-
divided, how disputes emerge, how research is funded and how findings are
published and used. In criminology, an understanding of these institutional
domains is especially important for knowledge is situated not just, or not even
primarily, in the 'pure' academic world but in the applied domains of the state's
crime control apparatus.[20]

From this starting point, Cohen described the various developments in
criminology from the end of the 1960s. In particular, he identified the
genesis and growth of the National Deviancy Conference (NDC), formed to
provide a radical critique of the theoretical and methodological underpinnings of mainstream positivist criminology and to establish connections
with new academic territories such as cultural studies, law and social policy.
Each of these areas had been directly or indirectly influenced by the work of
the new deviancy theorists. He ended his overview by raising a central
question, and one to which we shall return below, namely the relationship
between theoretical developments and policy innovations. There is little
doubt, he concluded, that 'the global fall-out from the last decade's ideas
have profoundly influenced the ways in which middle level control and
welfare institutions are being conceptualized. Whether this has, or will,
change their practice is another story'.[21]

In the second article Stuart Hall and Phil Scraton[22] traced the emergence
and consolidation of critical criminology and the subsequent fragmentation
of the critical paradigm into different and often hostile schools of thought.
Propelled, as we have described, by the major political upheavals and
confrontations that spread through the western world in the late 1960s, and
the fracturing of the mainstream paradigms in sociology itself, critical
criminology emerged as a radical response to both these wider political and
narrower academic schisms.

> In the political ferment of the 1960s, the dominant pluralist and structural–
> functional paradigms disintegrated and the sociological fraternity abandoned
> theoretical and methodological orthodoxy. Social scientists confronting this
> disintegration of their theoretical universe had finally to face what Alvin
> Gouldner defined as 'the coming crisis in western sociology'.... The weight of
> his critique ... rested on the role, position and consciousness of the social
> investigator. Social scientists could not abstract themselves from the
> conditions in which they worked. His critique bore down especially sharply on
> criminologists. Helping to operate programmes of social control, without
> questioning wider objectives they had made themselves into 'technicians of
> the welfare state'.[23]

Critical criminology's theoretical objectives, as exemplified by the NDC,
converged with radical political practice and 'took up a "politics of support"
for outsider groups – drug-users, prisoners, gypsies, welfare claimants,
homosexuals'.[24] A flavour of this perspective can be gleaned from the
collection of papers produced from two early NDC conferences under the
generic titles of *Images of Deviance*[25] and *Politics and Deviance*.[26] This conver-

gence, however, achieved its apotheosis in 1973 with the publication of *The New Criminology*.[27] It was a book which attempted to develop a 'fully social theory of deviance' by demonstrating the theoretical links between law, the state, legal and political relations, and the economic basis and functions of crime'.

> The most difficult set of problems confronting 'critical criminology' in the wake of the publications and reception of *The New Criminology* was how to conceptualize the relations between the law, crime and other processes in society. This problem arose from the principal domain assumptions of critical theory: the study of law and crime cannot be separated from the political, social and economic structures and relationship of society.[28]

Two things linked the Cohen and Hall–Scraton articles. First, because of when they were written, both pieces conclude their analyses at the end of the 1970s. Consequently, while they provided important background material concerning the development of radical criminology, the major criminological debates which have taken place in the harsh economic context of the 1980s are missing. In particular, the fragmentation of the radical paradigm in the 1970s had, by the mid-1980s, became concentrated still further around two opposing schools of criminological thought, inadequately and simplistically described as 'left idealism' and 'left realism'. We shall consider the nature, politics and implications of this debate later.

Second, both articles refer to, but do not develop substantively, the question of the interventions made by radical academics from the late 1960s onwards. For Stan Cohen such interventionism was important but he doubted 'whether many direct lines of influence can be traced. This is not to say that some key ideas have just percolated through and informed important institutional changes'.[29] Cohen's point is an important one. It raises a whole series of questions not only about the kind of interventions that were made, how these were theorized and how reforms were conceptualized, but also about the impact that they had in terms of confronting the state in particular and influencing the thrust of social policy in general. It is to the nature, extent and impact of these interventions that we now turn.

2. The Politics of Interventionism: Criminology from Below

Those who have regarded themselves as social scientists, sociologists and criminologists have long sought to make interventions into public debates about, and social policies on, a wide range of political issues. Such interventions, contrary to public belief, have not been carried out on behalf of the powerless. On the contrary, and as we discussed earlier, the history of social science has been, in the main, profoundly conservative. As Antonio Gramsci has pointed out, the rise of sociology, basing its methodology on the natural sciences, resulted in a theoretical tradition which limited the

scope and depth of the questions to be asked about society in general and the
state in particular:

> The rise of sociology is related to the decline of the concept of political science
> and the art of politics which took place in the nineteenth century, to be more
> accurate in the second half of that century with the success of evolutionary
> and positivist theories... 'Politics' becomes synonymous with parliamentary
> politics or the politics of personal cliques... And, lo and behold, society can
> now be studied with the methods of the natural sciences. Impoverishment of
> the concept of the state ensued from such views.[30]

The sub-discipline of criminology has followed a path. Both in its
theoretical orientation and its methodology, the questions asked and the
policies suggested have been equally circumspect in their concerns. This
criminological circumspection was crystallized around the attempt to find
the 'golden fleece' of criminology – the cause of crime – suggesting reforms
which improve the operational effectiveness of the criminal justice system
or supporting policies for reforming particular aspects of local environ-
ments which are believed to propel individuals into criminality. Either way,
structures of power, domination and control was left unresearched and
untouched. David Garland's recent history of the rise of criminology
demonstrates that when Cesare Lombroso, the so-called 'founding father'
of criminology, published *L'Uomo Delinquente* in 1876, purporting to show
the causes of crime, there was an immediate proliferation in criminological
works which within twenty years had 'become an explosion of interest in
the criminological enterprise'.[31] This in turn

> led to the publication of hundreds of texts, the formation of dozens of national
> and international congresses, conferences and associations and the assembly
> of an international social movement which pressed the claims of criminology
> upon the legislatures and penal institutions of virtually every Western
> nation.[32]

For his part, Lombroso was quite clear about the relationship between
criminology, structures of power and the social order. As he was to write in
a later work:

> nothing is more imprudent than to try to maintain theories... if they are
> going to upset the order of society... The sociologist must observe still
> greater circumspection, for if he puts into operation innovations of an
> upsetting nature he will simply succeed in demonstrating the uselessness and
> inefficiency of his science.[33]

It is important to note that not only did Lombroso give apparent scientific
support to 'current myths about the criminal', but also that 'the myths
found their way routinely into mass culture'.[34]

After the First World War, the interventions made by sociologists based
at the University of Chicago were, as Downes and Rock have argued, 'the
fruit of a carefully resolved philosophy thought and action, a philosophy

which emphasized the primacy of practice'.[35] As they point out, the Chicago School was very clear about what constituted a social problem, how it was to be defined and importantly, given the debates about criminal areas in the 1980s (see Gilroy and Sim in Chapter 2), where crime was located:

> Chicago sociology was a major co-operative enterprise which launched an intellectual assault of the study of the city. Part of that assault was occupied with social problems and social problems were typically confined to particular districts. The explanation of crime and deviance centred on the peculiar conditions of the zone in transition, a turbulent area which appeared to be out of joint with the rest of the city.[36]

By the 1950s, the dominant paradigm in sociology – indeed, throughout the social sciences – was structural–functionalism. Its central assumption was that society was an integrated, functioning whole, underpinned by a set of common values to which the great majority subscribed. The white, Anglo-Saxon, protestant mentality and ideology of this paradigm necessarily had as its converse the view that crime and deviance were aberrations, usually of an individual kind, in an otherwise smooth-running and benevolent system. It is no coincidence that many of the interventions which took place at this historical moment – the lobotomy being the classic example – were designed to obliterate criminal or deviant tendencies within individuals. As Conrad and Schneider indicate, two American surgeons, inspired by earlier work on chimpanzees, 'developed the technique of cutting the frontal lobes of the brain by inserting an icepick-like surgical instrument through the eye-socket'. Between 1935 and the early 1950s more than 50,000 people experienced psychosurgery of this kind. In short, they had been subjected to, 'irreversible destructive brain lesions to relieve symptoms thought to be associated with mental illness'.[38] Thus the submerged world of Big Nurse, Chief Bromden, Billy Bibbit and Randle McMurphy, brilliantly and poignantly evoked by Ken Kesey in *One Flew Over the Cuckoo's Nest*, was a reality for many people, usually the poor, caught up in the talons of institutional programmes whose theoretical purpose, professional training and organizational practice were geared to managing and controlling individual deviant propensities. Those who 'malfunctioned' would therefore be 'repaired' in places where

> a guy has to learn to get along in a group before he'll be able to function in a normal society; how the group can help the guy by showing him where he's out of place; how society is what decides who's sane and who isn't so you get to measure up.[39]

The supercession of the structural–functionalist paradigm in the 1960s, first by labelling theory and, subsequently, by critical theory ushered in not only radical and Marxist theoretical perspectives but also a new wave of criminologists committed both to making links with those who stood outside of the law and also to providing a rigorous theoretical analysis of the relationship between law, political economy and the state under advanced capitalism. Thus the politics of interventionism was placed on the 'academic' agenda. It was an interventionism with real commitment to the powerless in the context of an unjust and inequitable social order. The development of radical criminology, however, did not neutralize traditional positivist criminology. Today, the search for the 'cause of crime' persists. Researchers working within a positivist perspective continue to obtain research grants, teach in colleges and universities, and contribute to academic and popular forums. As recently as July 1986, for example, BBC Radio 4 broadcast a 30-minute programme on the biological basis of violent criminality. A supporting article, 'Inside the criminal brain', appeared in *The Listener* magazine on 24 July.[40] The article quoted, among others, the theories of Dr Sarnoff Mednick, who suggested 'that a large number of criminals are pushed into their lifestyle by virtue of their biological make-up'.

In presenting an alternative account to individualistic biological arguments radical criminology has not replaced them or their proponents. Both paradigms, their domain assumptions and their various sub-schools, still coexist uneasily. Yet through programmes of research, conferences, papers, pamphlets and books radical criminologists have provided a sustained and, in the main, rigorous challenge to these more traditional accounts. At the same time, a number of other issues which have profound political and tactical implications have become apparent. Of these two are particularly crucial. First, there is the question of reform: how it can be achieved and the limits of its achievements within a capitalist social structure. Second, there is the question of alliances with groups which do not support the accepted machinery of initiating change, either via the ballot box at 5-yearly intervals or through the often patronizing and deeply patriarchal parliamentary system.

The interventions made by radical criminologists from the late 1960s onwards covered a range of substantive areas. What linked them was a commitment to demystifying and exposing the workings of state power in its institutional forms through the police, courts and prisons in particular. Tactically those involved attempted to influence public debates about criminal justice issues by writing for and publishing in more popular journals and newspapers rather than in traditional academic forums such as the forensically based *British Journal of Criminology*. Also they made the results of their research available to different pressure groups while simultaneously, through the research, they challenged both state accounts and the more conservative and liberal criminological explanations about the nature of crime and punishment.

2.i Prisons of the State
In the early 1970s, a central focus of these interventions was the prison system. Up to that point in time, the prisons (apart from some very powerful autobiographical accounts) had remained the exclusive preserve

of the state and its conservative and liberal social scientists who, faced with a captive population, probed and prodded the heads and bodies of prisoners for the roots of their criminality or sought their reform through rehabilitation programmes. In 1972 there was fundamental challenge to that cosy academic and political relationship: Stan Cohen and Laurie Taylor published *Psychological Survival*.[41] The book provided a graphic account of the lives of a group of long-term male prisoners in Durham prison's E Wing whom Cohen and Taylor had met as teachers. The loneliness, solitude and pain for the long-termer were illustrated as the authors utilized their qualitative teaching experiences together with material gathered from interviews with over a hundred other long-termers. Crucially, Cohen and Taylor raised some critical questions about penal policy for long-termers in England and Wales. At the same time, and precisely because of this, they were confronted by an openly hostile Home Office Prison Department, which through a series of meetings and Kafka-esque twists and turns attempted to sabotage their whole project.[42]

This episode itself makes interesting reading, for the acceptability of criminology up to that point in time rested on its ability to stay within predefined limits. If criminologists were prepared to kiss the state then their research would be regarded as legitimate and 'scientific'. This was especially applicable to prison research. As Cohen and Taylor pointed out:

> The Home Office, and particularly the Prison Department, has used its obvious and legitimate identification with corrected aims to develop a highly circumscribed system for deciding what constitutes proper research. Either by carrying out its own research – through such bodies as the Home Office Research Unit – or simply by using it definitions of proper research to exclude outsiders, it has created a virtual monopoly of research on its own workings.[43]

In the end they abandoned their research. To have continued, they believed, would have given tacit support for the research policy of the Home Office. It was a policy which they considered to be 'a serious impediment to independent sociological inquiry'.[44] Cohen and Taylor's intervention, however, provided an important impetus to critical research on the prisons. It was an impetus which was consolidated in May 1972 when the pressure group, Preservation of the Rights of Prisoners (PROP), was founded. The organization was formed to, 'preserve, protect and to extend the rights of prisoners and ex-prisoners and to assist in their rehabilitation and re-integration into society, so as to bring about a reduction in crime'.[45] Initially, PROP issued 26 demands to extend the rights of prisoners and in the summer of 1972 helped to organize demonstrations at over one hundred prisons throughout Britain. Again there was academic involvement, principally through Mike Fitzgerald who was the organization's Publicity Officer. In 1977 Fitzgerald's book, *Prisoners in Revolt*, detailed the history and development of PROP's early years and the connection he saw between academics and the incarcerated:

it is essential to recognise that prisoners understand their own situation, and are aware where their best interests lie even though they are largely hidden behind walls and bars. Whilst acknowledging the important role that academics, penal reformists and other lay people involved might play in the administration of British justice, PROP was first and foremost an organisation of prisoners and ex-prisoners. To this end, full membership of the group including voting rights was opened only to people who are, or had been incarcerated.[46]

While Fitzgerald catalogued the problems surrounding the continuance of PROP through the mid-1970s, especially those of finance and personnel, the organization continued to work to provide a voice for those behind the walls. In May 1977 it held a four-day public inquiry into the Hull prison demonstration which had taken place in September 1976. In the aftermath of the demonstration information arrived from prisons throughout the country that prisoners had been subjected to a catalogue of abuse and brutality by prison officers.

PROP's public inquiry was important for two reasons. First, it went much further than the Home Office inquiry which stopped at the point when the prisoners came down from the prison roof. It was at this point that the violence of the prison officers began. In that sense, the inquiry provided an alternative and challenging account to the state's own internal version of events. Second, the inquiry was a forum for prisoners to provide their own accounts of what had happened. Together, they formed a devastating indictment of uncontrolled state violence:

Saturday morning, we were taken one at a time for breakfast and most prisoners punched or kicked by the screws lining the landings. Breakfast was either thrown at you or you had your breakfast rubbed into your face. I saw Michael King with blood streaming down his face. He shouted out of his window that the screws had kicked the shit out of him. Joe Duffy had large bruises on his face. Bailey a black prisoner next door to me was beaten in his cell, they came to my door but left when they saw me holding a piece of glass from the broken window. Guy Chatterton was being manhandled at his cell door across the wing from mine. Later, they came back to Bailey's cell for further 'fun'. The night before [Friday] they had gone into Peter Rajah's cell and beaten him, he was also black. He was in a cell below me but I could hear him screaming and the screws with their racial abuse, 'This is what we do to niggers', and 'National Front rule, O.K. nigger'.

Nigel Simmons and Mick Russell [another black man] were beaten and I also saw screws attempting to punch C. Beaumont. Jake Prescott was beaten up for shouting at the screws who were beating the Irish prisoners. These Irish prisoners were made a special case, they were forced onto hands and knees and told to sing 'God Save the Queen' and beaten for refusing. Intimidations continued for weeks in one form or another.[47]

Eventually, at the end of 1978, more than two years after the event, eight prison officers were found guilty of charges arising out of what had happened after the demonstration. They were given suspended prison sentences.

On 31 August 1979, 54 prisoners were injured when a riot-trained group of prison officers known as the Minimum Use of Force Tactical Intervention Squad (MUFTI) broke up a peaceful demonstration in D Wing at Wormwood Scrubs. On 1 September the Prison Department denied that anyone had been injured but on 10 September they admitted that five prisoners had been hurt. On 27 September PROP held a press conference which alleged that about 60 prisoners had been hurt, many with head injuries requiring stitching, and demanded an independent public inquiry. The following day, nearly all of the national press carried the story which led the department to admit that 53 prisoners had been injured. Finally, in a Parliamentary Answer on 21 October, the Home Secretary stated that 54 prisoners and 11 prison officers had incurred injuries consisting of cuts, bruises and abrasions.[48]

Thus the 1970s ended the way they began with PROP publishing detailed and accurate accounts of confrontations in British prisons. In 1973 it had published *Who Guards the Guards*,[49] Brian Stratton's chronicle of the violent events leading up to and following the Parkhurst disturbance in 1969, in 1976 there had been the violence at Hull, and in 1979 the Wormwood Scrubs incident. Between these major confrontations PROP's everyday activities revolved around collating and disseminating information on a range of issues around the prisons and providing support for the collective and individual actions taken by prisoners. The organization also mounted a number of campaigns, including the successful 1974 campaign against the infamous Control Units which were introduced in complete secrecy and were designed to break the spirit of prisoners regarded as subversive by keeping them for extended periods in conditions that amounted to virtual sensory deprivation. The campaign was supported by the publication of Mike Fitzgerald's *Control Units and the Shape of Things to Come*.[50]

Working alongside PROP in this and other campaigns was a second radical pressure group, Radical Alternatives to Prison (RAP). RAP was founded in 1970 and was influenced by the changes which were taking place in sociological theory which we discussed above, particularly the development of critical or Marxist approaches to the study of crime. At the same time, the organization's practice was determined by this critical perspective which meant that the questions it raised, and the answers it supplied about the state of the prisons, were different in political orientation to those of more traditional prison reform groups. As Mick Ryan, an academic member of the group, has explained:

Much of RAP's literature came to reflect these new perspectives, though its radical message varied in emphasis, sophistication and intensity. This is not to say that all its members were committed radical pluralists or Marxists. Indeed, it is arguable that many of them were not, that they were driven on by

'humanitarian' rather than overtly political concerns. However, their willingness to go along with a critical approach towards the criminal law, to view that
penal system in a much wider social context, inevitably led them into 'politics'.
It was just this progression which most other groups in the penal lobby,
notably NACRO and the Howard League, were keen to avoid, and it is this
which helps to divide them from RAP and explains the many tensions which
still exist between them. Thus, while RAP does not criticise NACRO's very
practical emphasis or question the Howard League's humanitarian principles,
to the extent that neither group is prepared to push the argument wider to
question the power structure of society, then the argument resolutely works
in the interests of the powerful.[51]

Ryan argued that RAP's contribution to the penal lobby in the early 1970s
was considerable.

> At that time when the rehabilitative ideal was beginning to falter, RAP's
> unambiguous message – its conviction that prison could not rehabilitate and
> therefore must be abolished and alternatives devised – helped to polarise
> opinion and force groups like the Howard League to re-think their commit-
> ment to prison and prison reform.[52]

In 1979 RAP's journal, *The Abolitionist*, was founded. It was designed to
provide a focus for the discussions and dissemination of ideas around prison
issues. Latterly it has widened its scope and now contains sections written
by different pressure groups. One of these is Inquest which was founded in
1980 by academics, friends and families of individuals who had died
suddenly, violently or inexplicably in police and prison custody. Since its
foundation members of the organization have:

> supported each other at pickets, at police stations and coroners' courts and
> spoken in solidarity at each other's meetings. The campaign held regular
> meetings and annually elected a committee to carry out policy decisions and
> co-ordinate activities. In 1982 Inquest applied to the GLC for funds to employ
> two workers to set up an office information centre and support team for the
> groups and campaigns. The Inquest office functions today with an ever-
> increasing workload. Attending the inquests of people who have died as a
> result of police activity in London, however directly or indirectly, supporting
> families and helping fund legal representation for inquests as well as
> campaigning for changes in the laws which govern inquests has proved
> time-consuming.[52]

In developing Inquest as a campaigning group the members have, by their
research and a wide range of publications,[54] forced into the public arena an
issue which hitherto has been neglected by academics and by the left in
general. The cases which have emerged have raised serious questions about
the nature and extent of institutionalized state violence towards confined
individuals. At the same time, they have made clear the lack of redress
afforded to relatives both because of the unsatisfactory and largely
unaccountable practices of the coroners' courts and because it is has proved

impossible to obtain even the most basic information about how their relative or friend died. Inquest's activists have challenged such state practices by helping sponsor a number of legislative changes (Administration of Justice Act 1982, The Coroner's Juries Act 1983); by demanding further reforms to the system such as legal aid to the relatives of the deceased, and by continuing to conduct research on and speak for those who because of their ascribed status as criminal or deviant have been denied legitimacy as human beings even in death.[55]

Besides PROP, RAP and Inquest, *The Abolitionist* provides space for a fourth pressure group in the form of Women in Prison. The question of women in prison had been raised sporadically by RAP since the early 1970s. In 1971 the organization had taken part in the campaign against the rebuilding of Holloway. In 1972, it had published *Alternatives to Holloway*. From that time, particularly with the publication of *The Abolitionist*, the position of women in prison had been raised in a series of articles.[56] However, it was only with the formation of Women in Prison (WIP) in 1983, that a concerted and systematic campaign developed. As their manifesto pointed out, 'during the last decade the number of British women prisoners has increased by 65 per cent'.[57] At the same time, the deprivations, indignities and violations which women prisoners underwent had to be set in the context of the sexist and racist discriminatory practices both of the criminal justice process and the wider society. The group was quite clear in its demands:

> Women in Prison ... seeks to unite women of all classes, ethnic backgrounds and sexual orientations in a campaign which whilst highlighting and attempting to redress the injustices presently suffered by Britain's hitherto neglected women prisoners will also campaign for democratic control of the criminal justice and penal system.[58]

These demands have again been supported by the work of academics, in this case by Pat Carlen working from the University of Keele. In 1983 Carlen's book *Women's Imprisonment: A Study in Social Control*[59] was published. The book was the first radical analysis of the state of women's imprisonment in the United Kingdom. In 1985 she and a number of ex-prisoners co-edited *Criminal Women*.[60] Both books powerfully describe the experiences of women in prison while simultaneously situating these experiences in a wider, political framework. As the Introduction to *Criminal Women* pointed out:

> These stories of criminal women are vivid chronicles of the times in which they lived. In presenting these chronicles we hope that they will not only destroy the mythology that inseminates contemporary stereotypes of criminal women, we hope also that they will contribute to the greater understanding of the complex and diverse responses which women can make when faced with the social disabilities imposed upon them by a class-riven and still deeply sexist society.[61]

The interventions by WIP since 1983, and the development of similar groups elsewhere, have been very important in focusing both political and public attention on imprisoned women. The media attention given to the appalling conditions in Holloway's C Wing in 1984 and 1985, and the screams of protest by the prisoners through self-mutilation, head-banging and suicide, would not have been possible or heard without the group's work. The publication in 1986 of a 225-page report from the GLC's Women's Committee on women in prison also had a strong input from the group.[62] The committee commissioned the report in order to redress the neglect in research

> specifically into women in prison, particularly Black women in prison. The women inside prison are becoming the most invisible, isolated and disadvantaged. The conditions of women in prison, the lack of accountability of the Home Office in relation to prisons and the secrecy surrounding prisons is a matter of grave concern.... The report... sets out nearly 200 recommendations. Some put forward radical changes, while others amount to minimal reforms based on basic human rights and the mere implementation of the law as it stands.[63]

While PROP, RAP and Inquest stand outside the sexist organization and bureaucratic formalism of mainstream parliamentary politics, they and WIP gave evidence to the House of Commons Social Services Committee in 1986. The Committee's report called for the abolition and complete replacement of Holloway's C Wing.[64]

In Scotland, similar interventions were being made by academics in the 1970s into the prisons debate. These interventions were initially spurred by a research project at the University of Stirling which began in August 1975. Until that point in time even less was known about the situation in Scotland, in comparison to the rest of Britain. At the same time, the prison authorities in 1966 had contrived to open the segregation unit at Inverness prison which became popularly known as 'The Cages'. The brutalization of long-term prisoners in this unit, the roof-top protests at Peterhead in 1972, the riot at the Cages in December 1972, and the opening of the Barlinnie Special Unit in February 1973, served as the context for the research project at Stirling. Within a year, academics from the project were making interventions via the media, especially concerning the conditions at Peterhead and in defence of the Barlinnie Unit which was under attack for being 'too liberal' in its regime. In November 1978 the Scottish Council for Civil Liberties organized a conference on Scottish penal policy which was attended by over two hundred people and at which it launched the first critical publication on Scottish prisons.[65] This was written by two members of the Stirling research team. In making these interventions those involved were committed to using the knowledge that they had gained first-hand from spending a year in the prisons by virtue of their academic position, to raising a series of critical questions about the nature and direction of penal policy in Scotland. Additionally, that knowledge was also utilized in a number of other critical criminological texts,[66] in disseminating informa-tion to groups such as the Scottish Council for Civil Liberties and in helping to prepare cases for individual prisoners to go to the European Commission on Human Rights. It laid the foundation for further work such as the exposure of conditions at the Glenochil Youth Custody Complex where there were eight suicides between 1984 and 1986[67] and for the taking up of cases by independent organizations such as the Gateway Exchange in Edinburgh.[68]

This research, in conjunction with the other projects outlined above, was quite explicit in its political and academic orientations. It fell under the more general rubric of what Thomas Mathiesen called 'action research'. Such research

> constitutes a conscious attempt to combine activities which researchers have traditionally tried to keep separate, a combination which has often been met by cries of anger. In this respect, action research is a follow-up of an insight which became common-place a few years ago, namely that research – at least in its consequences – cannot be value free. In action research we try to combine the disclosure of information with a conscious attempt to realise given practical or political values – the latter values being primary.[69]

It is important to consider the impact of the interventions discussed above in the realm of penal politics. Clearly these interventions were underpinned by wider philosophical and political questions concerning the nature of reform and how reforms could be implemented with regard to advanced capitalist social and state institutions. Mathiesen further argued that radical criminologists should engage in developing what he termed 'negative reforms'; that is, those that chip away at the system with a view to its eventual abolition. This he contrasted with 'positive reforms' which in the end are those incorporated into the system and, ultimately, which help to consolidate it. Indeed, as Stan Cohen pointed out, reformist politics not only faced the danger of co-option but by arguing for positive reforms criminologists were allowing society 'to present itself as more just and legitimate than it is'.[70] This distinction became very important for those criminologists engaged in the prisons debate and their efforts to avoid co-option into the system. In addition, others developed a more humanistic concern and awareness which centred on the suffering and brutalization experienced by individuals inside. This was a dimension which sociology in general was still ignoring in the face of theoretical point scoring. Thus the call, among other things, for better conditions, visiting facilities, the end to official secrecy and legal representation, tied to the final goal of the abolition of prisons, attempted to deal with these problems of reform while simultaneously making demands on the state that would have to be taken seriously. This is not to say that there were no disagreements over policy, or between individuals and groups, or that every tactic or strategy employed was successful. From the perspective of 1987 that would be patently incorrect. Under Thatcherism the new prison building programme, the increasing length of sentences, the record prison population (see Sim in Chapter 6) and the fragmentation of the prisoner's movement itself make it clear that the structure of power in prisons and in the state remains intact with the institutional centres of power consolidating their strength. At the same time, we should not fall into the politically pessimistic trap of feeling that nothing has been achieved in the last 15 years. This position has been taken, for example, by the editors of the influential criminology textbook *The Power to Punish*.[71] In their introductory article David Garland and Peter Young argue that in relation to the radicalization of criminology:

> The penal complex operates just as it did before without regard to this movement. In other words, the 'progress' made by radical criminology was never played back into an account of the actual nature of the penal system – except in broad generalities – nor into changing penal policy. Questions of penal policy remained the property of the very traditional penology that we have described. The findings and politics of radical criminology seem to evaporate before the reality of that which it says is central and abiding: the politics of control. This is all the more surprising as this period witnessed in many countries the emergence of a number of struggles and radical movements in the area of penality – prisoners' rights litigations, PROP, RAP, KRUM – and saw general talk of a crisis in penal affairs.[72]

Not only is this point academically facile in terms of the lack of appreciation of the complex history of opposition sketched out above, but also it misunderstands the operation of power and how it can be challenged. While agreeing with Poulantzas that the expansions and weight of state power 'are assuming proportions never seen before',[73] it is also important to note, as does Foucault, that there has been 'the development of power techniques oriented towards individuals and intended to rule them in a continuous and permanent way'.[74] In that sense the prisoners' movement, even at an individual level, in providing support and advice for prisoners and their families by acting as a reference point for the dissemination of information, challenged the imposition of power into their everyday lives. That individual prisoners could – and can – write to groups outside the walls and that cases do get taken up and publicized illustrates that the role played by prisoners' groups is not as politically ineffective as Garland and Young contend. The present success of Women in Prison in highlighting conditions in Holloway, for example, and in being there for women prisoners to contact is ample proof of this point.

There is a further dimension to this argument. The pessimistic defeatism of Garland and Young, and the political atrophy that their position implies, should not invalidate the continuation of strategies which challenge state power. Indeed, neither should the difficulties which radical pressure groups have experienced in the last 15 yesrs undermine the vision of a world without prisons in their present form. In a recent contribution to *Contemporary Crises* Thomas Mathiesen reviewed the work of the prisoners' movement in the last decade and a half. He acknowledged the shift towards greater repression in western capitalist democracies, the increase in the number of prisons and prisoners and the need for the further specification and development of what might constitute a politics of abolition. These problems, however, did not mean that 'the basic principles of a politics of abolition have become irrelevant or invalid'. On the contrary:

> as prison systems have expanded the importance of the goal has, to my mind, only increased. As people are being placed behind walls for longer periods of time, and/or as more people are being placed there, the long-range goal has become all the more significant. Among social scientists there seems to be considerable disillusionment, and, indeed, a turning away from the goal of abolition – more or less as if it were a youthful and confused prank from the late sixties which the middle aged and wise can hardly uphold. I have, however, never understood why a negative political trend – be it increased pollution, escalation of nuclear armaments or expanded prison systems – should lead one to conclude that the trend in question no longer constitutes a point of fundamental attack and final abolition from a radical position. To be sure, the issue of prison abolition is more complex than we thought 15 years ago. Among other things, and as suggested above, we see much more clearly today that prisons are a part of the state's apparatus for political repression, thus being much more integrated into the political system than some of us thought two decades ago. This however, should lead us to further and more refined analyses of strategy and tactics rather than disillusionment and despair. Much too often, sociological analyses stress the complexities of the issue without touching the issues of strategies and tactics.[75]

2. ii. The State of the Police

Until the 1970s much of the work developed from within the social sciences on the police focused on the organizational structure, management techniques and specialized training of the 'modern' force. Tacitly it assumed the liberal-democratic model of contemporary police work: that of the maintenance of order and the enforcement of the law within a democratic framework. Thus the concentration was around the effectiveness of the police as a corporate body, the diversity of the police as locally constituted forces and the occupational and professional culture of police work. While the 1962 Royal Commission on the police had been established in 1959 to consider the relationship between the police and the public, the handling of complaints and the pay and working conditions of the police within the frameworks of the 'constitution and function of local police authorities' and the 'status and accountability of members of police forces, including chief officers', it was assumed widely that the subsequent 1964 Police Act had ironed out the main problems. One of the most significant problems noted by the Royal Commission was that of 'controlling chief constables'. The Act, it appeared, had responded to this problem with the formation of new police authorities and had set the boundaries on police powers and political accountability.

The growth of public demonstrations, industrial conflict and the student movement in the late 1960s and early 1970s, however, raised renewed questions about the public order role of the police and the permissiveness of lawful discretion. Alongside this were revelations of wholesale corruption, to the extent of actual involvement in professional crime, by the CID in the Metropolitan Police. On the one hand the response was that 'society was becoming more violent' which demanded a more authoritarian form of police intervention. On the other were allegations that the police, as a matter of course, were overstepping the mark in their interventions against demonstrators, pickets and 'targeted' identifiable groups. In 1972 Derek Humphry published his *Police against Black People* which emphasized the consequences of targeting black communities.[76] This work challenged the fundamental liberal-democratic premises of equality-before-the-law and innocent-until-proved-guilty. On the contrary its powerful message was to expose these as myths of post-war consensual politics. Whoever the police represented, according to Humphry, they did not include black people on their list. It became increasingly evident that the targeting of black communities and the 'saturation' of identifiable neighbourhoods with 'high crime profiles' had become matters of policy rather than individual officers' discretion. The Special Patrol Group, established in 1964 to target areas of 'high crime', was fast becoming identified with differential policing strategies aimed almost exclusively at black neighbourhoods.

What this challenge provoked, together with the response of organized labour to the policing of industrial disputes under the Heath government, was the emergence of a critical body of research and writing on the role of the police, the controversial history of policing, the relationship between police powers and accountability and, eventually, the mythical status of the police as neutral arbiters in confrontations between competing interests. In 1976 the first contemporary critical text, Tony Bunyan's *The History and Practice of the Political Police in Britain*, was published and became an immediate alternative analysis of the history and development of police work.[77] For Bunyan, an investigative journalist and researcher, not an 'academic', examined and exposed the development and activities of those state agencies 'whose function is to counter and contain political movements in this country'. In particular he was concerned to analyse and establish the connections between the police, the Special Branch, MI5, and the military, considering them as, 'part of an interdependent matrix'.

Effectively Bunyan's contribution superseded previous writings on the police which had consisted mainly of police memoirs and liberal or conservative sociology/social history with a few civil libertarian critiques on the sidelines. Further it opened the way to a significant expansion of critical works on the police and to a new generation of 'police-watchers'. *The Political Police in Britain* was followed[78] by Ackroyd *et al.'s The Technology of Political*

Control, which considered the growth of technology and arms within policing in Northern Ireland and its inevitable adoption throughout Britain;[79] the Institute of Race Relations' *Police against Black People*,[80] which moved well beyond Humphrey's work to raise the issue of the structural relations of institutionalized racism; Peter Hain's two collections of essays, *Policing the Police*,[81] and Paul Gordon's *Policing Scotland*, emphasizing the significance of police policies and practices under a separate criminal justice system.[82]

While this work was being developed and consolidated there emerged a small but growing number of critical police watchers. The most significant 'specialized' group was the *State Research* group formed in 1977 to produce its regular monitoring bulletin. *State Research* was published from 1977 to 1983 and it produced the first systematic, critical monitor of the police and other state agencies. The group, through its library, its files and its personnel, developed and provided a unique source of critical information and research on policing and related issues. Although the group ceased publication in 1983 – due to financial reasons – a new network of police-watchers had emerged: critical researchers and writers' locally-based and publicly funded monitoring groups and full-time workers/researchers on policing issues, employed by local authorities (London (GLC), Manchester, Liverpool, and so on). Collectively these interventions followed the *State Research* commitment to programmes of police reform and public education on policing matters. Further to this was the development of campaigns around cases directed towards the objective of creating effective participation of communities in the police policies, priorities and practices adopted on their streets.

It has been on this issue – that of the political accountability of the police (see Chapters 4 and 5) – that the greatest expansion in critical research and publication has taken place. This work has highlighted specific confrontations between police authorities and chief constables, has raised powerfully questions of the implications of differential policing and has demonstrated conclusively the political autonomy of chief constables in the UK. While much of this work has developed directly from academic research and analysis it has retained an interventionist and applied emphasis. Critical criminologists have worked alongside community leaders, local politicians, union officials and church leaders in constructive attempts to pursue more accountable policing and to provide sensitive and appropriate police responses on the streets. This work has included the setting up and staffing of independent inquiries, the monitoring of individual cases and the provision of advice, the publication of reports, case studies and newsletters and the development of accessible critiques of the contemporary shifts in police operations and powers within the context of eight years of right-wing Thatcherite law and order policies.

As with the critical interventionist work on prisons, these initiatives on policing have been resisted strongly by central government, the Home

Office and the Association of Chief Police Officers (ACPO). While the priorities of paramilitary strategies have sharpened since the 1980–81 uprisings (riot-training, riot equipment, plastic bullets, CS gas, Police Support Units, specialist task forces, new technologies of surveillance and control), as predicted by Ackroyd *et al.*, the 'public face' has been one of community policing strategies (race awareness training; multi-agency initiatives; neighbourhood watch; 'bobbies on the beat'; police in schools/ youth clubs; victims' support schemes). What monitoring groups and critical research continues to show, however, is the surveillance potential of community policing and the persistence of differential responses by the police to particular groups: Asian communities over racial attacks; women over many aspects of male violence, particularly 'domestics'. Further (as discussed in Chapter 5) there has been the critical appraisal of new legislation, particularly the 1984 Police and Criminal Evidence Act and the 1986 Public Order Act, in terms of the substantive extension of police powers and the growing permissiveness of lawful discretion afforded to police officers by this legislation.

2. iii. *The Struggles in Northern Ireland*

Academic interventions, however, have not been restricted to the issues of police powers and prison politics. In a number of other substantive areas in criminal justice academics through research and publications have sought to question the politics of criminal justice and to document the experiences of those confronted by it. The case of Northern Ireland is important here, not simply because of the nature of the interventions made but also because the situation there has proved to be a political and academic blind-spot for sociologists and criminologists in England, Scotland and Wales. Even with the proliferation in Marxist and radical literature from the late 1960s onwards, interestingly at precisely the moment that 'the Troubles' flared again, academics generally have been reluctant both to understand the nature and role of the state in Northern Ireland and to assess the full implications of state policies in the six counties for the rest of the UK (see Chapter 10). As Michael Farrell has pointed out:

> Most commentators have failed to grasp the extent of British Government involvement in the establishment and underpinning of the Northern state; the degree of repression and violence maintained by that state and the extent to which the Unionist Party and the state had become one.[83]

In 1975, three academics, Kevin Boyle, Tom Hadden and Paddy Hillyard published *Law and State: The Case of Northern Ireland.*[84] The authors built on their earlier work most notably Hadden and Hillyard's 1973 Cobden Trust publication *Justice in Northern Ireland: A Study in Social Confidence*, and their submission to the 1974 Gardiner Committee which considered the operation of the Northern Ireland (Emergency Provisions) Act 1975. The book described the operation of various aspects of the legal system under the emergency conditions which prevailed in the North: the system for the arrest and interrogation of those suspected of political violence, the system of internment without trial and the operation of the ordinary courts of those cases in which normal criminal proceedings were brought. In the introduction to the book, the authors were categorical about its purpose:

> Much of the material on which the book is based was collected primarily to influence the course of events. Much of it has already been published or submitted to various governmental bodies. To that extent we do not claim to be wholly objective observers even if that were possible for anyone living in such a complex and emotionally charged situation as that now prevailing in Northern Ireland.[85]

The emphasis of the book was directed towards covering the nature and direction of criminal justice policy in the six counties and to examining rigorously

> the basic connection between the legal system and the state which it helps to support and the related fact that when that state is threatened the legal system will be used by those in power in whatever way seems to them most likely to restore stability.[86]

This emphasis on empirically demonstrating the nature of state power in Northern Ireland through rigorous research, and the increasing connections with state agencies in the rest of the UK through the normalization of special powers, was picked up by a number of other publications in the late 1970s. Most notable amongst these were Ackroyd *et al.*'s *The Technology of Political Control*,[87] Tony Bunyan's *The History and Practice of the Political Police in Britain*[88] and the State Research Collective's *Society and the State*.[89] In general, however, the issues raised by Boyle, Hadden and Hillyard were ignored by criminologists, radical or otherwise. In 1980, the three developed their work further when the Cobden Trust published *Ten Years on in Northern Ireland*.[90] Like their previous work it was based on 'detailed empirical investigations of the outcome of a sample of cases dealt with in the courts'.[91] The book itself was written from a traditional civil libertarian perspective in that it was concerned with 'individual justice and communal discrimination'. They were concerned also with broader matters, the consideration of socio-economic and political factors, the operations of the security forces and importantly how:

> certain emergency powers and practices have come to be regarded as almost normal and to stress how closely the development of these powers and practices is paralleled in other jurisdictions where there is no equivalent pressure of continuing political violence. In this respect our findings are as significant to other common law jurisdictions as they are to Northern Ireland. Our conclusions on the extent to which the criminal process has been 'bureaucratized' and the extent to which effective decision making on guilt or

innocence has been shifted back from the court-room to the police station are
of particular relevance to the current debate in Britain on the proceedings of
the Royal Commission on Criminal Procedure.[92]

The work of Boyle, Hadden and Hillyard was complemented in 1980 with
the publication of a substantive analysis of the history and form of Direct
Rule by three other left academics in Northern Ireland, Liam O'Dowd, Bill
Rolston and Mike Tomlinson.[93] Their work, *Northern Ireland: Between Civil
Rights and Civil War*, contributed significantly to the debate linking sectarian
division to the origins and development of capitalism in Northern Ireland.
Their detailed analysis of the economy, trade unionism, housing, local
politics, community struggles and law and order argued strongly that
through the interventions of the British state the 'underlying social
relationships' of post war reform were 'being reconstituted'. They
concluded, 'in a capitalist state these relationships must have a class form; in
the specific circumstances of Northern Ireland, however, class relations are
simultaneously sectarian.'[94] On this basis their argument proposed that 'the
Troubles' remain a persistent reminder of the inherent contradiction of the
British state in Northern Ireland, whose 'attempts to reform sectarianism
abstract it from class relations'. The work of Bill Rolston and Mike
Tomlinson has developed further with regular contributions to the annual
conference of the European Group for the Study of Deviance and Social
Control[95] and in 1981 they hosted the annual conference in Northern
Ireland. It has been in the development of this critical work in Northern
Ireland that the connections between theoretical analysis and political
intervention have been at their sharpest. For the personal, professional
risks and the isolation experienced in this work cannot be overestimated.

In 1984 Eileen Fairweather, Roisin McDonough and Melanie McFadyean
published a powerful account of Northern Ireland from the experiences of
Irish women.[96] Their work reminded commentators on Northern Ireland of
the particular and often deeply personal struggles experienced by women.
This is clearly evident in a chapter on Armagh Women's Prison and the
added pressures on women of imprisonment in extreme, often violent
circumstances.

All of this work has contributed significantly to the provision of a critical
analysis and alternative accounts on Northern Ireland. In the main the
issues have been ignored by traditional and radical academics alike and
successive governments, be they Labour or Conservative have maintained a
policy of minimal information and disinformation on all aspects of the
British state's involvement in Northern Ireland. Liz Curtis exposed the
extent of this policy in her comprehensive analysis: *Northern Ireland; The
Propaganda War*.[97] This work has continued through a campaign, Information on Ireland, which monitors the relationship between the British state
and the media and provides an alternative to mainstream media coverage on
all aspects of state intervention in the North of Ireland.

Paddy Hillyard's later work, as with that of Dermot Walsh,[98] has not only been concerned with monitoring and revealing the extent of the repressive state apparatus in the North of Ireland but also makes crucial connections between that apparatus and the introduction of legislation such as the 1984 Police and Criminal Evidence Act in England and Wales and the policing of the coal dispute.[99] Again, as with the prisons, this challenge by radical academics has not resulted in the overall curtailment of state power; none the less the discrediting of the supergrass strategy and the increasing calls for the abandonment of the Diplock Courts arguably would have been much more difficult without the initial and continuing interventions described above. Before concluding this section we wish to highlight three other areas which are important. In their own ways they illustrate the scope of the interventions that have been made, the relationship between academic work and powerless groups and they raise once more the question of tactics and strategies of reform when confronted by the power of the state on the one hand and institutionalized sexism and racism on the other, although all three very often come together on the same terrain.

2. iv. Threatening Women

In 1976 Carol Smart published *Women, Crime and Criminology*.[100] Her direct challenge to traditional and radical developments within criminology reflected a broader feminist critique of social sciences in general and sociology in particular. [101] For women and their experiences were marginal to the concerns of male-dominated disciplines. Patriarchy flourished (and persists) inside as well as outside the walls of academic institutions. Smart concluded her book with a call to situate future studies of female criminality in the 'wider moral, political economic and sexual spheres which influence women's status and position in society'.[102] This goal, she argued, should take place within a criminology and sociology of deviance which

> Must become more than a study of men and crime if it is to play any significant part in the development of our understanding of crime, law and the criminal process and play any role in the transformation of existing social practices.[103]

Since the publication of Smart's book there has been a proliferation of work on women, sexism and criminal justice although much 'mainstream' criminology has compounded years of neglect by marginalizing feminist work as 'women's studies'. The feminist critique has been developed both at theoretical and substantive levels to include: the relationship between patriarchy, the rule of law and underpinnings of theoretical criminology; the issue of violence against women and the state's response; women in institutions; women and crime; family law and the resistance of women to violence and to patriarchy.[104] This work has been of central importance in a number of different ways. First, in a sociological sense, it has moved the discipline of criminology into new theoretical and research areas. As Ann Jones has pointed out, 'the problem is not simply that the criminology of women is bigoted or biased, even that, as one feminist critic has noted, it is retarded. The problem is that it has never addressed the right questions.'[105] The body of work that has been established by criminologists writing from a feminist perspective has meant that the right questions are being raised in teaching and research (see: Chadwick and Little; Kelly and Radford below). The impact of this work has resulted in a clearer conceptualization of the totality and full complexity of the relationship between society, crime, the law and punishment. Second, in the face of the pervasive nature of violence against women, and the limited state response to it, the question of how research should be used and how reforms could be implemented have become ongoing issues. In her later book, *The Ties that Bind*,[106] Carol Smart attempted to conceptualize the dialectics of research projects in the relationship between women and the law. While she considered that the research for the book was 'unlikely to have very much impact', she concluded:

> All feminist work carries a political potential because it is a continuous challenge to the social order and because it may be taken up and used by feminist activists. Feminist work is never an end in itself, it is always a critique and it frequently imports strategies and policies for action. A fundamental feature of feminist research is that it is oriented towards a change in the social order... I would argue that the politics of the research are not simply contained in the 'doing' of the research: they have wider implications.[107]

These 'wider implications' have centred on the question of using the law as an arena of struggle. In a further contribution to the debate Smart and co-writer Julia Brophy have argued that there is in the 1980s 'little optimism about the way in which law can be used for progressive purposes'.[108] Despite this, they point out that many feminists work on two fronts. Priority is given to direct action in terms of setting up refuges for battered women or rape crisis centres, but at the same time, 'criticising the law and the agents of law enforcement. We find we cannot ignore the law because it affects our daily lives whether we choose it or not.'[109] Smart and Brophy argue that there is still a basic question to be answered, and one which has been integral to the various movements described above; that is, whether feminists

> embrace a totally negative view of law reacting to it only when it is essential to do so, or ... there should be a more positive approach that attempts to focus on law and legal practice and a campaign for a more progressive direction.[110]

This dilemma has been highlighted by feminists working directly with women in a number of legal spheres. In the arena of domestic violence, for example, Kathryn McCann has argued that all of the women in her study who related their experiences to her

> agreed that there was little real alternative to using the law to obtain relief from their husband's violence but that it was extremely difficult to obtain this

relief. Although the domestic violence legislation improved the formal legal rights of battered women, the *real* improvement in their position is substantially less.[111]

In the area of family law, Anne Bottomley contends that it is important to recognize the weaknesses in the way that formal justice operates. In particular, the fact that 'legal rights are fragile, lawyers have their own interests and the law has played a major role in enforcing women's position in society'.[112] Despite this, Bottomley argues that there are a number of contradictions and spaces within the law itself which can be exploited in order to pursue equality for women:

> it is important to recognize that there are many modes of discipline and regulation. In exposing one it is often useful to use the rhetoric of another, we have a language of jurisprudence which gives us concepts with which to critique the appeal of welfarism and informality. In doing so we do not need to believe that the law is all that it has pretended to be or that radical transformation can be achieved through law. Secondly, the law is not a unitary system, it is a complex and changing form which gives us some space to struggle within, if not to better our position at least to protect it. Thirdly, by arguing for the right to formal justice in family law we are maintaining a public profile and refusing to be privatised either into the hands of welfare agencies or into the dangers of private ordering.[113]

In taking this position Bottomley is supported by Smart and Brophy who agree that it is possible to find contradictions in the law, in legal practice and between different strata of the legal profession, 'which cast doubt upon the existence of a male legal conspiracy'.[114] In that sense, they do not see the law as if it were

> an homogeneous unit with a unitary purpose... Our argument is that it is important to distinguish between the law and the *effects* of law and legal processes in order to identify the contradictions which allow space for change.[115]

In reviewing the literature on violence against women Elizabeth Wilson has documented both the extent and importance of the campaigns conducted in the area in the 1970s and 1980s. She points out that most of these campaigns had three distinct but interrelated aspects to them – the grassroots organization of material resources and emotional support which have allowed some women freedom from male violence; the persistent campaigns which have been waged to change the law or to modify the way in which laws are interpreted, used or not used; and the struggle against ideology. On this latter point she states:

> This has been the hardest; the struggle against deep-seated 'common sense' assumptions built into our consciousness – assumptions about the nature of male and female sexuality, the ability of individuals to protect themselves, the extent of the violence and what causes it.[116]

The establishment of rape crisis centres and refuges for battered women has taken the issue beyond the interference of state servants and health services whose statutory basis has limited their freedom of action:

> It has always been one of the strengths of autonomous self-help groups that they are free from such restraints. Rape crisis centres are run by women for women... While there is still a long way to go it is important not to underestimate what has been achieved. And what feminists have achieved is to force society at large to reconsider its attitude to rape.[117]

While, as Kelly and Radford point out in Chapter 8, there exists the potential for state incorporation of women's struggles through the financial institutionalization of rape crisis centres, help-lines and refuges the development of these independent initiatives as sites of women's collective strength has sharply revealed the reluctance of state agencies to take women's oppression seriously. The radical feminist critique of the advanced capitalist state has provided a powerful and necessary corrective to critical analyses which consider the state primarily, even solely, in terms of the social relations derived in monopoly capitalism. For what this work has emphasized is the patriarchal nature of the state. Given the importance of the findings of recent studies of sexual violence and the state's persistent reluctance to respond to the needs of women as victims[118] the feminist critique of criminology, both traditional and critical, has placed the politics of sexuality at the centre of the analysis. Writing in 1975 Christine Delphy argued that 'only the women's struggle, and the simultaneous conceptualization of women's condition as oppression, has brought sexuality into the potential arena'.[119]

Pat Mahony, in explaining the limitations of a Marxist analysis and considering the universality of patriarchy, asks:

> What then is the material base of patriarchy – how do men control women? They do so through their control of women's access to production and by their control over biological reproduction, but this is not sufficient. A crucial third element which has been omitted from the Marxist account is male control of women's sexuality through a particular form of heterosexuality. The construction of male identity and in particular the social construction of male sexuality is crucial in the maintenance of male power.[120]

Recent work on the politics of sexuality has challenged 'the assertion that the association between sex and power is inevitable or desirable, and that dominance and submission are inherent in sexual activity and essential to sexual pleasure'.[121]

What the findings of the above studies show is that while not being inevitable the power exerted by men over women within the framework of the politics of sexuality remains universal. The exercise of aggression together with the ideological and legal construction of 'property rights' has created male sexuality in a generalized form which transcends the boundaries of class, race and cultural relations. Powerful investigative research on male violence against women as partners[122] or girl children[123] stands as an indictment not only of men's control over women but also of the neglect by criminologists and other social scientists of the centrality of the social relations of patriarchy to an understanding of the construction of legality and the workings of the criminal justice process. All women are controlled by the constant threat, both publicly and privately, of male power relations, but when they organize and engage directly with the rule of law it is they who become the perceived threat. Individual women who have defended themselves against the persistent attacks of husbands, partners or fathers, and women's collectives which have campaigned strongly around peace, sexual harassment, sex shops, pornography, safe streets and lesbian rights have been systematically marginalized, differentially policed and, ultimately, criminalized. This range of work, clearly combining the politics of women's struggles with research and publication, has provided a major contribution not only to critical analysis but also to the development and realization of a critical methodology which locates the everyday experiences of women within the broader structural relations of an advanced capitalist patriarchy.

2. v. The Struggle Against Institutionalized Racism

Some time before the emergence of a critical sociology or a radical interventionist criminology, the notion of objective research, 'value-free' and distanced and divorced from the reality being researched, had come under attack in a different area of sociological study – that of race relations. In January 1971, Robin Jenkins, a researcher in the International Race Studies Programme of the prestigious Institute of Race Relations [IRR], delivered a paper to the British Sociological Association. The subject of Jenkins's paper, 'The Production of Knowledge at the Institute of Race Relations', was the mammoth 1969 IRR study, *Colour and Citizenship*, the end result of a lengthy 'Survey of Race Relations'. Jenkins argued that the approach of the report was not scientific, as its authors and supporters claimed, but ideological, and that the knowledge contained in it made the power elite more powerful and the powerless more impotent. 'The IRR has worked to make the power elite relatively more powerful and knowledgeable and thereby to make the subject [immigrant] population relatively more impotent and ignored.'[124] But Jenkins went further to warn black people, the objects of such research studies, not to submit themselves to the scrutiny of white researchers who acted, in effect, as government spies. He advised that they should tell researchers from the IRR to 'fuck off'.

Jenkins was expressing what many IRR staff had felt for a long time. As a result they had developed their work so that it was more relevant to the situation of black people, becoming increasingly critical of government policy, the police, the courts, schools and other state institutions. In the process, the pages of the Institute's magazine, *Race Today*, began to be opened to black people themselves to talk about their own experiences and describe their own reality. Jenkins' critique, and the furore which followed as demands were made for his sacking, brought into the open the divisions within the IRR and the beginnings of a struggle over the purpose and direction of the Institute which was to last until April 1972 when the staff, with the support of sympathetic academics, researchers, community activists and others succeeded in wresting control of the Institute from its council. As an IRR researcher was to put it later:

> The dispute in the IRR ... had gone far beyond Jenkins' critique. Where the fundamental problem lay was now the issue. It was not black people who should be examined, but white society; it was not a question of educating blacks and whites for integration, but of fighting institutional racism; it was not race relations that was the field for study, but racism.[125]

The struggle at the IRR, and the development of the institute from an institute *of race relations* to an institute *against racism*, pointed the way for researchers and academics working in other disciplines to question their assumptions, theories, practices and political purposes.

These developments set the agenda within critical analyses of racism, shifting emphasis from the liberal-democratic constructions of attitudinal imperatives to the historical materialist process of institutions. Within critical criminology the main focus had centred on black people and their relationship to the law. That relationship, particularly, from the early 1970s onwards[126] has been one of conflict with and resistance to state agencies in general and the police in particular. In the last 15 years the question of the policing of black communities, either at individual officer level through the use of the sus laws or institutionally through the use of reactive fire-brigade techniques (though both, of course, are interrelated), has become a focal point for both academic dicussions and interventions in defence of individuals and communities. Again, running through these interventionist initiatives have been a number of different strands. First, at an academic level, the work of the Centre for Contemporary Cultural Studies at the University of Birmingham has yielded two major texts on the black experience in Britain. These texts, *Policing the Crisis* and *The Empire Strikes Back*,[127] have analysed the operation of contemporary legal relations within their specific political economic contexts. In that sense, black people's personal and collective direct experiences of the law, and the everyday struggles which are part of those experiences, have been harnessed to a theoretical framework which emphasizes the totality of the relationship between political economy, historical antecedents, institutionalized racism and the relative autonomy of state practices in their contribution to the legitimation of existing social relations and the maintenance of order. These publications and others, most notably from the Institute of Race Relations, have been important both in their own terms as academic texts and in challenging traditional academic accounts of black communities which have centred on the disorganization of black families and the disaffection of black communities.[128]

Second, in the wake of the major and frequent confrontations which have taken place between the police and black communities in the last 15 years, new forms and types of organization have emerged. They have developed as part of the different campaigns which had their genesis in the desire of black communities to defend those who had been arrested. Importantly, as we saw above, these grass-roots organizations also struggled within the law and used legal processes and institutions as platforms for political struggle and opposition. As Paul Gilroy has pointed out:

> Whilst the law was recognized as a repressive force there was no reluctance to use what institutional and democratic residues it contained. The strategy which was devised sought to reveal and then exploit the political dimensions of the legal process by using the dock as a platform for the critical perspectives of the defendant while combining this legal struggle with popular local agitation and organizing of community support. Those campaigns were aimed at maximizing mobilization rather than membership of the various organizations involved. This combination of tactics and the synchronization of protest inside and outside the law provided a model which was to become central to the political repertoire of black activism up and down this country.[129]

These campaigns and struggles have not been confined solely to the legal form. Black self-defence groups have organized against racist violence, local groups have monitored the activities of the police, action groups have been set up around specific cases such as the Anwar Ditta Defence Committee[130] and black women's groups, and the formation of a black women prisoners' group, have asserted the rights of black women. Collectively these campaigns have challenged the power of the state, in its various forms, to dictate the direction of the lives of black and brown people in Britain. More generally, other organizations have been formed to combat the institutionalized process of discrimination and rejection. These have taken various forms – schools, churches, community organizations, training schemes, youth clubs, social clubs, action groups, legal advisory and counselling services, translation and interpretation services, and as mentioned above, defence committees.[131]

The action taken by anti-racist groups is consistent with other organized struggles and reflects not only opposition to the power, authority and legitimacy of the state but also it points to the dissatisfaction and exclusion which black and brown people have experienced in relation to established pressure groups, political parties and the institutions of the British state. Indeed, the democratic process itself has been at the forefront, through immigration legislation for example, in its reinforcement of subordination. The traditional platform for white, working-class organization and resi-

stance in Parliament and local politics – the Labour Party – has been part of
that process. As Errol Lawrence has argued:

> the Labour Party, despite the wish for egalitarian solutions for the race-
> relations 'problem'... finds itself unable to counter the arguments of this
> rascist ideology, partly at least because Labour politicians share many of its
> commonsense assumptions.[132]

2. vi. Building Alternative Accounts

A further political dimension to the growth of community struggle has been
the demand for independent, community-based inquiries when a major
confrontation has occurred between police and people. Like PROP's inquiry
into the Hull prison disturbance, discussed above, such inquiries have been
important in terms of setting out alternative accounts of events. Further,
they provide a forum for those whose voices are not heard and, when
published, act as a challenge to the state's 'official' accounts. The major state
inquiries which have been set up in recent years, for example: Lord Widgery
into Bloody Sunday in 1972, Lord Scarman into Red Lion Square in 1974 and
Brixton in 1981, and Mr Justice May into the prison system in 1979, have
taken place on terrain laid down by the state, specifically the government of
the day, through the terms of reference set, the time-span in which they are
required to report, the role and position of the official secretary and the
inclusion in and exclusion of 'relevant' or 'significant' evidence. Ultimately,
they legitimate state practices and represent a form of 'official discourse'.[133]
Independent inquiries suffer no such constraints and increasingly have
become important in providing a voice for the powerless. When Blair Peach,
a demonstrator, was killed by an unknown member of the Special Patrol
Group at an anti-fascist demonstration in April 1979, the National Council
for Civil Liberties responded to approaches by the local community and set
up an unofficial committee of inquiry whose panel included three academics. The final 192-page report of the inquiry[134] provided a detailed and
powerful alternative account of the events which had taken place, particularly concerning the level of violence and intimidation perpetrated by the
police. Like PROP's 1976 inquiry into Hull, the inquiry documented a
chilling picture of uncontrolled state violence towards legitimate demonstrators whose primary motivation was to protect their community from a
racist presence on their streets:

> Our own analysis of 243 statements given to the Enquiry or to solicitors
> shows that, of 146 people charged with criminal offences, 83 complained of
> being assaulted by the police, including 36 of who complained of injuries to the
> head. Of those not charged with an offence, 10 complained of an assault,
> including 6 who said they had been hit on the head. Even this figure of 93
> people injured, including 42 who had suffered head injuries, is likely to be
> incomplete. Many who had suffered only minor injuries from kicks, hair-
> pulling or truncheon blows did not go to see a doctor and not all gave
> statements to Southall Rights, to solicitors or to this Enquiry. At least three

protestors were hit so hard on the head that their skulls were fractured. One was Blair Peach, who died from the blow. One was Clarence Baker, who suffered a blood clot on the brain. The third was a 35 year old man who said he was walking home and sustained his injury in Waverley Road. Many other people also suffered severe blows on the head. They included Vincent Conway, who was arrested in 6 Park View Road and acquitted on all charges and who had three stitches in his head, and Martin Craxton, arrested in Southall Park, who had two stitches to a wound which penetrated to the bone. Charges against him were dropped on his agreement to be bound over. Paul Seligman, who was arrested and taken to the police station but not charged, was kicked in the face and his teeth chipped. Gareth Peirce, who went to Southall Rights late in the evening to give legal advice, was appalled by the number of people she saw with head injuries and commented that 'they needed a doctor, not a lawyer'. One of the stewards, Inderjeet Singh Kohli, who was cornered, suffered a fractured pelvis and a young member of Peoples Unite suffered a severe eye injury in 6 Park View Road.[135]

The establishment of independent inquiries with academic involvement continued in the 1980s. After the Handsworth rebellion in the autumn of 1985, West Midlands County Council set up a review panel to inquire into the disturbances. The panel of six, two of whom were academics produced a 97-page report which described the harsh political economy of the local community and the experiences of black people both in that economy and at the hands of state services, that is, health, social welfare and the police; the last of which refused to give evidence to the panel.

> The Alternative Reality comprises a description of the Black experience in Britain today and locates it in a Birmingham context. It highlights the pattern of oppression and disadvantage, the imposition of law and order responses to Black resistance, deals with the myth that large amounts of money were going into Black areas, and examines the by-passing mechanisms which ensure that Black people always miss out.[136]

The events in Handsworth were paralleled in Tottenham where, following the death of a black woman after the police searched her home and the shooting of another black woman in Brixton, there was a major disturbance which centred on the Broadwater Farm estate. The London Borough of Haringey set up its own independent public inquiry after the Home Secretary refused to set up a government inquiry. Again academics were involved as the inquiry sought to 'provide a channel for the grievances and complaints of the local community and to investigate a number of disputed issues'.[137] In order to achieve this, the inquiry team went beyond the usual methods employed by official inquiries, a methodology which was important for widening the scope and detail of their analysis. The formal rigidity of conventional inquiries and the narrow political answers which they normally supplied was thus marginalized:

> we went far beyond the normal inquiry process whereby any interested

person or organization was invited to put in written submissions and give evidence at public hearings. We turned the Inquiry into an active process. Members of the the Inquiry panel themselves as well as the Inquiry staff knocked on doors, held interviews and attended meetings in the community. We published two newsletters which were distributed throughout the Broadwater Farm estate and neighbouring streets. At the public hearings we encouraged participation by members of the public. In all these ways we reached out into the community. We could not remove the cloud of fear, but by treating people's fears as being serious and reasonable, we believe we obtained far more information than a formal 'judicial' inquiry would have done.[138]

The final report was 256 pages in length. What emerged from this forum for the powerless was a complex picture which, as the Handsworth inquiry also indicated, is never documented in a racist media which chooses to rely on stereotypical images of disorganized black communities underpinned by sensationalist images of black criminality. At the heart of the matter in Tottenham, as with Handsworth, lay the community's relationship with the police:

Witness after witness to our Inquiry spoke of the indignities which they have suffered at the hands of police officers for no other reason than they were Black. The bitterness of their experience was shared by old and young, men and women, professional people and unemployed.[139]

The inquiry also provided a chilling picture of the aftermath of the disturbance when the police, supported by a supine and acquiescent magistracy put a legal stranglehold on those detained:

There was a uniform policy to forbid arrested people access to a solicitor ... the policy of refusing access to a solicitor was maintained on many occasions even after people had appeared in court when they were remanded in police custody for further questioning. It is hard to avoid the conclusion that the investigating officers denied access to solicitors because they wished to hold suspects incommunicado for long periods and thus put maximum pressure upon them to make a confession. Many allegations were made to us about the conditions of detention and the manner of questioning. Some concerned particular cases of actual maltreatment – deprivation of sleep, assaults and extreme threats.[140]

These statements raise crucial theoretical and political questions about the relationship between the police, the law and the state. Also they emphasize the importance and significance of these and other inquiries[141] in documenting alternative explanations for events, and providing a challenge to those whose voices are heard exclusively as part of government-backed official discourse. The involvement of academics in such inquiries is a further element to the interventionism which has been part of left academic work in the UK over the past 15 years.

The final arena of intervention which we wish to mention, and one which has shown once more the continuation of the radical strand in criminology, is the role of academics in the 1984–5 coal dispute.[142] It was during this dispute that the increased militarization of the police, which was clearly evident after the disturbances in 1981, was most obvious. The ruthlessness with which they responded to pickets and their families, especially at Orgreave and Armthorpe, the mobilization of the law to criminalize the Union collectively and miners individually, the use of social security legislation to debilitate mining communities still further, and the media representation of the strikers as wild, violent and lawless (the 'enemy within', to use Margaret Thatcher's phrase) illustrated the close inter-connection between law, the state and the powerful:

> The 1984–5 confrontation between the police and the miners has underlined the class nature of British policing. The law and order ideology so evident in the Margaret Thatcher/Leon Brittan speeches and so clear in the statements of senior police officers and ACPO showed a clear coincidence of interests. It permeated the thinking of the police involved on the picket lines and their selective enforcement of the law. It was present in the Courts, where bail conditions and payment of costs were used as forms of direct punishment. It was reinforced by an almost universally hostile media and a persistently biased news coverage of the dispute. As part of a process of regulation which controls and contains any resistance to the structural political and economic inequalities inherent in British society, police operations, priorities and practices are yet again firmly rooted in the interests of employers and their political representatives.[143]

As Janie Percy-Smith and Paddy Hillyard pointed out, the power of the state had not been used on such a massive scale this century 'against a clearly identified group of individuals, except in Northern Ireland against the nationalist community'.[144] Throughout the dispute, academics were involved in a number of different ways through writing, researching, publishing, addressing meetings, making media interventions and generally challenging the state's account of what was happening. Huw Beynon, for example, was not only a Reader in Sociology at Durham University but also was associated closely with the NUM as a lecturer and researcher in Durham and South Wales. During the dispute, he edited an important collection on the strike to which twelve academics contributed and this collection was complemented by two other texts which dealt with the police and the law.[145]

At another level the collection and dissemination of 'alternative information' by academics, particularly in relation to the question of violence, was important in challenging the media's portrayal of the strikers as being both mindless and aggressively violent. The statistics collected by Janie Percy-Smith and Paddy Hillyard, who worked closely with the NUM, showed clearly that far from being arrested for crimes of violence, the majority of miners were charged under Section 5 of the Public Order Act, for obstructing a police constable or for obstructing the highway. In their analysis of Home Office figures they showed that of 9,508 arrested, 6,429 (62%) were charged with these offences:

The meaning of Section 5 – 'the use of threatening, abusive or insulting words or behaviour likely to cause a breach of the peace' – is far from clear and will depend upon the views of the assessor. . . . There is considerable evidence to suggest that Section 5 charges laid during the dispute were frequently arbitrary, bearing no resemblance to the actual behaviour of the arrested person. The law was interpreted differently by different police forces and at different times of the day. What constituted 'threatening, abusive or insulting words and behaviour' appeared to be wholly a matter of discretion for the police who happened to be on duty at a particular picket line. It also provided the prosecutors with a very convenient charge to bring against anyone arrested on the picket line. The fact that it was used on such a scale illustrates the extent to which the authorities were prepared to use vague and ill-defined law to police public order incidents.[146]

Also significant and important from this analysis is the small proportion of offences relating to violence. Percy-Smith and Hillyard's figures show that only 877 (8.4%) of all charges were for offences involving violence. These included: assaulting a police officer (although even here there is a great deal of police discretion), actual bodily harm, grievous bodily harm, murder, wounding and possession of an offensive weapon (again open to permissive interpretation). As they make clear 'the proportion of persons charged with these offences was in fact less than the proportion of miners who were injured or roughly handled during arrest'.[147]

Such research interventions were important. First, they have provided a wide body of literature which documents the experiences of those who came into contact with the state for that year.[148] For many families the negative impact of that contact will live with them forever. Second, they have shown that despite the claims about the demise of radicalism within the 'intellectual left', critical academics did work closely with mining communities in order to present their cases against the Coal Board and the Government. Putting the powerless in print was in itself an important political commitment given the conservative stranglehold that the media generally exerted on the coverage of the dispute. Third, it showed also that academics could work both with established civil libertarian groups such as the National Council for Civil Liberties in the setting up of independent inquiries into the policing of the dispute[149] and, more pertinently, with groups outside the established civil libertarian lobby. The Sheffield Policewatch Group was an important example of this. The group's membership was two-thirds women and comprised of, among others, teachers, academics, students and unemployed. The main group was divided into three sections of approximately twenty people and each was linked to one of three local strike centres. Relays of two or three volunteers daily monitored policing at picket lines. From their observations they concluded that:

What we have seen of police behaviour has confirmed our view that effective and permanent police monitoring is necessary if civil liberties are to be protected... we stress that we are talking not just about the erosion of abstract rights, but about individuals being assaulted and abused by our police forces.... We are equally disturbed by the possibility that the type of policing we have seen evolve and being permitted during this dispute could become the norm.[150]

The joint report from the Welsh Campaign for Civil and Political Liberties and the NUM (South Wales Area)[151] had similar academic involvement. Again this report stood outside mainstream left and traditional civil libertarian perspectives. Through recording the catalogue of abuse, violence and repression which the police and the courts inflicted in South Wales it identified with different support networks within Britain. These included members of the peace movement, DHSS claimants, women, blacks, Welsh language activists, socialists, Irish people, gays, trade union activists, Britain's 5 million unemployed,

and those who live in Britain's industrial wastelands but refuse to become industrial itinerants chasing jobs already structured out of the British economy. The links forged through these support networks will continue beyond the strike and similarly we consider this report needs no conclusion because it is part of an on-going struggle for ordinary people's freedom to identify their common interests and fight for them against the power of the media and the increasingly overt forces of the capitalist state.[152]

Throughout this section we have attempted to document some of the contributions that left academics have made during the 1970s and 1980s. These contributions, and not all are listed here, represent an honourable tradition which until now has been unexplored. A number of critical questions have been at the centre of this tradition – limits to reform, civil liberties, the power of the state, the necessity of extra-parliamentary action, the relationship between the powerful and the powerless in a class-based and patriarchal society. As we intimated above it would be incorrect and dishonest to argue that all of these interventions have been successful or that all of the strategies pursued have brought political gains. Clearly that is not the case. On the other hand, they have challenged state practices, provided support for the powerless, influenced, to a limited extent, the introduction of more humane legislation and provided considerable opposition to the further encroachment of state institutions into the lives of the powerless. In this, critical academics have tried to exploit contradictions within both the state and legal institutions. The exploitation of these contradictions has been done not by seeing the state or its institutions as an homogeneous entity tied conspiratorially to the interests of a uniform ruling class. Rather the tactics adopted and the strategies employed have identified and developed those limited opportunities within academic work and other sites which allow for research, resistance and, occasionally, positive change. In developing these strategies it has been necessary to think beyond reform to the very organization, indeed reorganization, of society itself. This is well summarized by Thomas Mathiesen:

> We need visions of how society should be alternatively structured. Such visions are part of what sociologists might contribute to political movements although few sociologists have recently been such contributors. We need ideas of how human relationships might be alternatively organized so that conflicts are resolved in new and socially acceptable ways. In short, we need images of society or structures within society formulated as ideologies in a positive sense of that word, to work for. To me, a most important part of such a vision must necessarily be that of developing the conditions fostering and nurturing the anti-authoritarian features of human relationships. It will therefore be essential to provide maximum support for the anti-authoritarian components, find where they are today, develop the conditions for strengthening them further and provide support for giving them hegemony.[153]

Critical, interventionist criminology, however, is only one element of criminology in the 1980s. Those on the left of the discipline have been engaged in a major debate at the heart of which lies not only the role that criminologists might play but what kind of interventions should be made and how they should be theorized.

The issues are not new and the related questions of the relationship between 'radical criminology' and 'radical practice' and of what brand of left politics should be supported by radical criminologists formed the substance of many of the National Deviancy Conference debates in the 1970s. Ten years on, however, and under the economic 'libertarianism' and social 'authoritarianism' of a Thatcher administration these debates have a more fundamental meaning and there is an urgent need to develop common purpose and resolve differences. With the persistent attack on civil liberties, welfare rights, organized labour and all public sector services it might have been expected that radical criminology would have presented a united front. Instead there has been a major attack on the development of critical criminology, not only from 'new right' academics such as Scruton, Waddington and Dale, but from within the very heart of the radical movement initially inspired by the 'New Criminology'. This attack has been mounted and pursued with some vigour by the self-styled 'new realists' on the left.

The new realist criminologists, based at Middlesex Polytechnic and at the University of Edinburgh, have set out to expose the theoretical contradictions and over simplified practice of what they identify as the 'left idealist' position which has come to dominate critical criminology. Both the personal dynamics and the political form of this attack have emerged in such a way that many critical criminologists understandably have been compelled to defend their position which has served to give some credibility to the new realists' claim that an idealist–realist polarity does exist within critical criminology. Thus opposition to the theoretical and political directions of the new realists has been portrayed as proof of the existence of a left idealist position, the holders of which are anxious to defend 'their' ground. The critics of the new realists, however, reject their categorization as left idealists and argue forcefully that their interventionist work within critical criminology has responded to the realities of life under Thatcherism. Further, they challenge new realism on its misreading of history, under-theorization both of the structural contradictions within advanced capitalism and of the advanced capitalist state form and its rule of law, and on its essentially superficial approach to the complexities of crime, crime control and the criminal justice process. It is to a consideration of this debate that we now turn.

3. 'New Realism', 'Left Idealism' and the Development of Critical Criminology

The attack by the self-styled new realists on left idealism has its roots in a number of articles written by Jock Young in the 1970s. In 1979 he wrote the introductory chapter to a collection of essays, *Capitalist Discipline and the Rule of Law*,[154] and he used this opportunity to construct his interpretation of the left idealist position on crime and the law and to develop a critique. He chastised left idealists for their voluntaristic conception of human nature, their coercive conception of order and their functionalism. More specifically Young argued that idealists see 'the law as the direct expression of ruling class interests' and that crime is 'a first flicker of consciousness, a proto-revolutionary event which challenges property relations'.[155] He stated:

> The strategy of left idealism is exposé, it is to reveal the iron fist within the velvet glove, and then the final task if we list the parts of the apparatus of social control – the prison, the police, the school, the mass media and even the nuclear family – is their systematic abolition. Both the form and the content of these institutions are inimicable to working class interests; their form is undemocratic, manipulative and coercive, their content an illusion which pacifies the masses. As they are functional to capitalism, they must be removed: in its most invidious form, reform itself is seen to be functional and great lengths are gone to avoid the siren-like embraces of reformism.[156]

Young's characterization of left idealism set up what might be termed an 'idealist straw man'. While the qualities, and weaknesses, he linked with left idealism undoubtedly appeared in some left discussions about crime, as well as being applicable to elements of Marxist theory in general in its most reductionist manifestations, he over emphasized these elements and under estimated, indeed caricatured, the complexities of left interventionism in the 1970s and 1980s. In castigating left idealists for being anti-reformist (a position adopted by political parties such as the Socialist Workers Party and the International Marxist Group in the 1970s), he ignored the recent history of critical criminology in which individuals had worked within the state system, exploited the contradictions therein and struggled for effective reforms which were not undermined and turned to the advantage of the powerful. That political concern was not, as Young accused, an example of ultra-leftism, but a clear indication of a realistic awareness which attempted to utilize the contradictory spaces within the law and the state. It was a serious and difficult struggle to defend or to win rights within a class-based social system in which the notion of human rights never has been a fundamental element of its legal, political or social superstructure. In establishing caricatured arguments at a high level of generality Young ignored the depth, tempo and subtleties of left interventionist responses within the UK.

Young's portrayal of the significant trends in progressive criminology began with a failure to recognize that through the 1970s, as we have described, a considerable shift took place within radical analysis and interventionist practice. Its very objective had been to recognize and struggle with the complexities of locating analysis of crime and deviance within a political-economic framework. Through his early 1970s work Young had contributed to, even inspired, this project yet despite his proximity he missed the complexities. What he developed was the illusion of polarization between the two 'major socialist currents in criminology': reformism and left idealism.

It was never clear in Young's construction of left idealism exactly against whom his critique was levelled. One or two references to what conspicuously he termed 'typologies' gave no clear indication of the identity of the left idealists. At one point he appeared to drop a hint: 'it will be no revelation that the left idealist position is not a million miles away from the work of new criminologists whether they be Taylor, Walton and Young, Richard Quinney or Carol Smart; nor for that matter from the work of Michel Foucault'.[157] Given his liberal approach to geographical distance, how far each of these quite different positions stood from his portrayal of the most 'extreme' form of left idealism – 'unable to distinguish the factory from the prison; education from brain-washing; the anti-social from the social; fascism from democracy' – was never established. It was as if all critical theories which had emerged in their complexity during the 1970s were teetering on the brink of crude reductionism. It was significant that the extensive work of Hall *et al.* and their neo-Gramscian analysis of the state, class relations, ideology and the rule of law was absent from Young's critique.

By 1982, three years into the first Thatcher administration, anti-union laws had already been passed, the 'short sharp shock' was introduced in detention centres, uprisings in most of Britain's inner cities and many towns had occurred and new legislation to extend police powers were on the table. Following a conference on policing which focused on the police involvement with and response to the uprisings Richard Kinsey and Jock Young picked up on the left idealist theme but now their analysis introduced new labels. The 'reformer' remained intact and the 'conservative', rejected by Young in

1979 as 'beyond the pale', re-emerged as a third category. Left idealists, however, were now 'abolitionists'. Kinsey and Young, again without reference to specific authors, left no doubt as to the 'abolitionists' position:

> The abolitionists – whether anarchists or Marxists – argue that the institution is unretainable; that there is little that can be done this side of revolution other then attempt to monitor or control it; the only solution to the problem of policing is the abolition of the police.... For the abolitionist all crime is political. It has two forms: working class crime, which is born of poverty, desperation and unemployment; and crimes of the powerful, which are born of greed, guile and manipulation.[158]

The line of argument remained consistent with Young's earlier paper. Abolitionists were left idealists who simplified and reduced crime and policing to a rhetoric which proposed the exaggeration of working-class and the under-representation of ruling-class crime and that the criminal justice system, and the police in particular, simply function to protect the powerful and control the working class.

In a more recent interview for *Time Out* Jock Young was introduced as, 'a criminologist who believes in cutting through the ideological crap – from Right or Left'. This middle-of-the-spectrum 'realism', 'the hardest line of all', returned to the well-established theme and trod (almost) the same ground. For there had been two (not three, after all) 'brands of criminology'. The first was the 'conventional, Home Office sort designed by Cambridge scholars' (was this reformism or conservatism?).

> The other dominant brand came from the headbanging left. This postulates that it is the police – and only the police – who are beastly; in fact that crime – to quote one leading apostle – 'is merely a footnote in this history of policing'; and that notions of crime waves in working-class areas, perpetrated by the working-class, are the product of media-inspired moral panics.[159]

Variously labelled 'left idealists', 'extreme idealists', 'abolitionists' or the 'headbanging left' the thread has run through the 'new realists' work with a clear consistency. What has been created is an image of the critical debates in criminology and deviancy theory as being hijacked by ultra-leftists whose crude reductionism and determinism removed the possibility or perceived need to engage in responsible, constructive or interventionist dialogue around crime and policing. By building the 'straw man' of left idealism and distancing themselves from it the new realists have established, apparently to their own satisfaction, that they alone address the complexity and reality of the related issues of crime and policing.

Young's work has formed the basis of a series of articles and books written from the mid-1980s onwards. Three of the main texts which have been produced are *What is to be Done About Law and Order?*, *Confronting Crime* and *Losing the Fight against Crime*.[160] In each of these books, the realist position on a number of criminological issues is outlined. For the realists crime is a particular problem in deprived inner-city areas; it is predominantly intra-class and intra-racial; it is a reflection of those most basic of capitalist values, individualism and acquisitiveness and the policing of society must be made more effective and accountable so that it responds to the real needs of the community. They have supported these arguments by conducting a number of surveys, most notably in Islington and Merseyside. In outlining these issues the realists argue that radical criminology has neglected them to the detriment not only of individuals and communities but also to the development of a successful left political strategy as the right's success in playing the law-and-order card at elections guarantees them a winning hand. In the next part of this chapter we critically evaluate three main aspects of left realist criminology: their conceptualization of crime, their analysis of the police and the state, and finally the political context within which their ideas have developed.

3. i. Realism and the Question of Crime

> Let us state quite categorically that that the major task of radical criminology is to seek a solution to the problem of crime and that of a socialist policy is to substantially reduce the crime rate.[161]

The question of crime dominates much of left realist writing. Within that context, the impact of crime on working-class people is a pivotal element in their analysis. They attempt to dispel what they see as a 'Robin Hood' view of crime which they argue demonstrates left idealist views in the area. Indeed, Jock Young had been expressing such views as early as 1979 in *Capitalism and the Rule of Law*:

> A key feature of left idealism emerges here: it *plays down* the impact of working-class crime against the working class, it *maximizes* the anti-working-class effects of ruling-class crime; whilst at the same time stressing its endemic nature.[162]

Following the 1980–81 uprisings from within Britain's black communities the debate around police–community relations was reconstructed both in official discourse and in the media coverage as an issue of the escalation of black criminality. The clear evidence of institutionalized racism in the post-war policies and practices of the state, so stark in the case of operational policing,[163] became lost in the unquestioning acceptance of statistics and reports which had their origins in the partisan interests of the police. Press photographers and television news coverage of black 'rioters', 'looters' and 'arsonists' consolidated the images of 'muggers' and 'thugs'. Enoch Powell's late 1960s prophecy of 'rivers of blood' had been self-fulfilled by the 'evil' within the 'alien' cultures of the inner city. Given the theoretical and analytical sophistication of the challenge to these crude, reductionist explanations – noted earlier – the black communities might have expected 'radical' academics to shift the emphasis away from the genetic and cultural determinism of the New Right and its attendant media. It was in this climate that new realist criminology emerged. If the expectation was an analysis which directed attention towards white racism and its institutionalized forms of expression it was soon to be shattered by the immediate writings of John Lea and Jock Young and their theory of urban marginalization.[164]

At the heart of their thesis was a well-worn interpretation of post-war black history in Britain. This argued that the 'first generation of immigrants entering this country in the nineteen fifties and sixties more often than not had *lower* expectations of life than the indigenous population'. This is because the comparison was made by immigrants with their country of origin – thus 'cultural diversity' worked 'against instability and discontent'. The second-generation blacks, however, were schooled in the expectation of equality in jobs and in access to the consumer market but soon realized that by comparison with the 'indigenous population' they were 'manifestly unequal'. Thus it was not the 'separateness of cultures but in the process of their homogenization, through the school and the mass media that gives rise to discontent'. Lea and Young concluded that as a result West Indian youth formed a 'counter culture' not inherited from their parents but

> a culture of discontent resulting from the visibility of deprivation... highlighted by the very process of integration into British standards and expectations of life ... an improvised culture based on the import of elements from the West Indies.[165]

This 'culture of discontent' involved 'contradictory elements'. On the one hand it embodied a 'positive search for identity and survival in the harsh conditions of the inner city'; on the other:

> Street culture can be competitive, disorganized, anti-social ... Hustling is not the pursuit of angels. Cultures which grow out of adversity and oppression are as likely to be predatory as progressive. Crime abounds in such communities and whereas much of it has no significance (i.e. cannabis smoking) other elements such as street robbery and interpersonal violence is seriously anti-social.[166]

Lea and Young supported the cultural equation of 'discontent' and 'crime' not only by quoting from the police evidence to the Scarman Inquiry but also by an uncritical acceptance of the police statistics for 'mugging' and footpad robbery (such as the claimed 138% increase in 'mugging' in Brixton between 1976 and 1980). Once the equation had been drawn their description appeared little different in text to similar pronouncements from the right. For example: 'Inner city black youth culture is a counter culture of of despair and resistance to discrimination and deprivation which involves soaring rates of street crime.'[167] In turn this created 'a vicious circle whereby relations between the police and the community deteriorate in such a way that each step in deterioration increases pressure for deterioration'. Their emphasis, like that of the police, focused on the Afro-Caribbean community. They argued that Asian youths have been insulated from the process of relative deprivation because of the entrepreneurial, professional opportunity structure afforded by their community. Further, in an intriguing use of the notion of social distance, they argued that 'the distance between Asian culture and the indigenous British culture is greater than the distance between the West Indian and the indigenous British culture'. Thus they concluded that the 'assimilation to indigenous British standards and aspirations' was 'probably a more rigid process for youth of West Indian parentage'. This had led to Afro-Caribbean youth experiencing deprivation more severely and 'the consequent fostering of a deviant counter culture'.

While Lea and Young attempted to grapple with the relationship between class and subcultures, for they argued that late capitalism has produced 'some of the social and political features of early capitalism, particularly the economic and political marginalization of whole communities from the political process', their position on race ignored the historical, economic and political contexts in which immigration developed. Further, that 'first generation blacks' *internalized* the values of 'indigenous British culture' (whatever that is) is a common assumption seriously contested by black commentators and community leaders. They generalized their discussion of Brixton and ignored the fact that the black community in cities such as Liverpool is in its fourth and fifth generations. Finally, and most seriously, they ignored the proposition that British state institutions, including the police, have developed and now reinforce policies and practices based on the political and ideological construction of national identity. In the institutionalization of racism marginalization is not a 'condition' suddenly inflicted on the Afro-Caribbean or Asian community simply by a downturn in the economy. It is written into the statutory definitions of immigration law and reflected in the political management of identities throughout state practices.

Lea and Young failed to theorize the connections between class and race. They provided no analysis of the historical development of class fragmentation, particularly the use of migrant or immigrant labour as 'reserve armies'. Given the reliance of most advanced capitalist economies on 'guest workers' and, in Britain, the well-established practice of exploiting 'cheap' labour from the colonies (such as Irish immigration in the nineteenth century) it is difficult to understand Lea and Young's omission. It is a significant issue if the dynamics of post war immigration and the economic marginalization of black communities are to be understood. For the shift from labour-intensive production and the experience of an economic crisis within the UK together have produced long-term, structural unemployment. The reserve army of labour is no longer necessary and the growth of unemployment as a persistent condition of advanced capitalism has produced a relative surplus population. The inevitable consequence of the economic, political and ideological location of black communities is that they are over-represented in this surplus population. As with the late nineteenth century constructions of moral degeneracy and social contagion, black people have found themselves on the wrong end of the rough–respectable and non-deserving–deserving continua. This series of factors have created the preconditions in which black communities can be identified as the new 'dangerous classes'. We consider that Lea and Young contributed to that identification. Thus the first forays by the new realists into the race–crime debate brought an angry response both from within the black communities and from critical criminologists.

Thus the development of the realist work, particularly Lea and Young's book, *What is to be Done about Law and Order?*, centred on the question of black people's involvement in crime. In the book sixty-four out of 284 pages are devoted to what they term, 'The Race and Crime Debate'. Here Lea and Young consolidate their earlier position: 'black people have a higher crime rate than would be expected from their numbers as a proportion of the population'.[168] This view subsequently has been contested in a number of articles.[169] In Chapter 3 Paul Gilroy brings together some of these arguments. As he has written in another context, however, it is important also to acknowledge that:

> The argument against it should not be read as a denial of the fact that blacks engage in criminal acts, though there are a number of unresolved questions around the extent of black participation – in particular around the role of official statistics in verifying their involvement. It is no betrayal of black interests to say that blacks commit crime, or that black law-breaking may be related to black poverty as law-breaking is always related to poverty. The possibility of a direct relationship between ethnicity, black culture and crime is an altogether different and more complex issue.[170]

There are a number of more general points we wish to make concerning the realists' argument. First, they base much of their discussion on the idea that 'crime is of importance politically because unchecked it divides the working class community and is materially and morally the basis of disorganization'.[171] This abstract and undifferentiated view of crime is theoretically and politically problematic not only because it allows the already elastic concept of crime to become a catch-all category but also because it presents an idealized view of the working-class community as 'a homogenous group united by its fear of crime despite the everyday divisions of gender, race, craft, income and employment'.[172] This division, historically and contemporaneously, has been a fundamental part of working-class life. Its origins are clear in early industrial capitalism. Second, and related to this, while Lea and Young have argued that vandalism, rape, mugging, burglary and so on, constitute just one more factor in the burdens that working-class people have to suffer, and that there should be a police force that will respond effectively to these problems, they fail to differentiate the impact of these crimes on specific groups in the population and overemphasize both the ability and the willingness of the police to deal with them. As Tony Ward has explained:

> There are two objections to this which seem to me to go to the heart of this

version of 'realism'. Firstly, vandalism, rape etc. do not constitute a single
phenomenon (if the common denominator is supposed to be 'street crime' this
implies a gross misconception of rape). Secondly, policing is not *the* issue. *An*
issue is that in certain circumstances where the police could take effective
action – eg. rapes and racial attacks where the victim knows the attacker – they
fail to do so. It is a secondary issue in the wider context of racism and
patriarchy but a crucial one for the individuals concerned.[173]

In addition to this, as Phil Scraton has pointed out, there is no reason to
believe that the range of burdens identified by the new realists are seen by
victims as being similar. As he argued, 'just as it is probable that men from all
classes see street violence as a "problem" for them, they would not see most
actions of sexual harassment as a "problem" at all'.[174] Finally, as Gilroy and
Sim discuss in Chapter 2, public concerns about crime must be understood
as the outcome of a political process which necessitates breaking down the
abstract general category of crime into 'the particular experiences, images
and fear which correspond to city life'.[175] In turn this means understanding
the complex relationship between the police and fractions within the
working class, the struggles around criminalization and the depoliticization
of struggle.

3. ii. Realism, the Police and the State

We do not want to extend the role of the police but to restrict it. We are not
anti-police, just totally against undemocratic forms of policing.[176]

The second major point in the new realist position is their analysis of the
role of the police and their conception of the state in British society. In *What
Is to Be Done about Law and Order?* Lea and Young argue for a system of police
accountability the consequences of which would be that 'the relation
between police and public will change from the present one verging in
growing areas of our major cities on open warfare to one of mutual
confidence'.[177] This new-found accountability will ensure that the vicious
circle of alienation, the reduced flow of information to the police, rising
crime, militarization and more alienation will be broken; more information
will flow to the police, more crimes will be cleared up and there will be more
public confidence in the police as a service. This proposition, like their
position on crime, has a number of significant weaknesses. First, as we
argued above, the relationship between the police and the policed is more
complex than the realists appear to assume – that the long historical
confrontations and profound mistrust of the police within working-class,
black or Irish communities can be forgotten is misplaced. Second, the
proposition lacks historical specificity. Put simply, the realists do not
present any clear historical evidence as to when the 'flow of information' to
the police began to dry up. Lea and Young note:

It is our argument that, firstly, over the last decade and a half the signs have
been of a drift towards military policing in areas like Brixton; and secondly,

that this drift is self-reinforcing. It results in a vicious circle in which moves in the direction of military policing undermine whatever elements of consensus policing may remain, and lay the foundations for further moves in the direction of military policing.[178]

This argument implies that at some unspecified time prior to the mid-1960s consensus policing and the flow of information to the police was a reality. This is erroneous. In London, for example, in the 1930s the clear-up rate for crime was not only then low but the Commissioner was even then having to defend the use of stop-and-search powers because of the hostility they engendered from some of the population.[179] Third, and related to this, as Tony Ward has indicated:

the relationship between the flow of information and the crime rate is a highly complex issue which Lea and Young make little attempt to explore ... their position assumes that in a large proportion of crimes there are witnesses who a) could identify the offender, b) do not do so out of hostility to the police and c) would do so if the police were accountable and behaved better. Should any of these assumptions be false, the result of an increased flow of information could well be a higher rate of reported crime, and a lower 'clear-up rate' ... [also] they assume that the 'clear-up rate' is a major determinant of the 'real' crime rate, thus taking for granted the shakiest aspect of the theory of general deterrence, the relationship between 'objective' and perceived certainty of detection.[180]

Fourth the realists argue from their surveys that where crime is a real problem for communities, 'people want the police but they want them to get on with what they see to be the proper jobs of policing – the control and investigation of serious crime and offences like sexual assaults, robbery and burglary'.[181] This position, as Tony Jefferson has pointed out, is not only disarmingly simple, it is

simplistic. Quite aside from the fact that neither police numbers nor particular activities appear to bear much relationship to the clear-up rate beyond a certain bedrock of effectiveness, the difficult truth is that more effective crime control has implications for civil liberties.[182]

Fifth, there are methodological issues relating to the surveys raised by a number of critics: findings based solely on questionnaire interviews have to be treated with a degree of caution; surveys depend on how questions are asked and how well interviewers are trained;[183] the findings can be interpreted in a number of different ways. For example, as Kenan Malik has pointed out, while those involved in the Islington Crime Survey has contended that the public see crime as a major problem:

According to their own figures, twice as many people worry about unemployment as they do about crime. Barely a third see crime as a major problem – a figure that is statistically no different from that of vandalism, poor housing or the lack of facilities for young people.[184]

Sixth, and underpinning much of the above discussion, is whether the police as an organization and as a state institution is committed to doing something about crime. Sociologically, there is still little evidence to support the view that the police can, or indeed wish, to solve crime, especially those crimes which strike most viciously and selectively at the heart of communities, for example, racial attacks and sexual assaults. Also it is important to remember the historical evidence which shows that the police have been a force *against* rather than a service *for* working-class people. This is supported by a structural relationship of legal domination in which police power is dovetailed with the rule of law to prioritize the imposition of control and order within the criminal justice process.[185] This is not to deny that such power is unchallenged, without contradictions or without limitations. Neither does it propose the existence of a unified, homogeneous state apparatus. Clearly the disturbances of 1981 and 1985 illustrated the gaps in the ability of the police to deal with disorder, gaps which the police have been eager to plug through the introduction of CS gas, plastic bullets (despite the fact that in Northern Ireland the majority of people killed by them have been children and bystanders), more sophisticated riot equipment and greater powers of arrest, stop and search and detention. These developments, with concomitant ruthlessness, have taken place in the context of a more militarized state response to problems of dissent and disorder in the UK. The aggressive mobilization of the police at recent public-order situations – students, miners, peace campaigners, travellers, trade unionists and anti-apartheid demonstrators – has not been resisted by the force. On the contrary, interventions by senior police officers, in the media and in private and public lobbying of parliamentarians, have encouraged the view that society is under sustained threat from groups of anti-authority agitators who stand outside of, and indeed subvert, the lifestyles of right-thinking, decent, 'normal' people. This equation between police attitudes, crime and public order was captured by Geoffrey Dear, Chief Constable of the West Midlands on BBC's *Brass Tacks* in July 1986:

Geoffrey Dear: The majority of people that I dealt with nearly 30 years ago and indeed 20 years ago would largely do as they were told by authority whether it's police or schools or the government or whatever. We've changed you may well argue for the better, I don't know, I think that's the point at issue, the point is that society is more questioning, more demanding, more searching in its attitudes and adopts a whole range of attitudes now which were not there before and that makes a number of occupations much more difficult and of course the police is well in the forefront of that little batch.

Q.   The police are supposed to prevent crime and maintain order, which is more important to a Chief Constable?

Geoffrey Dear: They're both important but I suppose in the final analysis it's got to be the maintenance of public order or the prevention of disorder. You can encapsulate the whole thing I suppose in a not entirely flippant way by saying that crime can go up through the roof and no-one is too worried about it but a serious and continual outbreak of public disorder will bring governments down and Chief Constables will be lost and out of a job very quickly.[186]

In the context of the UK, the growing authoritarianism of state practices, which clearly allows the deeply conservative views and attitudes of the police to flourish, cannot be divorced from what is happening in Northern Ireland, nor from Britain's historical role in its colonies. The new realists do not address this question, nor do they appear to see it as a significant sociological or political variable. While we would avoid the simplistic position that whatever happens in Northern Ireland will *automatically* happen in England, Wales and Scotland, there is enough evidence to demonstrate the links between individual state servants and institutional state practices in the six counties and in Britain (see Hillyard in Chapter 10). Rather than considering the political significance of this and other issues for their sociological analysis, the new realists simply return to their caricature of left idealism and its response to the state. Thus, Kinsey, Lea and Young contend that left idealists

> conceive of the state as a unitary, monolithic structure organized to one end – namely the protection of ruling class interests. . . . [Left idealism] ignored both the social basis of conflict within the police and the degree of autonomy of the police in relation to other state agencies. In doing so it denies the existence of political space for reform and the possibility of alternative forces of organization and control.[187]

This generalized caricature, not only ignores but categorically is contradicted by the recent history of critical criminology, outlined above, whose interventions were and are intended to exploit the contradictions within the state and the legal form itself in order to facilitate reform and change. Put simply, if the state had been conceived as a monolithic entity, incapable of change – and the Northern Irish state could be seen as the best example – then criminologists and sociologists would not have been involved in working for reform. Indeed, in terms of the new realist programme for reforms of the criminal justice process, it could be argued that it is *their* conceptualization and political understanding of the nature of reform that simplifies complex political processes. As Maureen Snider pointed out in her review of *What Is to Be Done about Law and Order?*, the book is

> insufficiently informed by any consideration of the limitations of the capitalist state, a problem that mars the final chapter with its delineation of a more just prosecutorial and prison system even more strikingly.[188]

Snider poses a series of questions which point to the severe limitations of the new realist's position in the relationships between legal reform, the state and capitalism:

> Where did the solid body of knowledge on the nature of the state under capitalism go that two Marxist scholars could assert that the police can be made accountable to representatives of the marginal working class ... OR that they can be made to take the theft of £50 from an old age pensioner more seriously than a similar theft from Woolworths? OR that prisons can be changed, and life inside them made 'as free and as normal as possible', by well-meaning political pressure-group struggle as though the only function of prisons is to contain the bad guys and protect the community? Wherever is the realism in such a wholesale denial of all that we know about the problems of reforming the state and especially the criminal justice system under capitalism? The closest Lea and Young came to a serious discussion of this is an optimistic and superficial reference to the state as a 'site of contradicting interests'. While it is true that the limits of reform are presently the subject of hot debate ... the one thing which is clear is that making meaningful middle or macro-level changes in the absence of far-reaching political and economic change is a very problematic endeavour far more likely to backfire, to be used against the interests of the powerless, to enrich the professionals administering the scheme and to extend the state's net of social control, than to turn life around for the marginal working class.[189]

This underlines a central tenet of new realist thinking: that in arguing for reform they have tied their demands to a programme of action which is to be monitored by the Labour Party. As Kinsey, Lea and Young succinctly have put it, 'the reforms we suggest are, of course, a matter for a future Labour government determined to tackle the problem of crime and its impact on working class people'.[190] How far the Labour Party is capable of realising such reforms, is the subject of the next section of this paper.

3. iii. *Realism, the Labour Party and Politics – Back to the Centre*

> The terrible irony of the return in the 1980s to a widespread concern among 'realistic' socialists with the immediacy of the question of power is that it has embroiled itself in a beside-the-point attack on vulgar Marxism while ignoring and even caricaturing the enormous contributions that were set in motion in the 1970s by the developments in Marxist writings on the state which were just reaching towards breaking the theoretical logjam of Marxist politics when the tide among socialist intellectuals turned back towards reformism.[191]

The period from the early 1970s onwards has been dominated both by the question of Britain's economic decline and by the ongoing struggle to maintain order and cohesion on a number of fronts. The uprisings in 1981 and 1985 and the confrontations between the police and different groups and communities have demonstrated both the fragility of that order and the limitations in the repertoire of the state's response. These limitations have been illustrated clearly in the ongoing struggle to maintain order in

Northern Ireland. The political tensions in the 1980s for the left have been underpinned by the continuing debate about the rise of what has been termed the New Right,[192] the development and consolidation of Thatcherism, and what an appropriate left response should be to these events if it is not to find itself fighting on the terrain mapped out by the right. While we do not intend to cover the full range of this debate, we emphasize that the key to understanding the Labour Party's analysis of crime and punishment is heavily influenced, if not determined, by these events. The Party on a range of social issues, has attempted the re-conceptualization of its analysis to take account of the right's ascendency. This has been done under the general umbrella of new realism while at the same time maintaining, indeed vigorously promoting, the idea that the Party is still wholly committed to social democracy and the parliamentary road to socialism. The new realism in criminology has nailed its colours to the Labour Party's mast. One of the earliest works produced by the realist school was Ian Taylor's *Law and Order: Arguments for Socialism*,[193] published in 1981. Taylor's analysis was influenced heavily by the writings of Tony Benn and the struggle at that point to 'democratize' the party:

> Direct and practical involvement in democratic socialist policies as currently organized (*therefore in Labour Party politics at local and national level*) is essential in order that the objective socialism can be reconnected to the various – frequently fragmentary – social groups which now make up the working class. Socialists in the Labour party have begun to take seriously the popular anxieties and fears which fed and sustained the growth of the radical Right. They must begin to construct and articulate policies that prefigure a genuine social order for all.[194]

In a range of writings during this period Taylor made several interventions outlining his position. In the American radical criminology journal *Crime and Social Justice* he made the unsupported assertion that

> in Britain mugging is indeed a form of self-employment (and may be a primitive form of street-level anti-white politics) that is disproportionately practiced by unemployed West Indians.[195]

Taylor's concern about 'muggings' and his view that it is 'disproportionately practised by unemployed West Indians', as we have seen, has been a central element in the new realist attempt to take crime seriously. His answer was for a full democratization of the social order, including the state, and for the mobilization of local communities into forums where popular justice would be a priority. In making the Labour Party the vehicle for this democratization Taylor's analysis was, as Tony Platt has pointed out:

> not a class analysis, it is dogmatism for it is at least questionable whether or not a transformed Labour party will become the vehicle of popular democracy in England.[196]

At the time of publication of Taylor's book Roy Hattersley, then Shadow Home Secretary, voiced the collective opinion for his Shadow Cabinet colleagues, and undoubtedly many others in the Party and the trade union movement, when he said that Labour must adopt a 'sensitive approach' to the police, an approach that would avoid the Party being labelled 'the anti-police party':

> We have made it clear that we want an effective police force (because it works with and for the people) which is able to produce the more peaceful society that Mrs Thatcher promised at the last election but was unable to provide . . . We will not achieve that end if we allow ourselves to become the anti-police party, better known for our unfair attacks than our constructive criticism.[197]

The centrality of Labour politics to the new realist position, and their belief in the party's political strategy for reforming the state was developed further by John Lea and Jock Young in a series of articles[198] and in *What is to Be Done about Law and Order?* We have outlined a number of critical points with regard to this work. Here we pay particular attention to their analysis of 'riot' and what should be done about it. For it is on this issue that their dependence on social-democratic politics is most clear.

The basis of their analysis of the 'riots' is to be found, they argue, in the complex interplay between relative deprivation, political marginalization and economic marginalization. Young blacks, in particular, through this interplay lack any effective outlet for their grievances and so engage in riotous behaviour. Crucially for Lea and Young:

> Riots only initiate changes and reforms in society to the extent that they force others (like Lord Scarman) to respond and inevitably define the issues. Precisely because they remain a form of reaction not a process whereby political changes and developments at the level of society as a whole can rationally be evolved, the riots signify that a large number of people are outside politics. The real issue of political reform facing us now is not that of how to define riots but how to adapt our political system in such a way that those previously driven to riot can be re-included in the organs of political discourse.[199]

For Lea and Young the 'organs of political discourse' ultimately depend on the participation of the Labour Party within the framework of social democratic politics. A number of critical points can be raised concerning this argument.

First, there is a very real neglect of the Labour Party's role in strengthening and consolidating, rather than challenging, state practices (see Gilroy and Sim in Chapter 2). Within social democratic discourse there are acceptable levels of debate and criticism beyond which those involved do not go. For black communities in particular, racism in the Labour Party and in the trade union movement in general has been a major factor which has led to the 'political isolation of the black community'. As Lee Bridges has pointed out:

Lea and Young talk of the necessity for a 'more radical reorganization of the political system' without apparently realizing that it is already well advanced under Thatcherism. In this situation it is increasingly the Labour Party and the 'socialist' Left and their popular democratic politics that are becoming marginalized, while the state proceeds in fulfilling its need for more effective policing against the community.[200]

Second, Lea and Young's position on riotous behaviour is underpinned by their conception of what constitutes *acceptable* political behaviour, a conception which centres on the narrow terrain of social democratic parliamentarianism. This ignores, as we have argued, the fact that this institutional arrangement has failed to represent not only black people but also the working class 'as a class at all'.[201] As Paul Gilroy has pointed out 'the failures of these institutions must be compared to the rapid growth of new movements with an autonomy from capitalist command as well as from the constricting repertoire of the "labour movement"'.[202] A third objection to the centrality of social democratic parties as political forces for social change, and one which is related to the point above, is the limitation in the vision of Labourist politics:

Social democracy, as a political force, has ... long since abandoned (if it ever had any conception of) the moral–social leadership ... over the classes it claims to represent. It has long ago ceased to work the 'good sense' of the class, its 'spontaneous' class instinct, its sense of the world as unjustly divided into the oppressed and the oppressing classes: it has limited itself to making tactically pragmatic accommodation with the most traditionalist and conservative elements in popular morality.[203]

From the perspective of 1987, the dynamic of Labour Party policy (and organized trade unions) is towards a realistic acceptance of the crisis confronting the country, in the hope of returning a future Labour government. In Leo Panitch's perceptive phrase the party is concerned with the 'immediacy of the question of power'.[204] For Panitch this concern has had dire consequences for the working class, consequences for which the intellectual left must share the responsibility:

The response of workers to the crisis must not be seen mechanistically or ahistorically as something inevitable, or as 'natural' or 'given'. It is *rather a product of a range of previous practices that fostered* certain structures and ideas that blocked the development of a viable socialist response to the crisis, and that excluded socialist options as 'unrealistic'. If we see the impasse in this way, as something constructed rather than given, we may also see that the impasse pertains not only, indeed only so much, to the drag that the working class or Marxism imposes on the socialist project, as many would have it today, as to the drag that social democracy continues to exercise on the working class and the intellectual left. For even though the Keynesianism and corporatism of social democracy have exhausted the limits of their reformist and electoral possibilities in the current crisis, they retain deep ideological and organizational supports which recent intellectual and party political experience indicates cannot be easily transcended.[205]

In the narrower field of criminology the social democratic strategies of new realism continue to work themselves through. Within the Labour Party the construction of the debate concerning the 'seriousness of crime' has accepted the premises of new realist criminology while underplaying the seriousness of the authoritarian shift within the state and its consequences for the furtherance of class domination and fragmentation. The Party's position on the state became clear during and after the 1984–5 coal dispute. Despite the evidence from the coalfields,

> Labour's leaders continued to see the state as an essentially neutral instrument capable of fulfilling a reconciling role. At one level the state was seen as an essential tool for the settlement of such conflicts, at another, a faith in the underlying liberalism of the British State, helped to ensure that Labour's leaders failed to come to terms with the reality of police actions in the coalfield. Such an approach to the state is not only to be found in Labour's responses to industrial disputes; it has dominated party thinking from the beginning.[206]

Further, is the tacit acceptance of the very terrain on which the law and order debate has been constructed and developed by the right and by state spokespeople. Thus the new realists have not challenged conventional criminological explanations and, more importantly, their policy prescriptions have become no more than 'constructive criticism' welcomed by the police and incorporated as an integral part of social democratic politics. After the police–community confrontation at Broadwater Farm in 1985 Bernie Grant, the Haringey Council leader, was uncompromising in his criticism of the police. The response from within the Party was to damn him with others on the 'loony left'. As Lee Bridges has stated:

> In effect, Labour Party policy is no longer addressed primarily to challenging police power *per se* but rather to reordering police priorities away from public order and towards crime prevention and control. The difficulty with this approach, on a political level, is that it moves some way towards accepting the Tory agenda for 'law and order' and places Labour spokesmen in open competition with their opponents in bidding up public anxieties about crime, with all the racist overtones that entails. Moreover, Labour's current policy, insofar as it relies on legal reforms and formal accountability to alter policing practices, seems to accept at face value the constitutional basis of police power and the supposed authority of chief constables over their forces. Certainly, without a strong line of command between senior officers and the police rank-and-file it is difficult to see what practical effect formal accountability will have in reducing police abuses of the black community.[207]

The new realists themselves now find their arguments being used by criminologists of the right.[208] The Labour Party, through its spokespeople, continues to tread the tightrope of assuaging 'public opinion' and making peace with the state. On 6 June 1986, the Shadow Home Secretary, Gerald

Kaufman, addressed a crime prevention seminar organized by Humberside Police at Hull University. He detailed the extent of crime committed in Britain in 1985. For Kaufman, his analysis of the official criminal statistics led to one unavoidable conclusion: that Britain was 'suffering from the worst crime wave ever known', and that under Thatcherism Britain had become 'a more dangerous and violent country'.[209] He went on:

> Under Margaret Thatcher Britain has become a family divided against itself. Division is deliberately stirred up between old and young, between the retired and those still at work, between employed and unemployed, North and South, black and white, inner city and suburbs. No family can prosper when some of its members feel neglected and despised.... Despite all their best and most dedicated efforts the police cannot cope with this crime wave.[210]

Kaufman's vision of a happy British family disunited and disrupted by the appearance of the evil and strange spirit of Thatcherism strikes a deep chord in the ideology of Labourist politics. His ahistoricism is compounded once more by accommodating the police as a service which, despite its best efforts, cannot swim against the criminal tide. While he rightly committed the Labour Party to the repeal of the Police and Criminal Evidence Act and the Public Order Act he was careful not to criticize the police role in the demand for such powers or the ways they have used and abused their new powers, as was revealed by the Broadwater Farm Independent Inquiry. The Government, in his view, had failed 'to recognize the importance of maintaining community support for the police. The result has been increasing confrontations between the police, and the community, greater likelihood of injustice and reduced police effectiveness.'[211] Kaufman's Hull speech followed his visit to the annual conference of the Police Federation where he assured delegates that a future Labour government would seek to work closely with the police. This assurance was made to dispel claims by the federation that anti-police attitudes were growing in the party. His attitude, however, was given the seal of approval by Sir Kenneth Newman at the beginning of June. Speaking on TV-am Newman stated that he detected a 'change of tack' in the Labour Party's position on the police:[212]

> If you look at what the Labour Party are actually proposing on law and order – leaving the issue of accountability on one side then it doesn't sound all that much different to me from what the Conservative Party is doing.

By the end of the 1986 summer the wheel had turned full circle. Norman Tebbit's attacks on the evils of the permissive society and post-war 'funk', widely quoted earlier in the year, were echoed by Neil Kinnock. Under the banner front-page headline of 'THE PERMISSIVE SOCIETY' the *Sunday Mirror* repeated the crime statistics: a burglary every 30 seconds; a violent crime every four minutes; rape up by 29% from the previous year. Inside, next to a cartoon of a denim-clad, long-haired hippie couple standing over a young boy and girl, clearly haunted by the spectre of drugs, Kinnock made the following statement on the notion of permissiveness (it could have been Tebbit talking):

> I am a reactionary. No matter how hard I try to convince myself towards the course of enlightenment I know damn well that, put to the test, it's no good.[213]

Despite the strength of the law and order lobby, the introduction of new punitive legislation, a contrived war in the South Atlantic and the militarization of the British police, successive Thatcher Governments were criticized from different ends of the political spectrum for failing to turn the tide of lawlessness. In one of his final speeches as Metropolitan Commissioner Sir Kenneth Newman talked of the 'multi-ethnic inner city' as presenting the 'greatest current difficulties for policing... the greatest challenge to government'.[214] Newman painted a clear backcloth to the deep-seated problems of the 'deprived inner city areas': a trebling of crime in 20 years with three-quarters of a million crimes reported in 1986; a sharp increase in violent crime, especially the use of knives which had doubled in 4 years; a *'general'* increase in violence – murders, assaults, robberies, and assaults on police officers. For Newman there was no doubt as to the centre of lawlessness:

> The tradition is that the policeman works with the consent of the community. But how does this apply to Broadwater Farm, where over half the households have members with criminal convictions, where the population is 42% black, and in 52% of households no-one has a job? Is there any form of social consensus in such places? The answer is, I think, that the local officer can have no confidence that local people will help him if he gets into trouble. Indeed, his experience if he lays a hand on a black man may well be that others will unite to prevent the arrest, and perhaps to assault him.[215]

The picture, reminiscent of Lea and Young's construction of the breakdown of consensus, is clear. Crime, violence and the black communities have become inextricably linked and the real power of the black communities is their ability to persist in their lawlessness free from police intervention – the creation of 'no-go' areas. He listed Railton Road in Brixton, All Saints Road in Notting Hill and Sandringham Road in Hackney as examples of centres 'where crime is at its worst, where drug dealing is intolerably overt, and where the racial ingredient is at its most potent.... These are the flashpoints of policing the inner city.'[216] Newman argued that in these centres the 'law abiding majority' and the police were beleaguered and isolated not only by spiralling crime but also by 'hypercriticism' from community leaders and local politicians. Once again the social construction is that of the minority 'enemy within' threatening the very fabric of city-based community life. Newman was not alone in holding this position.

In March 1987 one of the Old Bailey's most eminent judges, Michael Argyle, gave what he thought would be an unreported speech to law students at Trent Polytechnic. He argued strongly that despite its promises to apply a firm hand to law and order the 'Government has fallen flat on its face in dealing with the situation ... law and order does not exist in this country at the moment. The criminals are walking all over us.'[217] For Argyle the issue of lawlessness was juxtaposed with black immigration. He argued that there were probably 5 million illegal immigrants in Britain and he answered a request for proof with the comment: 'I do not have the figures but just go to Bradford'.

These views, reflecting a commonly held belief that crimes of violence, political disorder and industrial conflict now threaten the foundations of British society, have a broad constituency among Conservative Party politicians, chief constables, the judiciary and magistracy, and are given constant reinforcement by a reactionary media. As Stuart Hall has pointed out, law and order rhetoric and ideology has established and fed a climate of authoritarianism which has real populist appeal. Yet having contributed significantly to that climate the Conservative Government has found itself criticized for failing to deal with the lawlessness of the 'enemy within'. The Labour Party, presenting the political face of new realist criminology, made its own contribution to fuelling the moral panic. In September 1986 Gerald Kaufmann, the Shadow Home Secretary, launched Labour's new policy on crime and policing. His comments on the 'crime problem' were indistinguishable from those of Newman and Argyle. He stated:

> After seven years of failed Tory promises on law and order and relentlessly rising crime ... [in half an hour] 8 people will have become victims of violent crime; 38 people will have suffered from vandalism or criminal damage; 60 people will have been burgled; 128 people will have suffered a theft; 248 people will have been the victims of some kind of crime ... Thousands more endure the fear of crime.[218]

The Labour Party policy statement, entitled *Protecting our People*, went on to catalogue the breakdown in law and order and the devastating effects of the fear of crime under the years of Conservative rule. Its main theme was that it had become essential to make communities more safe with practical changes to the environment and better security in people's homes. It established the 'right' of people to live free from crime and its attendant fears. Yet in its acceptance of the rhetoric of law and order and in its uncritical response to the official statistics the new realist approach reinforced the very fears it was seeking to alleviate. This became even more apparent after the release of the 1986 criminal statistics in March 1987. Claiming the main story-line on all news bulletins and banner headlines in the following day's newspapers the 'escalation' in crime was presented to the nation as yet further evidence of the tightening grip of lawlessness and violence which threatened every individual, especially people not able to defend themselves.

Rather than responding to the release of the figures in a measured and responsible manner the opposition parties vied with each other to score pre-election political points. Gerald Kaufmann stated that the Conservative promise to deal with crime and its effects had been exposed finally as a 'real sham'. The Alliance spokesperson, Shirley Williams, said that the rising crime rates, 'shattered the Conservatives' claim to be the party of law and order'. Using a metaphor which was at best unfortunate the *Guardian* leader writer commented; 'Those record figures reveal the darkening side of life in Britain'.[219] Yet there was no attempt to consider the breakdown of the official statistics. As with the 1984–5 coal dispute the official line which gave the appearance that Britain was under threat from a wave of personal violence was not born out by the statistics. In fact the official statistics showed that the most common crime was motor vehicle theft (29.4%). Taken together with burglary (20.6%) and 'other theft and handling' (24.4%) crimes involving theft of property, money or valuables accounted for 94.4% of the total of reported crimes. Offences against the person, to which so much time was given in media and political statements, totalled 5.2% of all reported crime. Clearly this is a gross underestimate, given the under-reporting of violence against women and racist attacks, but these categories are given little priority in either the media or political debate.

It is difficult to establish a direct correlation between poverty and increases in property crime. Examining that relationship during the inter-war period Herbert Mannheim used unemployment as the 'more reliable factor for the measurement of the economic position' and found that fluctuations in crime and unemployment corresponded throughout the inter-war period.[220] Apart from statistical correlation Mannheim used official accounts which provided evidence that unemployment was an 'overwhelming force' as a 'crime-producing agency'. These reports indicated that long-term or 'structured' unemployment among adult men, coupled with a reduction in the real value of unemployment relief, produced widespread demoralization particularly in the inner cities where the class divisions were most obvious. He emphasized that the harshest effects were on youth, with people leaving school at 14 facing low pay, poor working conditions and unemployment. The climate in which young working-class people lived was 'one of despair'. He concluded that 'a very considerable part of the total crime rate in this country is due to unemployment'.

Rather than concentrating on the relationship between material conditions and the processes by which people become pushed into property crime, however, it seemed to suit the opposition parties to emphasize the failure of Conservative policies on law and order. Without a critical analysis of the political, economic and social forces which contextualize the growth in property crime the Tory, reactionary ideology of authoritarianism remains intact. As Jeremy Seabrook argued in his dramatic analysis of the 'real meaning of the Aids crusade':

> In the same week as this particular Aids scare, it was also reported that crime figures have reached record levels. The law and order rhetoric of eight years of

Thatcherism has failed, and it is time for a further turn of the ideological screw... the deliverer will come, St George, the bringer of order and the restorer of things... a role not a million miles from that which Thatcher assumed in the distant days of 1979.... Yet Thatcherism is too genteel in its brutalities; the velvet glove is too caressing and protective. When her mission is more widely seen to have failed, that is when we shall await the millenarian deliverance of the Strong Man, who will not only bring forth se.se out of universal chaos, but at the same time will restore Britain to her former greatness.[221]

For Seabrook the 'outlines of what will replace the demise of Thatcher' are founded on the established platforms of racism, homophobia and the intolerance of dissent. In the wings awaits fascism and the sights have been set accurately on its targets. What has been absent from the new realist analysis and its political pronouncements have been analyses of the processes by which specific groups become economically marginalized and politically targeted on the basis of ideological justifications which equate their struggles with the breakdown in moral values and social discipline. While critical criminology has sought to locate the processes of criminalization within a critique of the advanced capitalist state and its institutions of regulation and control the new realists appear to have faith in the potential of political reform under a Labour government.

In highlighting these connections we are not arguing that everyone in the Labour Party or the trade union movement necessarily subscribes to these views. Clearly, that would be indefensible. What is clear, however, is that new realism has led to a political cul-de-sac where 'realistic' policies on crime, welfare, housing, wages, health and schooling predominate over a class analysis. Consequently policies accept rather than challenge the terrain of the powerful. Also we should be quite categorical about what we are *not* saying: we are not saying that crime is not a problem for working-class people or that, contrary to the innuendo in some new realist writing, that the terrible brutality suffered by many women is not a problem for them. Neither are we saying that the state cannot be reformed. Clearly, as we have outlined above, this is possible within limits. What we are saying is that the new realist position on law and order is theoretically flawed and, from a socialist perspective, it remains politically conservative in its conclusions about what can be done about the state.

4. Conclusion: Interpreting the State, Understanding Criminalization

We are now in the middle of a deep and decisive movement towards a more disciplinary, authoritarian kind of society. This shift has been in progress since the 1960s; but has gathered pace through the 1970s and is heading, given the spate of disciplinary legislation now on the parliamentary agenda, towards some sort of interim climax.[222]

For Stuart Hall a 'repression to a stone-age morality' and the 'blind spasm of control' were the twin constructs of an 'authoritarian populism' used to justify and rationalize the deep political and institutional shifts towards a strong, authoritarian and coercive state given credibility in 1979 with the return of a Conservative Government under the leadership of Margaret Thatcher. As Hall noted, the foundations of this fundamentalist, authoritarian shift were laid in the Heath period of the early 1970s. They drew together several folk-devils which became plausible explanations for the economic and social 'decline' of Great Britain: the power of the unions; the rise of the scrounger; the escalation of crime; the threat of terrorism; the decline of moral values; the subversion of democracy. Each of these carefully constructed images, emphasized and reinforced by a right-wing media eager to cultivate and mobilize prejudices against any progressive developments around race, gender, class, unemployment and poverty, became synonomous with the 'breakdown' of British society. The demand was for a return to an old order – one based on the pillars of 'morality' and 'discipline' – the claimed values of Victorian Britain. Without so much as a cursory glance towards the realities of life in the Victorian period Thatcherite rhetoric became realized in policies directed to the achievement of the goals of the New Right: economic libertarianism and social authoritarianism.

Within a year of election the Conservative Government had cast its pre-election folk-devils as the 'enemy within'. It established new forms of surveillance, regulation and control in all areas of social policy, welfare and criminal justice. Substantial wage increases were given to military personnel and to the police. While the tax inspectorate deplored cuts in its serious fraud section specialist claims control units were set up within the DHSS as part of a well-publicized clampdown on welfare fraud. New legislation, imposing major controls on the unions and extending special powers and police powers, was drafted and passed. Harsh regimes were introduced in Youth Detention Centres and directed towards first-time offenders under the slogan of 'short sharp shock'. Heavier prison sentences were introduced, parole dates were pushed back overnight and a new prison-building programme announced. By 1986 Britain topped the West European league table for sending people to prison proportionate to its population. These initiatives, introduced amid scenes of joy verging on hysteria at successive Conservative Party conferences, consolidated the law and order bandwagon. Lawlessness meant the 'rising tide' of crime, industrial conflict, public disorder and political terrorism. Toryism meant a victory for common-sense, traditional values and a 'firm hand on the tiller'.

The Thatcherites know that they must 'win' in civil society as well as in the state. They understand, as the left generally does not, the consequences of the generalization of the class struggle to new arenas and the need to have a strategy for them too. They mean, if possible, to reconstruct the 'terrain' of what is taken-for-granted in social and political thought – and so to form a new common sense. If one watches how, in the face of a teeth-gritting opposition, they have steadily used the unpopularity of some aspects of trade union practice with their own members to inflict massive wounds on the whole labour movement, or how they have steadily not only pursued the 'privatization' of the public sector but installed 'value for money' at the heart of the calculations of every Labour council and every other social institution – health service, school meals, universities, street cleaning, unemployment benefit offices, social-services – one will take this politico-ideological level of struggle somewhat more seriously than the left currently does.[223]

Stuart Hall's lucid and searching reply to his critics reaffirmed an analytical commitment to the significance of what he termed previously the, 'death of the rightward turn' within the politics of Thatcherism.[224] The domination of 'domestic politics' by processes of 'crisis-management and containment strategies', had been set against a 'language of law and order ... sustained by moralisms'. Stuart Hall referred to this as the syntax of 'good' against 'evil', the standards of 'civilized' against 'uncivilized' and the choice of 'anarchy' against 'order'. He concluded: 'the play on "values" and on moral issues ... is what gives to the law and order crusade much of its grasp on popular morality and common-sense conscience'.[225] The consolidation and selective enforcement of repressive law, the acceptance – however grudging – of the operational independence of the police and the level of tolerance of reactionary court processes and decisions are manifestations of the grip of the New Right's law and order ideology. While there has been major resistance to authoritarian populism – the inner-city uprisings of 1980–81 and since; the direct action responses of women's groups; the peace movement and Greenham; the coal dispute – there remains substantial support for the police, the courts and the processes of criminal justice.

What the New Right has understood, certainly more sharply than the romanticized versions of a united homogeneous working class implicit in a broad range of left analyses, is the significance and depth of the political and ideological differences within working-class experiences. The fractures and divisions in neighbourhoods and workplaces have as such to do with the ideas and politics of patriotism and race, of masculinity and gender, of jobs and materialism as they have to do with the objective location of paid work, domestic labour or unemployment within the economy. As Paul Gilroy and Joe Sim establish in Chapter 2, selective enforcement and authoritarian responses have been central to the historical development of the legal process and are not to be seen as specific to Thatcherism. What the Thatcher administrations have sustained, however, is a high level of consensus between senior police officers, the magistracy, the judiciary and the government in the mobilization of the law against those well-established 'opponents' of liberal-democracy: political protestors, pickets, anti-nuclear demonstrators and 'alien' populations.

Law and order rhetoric, as an expression of deep-seated ideologies, has its strength in its broad appeal as part of the development of popular consent.

The level of resistance to government policies throughout the 1970s and since is clear evidence that dominant ideologies are not wholly internalized. A further strength of ideology, however, which is reflected in the well-established differential policies and practices of the police, the welfare agencies and the courts, is its institutionalization and central role in the management, containment and control of conflict.

The recent debates around the state and the rule of law have ranged from important contributions on left idealism[226] to naive, schematic and crude misinterpretations of the 'Marxist' model.[227] Beyond the contributions primarily concerned with crime and the rule of law, others have proved to be so academically dense and remote that they appear to restrict any potential for political action.[228] What has become clear is that there are quite substantive differences separating critical, neo-Marxist analyses of the state.[229] Most of these positions move beyond a simple interpretation of the rule of law merely as an instrument of class oppression and regulation although examples of this persist.

Hall *et al.*[230] paid specific attention to the centrality of legal relations in the achievement of a consensus for the social authority of a class alliance. The law does not simply correspond to the needs or demands of economic relations but through the intervention of its institutions it is essentially educative: it 'manages' consent, 'organizes' domination and 'secures' hegemony. This position owes much to the work of Gramsci who argued the centrality of the law in the shaping of society. In this process the state and its legal institutions are sites of class struggle while also being essential to the anticipation and resolution of such struggles.

The significance of these important, yet frequently inaccessible debates, has been the varying degree of emphasis placed on the state as a relation. In fact the state comprises a series of relations which exist at different levels. It is its very complexity, encompassing contradictory elements, which enables opposition to emerge within the state while defending established positions through internal alliances. It does matter that senior personnel share educational backgrounds and contemporary world-views. Yet those personnel operate within the confines and regulation of structural forms – the institution and practices of the state. These institutionalized practices reflect a history of confronting political struggle and opposition, a legacy of containment and political management. While each confrontation; internally or externally, develops and changes the state – policy makers and policy advisers do learn from their experiences – its shifts are more likely to be protective of social relations laid down in the economy than they are to be antagonistic. Advanced capitalism, with the added complexity of managerial relations and class fractions, is served and serviced but rarely confronted by the state's institutions whose members share its ends, if not always its means, in a common ideology. It is at this level that the function of institutions, exemplified by the rule of law, tutors and guides the broad membership of society.

Class fragmentation and the political and economic marginalization of fragmented elements within the working class, the oppression of women within the long and common history of patriarchal societies, and the post-colonial exploitation of immigrant and migrant labour are not solely manifestations of economic determinants. Patriarchy and colonization take political forms and engender political opposition – but also they generate ideological constructions of reality which justify, defend and reinforce the political-economic relations of dominance. It is at this point that the state and its institutions regenerate and reconstruct ideas as well as policies which serve to defend the structural contradictions – and their consequences – of a developing or receding national economy. Clearly, then, what critical analyses in criminology provide – and this constitutes the basis upon which each of these papers is founded – is an understanding of the processes of criminalization through which consensus is forced rather than forged.[231]

Notes

1 Antonio Gramsci cited in R. Simon, *Gramsci's Political Thought: An Introduction*, London, Lawrence & Wishart, 1982, p 100.

2 C. Wright Mills, *The Sociological Imagination*, New York, Oxford University Press, 1959.

3 A.W. Gouldner, *The Coming Crisis in Western Sociology*, London, Heinemann, 1970.

4 H.S. Becker, *Outsiders: Studies in the Sociology of Deviance*, New York, Free Press, 1963.

5 E.M. Lemert, *Human Deviance, Social Problems and Social Control*, Englewood Cliffs, NJ, Prentice-Hall, 1967.

6 D. Matza, *Becoming Deviant*, Englewood Cliffs, NJ, Prentice-Hall, 1969.

7 In July 1972 after already publishing a symposium on Gouldner's 'Coming Crisis' the *American Journal of Sociology* published a wide-ranging attack on radical sociology which focused specifically and harshly on Gouldner's work.

8 H.S. Becker and I.L. Horowitz, 'Radical politics and sociological research', *American Journal of Sociology*, Vol. 78, no. 1, 1972.

9 R. Blackburn, 'A brief guide to bourgeois ideology' in A. Cockburn and R. Blackburn, *Student Power: Problems, Diagnosis, Action*, Harmondsworth, Middx, Penguin, 1969, p. 163.

10 M. Shaw, 'The coming crisis of radical sociology' in R. Blackburn (ed.), *Ideology in Social Science: Readings in Critical Social Theory*, London, Fontana, 1972, p. 33.

11 M. Shaw, *Marxism and Social Science: The Roots of Social Knowledge*, London, Pluto, 1975, p. 33.

12 M. Nicolaus, 'The professional organisation of sociology: a view from below' in R. Blackburn (ed.), op. cit. p. 45.

13 N. Poulantzas, *Political Power and Social Classes*, London, New Left Books, 1973. See Part III, sec. 3 on 'The capitalist state and force', pp. 225–8.

14 A.W. Gouldner, *For Sociology: Renewal and Critique in Sociology Today*, Harmondsworth, Middx, Penguin, 1973.

15 A.W. Gouldner, Foreword to I. Taylor, P. Walton and J. Young, *The New Criminology*, London, Routledge & Kegan Paul, 1973.

16 A.W. Gouldner, op. cit. 1970, p. 57.

17 M. Fitzgerald, G. McLennan and J. Pawson, (eds), *Crime and Society: Readings in History and Theory*, London, Routledge & Kegan Paul, 1981.

18 S. Cohen, 'Footprints in the sand: a further report on criminology and the sociology of deviance in Britain', in M. Fitzgerald *et al.*, op. cit., pp. 220–47.

19 Ibid. p 220.

20 Ibid. pp. 220–1.

21 Ibid. p. 242.

22 S. Hall and P. Scraton, 'Law, class and control', in M. Fitzgerald *et al.* op. cit., pp. 460–97.

23 Ibid. p. 464.

24 Ibid. p. 465.

25 S. Cohen (ed.), *Images of Deviance*, Harmondsworth, Middx, Penguin, 1971.

26 I. Taylor and L. Taylor (eds), *Politics and Deviance*, Harmondsworth, Middx, Penguin, 1973.

27 I. Taylor, P. Walton and J. Young, *The New Criminology*, London, Routledge & Kegan Paul, 1973.

28 Hall and Scraton, op. cit., p. 471.

29 Cohen, op. cit. p. 242.

30 Cited in Buci – Glucksman, C., *Gramsci and the State*, London, Lawrence & Wishart, 1980, p. 108.

31 D. Garland, *Punishment and Welfare*, Aldershot, Hants, Gower, 1985, p. 77.

32 Ibid. p. 77.

33 Cited in D. Garland, 'Politics and policy in criminological discourse: a study of tendentious reasoning and rhetoric', *International Journal of Sociology of Law*, vol. 13, no. 1 February 1985, p. 27.

34 S. Rose, L. Kamin and R. Lewentin, *Not in our Genes*, Harmondsworth, Middx, Penguin, 1984, p. 54.

35 D. Downes and P. Rock, *Understanding Deviance*, Oxford, Clarendon Press, 1982, p. 55.

36 Ibid. pp. 73–4.

37 P. Conrad and J. Schneider, *Deviance and Medicalisation: From Badness to Sickness*, C.V. Mosby, 1980, p. 224.

38 Ibid. p. 226.

39 K. Kesey, *One flew over the Cuckoo's Nest*, London, Picador, 1973, p. 43.

40 P. Evans, 'Inside the criminal brain', in *The Listener*, 24 July 1986, pp. 4–5.

41 S. Cohen and L. Taylor, *Psychological Survival*, Harmondsworth, Middx, Penguin, 1972.

42 S. Cohen and L. Taylor, 'Talking about prison blues' in C. Bell and H. Newby (eds), *Doing Sociological Research*, London, Allen & Unwin, 1977, pp. 67–86.

43 Ibid. p 77.

44 Ibid. p. 85.

45 M. Fitzgerald, M. 'Prisoners in Revolt' Harmondsworth, Middx, Penguin, 1977, p. 137.

46 Ibid. p. 140.

47 PROP, *Don't Mark his Face*, PROP, (undated), p. 44.

48 'Whitelaw's whitewash' in *The Abolitionist*, 1982, No. 11, Vol. 2, p. 5.

49 B. Stratton, *Who Guards the Guards?*, PROP, 1973.

50 M. Fitzgerald, *Control Units and the Shape of Things to Come*, RAP, 1974.

51 M. Ryan, *The Politics of Penal Reform*, London, Longman, 1983, pp. 112–13.
52 Ibid. pp. 110–11.
53 M. Benn and K. Worpole, *Death in the City*, London, Canary Press, 1986, p. 1.
54 See, for example, *Inquest Annual Report 1982–83*, Inquest 1983, *Murder Near the Cathedral* Inquest 1983. Also related to these works are G. Coggan and M. Walker, *Frightened for My Life*, Fontana, 1982 T. Ward, *Death and Disorder*, Inquest 1986; P. Scraton and K. Chadwick, *In the Arms of the Law: Coroner's Inquests and Deaths in Custody*, London, Pluto, 1987.
55 P. Scraton and K. Chadwick, 'Speaking ill of the dead: institutional responses to deaths in custody', in *Journal of Law and Society*, Vol. 13, No. 1, Spring, 1986.
56 See, for example, *The Abolitionist* no. 5 and no. 8.
57 Cited in P. Carlen, J. Hicks, J. O'Dwyer, D. Christina and C. Tchaikovsky, *Criminal Women*, Cambridge, Polity Press, 1985, p. 187.
58 Ibid. p. 190.
59 P. Carlen, *Women's Imprisonment: A Study in Social Control*, London, Routledge & Kegan Paul, 1983.
60 P. Carlen *et al.* op. cit.
61 Ibid. p. 13.
62 Greater London Council Women's Committee, *Women's Imprisonment: Breaking the Silence*, GLC, 1987.
63 Ibid. Foreword p. i.
64 *Third Report from the Social Services Committee Session 1986–6*, Prison Medical Service Volume 1, HMSO, 1986.
65 D. MacDonald and J. Sim, *Scottish Prisons and the Special Unit*, Scottish Council for Civil Liberties, 1978.
66 M. Fitzgerald and J. Sim, *British Prisons*, Oxford, Basil Blackwell, 1979.
67 See P. Scraton and K. Chadwick, 'The experiment that went wrong: the crisis of deaths in youth custody at the Glenochil Complex', in B. Rolston and R. Tomlinson, *The Expansion of European Prison Systems*, European Group for the Study of Deviance and Social Control, 1986.
68 In 1985 the Gateway Exchange held public meetings concerning Glenochil in Edinburgh and Glasgow.
69 T. Mathiesen, *The Politics of Abolition*, London, Martin Robertson, 1974, p. 30.
70 S. Cohen, 'Guilt, justice and tolerance: some old concepts for a new criminology', in D. Downes and P. Rock (eds), *Deviant Interpretations*, Oxford, Martin Robertson, 1979, p. 49.
71 D. Garland and P. Young (eds), *The Power to Punish*, London, Heinemann, 1983.
72 Ibid. pp. 6–7.
78 Cited in B. Smart *Michel Foucault*, London, Tavistock, 1985.
74 Ibid. p. 26.
75 T. Mathiesen, 'The politics of abolition', in *Contemporary Crises*, vol. 10, 1986, p. 84.
76 D. Humphry, *Police Power and Black People*, London, Panther, 1972.
77 T. Bunyan, *The History and Practice of the Political Police in Britain*, London, Quartet, 1977.
78 By 'followed' we are not suggesting a direct connection.
79 C. Ackroyd *et al.*, *The Technology of Political Control*, Harmondsworth, Middx, Penguin, 1977; Pluto, 1981 (2nd edn).
80 Institute of Race Relations, *Police against Black People*, IRR Race and Class

Pamphlet, no. 6, 1978.

81 P. Hain (ed.), *Policing the Police*, Vols. I and II, London, John Calder, 1979 and 1980.

82 P. Gordon, *Policing Scotland*, SCC, 1980.

83 M. Farrell, *Northern Ireland: The Orange State*, London, Pluto, 1976, preface.

84 K. Boyle, T. Hadden and P. Hillyard, *Law and State: The Case of Northern Ireland*, London, Martin Robertson, 1975.

85 Ibid. p. 5.

86 Ibid. p. 3.

87 C. Ackroyd, K. Margolis, J. Rosenhead and T. Shallice, *The Technology of Political Control*, Harmondsworth, Middx, Penguin, 1977.

88 T. Bunyan, *The History and Practice of the Political Police in Britain*, London, Quartet, 1977.

89 State Research, *Security and the State*, 3 vols. London, Julian Friedman, 1980.

90 K. Boyle, T. Hadden and P. Hillyard, *Ten Years on in Northern Ireland*, The Cobden Trust, 1980.

91 Ibid. p. 5.

92 Ibid. pp. 5–6.

93 L. O'Dowd, B. Rolston and M. Tomlinson, *Northern Ireland: Between Civil Rights and Civil War*, London CSE Books, 1980.

94 Ibid. p. 205.

95 See B. Rolston, 'The Republican movement and elections: an historical account' and P. Hillyard, 'Popular justice in Northern Ireland', in *Working Papers in European Criminology*, no. 5, 1984; B. Rolston and M. Tomlinson, 'Long-term imprisonment in Northern Ireland: psychological or political survival', in *Working Papers in European Criminology*, no. 7, 1986.

96 E. Fairweather, R. McDonough and M. McFadyean, *Only the Rivers Run Free. Northern Ireland: The Women's War*, London, Pluto, 1984.

97 L. Curtis, *Ireland: The Propaganda War*, London, Pluto, 1984.

98 D.P.J. Walsh, *The Use and Abuse of Emergency Legislation in Northern Ireland*, The Cobden Trust, 1983.

99 See, for example, P. Hillyard, 'From Belfast to Britain: some thoughts on the Royal Commission on Criminal Procedure', in *Politics and Power*, vol. 4, London, Routledge & Kegan Paul, 1983; P. Hillyard, 'Lessons from Ireland', in B. Fine and R. Millar (eds), *Policing the Miners' Strike*, London, Lawrence & Wishart, 1985.

100 C. Smart, *Women, Crime and Criminology*, London, Routledge & Kegan Paul, 1976.

101 See D. Smith, 'The social construction of documentary reality', *Sociological Inquiry*, no. 44, pp. 257–68.

102 C. Smart, op. cit. p. 185.

103 Ibid. p. 185.

104 See, for example, S. Atkins and B. Hogett, *Women and the Law*, Oxford, Basil Blackwell, 1984, K. O'Donovan, *Sexual Divisions in Law*, London, Weidenfeld & Nicolson, 1985, E. Leonard *Women, Crime and Society*, London, Longman, 1982; S. Edwards, *Women on Trial*, Manchester, Manchester University Press, 1984; B. Hutter and G. Williams (eds), *Controlling Women*, London, Croom Helm, 1981; F. Heidensohn, *Women and Crime*, London, Macmillan, 1985; R. Dobash and R. Dobash, *Violence against Wives*, Open Books, 1979; J. Brophy and C. Smart (eds), *Women in Law*, London, Routledge & Kegan Paul, 1985.

105 A. Jones, *Women who Kill*, New York, Holt, Rinehart and Winston, 1980, p. 11.

106 C. Smart, *The Ties that Bind*, London, Routledge & Kegan Paul, 1984.

107 Ibid. pp. 158–9.

108 J. Brophy and C. Smart, op. cit. p. 16.

109 Ibid. p. 16.

110 Ibid. p. 17.

111 K. McCarne, 'Battered women and the law: the limits of the legislature', in J. Brophy and C. Smart, op. cit. p. 94 (emphasis in original).

112 A. Bottomley, 'What is happening to family law? A feminist critique of conciliation', Ibid. p. 184.

113 Ibid. pp. 184–5.

114 Smart and Brophy, op. cit. p. 17.

115 Ibid. (emphasis in original).

116 E. Wilson, *What is to Be Done about Violence against Women?*, Harmondsworth, Middx, Penguin, 1983, p. 222.

117 Ibid. pp. 185–94.

118 See C. Smart, op. cit. 1977; F. Heidonsohn, *Women and Crime*, London, Macmillan, 1985.

119 C. Delphy, *Close to Home: A Materialist Analysis of Women's Oppression*, London Hutchinson, 1984, p. 217.

120 P. Mayony, *Schools for the Boys: Co-education Reassured*, London, Hutchinson, 1985, p. 70.

121 L. Coveney et al., *The Sexuality Papers: Male Sexuality and the Social Control of Women*, London, Hutchinson, 1984, p. 83.

122 See J. Hanmer and S. Saunders, *Well-Founded Fear*, London, Hutchinson, 1984; R. Hall, *Ask Any Woman*, Bristol, Falling Wall Press, 1985; R. Hall et al., *The Rapist who Pays the Rent*, Falling Wall Press, 1981; D. Russell, *Rape in Marriage*, New York, Macmillan, 1982; E. Stanko, *Intimate Intrusions*, London, Routledge & Kegan Paul, 1985.

123 See E. Ward, *Father–Daughter Rape*, London, The Women's Press, 1984.

124 R. Jenkins, *The Production of Knowledge at the Institute of Race Relations*, Independent Labour Party, 1971.

125 J. Bourne, 'Cheerleaders and ombudsmen: the sociology of race relations in Britain', *Race and Class*, vol. XXI, no. 4, 1980. See also: Sivanandan, A. *Race and Resistance: The I.R.R. Story*, Race Today, 1974 and: Mullard, C. *Race, Power and Resistance*, London, Routledge & Kegan Paul, 1985.

126 P. Gilroy *There Ain't no Black in the Union Jack*, London, Hutchinson, 1987.

127 S. Hall et al., *Policing the Crisis*, London, Macmillan, 1978; Centre for Contemporary Cultural Studies, *The Empire Strikes Back*, London, Hutchinson, 1982.

128 E. Lawrence, 'Just plain common sense: the 'roots' of racism', in Centre for Contemporary Cultural Studies, op. cit. pp. 47–96.

129 P. Gilroy, op. cit. pp. 125–6.

130 P. Gordon, 'Outlawing immigrants!: Anwar Ditta and Britain's immigration laws', in P. Scraton and P. Gordon, (eds), *Causes for Concern*, Harmondsworth, Middx, Penguin, 1984, pp. 114–34.

131 Report on the Review Panel, *A Different Reality*, West Midlands County Council, 1986, p. 60.

132 E. Lawrence, op. cit. p. 88.

133 M. Fitzgerald and J. Sim, 'Legitimating the prison crisis: a critical review of the May Report', in *The Howard Journal*, vol. XIX, 1980, pp. 73–84.

134 National Council for Civil Liberties, *Southall 23 April 1979*, NCCL, 1980.

135 Ibid. pp. 163 4.
136 Report of the Review Panel, op. cit. p. 7.
137 Report on the Independent Inquiry, 1956.
138 Ibid. p. 7.
139 Ibid. pp. 36–7.
140 Ibid. pp. 185–94.
141 See also Report of the Independent Inquiry Panel, *Leon Brittan's Visit to Manchester University Students' Union 1st March 1985*, Manchester City Council, 1985. Two academics sat on this panel.
142 Thanks to Paddy Hillyard for discussing and clarifying these points with us.
143 P. Scraton, *The State of the Police*, London, Pluto, 1985, pp. 162–3.
144 J. Percy-Smith and P. Hillyard, 'Miners in the arms of the law: a statistical analysis', in P. Scraton and P. Thomas (eds), *The State v The People: Lessons from the Coal Dispute*, Oxford, Basil Blackwell, 1985, p. 345.
145 H. Beynon, (ed.), *Digging Deeper: Issues in the Miners' Strike*, London, Verso, 1985. Also combining academics, campaigners and civil libertarians were: B. Fine and R. Millar (eds), *Policing the Miners' Strike*, London, Lawrence Wishart, 1985; P. Scraton and P. Thomas, (eds), *The State v The People: Lessons from the Coal Dispute*, Oxford, Basil Blackwell, 1985.
146 J. Percy-Smith and P. Hillyard, op. cit. p. 349.
147 Ibid. p. 350.
148 See, for example, H. Beynon, op. cit.; P. Scraton and P. Thomas (eds), op. cit.; B. Fine and B. Millar, (ed.), op. cit.; WCCPL and NUM, *Striking Back*, WCCP and NUM, 1985; J. Coulter, S. Miller and M. Walker, *A State of Siege*, London, Canary press, 1985.
149 National Council for Civil Liberties, *Civil Liberties and the Miners' Dispute*, NCCL, 1984.
150 Sheffield Policewatch, *Taking Liberties! Policing during the Miners' Strike April–October 1984*, Sheffield Policewatch, 1984, p. 15.
151 WCCPL and NUM, op. cit.
152 Ibid. pp. 8–9.
153 T. Mathiesen, op. cit. pp. 86–7.
154 J. Young, 'Left idealism, reformism and beyond: from new criminology to Marxism', in NDC/CSE, *Capitalism and the Rule of Law*, London, Hutchinson, 1979, pp. 11–28.
155 Ibid. pp. 12–15.
156 Ibid. pp. 15–16.
157 Ibid. p. 19.
158 R. Kinsey and J. Young, 'Police autonomy and the politics of discretion', in D. Cowell *et al.*, *Policing the Riots*, Junction Books, 1982, p. 118.
159 A. Tyler, 'Police and thieves' a 'Face to Face Interview with Jock Young', *Time Out*, September 1986.
160 J. Lea and J. Young, *What is to Be Done about Law and Order?* Harmondsworth, Middx, Penguin, 1984; R. Matthews and J. Young (eds), *Confronting Crime*, Beverley Hills, Calif., Sage, 1986; R. Kinsey, J. Lea and J. Young, *Losing the Fight against Crime*, Oxford, Basil Blackwell, 1986.
161 J. Young, 'The future of criminology: the need for radical realism', in R. Matthews and J. Young, op. cit. p. 28.
162 J. Young, op. cit. 1979, p. 15.

163 D. Humphry, *Police Power and Black People*, London, Panther, 1972; R. Moore, *Racism and Resistance in Britain*, London, Pluto, 1975.

164 J. Lea and J. Young, 'The riots in Britain 1981: urban violence and political marginalisation', in D. Cowell *et al.*, op. cit.

165 Ibid. p. 8.

166 Ibid. pp. 8–9.

167 Ibid. p. 10.

168 J. Lea and J. Young, op. cit. 1984, p. 165.

169 See, in particular, L. Bridges and P. Gilroy, 'Striking back', *Marxism Today*, June 1982; L. Bridges, untitled, *Social Abstracts*, February 1983; P. Gilroy and J. Sims, 'Labour and crime', in *New Statesman*, 21 October 1983.

170 P. Gilroy, op. cit. p. 99.

171 J. Young, op. cit. 1979, p. 19.

172 P. Gilroy and J. Sim, op. cit. 1985, p. 14.

173 T. Ward, 'Armchair policing: a review of "What Is to Be Done about Law and Order"', *The Abolitionist*, no. 17 (1984 no. 2), p. 35.

174 P. Scraton, op. cit. 1985, p. 168.

175 P. Gilroy and J. Sim, 'Law, order and the state of the left', *Capital and Class*, no. 25, Spring 1985, p. 46.

176 R. Kinsey, J. Lea and J. Young, op. cit. 1985, p. 215.

177 Ibid. pp. 222–3.

178 J. Lea and J. Young, op. cit. 1984, p. 175.

179 See, as an example, *Report of the Commissioner of Police 1935*, pp. 8–10.

180 T. Ward op. cit. 1984, p. 35.

181 R. Kinsey, 'Crime in the city', in *Marxism Today*, May 1986, p. 8.

182 T. Jefferson, 'Unpopular perceptions: a reply to Richard Kinsey', *Marxism Today*, July 1986, p. 39.

183 R. Carr-Hill, 'Law and tory order: a reply to Richard Kinsey', *New Statesman*, 14 February 1986, p. 20.

184 K. Malik, 'Crime, police and people: a reply to Trevor Jones and Jock Young, *New Society*, 14 February 1986, p. 294.

185 D. McBarnet, *Conviction: Law, the State and the Construction of Justice*, London, Macmillan, 1981.

186 *Brass Tacks*, BBC, 12 July 1986.

187 R. Kinsey, J. Lea and J. Young, op. cit. 1986, pp. 168–9.

188 L. Snider 'Review of "What Is to Be Done about Law and Order"', *International Journal of the Sociology of Law*, vol. 13, 1985, p. 435.

189 Ibid. p. 433.

190 R. Kinsey, J. Lea and J. Young, op. cit. 1986, p. 212.

191 L. Panitch, *Working Class Politics in Crisis, Essays on Labour and the State*, London, Verso, 1986, p. 46.

192 See R. Levitas (ed.), *The Ideology of the New Right*, Cambridge, Polity Press, 1986.

193 I. Taylor, *Law and Order: Arguments for Socialism*, London, Macmillan, 1981.

194 Ibid. p. 123 (emphasis added).

195 I. Taylor, 'Against crime and for socialism', in *Crime and Social Justice*, Winter 1982, p. 9.

196 T. Platt, 'Criminology in the 1980s: progressive alternatives to "law and order", in *Crime and Social Justice*, no. 21–2, p. 196.

197 Cited in *Labour Herald*, 5 November 1982.

198 See, in particular, J. Lea and J. Young, 'Urban violence and political marginalisation: the riots in Britain summer 1981', in *Critical Social Policy*, no. 3, 1982.

199 J. Lea and J. Young, op. cit. 1984, p. 232.

200 L. Bridges, untitled paper for *Social Abstracts*, February 1983. p. 9.

201 P. Gilroy, 'Steppin' out of Babylon – race, class and autonomy', in Centre for Contemporary Cultural Studies, op. cit. 1982, p. 305.

202 Ibid. p. 306.

203 S. Hall, 'Popular-Democratic vs. Authoritarian Populism: two ways of "taking democracy seriously"', in A. Hunt (ed.), *Marxism and Democracy*, London, Lawrence and Wishart, 1980, p. 178.

204 L. Panitch, op. cit. p. 46.

205 Ibid. pp. 3–4.

206 D. Howell, '"Where's Ramsay MacKinnock?" Labour Leadership and the miners', in H. Beynon (ed.), op. cit. pp. 195–6.

207 L. Bridges, 'Beyond accountability: Labour and policing after the 1985 rebellions' in *Race and Class*, vol. XXVII, no. 4, Spring 1986, p. 80.

208 See P.A.J. Waddington, 'Mugging as a moral panic: a question of proportion', in *British Journal of Sociology*, vol. XXXVII, no. 2, 1986, p. 255.

209 Text of a speech at a Crime Prevention Seminar Organized by Humberside Police at Middleton Hall, University of Hull, 6 June 1986, p. 1.

210 Ibid. p. 3.

211 Ibid. pp. 23–4.

212 *The Guardian*, 2 June 1986.

213 *Sunday Mirror*, 31 August 1986.

214 Sir Kenneth Newman, 'Policing the inner city', speech to the Society of Conservative Lawyers, 16 February 1987, p. 9.

215 Ibid. p. 3.

216 Ibid. pp. 7–8.

217 *The Observer*, 15 March 1987.

218 G. Kaufman, press release on *Protecting our People*, Labour Party policy 25 September 1986.

219 *The Guardian*, 17 March 1987.

220 H. Mannheim, *Social Aspects of Crime in England between the Wars*, London, Allen & Unwin, 1940.

221 J. Seabrook, 'The disease waiting in the wings', 'Guardian Agenda', in *The Guardian*, 22 December 1986.

222 S. Hall, *Drifting into a Law and Order Society*, Cobden Trust, 1980, p. 3.

223 S. Hall, 'Authoritarian populism: a reply to Jessop *et al.*', *New Left Review*, 151, May/June 1985, p. 119.

224 S. Hall, 'The great moving right show', *Marxism Today*, January 1979, pp. 14–19.

225 Ibid. p. 19.

226 J. Young, 'Working-class criminology', in I. Taylor, P. Walton and J. Young, (eds), *Critical Criminology*, London, Routledge & Kegan Paul, 1975.

227 R. Kinsey and J. Young, op. cit. 1982.

228 An example of this is B. Jessop *et al.* 'Authoritarian populism, two nations and Thatcherism', *New Left Review*, 147, 1984.

229 A more considered overview is S. Hall and P. Scraton, op. cit. 1981.

230 S. Hall *et al.*, op. cit. 1978.

231 This conclusion is taken, in part, from P. Scraton, 'The State v. The People: an introduction', *Journal of Law and Society*, vol. 12, no. 3, Winter 1985.

2

Law, Order and the State of the Left

Paul Gilroy and Joe Sim

This chapter looks at the left's orientation to law and order issues and challenges it on the basis of historical evidence. The concept of 'Thatcherism' and its attendant view of the authoritarian state is heavily criticized for obscuring important continuities which bind the practice of this government to that of previous administrations. It is argued that an adequate account of Britain's increasing authoritarianism must include reference to the war in Northern Ireland, the junction of race and crime themes and most importantly, the autonomy of the police service which has generated distinct and consistent patterns of political intervention.

We suggest that socialists make a fundamental mistake in falsely trying to separate policing from consideration of the criminal justice system as a whole. The political effects of legality, the way that legal ideology shapes police activity and the gap between the rhetoric and the actual practice of justice are all examined in a way which highlights some problems in current socialist initiatives around police accountability.

We argue that the left undermines its own position by colluding in the idea that policing is primarily concerned with the prevention and detection of crime. An alternative approach, premised on the idea that policing is an essentially symbolic rather than instrumental activity is outlined as part of our argument that for police, the maintenance of social order has always taken priority over the pursuit of criminals.

Finally, we locate concern about crime, law and policing at the core of political conflicts which express important changes in the division of labour and in civil society itself. These struggles reflect not only the management of national crisis, but the development of a post-industrial state. In these circumstances, law-breaking is central to processes of class formation and decomposition, and lines of legality differentiate the fractions of a hetero-geneous, non-working class.

The Limits of 'Thatcherism'

The riots of 1981, the 1984–5 miners' strike, and the Wapping dispute confirmed the centrality of law and policing to contemporary British politics. On the left, it has become commonplace to identify this situation as a novel aspect of unfolding, authoritarian, 'neo-liberal' statism. Or at least as a rightward drift in national politics. As the crises deepen, so the drift accelerates. This fashionable view is often supported by a concept of 'Thatcherism' which dates the arrival of authoritarianism and its new right forces in the spring of 1979. There is more than a suggestion that it is the dead hand of monetarism which rests on the throttle of statism. The balmy days of post-war consensus have been lost in the autumn mist of economic recession. A winter of repression awaits us. Britain, so the argument continues, is under the heel of its most vicious and repressive government. The Thatcher record on law and order is revealed to be a series of signposts on the road to a police state.

The administration and practice of the criminal justice system has certainly seen changes which have been designed to strengthen the coercive power of the forces and institutions of law and order. New Acts and Bills covering police powers in Scotland, England and Wales, picketing practices, juvenile justice, Contempt of Court, and Prevention of Terrorism have been introduced. In July 1984 the Juries Disqualification Act was passed which debars from jury service anyone who has served any period of imprisonment during the previous 10 years, or who has received a suspended sentence or has had a community service order. In addition, anyone who has been placed on probation will be debarred for 5 years. The amount of money spent on the criminal justice system has increased to the point where the police's budget in England and Wales alone was £2.5 billion in 1983/4. The force has been increased by some 9,000 officers since 1979 and riot equipment such as CS gas and plastic bullets have been made available. Twenty new prisons are to be built, parole has been effectively abolished for certain categories of long-term prisoners and changes have been established by the 1986 Public Order Act which could result in the jailing of individuals for up to 10 years. In Northern Ireland, in addition to the use of supergrasses and Diplock Courts, a shoot-to-kill policy is said to be in operation by the security forces. Furthermore, the amount of money spent on the police service there increased from over £124 million in 1979/80 to nearly £218 million in 1982/3, while in 1983 there were 655 full-time police officers per 100,000 of the population.[1] This compared with 255 officers per 100,000 of the population in Scotland[2] and 241 per 100,000 of the population in England and Wales.[3]

There has also been increased activity by the Special Branch ranging from the use of technology such as the Police National Computer to store information on individuals and groups to the arrests and trials of women at Greenham Common with scant regard to any due process of law. The increase in the number and activities of Specialist Claims Control Units at the DHSS and the criminalization of the claims of welfare recipients and the six-month jail sentence given to Sarah Tisdall are all part of a tendency to define those who challenge the legitimacy of either government or state practices to be striking at the heart of democracy itself. In other words, as subversive. This view was expressed by Harold Salisbury, the former Chief Constable of York, North East Yorkshire, who in 1981 defined subversives as:

> Anyone who shows affinity towards communism, that's common sense, the IRA, the PLO and I would say anyone who's decrying marriage, family life, trying to break it up, pushing drugs, homosexuality, indiscipline in schools, weak penalties for anti-social crimes ... a whole gamut of things that could be pecking away at the foundations of our society and weakening it.[4]

Against this, the policing of crimes committed by the more powerful has become even more curtailed in recent years. The number of Factory Inspectors fell from 978 in 1979 to 833 in 1983 while the number of prosecutions for contraventions of the Health and Safety at Work Act fell from 2,127 to 2,022 in the same period. The average penalty for prosecutions under the Act was £205. In addition, the number of workplaces inspected fell from 22.5% in 1979 to 15.5% in 1983. In the mining industry there were 1.03 people killed or seriously injured per 100,000 shifts in 1979 and 'by 1983 it had gone up to 1.97 ... in other words there has been a 12% increase in the number of people killed or seriously injured in the mines even in the last year'.[5]

Without wishing to minimize the seriousness of the situation which confronts us, nor to play down the significance of these changes in the criminal justice and welfare state systems, we want to challenge this framework of analysis. We will examine some of the errors and misconceptions regarding law, policing and the state itself on which the authoritarian drift thesis depends. We do not however intend to abandon the idea of authoritarian statism which does have an important place in understanding the formation of the post-industrial state in Britain. It is essential though to qualify and restrict the looseness with which the concept has been used in the past. This lack of rigour may be rooted in the desire to emphasize the horrors of 'Thatcherism' and demonstrate the extent to which it marks a departure from the fudged social democracy of the Wilson, Heath and Callaghan years. Yet as far as law and order, policing and criminal justice matters are concerned, the Thatcher governments do not represent a decisive break with patterns set in preceding years.

The centralization and militarization of policing and the growth of repressive legal regulation have longer histories than most advocates of the Thatcherism concept would like to admit. This is principally because they are histories in which the Labour Party at every level has been extensively and intimately involved. Thus the horrors of 'Thatcherism' are only half the story. They are balanced by an idealized view of the post-war period, particularly the 1945–51 years when Labour took power. This moment is judged to be something of a golden age for socialist thought and radical policy. The strands in social democracy which link the immediate post-war phase, 'Butskellism' and the emergence of popular authoritarianism during the 1970s are ignored, and the name of democracy is invoked as part of a plea to return to the spirit of progressive reform which these Labour governments embody. However, careful consideration of policing and criminal justice policies completely disrupts this revisionist history.

Labour and State Power

1945–1951: The Golden Age

In the arena of law, order and criminal justice, the post-war Labour government was hardly a reforming one. Indeed, in some areas it was more authoritarian than its pre-war Conservative predecessor. In others, it either laid the foundations for, or gave support to, policies and practices which increased the power of the criminal justice system to punish, discipline and maintain order by force. James Chuter Ede who became Labour Home Secretary on 3 August 1945 was an ex-schoolmaster and infantry sergeant. While he had been an MP intermittently between the wars, his 'only experience of government had been Parliamentary Secretary to the Ministry of Education from 1940 to 1945'.[6]

Under Ede's regime police practices and procedures were left intact. Under pressure from the Police Federation the old police training college was not re-established 'while the fabric of local government was left undisturbed as it had been since created by the government of the Marquess of Salisbury in 1888'.[7] He also introduced a Criminal Justice Bill in 1948, which in some of its recommendations was more conservative than its 1939 predecessor which fell with the outbreak of war. For example, proposals for community-based hostels, to be known as Howard Hostels, were jettisoned and replaced by the introduction of detention centres whose 'regime was to be deliberately deterrent in nature so as to provide sentencers with the option of imposing a "short, sharp, shock" '.[8] While the 1939 Bill had banned the imprisonment of offenders under the age of 16, Ede's Bill lowered this age to 15 for higher courts. It also raised the maximum period of preventive detention from 10 to 14 years. Finally, the Bill contained no commitment to the abolition of capital punishment despite the fact that 'the 1934 Conference had passed an abolitionist motion and the 1945 Parliamentary Party contained many abolitionists'.[9]

Ede himself had been in favour of abolition at one time but by 1947 was set against it, 'having been influenced in this direction by Senior Home Office civil servants, particularly Sir Frank Newsam. In short there was a departmental view against abolition and Ede had been persuaded to accept it.'[10] Ede's time at the Home Office was given the seal of approval by Sir Harold Scott, the Commissioner of the Metropolitan Police from 1945 to 1953. In his account of Scotland Yard during these years Scott pointed out that:

> During my eight years at Scotland Yard there were never any serious differences of opinion between myself and Mr Chuter Ede or Sir David Maxwell-Fyfe (his Conservative successor). Their different political views were never allowed to influence their approach to police questions.[11]

In other areas the government was not slow to act against disorder. Within a month of taking office, troops were used at Surrey Docks in London to break up a dockers' strike which had been in progress for 10 weeks. This pattern was to be repeated throughout their term of office. Troops were sent to Smithfield Market in April 1946, to Avonmouth in May 1949, to Belfast in September 1949, to the Royal Group of Docks in London in March 1950 and to Smithfield again in June 1950.[12] It is also worth noting that while it proved difficult to enforce the law regarding strikes and while there was widespread rank and file resistance to the use of law in the arena of industrial relations, 'virtually every strike between 1940 and 1951 was a criminal offence'.[13] Strikes by the dockers, and others, motivated Attlee's government to pursue a policy of emergency planning which among other things involved reconstituting an Emergencies Committee in April 1947. The remit of this committee was to supervise plans for providing and maintaining supplies and services in any emergency and to co-ordinate action for just such a purpose. This Emergencies Committee has 'remained a standing Committee of the Cabinet ever since'.[14] The apparent threat of domestic subversion and communism lay behind the government's enthusiasm for the committee:

> After five years in power Attlee's Cabinet, which began its emergency planning with such careful deliberation, had convinced itself that virtually all industrial unrest stemmed from a subversive challenge to established order. In these circumstances, detailed and systematic emergency planning seemed both necessary and desirable. Ironically, fear of revolution, or at least subversion, which had been the initial stimulant for the establishment of a strike-breaking machine after the First World War, did much to sustain the development of a similar organization after the Second.[15]

The Special Branch and other detectives were integral to the government's strategy during these strikes. At first reluctant to use secret state agencies, their use blossomed from October 1945, as they exercised surveillance on 'unofficial strike leaders as a matter of course'.[16] According to Ellen, this practice had been a regular feature of Bevan's regime at the Ministry of Labour during the Second World War.[17]

Labour's nostalgia for 1945–51 is also important because it locates the past golden age of 'consensus policing' against which contemporary Thatcherite horrors are to be measured and found wanting. The resulting Dixon of Dock Green view of history suggests that the police, if they were not actually loved, were respected and supported and that officers kept a paternalistic eye on the people that they policed. Occasionally, those who stepped out of line, usually young people, would be given a 'clip round the ear' and sent on their way. Crime was therefore held in check, kept under control by the activities of the police who were usually bobbies on the beat.

This mythology remains potent. Time and again during the 1983 general election campaign, spokespeople for the party, especially Roy Hattersley, referred back to pre-war days as a response to the Conservative Party's tough line on the law and order issue. Yet, this version of the history of policing has been discredited by the work of historians such as Robert Storch,[18] John Field,[19] Barbara Weinberger[20] and Phil Cohen.[21] Their work shows that throughout the nineteenth century the police were not accepted in many communities, that there was widespread resistance to and conflict between the force and local people, and that these conflicts could spill over into serious disorder at any time. This conflict continued into the twentieth century. Jerry White's description of Campbell Bunk, a community in Finsbury Park in London between the wars, captures what was happening between the police and the policed. When in the area the police would often attempt to crack down on gambling in the street or other recreational activities. It was then that trouble would erupt. In the summer of 1930, two police officers attempted to arrest a gambler named Musgrove:

> He resisted and threw the arresting officer to the ground. A crowd estimated at 200 surrounded the police, urged on by another Bunk character well-known to the police, called Bill Hagger. He kicked a PC in the back and Musgrove escaped into a house where he was later arrested. . . . Simiar collective efforts were made when the police tried to arrest either of the street bookmakers. . . The police had similar trouble breaking up fights in Campbell Road and risked a serious assault if they tried to do so.[22]

The question of police powers to stop and search people in the Metropolitan area, was also a matter of controversy at this time. The Report of the Commissioner for 1935 devoted two and a half pages to discussing the fact that 'a good deal of attention has been given in the press during the year to the use by the police of their powers to stop, search and detain persons suspected of carrying stolen property'.[23] According to the report, Met officers were stopping 1,000 people a week. Without giving figures, the Commissioner intimated that 'a very considerable number of thieves are caught in this way'[24] but conceded that there would always be a certain number who resented the police engaging in such behaviour. The report goes on to discuss the problem of arresting individuals who were loitering with intent to commit a felony and points out that in the light of a number of these cases being dismissed 'the suggestion has been made that police are employing their powers with an excess of zeal or even oppressively'.[25] The Commissioner concluded that:

> Put shortly, the position is that complete freedom for the individual is not compatible with adequate protection for the community. The police do their best to maintain the one without infringing the other. It is not an easy task and a reasonable amount of criticism is to be expected and is indeed helpful.[26]

Two pages of the 1937 report address a similar theme, indicating that 'thousands of ... persons are "stopped" every year'.[27] The Commissioner tried to allay the fears of the public by arguing that these powers were necessary if crime was to be held in check:

> if the liberty of the subject is to be regarded as so sacred that no one can be asked a reasonable question regarding his movements or anything he happens to be carrying, criminals must perforce have their share of such liberty.[28]

Two other ideas are central to Labour's mythology of policing. First, the notion that the police were under some sort of local control in times past. This control, so the argument goes, was eroded and finally destroyed with the increasing centralization of the police from the 1960s onwards. Again, during the 1983 general election campaign Roy Hattersley held up local watch committees as an example of the kind of police accountability to which the country should be directed. While much historical work remains to be done on the issue, a major piece of research by Mike Brogden[29] has shown that in Liverpool at least, the police were never under the control of the local authority. When it comes to major police decisions, the police are, and have always been, their own bosses.

The second idea is that crime in the past was not the problem that it is today. This idea was central to major changes in sentencing and penal policy announced by Leon Brittan at the Conservative Party Conference in October 1983. We do not wish at this point to enter into a debate about the complexities of criminal statistics. What we do wish to point out, however, is that Labour's continuing reliance on the statistical evidence of a rising crime rate does not take into account the fact that 'criminal statistics are notoriously unreliable as measures of the actual extent of criminal activity, to such a degree that it is not unknown for historians to discount them altogether'.[30] Rather than being 'cast in the historical idiom of *change* ... the facts of crime and disorder must be re-allocated within the idiom of *continuity*'.[31] Geoff Pearson's work shows that the popular concern, indeed obsession, with crime and disorder has a history which can be traced back to the nineteenth century. He situates this concern in a wider, political context where crime is seen as a metaphor for a more general feeling of social apprehension.

> The preoccupation with mounting disorder seems to serve a specific ideological function within British public life, as a convenient metaphor for wider social tensions which attend the advance of democratisation . . . this preoccupation returns to a cluster of themes bearing on the production and reproduction of consent and social discipline among the working class – and more particularly among the rising generation, the bearers of the future.[32]

1951–1979: Consolidating the Past

The tendencies within government to either strengthen the various arms of the criminal justice system or to turn a benevolent blind eye to their activities have not spared post-1951 Labour administrations. It was during the Wilson government of 1964–70 that the Special Patrol Group was first deployed in London. In 1967, the government introduced its Criminal Justice Act which allowed jurors to convict or acquit by a majority of ten to two, whereas until then juries had to consider a case until all of them agreed. Within the prisons, as a result of the Mountbatten and Razinowicz Committees, regimes for long-term prisoners were tightened, security and control massively increased and prisoners increasingly classified and segregated. The number of warrants which allowed telephones to be tapped increased from 253 in 1964 to 395 by the end of the first Wilson government.

The Wilson and Callaghan administration of 1974–9 was also important in the drive towards giving more power to the criminal justice system. Roy Jenkins, as Home Secretary, introduced the 1974 Prevention of Terrorism Act, which was augmented by its 1976 successor. The Atomic Energy (Special Constables) Act 1976 gave the Atomic Energy police new and exceptional powers including the power to carry arms at all times, the right to enter premises at will and the power to arrest on suspicion. The Special Branch continued to increase both its numbers and its activities; it numbered 1,180 by 1977, a rise from around 200 in the early 1960s. There was continued militarization of the police including greater training in the use of firearms and public order duties. In 1976–7 new technology was introduced in the form of a computer in C Department of the Metropolitan Police which had the capacity to store information on 1,300,000 people; half this space was allocated to the Special Branch. The 1977 Criminal Law Bill reduced the right of peremptory challenges by defence lawyers at jury trials to three and removed a number of offences from courts with juries, allowing them to be tried only before magistrates. The Act also removed the requirement for a coroner to summon a jury in cases of sudden or violent death. This subsequently allowed the High Court to allow the holding of the inquest on Blair Peach without a jury. September 1977 saw the use of the Official Secrets Act in the notorious ABC trial and the subsequent vetting of the jury. The introduction of the Minimum Use of Force Tactical

Intervention Squad (MUFTI) into the prison system in the late 1970s meant that prison officers, like the police, were trained in riot control techniques. Part 1 of the Criminal Law Act (1977) rendered it an indictable offence, punishable with a fine or imprisonment, for trade unionists to plan 'intimidatory' mass picketing. The Labour Scottish Criminal Justice Bill which fell at the 1979 general election was similar in scope and design to the one that became law under the Tories in 1981. In Northern Ireland, amongst other things, both Amnesty International and the Bennett Committee found that confessions made to the RUC by detainees were obtained by violence and intimidation. Complaints against the police there increased rapidly in 1976 and 1977, principally under the stewardship of Roy Mason at the Northern Ireland Office.[33] Finally, as Jimmy Boyle has recently indicated,[34] an important prison reform, the Barlinnie Special Unit, was continually undermined and criticized by both the Labour Secretary of State for Scotland, Bruce Millan, and Harry Ewing, the minister in charge of the Scottish prison system.

This is not a complete list of the changes made under the two most recent Labour administrations or under the 1945–51 'reforming' Labour government. It is sufficient though to move the debate away from the continued concentration on Thatcherism as the instrument which has ushered in a newly authoritarian state. The emergence of these tendencies within the state has a much longer history in which the socialist movement has been deeply implicated.

Policing and Politics

Crisis Management and the Rule of Law

Policing is a profoundly political process. Police work entails the use, often in a very arbitrary way, of violence and coercion. It is important for the left to come to terms with this aspect of police power and the complex interrelationships between the force and other sectors of the criminal justice system as well as other state agencies, welfare services, and the media. As Michael Brown has pointed out:

> It is a fundamental misunderstanding of what the police do to evaluate them as just another municipal agency delivering services. To be overly-preoccupied with whether or not patrolmen respond as quickly as they should to calls for service, with the efficiency of the police in allocating resources, or with their effectiveness in dealing with crime – whether that is measured by crime rates, clearance rates or victimization studies – is only to perpetuate, albeit in a far more sophisticated way, the flawed vision of the Progressive Reformers. The important question is whom the police serve and how they serve them. Even the most obtuse patrolmen understand that they deal, day in and day out, with the primordial political issues – justice, equality, liberty – that their decisions have momentous consequences for the fate of groups and individuals. The police may be nonpartisan in some sense but they are not apolitical.[35]

Before an alternative periodization of authoritarian development can be built up, it is important to register that we also dispute the idea that these processes are best understood as a drift. This notion is useful in suggesting a steady and sometimes imperceptible rate of change, but is misleading in that it tends to obscure the struggles and resistances which have challenged, blocked and diverted the designs of authoritarian planning at every turn. These struggles have occurred inside and outside state institutions and they will continue wherever DHSS staff refuse to co-operate with the snoopers, welfare state professionals deny police interventions the stamp of profes- sional authenticity, and people on the receiving end organize to reject the positions of subordination to which the law assigns them. A full periodiza- tion of Britain's authoritarian state has been attempted by other authors and cannot be repeated here.[36] It is possible however to identify several key factors which combine to undermine the view of 1979 as a watershed. For example, a more adequate account ought to register the significance of the expansion of police autonomy which followed the Royal Commission of 1962 and the relationship between police professionalization and politiciza- tion. Many of the indications of authoritarian policing can also be interpreted as by-products of the creation of police professionalism and of the bureaucratization of police work. Similarly, the dispatch of troops to the six counties of Northern Ireland triggered not only profound changes in the strategies and goals of the police but in the legal procedures of the country as a whole. Finally, the association of race and crime which followed Enoch Powell's populist pronouncements on the subject of race and nation and which identified black settlement as a threatening, alien presence has made an important contribution towards securing the popularity of authoritarian criminal justice policies. It has also justified an elaborate system of internal control and surveillance on the black settler populations on whom the labels of illegal immigrant and street criminal are equally burdensome.

Each of these headings: politicization/professionalization, the impact of conflict in Northern Ireland and the race/crime couplet refers to a history of struggle with its own pace and characteristics. Considered together, these histories can be used to illustrate that the anxieties, themes and values identified as 'Thatcherism', its techniques of policing and judicial reasoning and its recruitment of the law into political control are not exceptional but normal events. In each of these areas the practice of post-1979 governments has a degree of continuity with the practice of previous governments of varying political hues. This suggests that there is scope within the overall framework of liberal democracy for authoritarian policy and practice to germinate. Adherents of the drift scenario have been generally unin- terested in exploring the fundamental ambiguities in the post-war British state on which its authoritarian features can be shown to operate. These ambiguities are displayed with special clarity in legal processes. The specificity of law is in part its ability to reconcile the potential contradictions between liberal-democratic and repressive orders of public authority.

However, any strategic decision to use formal legal rationality in an instrumentally repressive manner is likely to make the reconciliation of the competing demands for order and legitimacy very difficult. State theorists and intellectuals charged with the task of planning to combat the civil disorder which they see as the inevitable counterpart to recession and de-industrialization appreciate these points. Both are central to understanding the British post-internment strategy in Northern Ireland.

In his book *Peace Keeping in a Democratic Society – The Lessons of Northern Ireland*[37] Colonel Robin Evelegh, an ex-commander of troops in Belfast, outlines the legal obstacles to successful policing of the province. His view of the law's shortcomings regarding the detection of crime foreshadows the government's rationalization of the Police and Criminal Evidence Bill and creation of a legal and constitutional structure which would legalize and therefore legitimate the requirements of the security forces. His critique and revision of Frank Kitson's better-known theories can be identified as the inspiration behind many current 'security' initiatives. For example, Evelegh theorizes the value of informers at great length and outlines a plan for developing them out of terrorist or criminal organizations. He also proposes the preparation of 'dormant emergency legislation for combating disorder and terrorism, that can be invoked when the need arises'. His proposals are not limited by the Northern Ireland situation but offer a general theory of 'the constitutional framework and operational laws that are necessary to make the military and to some extent the police, effective in countering rioting and terrorism in any democratic society that finds itself in a situation similar to that in Northern Ireland'. His conflation of terrorism and rioting is also significant, particularly if placed in the context of the Met Commissioner's recent remarks:

> There are two particular problems in Western societies which have the potential to affect the balance between order and freedom. The first is concerned with the growth of multi-ethnic communities. The second is related to indigenous terrorist movements.[38]

Unlike many on the left, these thinkers appreciate that public disorder is becoming a routine expression of profound changes in civil society and the division of labour. They correctly recognize that police and the rule of law are central to the practice of contemporary crisis management. The tactics and strategy being used by police in this series of struggles are again informed by longer histories than the concept 'Thatcherism' allows. The miner's dispute, which has focused attention on the suggestion that police have abused their powers, needs to be seen in the context of earlier patterns of public order policing. The issue of police violence and the question of their surveillance of strikers and demonstrators reveal a remarkable degree of continuity with police practice in previous eras.

Policing Disorder

From the Suffragettes to Grunwick·— via Harmworth Colliery

Surveillance by both Special Branch and ordinary police officers has been an integral element in policing industrial disputes since the turn of the century, if not before. During the 1910 South Wales Coal Strike, plain-clothes police officers, in this case officers from the CID at Scotland Yard, attended a miners' meeting and recorded statements made by members of the strike committee. Both officers could speak Welsh and had knowledge of the local community. A Home Office official was posted to the strike area and he sent 13 of his own reports and assessments back to the Home Office. Metropolitan police officers were also sent to the area. Home Office intervention, however, 'was not simply limited to sending police. The assumption of overall control of both police and the military was a major policy innovation which markedly contrasted with the purely local control exercised during earlier disputes'.[39] Tony Bunyan has made it clear that this surveillance continued over the next six decades into the 1970s.[40] In September 1974, for example, the magazine *Time Out* published extracts from general orders for London police which related to 'Public and other events', 'these extracts confirmed that the Branch is informed in advance of *all* political meetings known to the local police, and that – should Branch officers not attend – a report on all meetings is forwarded to them'.[41]

If state violence on picket lines is considered historically, a different emphasis emerges. For example, condemnation of the violence on the picket lines has usually had cross-party agreement while individual police officers were condemned by Labour Party spokespersons. The party has drawn back from the suggestion that violence might be institutionalized within the police force in Britain. A brief glimpse at some of the major public order confrontations this century indicates both that violence by the state is not unique either to Thatcherism or to the aberrations of individual police officers overcome by the tension of the situation provoked by protestors. The history of the Suffragette Movement is rich with personal accounts of the treatment that women received at the hands of police and prison officials. For example, on 18 November 1910, the suffragettes sent deputations from Caxton Hall to see the Prime Minister Asquith. When they approached Parliament Square, they were confronted by police who according to Hertha Ayrton, one of the marchers, made them:

> All run the gauntlet of organized gangs of policemen in plain clothes, dressed like roughs who nearly squeezed the breath out of our bodies, the policeman in official clothes helping them.... Women were thrown from policemen in uniform to policemen in plain clothes literally till they fainted.[42]

Ada Wright, another marcher told a similar story about police behaviour and pointed out the interrelationship between government and media when it came to censorship:

When we reached Parliament Square, plain-clothes men mingling with the crowds kicked us, and added to the horror and anguish of the day by dragging some of our women down side-streets. There were many attempts of indecent assault. The police rode at us with their horses so I caught hold of one of the horses and would not let go. A policeman grabbed my arm and twisted it round and round until I felt the bone almost breaking and I sank to the pavement helpless.... The next morning I found I had been photographed lying on the ground where I had been flung, and the photograph occupied the front page of the *Daily Mirror*. As soon as this became known to the Government, an order to have the picture suppressed was sent to the office of the newspapers, but they could not suppress the copies which had been sold.[43]

The marchers also indicated that it was the old, the frail and the weak who came in for particular attention from the police. May Bellingham, a disabled woman who was confined to an invalid tricycle, provided a moving account of her experience:

At first police threw me out of the machine on to the ground in a very brutal manner. Secondly when on the machine again, they tried to push me along with my arms twisted behind me in a very painful position.... Thirdly they took me down a side road and left me in the middle of a hooligan crowd, first taking all the valves out of the wheels and pocketing them, so that I could not move the machine.[44]

Two deaths were attributed to the violence which the women experience that day.

Twenty years later, the Hunger Marchers in Hyde Park also felt the blunt force of police violence. On 5 November 1932, the *New Statesman and Nation* carried a story concerning police behaviour towards the Hunger March demonstration in London:

Suddenly for no apparent reason, the mounted police, accompanied by foot police, began to charge the crowd right and left... both unemployed and innocent spectators and passers-by.... The next performance of these riders was to charge into the peaceful groups standing around the meetings. People were forced to run for their lives in order to escape being trampled upon by the police horses or beaten by staves. There was no kind of disorder at any of these meetings, and no reason at all for the police to charge into them in the wanton way they did.[45]

Five years after this incident a similar story was told to the National Council for Civil Liberties by striking miners and their families in the pit village of Harmworth in Nottinghamshire. Their accounts were similar to the recent miners' dispute. In March 1937 the newly formed National Council for Civil Liberties produced a report by Ronald Kidd, the secretary of the organization. Kidd had been sent to Harmworth Colliery to investigate 'the situation in relation to allegations made to the National Council for Civil Liberties of the infringements of civil rights in the trade dispute now taking place'.[46] The dispute centred around the dismissal of the miners who refused to accept a modification in their 'snap' time. On 2

September 1936, the miners at the colliery downed tools in support of their sacked comrades. From there, the dispute widened into a conflict between the Notts Miners Association, which was affiliated to the Miners Federation of Great Britain and the Spencer Union which many of those involved felt was a company union. The police were at the centre of the dispute. Between 100 and 150 of them were drafted into the village from every part of the country at an average extra charge on police funds of £120 a week. According to Kidd:

> I received a large number of complaints that the police have exceeded their authority in ordering law-abiding men and women not to be seen in the streets at certain times . . . the police have adopted a threatening attitude to persons who are not in any way disorderly, and it is widely believed that this threatening attitude is an attempt to interfere with the rights of assembly and to render it difficult for peaceful picketing to be carried out.[47]

First-hand accounts provide graphic illustrations of the role that the police were playing. Mr B was told by a superintendent that he 'was not going to allow our men to walk the streets at night when the other men were going back to work. He was going to make it hot for anyone who followed the crowd.'[48] Mr R was told that he and a group of other men walking at 10.15 in the evening were to stop parading in the street and the best thing that they could do was to 'clear out of the village'.[49] Mr B made the following statement to Kidd:

> On December the 13th 1936 I was turning into the Crescent when a police officer stopped me. I told the officer I lived along the Crescent and was going home. The officer replied, 'you'll f— well go where I want you to go'.[50]

Mrs S a 25-year old Salvation Army officer told her story:

> On December 16th 1936, three police officers were round inside my house on my return from fetching fish and chips from a motor van which stopped at the top of the road. I had to wait some little time at the van for a second frying. During my absence my husband, who was emptying a teapot in the outside lavatory, returned to find two police officers standing inside the passage where it leads into the sitting room. He expressed surprise at their presence and they followed him into the sitting room uninvited. Later, a third officer entered. All three officers were interviewing my husband when I returned. Next morning a large number of footprints of police boots were visible in the garden and a number of cabbage plants had been destroyed by being trampled on. On December 26th 1936, at 11.30 p.m. Sergeant Weaver and Inspector Eyley and a constable came to my house and told me I must not be seen on the streets when the men are coming from and going to work.[51]

Kidd listed a whole series of other 'irregularities' in the administration of justice during this dispute. These included a marked partiality on the part of the police towards those still at work; the wrongful detention of individuals while the police made up their mind which charges to bring (an illegal practice according to the 1929 Royal Commission on Police Powers and Procedures); abuse of power to stop and search; summoning individuals to appear in court 10 miles away, 12 or 36 hours after an incident thereby rendering it very difficult both in terms of time and distance to collect witnesses; the class background of the local magistrates bench being the same as the mine-owners themselves; and the use of the new Public Order Act whereby individuals were charged under the section of the Act which dealt with the offence of using insulting words and behaviour, this section itself having been extended from London to apply to the rest of England with a simultaneous increase in penalties. Kidd concluded his report thus:

> Whatever the cause, there can be no reasonable doubt, I think, that there have been serious irregularities in the conduct of the police during the dispute and this, coupled with the attitude and composition of the local Bench and with the methods of serving summonses and making charges, had led to a feeling throughout the district that the general administration of law and order in the County is being used in manner which must do infinite harm to a belief in the traditions of public administration and justice.[52]

The NCCL's enthusiasm for inquiries resulted in the organization's setting up another in connection with the disorders in Thurloe Square in London on 22 March 1936. The disturbances were a result of clashes between anti-Fascist and British Union of Fascist supporters. The BUF had announced that they intended to hold a demonstration in the Albert Hall. Anti-Fascist supporters called for a mass mobilization and were met by 2,500 police who also had 400 men and women in reserve. When the anti-Fascist group moved to Thurloe Square and the speeches started 'the police assembled and without warning forced their way into the crowd'.[53] One of those involved later wrote:

> As soon as the mounted police were well inside the crowd, they drew their staves and began beating all those members of the public who were within their reach upon the head and shoulders. It was then observed that the foot police had also drawn their staves and were also using them on those members of the public whom they could reach. The crowd dispersed very rapidly making no resistance whatever to the police.[54]

At Tonypandy, in Wales, the same year, the police were in action again at an anti-Fascist meeting. They arrested 36 people who were charged with riot, incitement to riot, unlawful assembly and breaches of the peace. Police evidence to the court described one of the accused as 'a most violent man and extremely lawless in outlook' and another as 'the most subversive agitator in the Rhondda, with a fanatical outlook on life'.[55] In a letter to the *Guardian*, Harold Laski made a number of points again concerning the question of police neutrality and the court procedures involved:

> He queried whether thirty people accused of different offences and tried simultaneously could lead to a 'sense of discrimination' by the jury, especially

over six days of conflicting evidence. He also criticized the length of the judge's summing up. He expressed concern on these points for this had been the third 'mass' trial in Wales in recent years. Laski pointed out that the police denied that they could hear the provocative remarks attributed to Moran [one of the Fascist speakers] although he had the use of loudspeakers. Yet, they were able to detail what the accused were doing and saying. Laski also criticized the police for drawing attention to the political views of the accused, which were not a crime, and suggested that the police differentiated between the 'extreme' views of the left and the views of the right. Professor Laski felt that it was dangerous to convict accused persons on the evidence of police, who assume that certain political beliefs make a man a bad citizen. He called for an inquiry into the habits of the police in these matters.[56]

During the 1950s the police were again involved in a number of industrial disputes which included 'a tendency to declare that more than two pickets are illegal'.[57] In June 1959 during the printing strike, 50 pickets gathered to demonstrate against the use of scab labour in the printing of the *South London Press*. The police, who numbered about 70, used dogs to clear the path for a lorry loaded with newspaper. The appearance of the dogs:

> at once incensed them [the pickets] and turned an orderly crowd into an ugly scene with the possibility of a serious clash with the police. The atmosphere was so charged that I am sure that if the van and lorry had come out there would have been casualties.[58]

A year earlier, during a strike at the Levine Manufacturing Company's factory in Cricklewood Lane, police officers were again asking strikers to reduce the number of pickets 'in order to ensure compliance with the law and peaceful picketing'.[59] The strike also saw the use of plain-clothes officers on the picket lines. One of the pickets described the following incident:

> My attention was drawn to an incident at the gate involving a fellow picket who was attacked by two men dressed in civilian clothes leaving the factory with the rest of the workers. I immediately appealed to the uniformed police on duty to apprehend the said assailants who were forcibly marching the picket past us. The police informed me that the 'civilians' were police officers. I then asked for their warrants and authority for such action but I was ignored and brushed aside. The wife of the arrested picket throughout the entire event was pleading for their warrant to be shown, but she received the same treatment as myself, i.e. no satisfactory reply and contemptuous evasions. Another picket made the appeal for authority but with the same success.[60]

During the Grunwick dispute in 1976/7, the striking workers told of how they had been continuously harassed by the police and how the force behaved in a manner that was partial to the employer. As Phil Scraton has commented:

> What angered the pickets ... was the 'special relationship' which appeared to exist between Grunwick management and the police on duty at the picket. The

police were seen to be on 'first name terms' with management staff, drank tea in the Grunwick canteen and refused to act on threats or 'accidents' involving management staff. Yet at the same time they tried to limit the pickets to six strikers and they arrested pickets for obstruction.[61]

The Politics of Legality

Legal Process in Practice

This is not a complete account of the police in public order situations nor of their involvement in industrial disputes. Yet even this history can provide evidence that the authoritarian tendencies within the British state go beyond the period of Margaret Thatcher's administrations. These examples also suggest that the notion of civil liberties, and the related belief that police violence, surveillance and manipulation of the law can be explained by the deviancy of individual officers, are not adequate to the scale of the problem. It is important to avoid the implication that policing has not changed in the years since the struggle for women's suffrage. Police practices have been modified and rationalized to take account of contemporary problems. However, it does seem worth pointing out that the repertoire of police strategies appears small, and that the number of permutations in the way that crime is presented is inherently limited. Rather than marking a qualitative change, the developments misrecognized as Thatcherism merely intensify tendencies which pre-date Mrs Thatcher's premiership. The modern force is still marked by its origins and by the complex processes of state formation and consolidation in which it assumed recognizable modern shape and duties. If we are to argue that a post-industrial state is emerging, we cannot afford to retreat from detailed examination of its legal system, particularly the extent of its continuity with the past. As Anderson and Greenberg correctly point out, 'There have been several capitalist state forms, not one. These variations have had major ramifications both for the substance of legal codes and their social effects.'[62] It is possible to identify the coercive power of legal procedures which rely on a gap between the democratic rhetoric of law and the actual practice of justice as one important site of this continuity. This gap is expressed day by day in the manner that, for example, the right to silence is not a right at all and Judges' Rules are not in a meaningful sense rules. It is reinforced and reproduced in police and courtroom cultures which treat suspects, formally innocent until proven otherwise – as prisoners, and in the routine brutality and machismo in the work of police and prison officers which also preceded 'Thatcherism'. This violence is not a simple matter of deviancy. We must begin to address the question of why behaviour of this type has become congruent with the job of imposing order and control. State brutality provides the perfect example of how, even under liberal democracy, legality and illegality become part of the same institutional structure. It is worth studying because it confirms that violence continues to occupy a determining position in the exercise of state power.

The complexity of judicial structures and procedures, particularly the law's bureaucratic and theatrical elements, can obscure the simple fact that the production, preparation and presentation of evidence does not match up to the rhetoric of justice. This rhetoric is routinely undermined by the operation of the legal system. The point bears repetition because it indicates that socialists must move beyond the superficial view that bad or repressive laws are essentially different from laws of which they approve. Specific laws to which leftists tend to object, governing pickets or demonstrations for example, should not be isolated from consideration of processes of legality in general.[63] Doreen McBarnet has correctly castigated radicals for their reluctance to look at the legal process as an integrated system and the consequent inability to appreciate that the problems of capitalist legality consist of more than occasional deviations from an otherwise acceptable legal or constitutional standard. Her approach demonstrates the false nature of distinctions between crime control and due process models of law enforcement. Due process, she rightly argues, is *for* crime control and rather than inhibiting the prosecution, legal rules are legitimately used to secure convictions. Law expressed in rules and codified by textbooks is not necessarily at odds with its summary expression in the magistrate's court. The frameworks and techniques of legality are therefore neither a mere backdrop nor a simple instrument of political struggle. Our starting point is that the legal form must be seen as a problem in itself.

In political terms, this is not an argument for retreat from conflicts in and around the courts. To the contrary, it is a plea that such struggles are conducted in a spirit which demands more of justice than an apparent fairness rooted in the internal coherence of legal procedures. The recent history of black community struggles, of the Greenham women and of prisoners offers important points towards how extra-legal and legal elements in a political campaign can be balanced and blended in new ways which exploit any residual contradictions in legal rights and dramatize the power relations involved. E.P. Thompson's[64] well-known suggestion that the rule of law is an 'unqualified human good' is echoed by many on the left inside and outside Parliament. It should be challenged not only because the level of abstraction at which it functions makes its kernel of truth banal. Like many left thinkers, Thompson overemphasizes the significance of formal legal rationality and as a result ends up taking existing legality on trust. The recent use of bail procedures during the miners' strike is an example of how readily formal legal rationality can be qualified by the need to maintain order and control the accused.

This points to the wisdom of considering law and policing together as intermeshing aspects of a complex and sometimes contradictory bureaucratic system. The price of falsely separating law from police and court practice is that it ascends to abstract philosophical heights from which it is unlikely to return.[65] It makes better sense to develop a view of legality as a process made up of different elements. Police are therefore only one part of the overall pattern and it should not be assumed that they are able or wish to achieve complete control over the others. Looking at law in this way must also reckon with the relationship between trial procedures and the actual events which lead to arrest in the first place. Police officers, giving evidence or prosecuting, reconstruct events so that their actions are seen to be consistent with police regulations, legal rules, the occupational cultures of both police and court officers and judicial discourse. Their accounts and definitions are accorded a special, privileged status. It is with this reconstructed reality that the defence must take issue; 'attempts by defendants to discuss what really happened . . . miss what the court regards as the point'.[66] This is part of the explanation of how legal processes routinely support and endorse outcomes favoured by the police. Rather than guaranteeing space in which the defence can manoeuvre, formal legal rationality can itself become another obstacle to the realization of the rhetoric of justice.

The riots of 1981 kindled an interest in policing and legality among many activists whose campaigning work had not previously recognized these issues. The growth of the peace movement, and consequent interest in various forms of direct action strengthened this concern. The political value of symbolic, illegal actions was highlighted simultaneously with a sense that the police were developing a better organized, more flexible and inevitably more ruthless response to disorderly protest. If policing has become a familiar problem for inner-city dwellers, peace activists, animal rights group and trade union militants, this has not been reflected in the analytical writings of the socialist movement in either its Labour or non-Labour incarnations. These remain dominated by the belief that the real problems with police originate from outside their ranks, specifically in the role which they have been given in the enforcement of 'Thatcherite' government policy. In the words of Robert Reiner, 'It is heightened political conflict which contains the dangers of a police state, rather than developments within the police force itself.'[67]

This basic proposition is expanded by the equally erroneous belief that police misdeeds are not only rare but also technically illegal. The problem of police reform is then reduced to the complex task of creating a framework of legal safeguards capable of inhibiting the deviant urges of the force's bad apples. This perspective acknowledges the basic problem as it is defined by senior policemen who have attacked the restrictive effect of the existing legal framework which forces police to operate outside the law if they are to be effective.[68] The coercive force of common law powers and of the case law systems are thus glossed over. The impact of police professionalism which has specifically encouraged the development of an 'informed discretion' in the way officers use their powers at street level is minimized. This legalistic approach is locked in place by a definition of 'police accountability' as an exclusively administrative and institutional use. Yet it is precisely the

exercise of flexible, discretionary power by police which reveals the
limitations of the idea that police are directly accountable to the law. It
demonstrates that the effect of law on police practice at street level is
permissive rather than restrictive. Law in general offers no formula for
calculating police priorities or practical guidelines as to what, for example,
patrolling officers ought to do. Instead, legal powers which were framed
with the control of particular street populations in mind, become a unified
resource with which officers are able to legitimate any course of action they
engage in. This is vividly conveyed in ethnographies of police work and by
officers who boast 'Whatever [powers] they give us, it doesn't really matter
we'll find a way round it' or 'Believe me, from experience there is a statute to
fit almost every situation encountered by the police'.[69] This confidence
originates in far more than just the lower ranks' moulding of official policy
around the alternative priorities of their occupational culture. In organizational terms, the balance of power in the force inverts its military hierarchy.
In a discussion of new management initiatives, a constable from the
North Wales force spells out the importance of organizational factors in
determining the eventual shape of police practice:

> Information is passed up not down. Police management must control the flow
> because this increases its capacity to regulate those being controlled [the
> junior ranks].... The greatest amount of discretionary decision making is
> practised at the lowest level ... police management leads from behind or does
> not lead at all. Police leaders lack a comprehensive appreciation of what is
> really happening on the streets. The higher the rank, the less is known.[70]

The 'Left' Response

Myths and Misconceptions

E.P. Thompson's work typified other problems in how socialists approach
the role of the police in society. These run parallel with his tendency to
idealize legality and become mesmerized by constitutional archisms.

In an important, and highly influential piece, written in 1978 he attacked
those on the left who took the position that all law and all police were bad
and saw crime as some sort of displaced revolutionary activity. Without
naming individuals or groups he went on to argue that 'there are half-truths
which have a continual tendency to degenerate into rubbish, and moreover,
into rubbish which has a particular appeal to a certain kind of elitist
bourgeois intellectual'.[71] Citing the case of the police in particular,
Thompson pointed out that:

> In any known society, some of the functions of the police are as necessary and
> legitimate as those of firemen and of ambulance-men; and these legitimate
> functions include not only helping old ladies across the road (which I do not
> often notice them doing during the day) but enforcing the law and protecting
> citizens against offenders.[72]

The piece described his participation in street demonstrations over the last 30 years. He often found his companion to be a police officer who, after a few grumpy exchanges, was found to be 'seriously interested in the issue of the march, nuclear disarmament, or the Vietnam War or even racialism itself'.[73] While pointing out that this is a sentimental picture and that Grunwick showed the police up in a less endearing light, Thompson maintained that 'a wholly indiscriminate attitude of "bash the fuzz" is very much more sentimental, more self-indulgent and counter-productive'.[74]

Thompson's support for the police, particularly in the fight against rising crime has been reiterated continuously in broadcasts, statements, speeches, debates and books by supporters, thinkers and politicians in and around the Labour Party. This approach to crime control and the police has been advocated by Neil Kinnock in an article in the *Daily Mirror* in January 1984. He uncritically accepted official Home Office statistics about the rising crime rate despite the major methodological and theoretical weaknesses which can be identified in the use of such statistics. He accused the Thatcher government of presiding over major percentage increases in violent offences, criminal damage, burglary and robbery. Kinnock, finally, resurrected his youth in the 1950s when 'everybody shared the duty of keeping an eye on the kids and on each others' homes'.[75] What we need, he concluded, was 'the police back on the beat in touch, in contact, not riding around in Panda cars'.[76]

This notion of getting back to how 'things used to be' is underpinned by the idea that the police force is a fundamentally benevolent institution and that while there might be the odd abuse of power and the individual 'bad apple', the barrel is sound. Police should therefore be supported across party lines. For example, in June 1983 in the debate on the Queen's Speech Roy Hattersley was quick to point to his party's success in obtaining more resources for the force:

> Not only I do support the notion that more resources are necessary for the police and the police service. The increase in police pay, for which the previous Home Secretary took so much credit, was the direct result of an inquiry into police pay which I set up in the dying days of the Labour Government. If we want to take credit for these matters, I am prepared for the first time in three years to remind the House that that is what happened. The idea that the Edmund-Davies Committee should be set up and that its recommendations should be implemented was a matter not of party controversy but of agreement between the parties.[77]

Cross-party agreement extends beyond the issues of police pay and conditions. In February 1983, in the debate on the original Police and Criminal Evidence Bill in Standing Committee J of the House of Commons, while complaining about some of the clauses contained in the Bill, Roy Hattersley pointed out that the committee was 'one of the most tractable' that he could recall and that he 'never sat on a committee where the opposition and the government, over time have co-operated in such a friendly fashion'.[78] This view was supported by James Callaghan in the Home Office bicentenary lectures in 1982. He argued that on issues of law and freedom:

> There had always to be some approach towards the centre because, whatever their politics, Home Secretaries sprang from the same culture, a culture it was their duty to preserve if the country was to remain a good place to live in.[79]

The argument that more police are needed in order to combat crime wilfully ignores the proven inability of the police to detect, deter or solve crime. As far back as 1933, Lord Trenchard, the Commissioner of Police in London pointed out in his yearly report that it was important to bear in mind the distinction between what he called 'preventable' crime and 'detectable' crime. Trenchard argued that:

> It is perhaps obvious that there are certain types of crime which cannot be prevented by any possible police action. They can be discouraged by good detection but no amount of police vigilance can prevent such crimes as murder, fraud, forgery, embezzlement or the various forms of theft (such as shoplifting) which occurs when no police are present.... On the other hand, there are types of crime which police vigilance can do much to keep in check. They include all kinds of 'breakings', many kinds of larceny, such as bag-snatching, the picking of pockets, bicycle stealing and thefts from cars and telephone boxes and also receiving.[80]

Trenchard repeated his assertion in his 1935 report arguing that 'certain types of crime cannot be prevented, obstructed or made more difficult of performance by police action'.[81] The Commissioner was even more forthright later in the report maintaining that the public were beginning to realize that police protection nowadays is not to be measured by the frequency (or infrequency) of the appearance of officers on foot. The idea of 'going out and finding a policeman should now be out of date'.[82]

The Met discontinued these distinctions between different crimes in 1947 but by the late 1970s researchers at the Home Office Research Unit were again pointing to the inherent limitations in police capacity. Two of the unit's researchers, Ron Clarke and Kevin Heal, concluded that 'the crime prevention value of the police force rests less precisely on what it does than on the symbolic effect of its presence and public belief in its effectiveness'.[83] Three years later, Heal again surveyed approaches to crime control and highlighted the complexity of the issues involved. The Home Office has moved far beyond the over-simplified sloganeering of the left on the question of law and order:

> Over the last decade or so, research has called into question the effectiveness of conventional policing methods. This research does not indicate that

patrolling and detective work are without impact, though it is sometimes construed to be so, both by critics and defenders of conventional policing. However it suggests that the marginal gains from additional deterrent policing will be negligible.[84]

Heal argued that there were number of possible reasons for this, including the fact that it was difficult to achieve significant increases in the chances of offenders being caught. He pointed out that deterrent policing itself may actually amplify criminal behaviour by

> reducing the opportunities of convicted offenders for 'going straight', by fuelling resentment against authority or by confirming people's conceptions of themselves as law-breakers. It is also possible that extension of formal systems of social control may erode rather than supplement communities' informal self-policing mechanisms.[85]

In 1984, Clarke and Hough reviewed much of the research evidence and indicated that while for the first time in many years the police service was up to complement with the number of officers rising by 10% in the previous five years, 'crime will not be significantly reduced simply by devoting more manpower to conventional police strategies'.[86]

The authors found that there was no evidence that either more patrol cars or officers on the beat could reduce crime. In fact, given the present rate of burglaries, the average officer patrolling on foot in London would expect to pass within 100 yards of a burgarly once every 8 years. Significantly, they also indicated this kind of research had influenced the thinking of senior police officers,

> many of whom have accepated the limited effectiveness of conventional deterrent policing – foot patrol, car patrol and criminal investigation – and are now devoting considerable effort to the search for new solutions.[87]

Sir Robert Mark was one of these chiefs of police who had accepted this view. He had this to say about crime in 1982:

> A great deal of crime is simply not preventable. Even the biggest police force that society could want or afford to pay would be unlikely to have any significant effect on the numbers of thefts, burglaries or on crimes of violence between people who know each other.[88]

Mark has also been very vocal about the 'problem' of crime: 'seen objectively against the background and problems of 50 million people it is not even amongst the more serious of our difficulties'.[89] This refrain has been taken up by other chief constables to justify the police concern for public order and anti-subversion activities.

But it is an insight which does not lead inevitably in this direction. It could, for example, inform left discourse on crime which recognizes that public fear relates to the intermittent nature of social solidarity in some inner-city areas rather than to any risk of becoming a victim of crime. Its emphasis on the symbolic functions of routine police work is also important. It suggests that these fears may be reduced by other symbolic means. Similarly, the idea that policing ought not to be left to the police alone which has become a motto for intelligence gathering and surveillance, can be used to raise the question of self-policing. It contains an acknowledgement of popular capacity for mutual aid and protection which might become the means to advocate credible self-policing schemes, divorced from police practice, in some neighbourhoods.

A second misconception in the left's thinking about crime and the police, is the failure to acknowledge the crucial importance of the police subculture as the primary factor in deciding police priorities and practices. Power in the police force resides very much with the 'canteen cowboys', the rank-and-file constables and sergeants. As the Policy Studies Institute Report on the police in London showed, it is these officers who are the driving force behind the nature and style of policing. The study revealed that violence, racism and sexism are institutionalized in the Met where officers prove themselves by drinking 'large quantities of alcohol and recounting stories of violence, conflict and physical prowess'.[90] The report cast grave doubts on the traditional view of detective work and confirmed that:

> Comparatively little time is spent on investigation and that a high proportion of offences do not require the deployment of detective skills. Secondly, the research shows how the police on occasion, use their powers not for investigation but for retribution. Thirdly, the report looks at investigation in practice and concludes that in most instances police hands are tied not by the Judges' Rules which they ignore with impunity, but by their own incompetence and prejudices. Finally the researchers look at how the police use their position to persuade or intimidate people into creating evidence favourable to the prosecution.[91]

The report's four volumes show that the 'rights' of individuals are subservient to getting a 'result', that is, an arrest or a prosecution case that will stand up in court. Thus, the use of informal questioning, threats and inducements and the adjustment of statements are all part of a process which was regarded as necessary to obtain conviction.[92] One of those interviewed by the researchers described their experience in this way: 'They put me in a cell for two days. It only had a bench in it, no bed, no blankets. I claimed Habeus Corpus but they said they didn't understand Latin'.[93] The report found that it was common practice to manipulate evidence or statements which would be to the prosecution's advantage. Suspects were informally questioned on the way to the police station, juveniles questioned without the presence of parent or another adult (as the law requires), and individuals only told at the beginning of the formal interview of their right to silence. Police would then suggest a form of words to the interviewee. Thus, as the researchers pointed out:

> While the officer takes a statement in good faith and with the intention of

being fair, he will still tend to frame it in a way that is helpful to the prosecution and if he wishes to end the evidence to some extent, it is fairly easy for him to do so while drafting the statement in a form that the suspect will be ready to approve.[94]

The researchers found that very few people routinely come into contact with the police. The force orientate themselves towards policing what they see as the 'slags' of society, an 'underclass' of the poor and rootless whom the police continually subject to harrassment and arrest. They do not enforce the law impartially or without prejudice and officers sharply define who will be their target when on patrol according to:

> A special conception of social class, mixed with an idea of conventional or proper behaviour [which] is just as important to police officers as racial or ethnic groups. In this scale, the 'respectable' working class and the suburban middle class stand highest while the 'underclass' of the poor and rootless, together with groups regarded as deviant, such as homosexuals or hippies, stand lowest.[95]

This police subculture is not confined to London. In 1983, Simon Holdaway, an ex-police sergeant, published *Inside the British Police*. The book was his account of policing 'Hilton' subdivision, an area close to the centre of one of Britian's major cities which remained unnamed throughout the book. His account confirms much of what the PSI found in London. Hilton had a police subculture in which power again lay at the bottom of the hierarchy with the constables and sergeants. Racism and sexism were institutionalized, force was often used both to retain control or to mete out retribution, and 'verballing' remained an important strategy. Holdaway argues that tactics utilized in policing Hilton were supported by the view that the area was a place where the people were going to get 'out of hand' unless the police did something about it. For the force, these strategies:

> emphasize control, hedonism, action and challenge – constituents of the occupational culture. These cultural strands of policing are woven together as practical skills employed on the streets . . . these strategies seem to distance Hilton's officers from the constraints of legal rules and force directives, from the criticisms of the public that is policed, from the influence of the least powerful groups living and working in Hilton. Hilton's rank-and-file officers are free to police in their own style, with their own strategies and assumptions intact.[96]

The left's inability to come to terms with the power of the police subculture confines their discussions of policing and law to either the abuse of civil liberties and prisoners' rights or to a demand for greater police accountability. They do not take account of the police as an independent force within society, nor of the complex interaction between individual officers, their particular force, the law and the criminal justice system in general.

A third misconception which often underpins left discussion about the police is the idea that they do a difficult and dangerous job. This is reiterated by the Police Federation, who argue that officers work on violent, mean streets at great risk to their personal safety. Yet, as both Holdaway and the PSI researchers show, police officers spend a great deal of their time doing nothing. As Holdaway put it:

> Contrary to what you may have gleaned from *Sweeney* and *Operation Carter* police work is really a very quiet occupation.... Long periods of walking around and waiting are interspersed with occasional incidents, usually mundane. The reality does not match the popular image of a world pulsating with action and excitement.[97]

Even in police terms, the idea of policing dangerous streets is contradicted by the evidence. A study conducted in 1982, calculated that the risk of a police officer being murdered in England and Wales for the years 1970–77 was 1.4 per 100,000 of the population. This compared with 2.5 per 100,000 for the Federal German Republic, 4.5 for France, 6.6 for Switzerland, 20 for Italy and 22 for the USA.[98] It should be noted that while 19 police officers were killed on duty between 1972 and 1982, between 1970 and 1980 at least 12 people died in England and Wales as a result of force by police officers such as shootings and deaths on demonstrations.[99] Between 1972 and 1982 there were 411 deaths in police custody (or otherwise with the police) including 275 (67%) due to unnatural causes or suicide.[100] Finally, it is worth considering that in 1981, the year of summer disturbances, the number of days lost through officers being injured on and off duty in London were almost the same – some 59,000 days in each category. In terms of days lost through injuries sustained *on* duty, just over 4,000 were lost through officers being injured in public order situations (7% of the total) but 8,500 days were lost due to officers being involved in motor-cycle accidents (14% of the total) and a further 8,100 days were lost due to accidents when the injured officer was in a car (13% of the total).

Discussion of the left's orthodoxies is incomplete without consideration of the conspiratorial view which provides the main alternative to the dominant constitutional perspective. The conspiracy theory of police practice to which it refers has been given a boost by the policing of the miners' dispute which, it is argued, confirms that Britain has acquired the characteristics of a 'police state'. As in the constitutional view, it is believed that until Mrs Thatcher came on the scene, politics were somehow external to policing. However, in this approach, the nub of the problem becomes the newly conspiratorial relationship between senior police, Home Office and government. This, it is argued, explains the recent militarization of policing and the creation of repressive legislation such as the Police and Criminal Evidence Bill. This is presented as functional to the creation of a monetarist social order. The Bill tends to be understood as a clear and decisive break with the common law powers which preceded it. To the extent that police are identified as the junior partners in the conspiratorial partnership, this position lets them off the hook. Its advocates are spared the task of reckoning seriously with the politics of the force in either its ACPO or its Police Federation guise, let alone explaining the clear conflicts and contradictions which exist between these organizations and the Home Office. Though the variety of police responses to protest, demonstrations and campaigns – mass caution, mass arrest, mass violence – can sometimes suggest a political calculation, the level at which this takes place is hard to specify. Police refusal to charge peace demonstrators or enthusiasm for arresting and beating miners may be explained as much by the protestors' choice of tactics, the location of their action, or the presentation of their grievance and ideology as by tactical policing. In any case, the legal powers and organizational structure which encourage flexible, *ad hoc* police strategies are a more profound problem than nebulous conspiracies.

Attention must therefore be paid to forms of political action which in themselves restrict the range of acceptable tactics open to police in public order situations. Non-violent direct action has a role to play here and is one issue where the trade union movement clearly has something to learn from activist women.

Conclusions

In practice, the left's orientation towards policing often depends on a distinct but thoroughly subjective assessment of the extent to which anti-police activity by individuals or groups expresses an identifiable class interest. Waged workers or strikers who engage in violence or sabotage in the course of trades union activity will be viewed more sympathetically than 'marginalized' or 'alienated' youth who do the same. The latter are widely condemned for their 'nihilism' and their anti-social tendencies.[101] This socialist perspective is weakened by the idea that policing is primarily about crime control. In turn, this becomes the rationale for confining police activity to areas which accord with the political priorities and calculations of the moment. Policing, already defined as an instrumental rather than symbolic activity is given still greater importance by the idea that there is a continued and inexorable rise in crime. In this atmosphere, the real complexity of crime is disregarded by socialists who regard the Thatcherism monopoly of the law and order issue with near hysterical envy. Rather than reflecting any genuine interest, concern about crime has become more important as a talisman of populist politics. The issue of any relationship between recorded crime and unemployment rates suffers from the need to score vulgar political points. 'Tough' police tactics which target 'high crime' areas are welcomed if they can be balanced by the appropriate safeguards, though the vaguest familiarity with the working of the police force make this suggestion laughable. The 'new realists' of Labour's criminological fraternity have made the slogan 'heavy but accountable policing' their rallying cry.[102] As with the right, much of the Labour left sees the issue of crime as a potent symbol of the degeneration of the inner cities. Pronounce-ments on crime tend to invoke an anti-urbanism which sees the city itself as a stultifying brutal space in which fratricide and despair are more likely to develop than solidarity and community. The populist element in being seen to take crime seriously has been identified as the means to repair Labour's decaying relationship with its natural supporters – the respectable, white, productive working class.

Thus the issues of policing, legality and criminal justice are being brought to the centre of Labour's organizational and ideological crises. This is being done without apparent consideration of where, when and why the crime issue acquires its awesome power to mobilize and animate. Addressing these questions is urgent lest the party slips into a deeper embrace with the right by seeking to daub the populist package a shabby shade of red. Rather than being accepted as a straightforward reflection of entropic inner-city reality, public concern about crime must be understood as the outcome of a political process. This necessitates breaking down the abstract, general category 'crime' into the particular experiences, images and fear, which correspond to city life.

Few urban residents worry about crime in general. Any anxiety they have is likely to specify the crimes which have become a focus of concern – burglary, rape, car theft or perhaps 'mugging'. The easy resort to crime as an abstraction increases rather than diminishes the distance which the left has to travel if it is to articulate a credible politics of everyday life. Local factors are central to the pattern of fear about crime. This is always discontinuous, fluid and specific. Its unevenness points to another uneven-ness, in policing itself, which political organizing around the law and order issues must begin to recognize. Apart from the effect of police interventions in local and national political life which have become routine, perceptions of police and the degree of support for them relate directly to the quality of contact (if any) which people have with them. The majority of citizens may never have an unsatisfactory encounter with police while a large minority are the object of persistent police interest. In 1983, 1,257,000 people were arrested and 2,260,000 found guilty or cautioned in England and Wales. The success of local organizing is likely to be dependent on local circumstances, police deployment and priorities.

This ought to be a reminder that as far as 'law and order' is concerned, there are no ready-made answers waiting to be produced from the socialist hat by skilled conjuring. Popular sentiment about crime which develops without the experience of being a victim and without any contact with the police is obviously prone to panic and manipulation which flow from the symbolism inherent in police activity.

These problems are merely compounded by left writers whose simplistic, abstract view of crime is matched by a similarly crude portrait of the working class. The unevenness of experience and perception creates a wide variety of needs and expectations with regard to policing. There are for example substantive contradictions between the interests of men and women, young and old, black and white, and employed and unemployed people. These differences cannot be banished by the refusal to accommodate the heterogeneity of the working class as presently constituted or by the reluctance to look at the way that law fractures and reproduces class relations. It is not only in the industrial disputes discussed above that police practice contributes to the meaning of class and plays a central role in complex processes of class formation and decomposition which have eclipsed the idea of a simple progression from class in itself to class for itself. In this context, the lines of legality and the sites of police activity often mark significant struggles over social space or resources and freedom to exist without being subjected to continued surveillance or intimidation. Even today, these struggles relate directly to the character and meaning of 'working class'. Indeed, the political communities which emerge in the course of such struggles must be carefully evaluated and positioned. It is not sufficient to dismiss them under the heading of marginality. Socialists must remember not only that the processes which turn workers into a class are inextricably tied to the processes by which surplus labour is distributed and organized in politics; but also that, throughout its short institutional life, policing has been preoccupied with divisions among people – the reproduction of class relations. The history of police differentiating between deserving and casual poor or between labouring and criminal classes makes their more modern attempts to sort reputable from slag citizenry appear less surprising. A left theory of policing will also have to contend with the legacy of Victorian moralism expressed in socialist writing which regards the existence of surplus labour (the lumpenproletariat) as an embarrassment to the idea of class analysis. The expansion of the state's role in the provision of income and changes in the division of labour precipitated by de-industrialization and new technology have underlined this failure. This surplus increases but the political consciousness of the approved 'classically conceived' working class fails to match the predictive logic. Many of this group have articulated their interests in 'Thatcherite' terms.

The urban phenomenon crudely caricatured as the lumpenproletariat must be studied on its own and in its relation to other more politically attractive class fractions. Both histories will be centrally concerned with policing. Socialists must also accept that the struggle to impose legal regulation on working-class populations involves both criminalization and depoliticization. The years ahead are likely to witness many struggles to resist the imposition of criminal labels on individual and collective acts which have a normative and explicitly political though seldom revolutionary dimension. Working covertly while drawing the dole, drinking on unlicensed premises or harassing blacks for sport are as much a feature of this category as stoning police and burning their cars. The normative sanction of these acts is a reminder that the communities involved have their own sophisticated ideas about what justice and freedom consist of.[103] At times these norms may coincide with the priorities and sanctions of the police but recent history suggests that this is the exception rather than the rule. Authoritarian statism manifest in law and order politics may increase the extent to which officially defined crime, for example scrounging, picketing or mugging, is synonymous with crime as it is defined by the working and non-working classes. If this is so, it is not an inevitable or permanent state of affairs. There will also be wide variations in opinion and in levels of organization around policing; these will be expressed geographically.

The new initiatives organized by Sir Kenneth Newman at the Metropolitan Police recognize the patchy and intermittent character of anti-police consciousness and resistance. Their overall context is a shift towards police strategies based on area rather than offence categories which heralds the creation of a 'multi-agency' approach to crime prevention and control.[104] This sets out to synchronize a broad range of state agencies under police direction and co-ordinate their efforts towards the establishment of an 'ethos in society which makes crime unacceptable'. Newman has identified the areas which gave his force the greatest concern:

> Throughout London there are locations where unemployed youth – often black youths – congregate; where the sale and purchase of drugs, the exchange of stolen property and illegal drinking and gaming is not uncommon [sic]. The youths regard these locations as their territory. Police are viewed as intruders, the symbol of authority – largely white authority – in a society that is responsible for all their grievances about unemployment, prejudice and discrimination. They equate closely with the criminal 'rookeries' of Dickensian London.[105]

The existence of these areas comprises a threat which is less to do with any immediate lawlessness they contain than with their capacity to convey the limitations of police power and to signify the fragility of the order which police are able to impose:

> If allowed to continue, locations with these characteristics assume symbolic importance – a negative symbolism of the inability of the police to maintain order. Their existence encourages law breaking elsewhere, affects public perceptions of police effectiveness, heightens fear of crime and reinforces the phenomenon of urban decay.[106]

In earlier phases, the concept of 'mugging' focused popular panic around the activities of first black youth and then youth in general. In Newman's discourse, the concept 'street crime' is used to link street robberies with street riots and disorders so that each expresses the other and both become symptoms of the same criminal and environmental malaise. The development of the area-based notions of control and the resultant targeting of specific populations and groups is an important step towards the co-ordination of state interventions which Newman's Met identified as the true practice of what it now calls 'social control'. It is important to grasp that the 'multi-agency' initiative is only part of the Met's response to the challenge of policing the 1980s. Its corporate approach is inseparable from, indeed relies on, the existence of a ruthless militarized capability which has the primary function of 'nipping disorder in the bud'. In October 1984 Sir Kenneth told Westminster Chamber of Commerce:

> During the summer this year there were many mini-riots which had the potential to escalate to Brixton 1981 proportions. But they were quickly and effectively extinguished. So effectively indeed, that they hardly rated a mention in the press.[107]

Rather than setting these twin strategies at opposite poles of the policing spectrum the left must accept their interrelationship and examine how, in the present period, each has come to require the other. Both have profound implications for the police organization as a whole and each expresses the lessons learned by the force in 1981: a bitter experience which Geoffrey Dear, Assistant Commissioner at the Met described as having 'shaken the apathy out of the system'.

The seamless integration of state agencies as diverse and contradictory as schools, housing departments, social services, probation and the youth service remains unlikely if not impossible. However, the forms of social and political planning which are aimed at have a genuine appeal to sections of the left. This is particularly true of currents in local government and social work bureaucracy where administrative and statist conceptions of socialism and social change have taken root. The idea that the relevant professionals should sit down together and unify their work is clearly congruent with elements of Fabian thought which are once again popular among the self-styled 'new urban left'.[108]

The idea that the transformation of society can be administered from above in this way stands in stark contradiction to approaches which emphasize its origins in long and complex processes of popular self-organization. At this point, many who do not go all the way down the neo-Fabian road will want to argue that law and order is one area of life where orchestrated bureaucratic intervention is necessary to ensure the maximization of justice, albeit in modified forms. We believe that this position is insufficiently radical and an inappropriate starting point for effective and meaningful political action. At best, such an approach is premature, at worst it leads to the cynical attempt to incorporate unmodified 'Thatcherite' law and order politics into the work of Labour parties.

As an alternative, we have pointed to the existence of normative conceptions of crime and wrongdoing which compete for popular allegiance with those which originate in police practice. It is important to apply this insight and identify where such norms connect with a capacity for self-policing. Police initiatives like 'neighbourhood watch' schemes recognize this capacity but seek to subordinate it to the gathering of local intelligence and the obvious public relations value these schemes have for the force. Socialists must began to affirm and extend the belief that people are able to regulate their own community space and protect their lives and property without lapsing into vigilantism.

To be effective, the commitment to self-organization must go hand in hand with a combination of making demands on the police and carefully documented criticism of their failures and political stances. Left writers who have suggested that this mixture of tactics amounts to schizophrenia are closing off the only route out of a situation in which socialists are being dragged – with varying degrees of reluctance – to the right by the attempt to even speak about policing and crime. The balance between the three essential components – organization, demands and criticism – will be determined by local circumstances and may vary widely across a city.

If we are able to admit that 'law and order' issues express regret at the collapse of social solidarity in some areas it also follows that the re-creation of that solidarity will do something to decrease fear. We could do worse than follow Michael Ignatieff's advice:

> [Labour] ought to talk less about prisons and policemen and more about rebuilding civic trust among strangers in public places – by giving tenants control over their estates; by creating clubs, bars, gyms and small businessess where kids can create a civic space of their own between the institutions of home, school and dole office; by creating parks, public monuments and estates which, as the Victorians had the confidence to do, have the kind of beauty and respect for human scale which demands pride and trust from those who use them.[109]

The political challenge posed by this is twofold. The left must adapt itself so that it can correspond to the needs and aspirations of communities in which the police are a problem rather than a solution. The restriction of police autonomy and the reduction of their power must be brought to the centre of socialist organizing.

Acknowledgements

We would like to thank Clare DeMuth, Phil Scraton, Paul Gordon, Vron Ware and Marcus Gilroy-Ware for their criticism, encouragement and support during the preparation of this article.

An earlier version of this paper was published in Capital and Class, No. 25, Spring 1985.

Notes

1 Hansard, 14 November 1983, cols. 341–2.
2 Hansard, 8 November 1983, cols. 341–2.
2 Ibid, col. 90.
3 Cited in J. Sim and P. Thomas, 'The Prevention of Terrorism Act: Normalising the politics of repression' *Journal of Law and Society*, Summer 1983, p. 80. See also

Criminal Justice: A Working Paper, Home Office, 1984.

5 Hansard, 3 February 1984, cols. 508–12.

6 K. Jeffrey and P. Hennessy, *States of Emergency*, London, Routledge & Kegan Paul, 1983, p. 150.

7 K.O. Morgan, *Labour in Power 1945–51*, Oxford, Clarendon Press, 1984, pp. 55–6.

8 A. Rutherford, *Prisons and the Process of Justice: The Reductionist Challenge*, London; Heinemann 1984, p. 53.

9 M. Ryan, *Politics of Penal Reform*, London; Longman, 1983, pp. 10–11.

10 Ibid.

11 H. Scott, *Scotland Yard*, Harmondsworth, Penguin, Middx, 1957, p. 22.

12 *Labour Government vs. the Dockers 1945–51*, Solidarity Pamphlet 19, Summer 1966.

13 Cited in D. Strinatti, *Capitalism the State and Industrial Relations*, London, Croom Helm, 1982, p. 52.

14 Jeffrey and Hennessy, op. cit. p. 180.

15 Ibid, p. 220–1.

16 G. Ellen, 'Labour and Strike Breaking', *International Socialist*, 24, Summer 1984, p. 58.

17 Ibid, footnote 99.

18 R.D. Storch, 'The Plague of the Blue Locusts: police reform and popular resistance in Northern England 1840–57', *International Review of Social History*, 20, 1975, pp. 61–90.

19 J. Field, 'Police power and community in a provincial English town', in V. Bailey (ed.), *Policing and Punishment in Nineteenth Century Britain*, London, Croom Helm, 1981, pp. 42–64.

20 B. Weinberger, 'The police and the public in mid nineteenth century Warwickshire', in V. Bailey, op. cit. pp. 65–93.

21 P. Cohen, 'Policing the working class city', in NDC/CSE (eds), *Capitalism and the Rule of Law*, London, Hutchinson, 1979, pp. 120–36.

22 J. White, 'Campbell Bunk: a lumpen community in London between the wars', *History Workshop*, 8, Autumn 1979, pp. 33–4.

23 Report of the Commissioner of Police of the Metropolis, 1935, p. 8.

24 Ibid. p. 9.

25 Ibid. p. 10.

26 Ibid.

27 Report of the Commissioner of Police of the Metropolis, 1937, p. 8.

28 Ibid, p. 9.

29 M. Brogden, *The Police; Autonomy and Consent*, London, Academic Press, 1983.

30 G. Pearson, *Hooligan: A History of Respectable Fears*, London, Macmillan, 1983, p. 213.

31 Ibid. p. 212 (emphasis in original).

32 Ibid. p. 230.

33 For documentation of many of these changes see *State Research, Review of Security and State*, 3 vols, London, Julian Friedman, 1978–80.

34 J. Boyle, *The Pain of Confinement*, Edinburgh, Canongate Press, 1984.

35 M. Brown, *Working the Street: Police Discretion and the Dilemmas of Reform*, Russell Sage Foundation, 1981, pp. 283–4.

36 S. Hall *et al.*, *Policing the Crisis*, London, Macmillan, 1978; Anthony Barnett, 'Fortress Thatcher', in P. Ayrton, T. Englehart and V. Ware (eds), *World View*

1985, London, Pluto Press, 1984; Colin Leys, 'Neo-Conservatism and the organic crisis in Britain, *Studies In Political Economy*, 4, 1980.

37 Robin Evelegh, *Peace Keeping in a Democratic Society – The Lessons of Northern Ireland*, London, C. Hurst, 1978.

38 Kenneth Newman, 'Public order in free societies', speech to The European Atlantic Group, 24 October 1983.

39 R. Geary, 'From battle to march: the changing nature of industrial confrontations', *The Police Journal*, vol. LV 11, no. 2, April–June 1984, p. 151.

40 T. Bunyan, *The History and Practice of the Political Police in Britain*, London, Julian Friedman, 1978.

41 Ibid. p. 141.

42 Cited in A. Raeburn, *The Militant Suffragettes*, London, Michael Joseph, 1973, pp. 153–5.

43 Ibid.

44 Cited in C. Morrell, *Black Friday: Violence against Women in the Suffragette Movement*, Women's Research and Resource Centre, 1981, p. 35.

45 A. Hutt, *The Condition of Working Class in Britain*, London, Martin Lawrence, 1933, p. 244.

46 The Harmworth Colliery Strike: A Report to the Executive Committee of NCCL by the Secretary of the Council, 1937, Introduction.

47 Ibid. p. 7.

48 Ibid. p. 12.

49 Ibid. p. 13.

50 Ibid. p. 14.

51 Ibid. p. 13.

52 Ibid. p. 11.

53 R. Benewick, *Political Violence and Public Order*, London, Allen Lane, 1969, p. 205.

54 Cited in Ibid.

55 Ibid. p. 212.

56 Ibid. p. 213.

57 NCCL, Minutes of Evidence Taken before the Royal Commission on the Police, 24 January 1961, p. 745.

58 Ibid.

59 Ibid.

60 Ibid.

61 P. Scraton (n.d.) 'Industrial disputes, picketing and public order', in 'Decision Making In Britain' Open University Course p. 208; Block IV, Part 5, First Draft, p. 47.

62 Nancy E. Anderson and David Greenberg, 'The legal theories of Pashukanis and Edelman', *Social Text*, 7, 1983.

63 Doreen McBarnet, *Conviction-Law, The State and the Construction of Justice*, London, Macmillan, 1981.

64 E.P. Thompson, *Whigs and Hunters*, London, Allen Lane, 1975.

65 Bob Fine, *Democracy and the Rule of Law*, London, Pluto Press, 1984.

66 M. Brogden and A. Brogden, 'From Henry III to Liverpool 8 – The Unity of Police Street Powers', *International Journal of the Sociology of Law*, 12, 1984.

67 Robert Reiner, 'Is Britain turning into a police state?', *New Society*, 2 August 1984.

68 David McNee's evidence to The Royal Commission on Criminal Procedure and

David McNee, *McNee's Law*, London, Collins, 1983.

69 John Smith, an ex-Met officer quoted in *The Guardian*, 28 January 1984. Interview with Martin Young in *The Listener*, 5 July 1984.

70 Harry Templeton, 'Something is wrong, do we need medicine or the surgeon's knife?', *Police* vol. XVI, May 1984.

71 E.P. Thompson, 'Introduction' in *State Research, Review of Security and the State*, London, Julian Friedman, 1978, p. XI.

72 Ibid, p. XV.

73 Ibid.

74 Ibid.

75 *Daily Mirror*, 26 January 1984.

76 Ibid.

77 Hansard, 23 June 1983, col. 190.

78 Hansard, 10 February 1983, col. 601.

79 Cited in The Home Office Perspectives in Policy and Administration Bicentenary Lectures, 1982, RIPA, p. 21.

80 Report of the Commissioner of Police of the Metropolis for the Year 1933, Cmnd 4562, pp. 15–16.

81 Report of the Commissioner of Police of the Metropolis, 1935, Cmnd 5165, p. 5.

82 Ibid. p. 15.

83 *Police Journal*, Vol. L11, No. 1., January/March 1979.

84 M. Hough and K. Heal, 'Police strategies of crime control', in F. Feldman (ed.), *Developments in the Study of Criminal Behaviour Vol. 1: The Preventions and Control of Offending*, 1982, p. 46 (emphasis in original.)

85 Ibid.

86 R.V. Clarke and M. Hough, *Crime and Police Effectiveness*, Home Office Research Study, no. 79, 1984, p. 1.

87 Ibid.

88 Cited in P. Gilroy, 'The myth of black criminality', in M. Eve and D. Musson (eds), *The Socialist Register* 1982, London, Merlin Press, p. 56.

89 R. Mark, *In the Office of Constable*, London, Collins, 1978, p. 24.

90 *Policing London*, no. 11, p. 35.

91 Ibid. p. 44.

92 Ibid. p. 45.

93 Policy Studies Institute, *Police and People in London*, vol. 1, 1983, p. 146.

94 Ibid. vol. IV, p. 212.

95 Ibid, p. 111.

96 S. Holdaway, *Inside the British Police*, Oxford, Basil Blackwell, 1983, pp. 100–1.

97 Ibid, p. 146.

98 Cited in D. Lester, 'The use of deadly force by police', *Police Journal*, vol. LV 11, no. 2, April–June 1984, p. 170.

99 Figures supplied by Inquest cited in *Policing London*, no. 10, December 1983, p. 21.

100 Third Report From the Home Affairs Committee, 1980, H/C 631:Home Office Statistical Bulletin, 9/83.

101 Ian Taylor, 'Against crime and for socialism', *Crime and Social Justice*, Winter 1982.

102 Jock Young and Richard Kinsey, 'Life and crimes', *New Statesman*, 7 October 1983.

103 S.D. Reicher, 'The Bristol Riot: an explanation of the limits of crowd action in terms of a social identity model', *European Journal of Social Psychology*, 14, 1984.

104 See Lord Elton's introduction to 'Crime Prevention: a co-ordinated approach' Home Office, 1983. The Parliamentary All-Party Penal Affairs Group, 'The Prevention of Crime Among Young People', Barry Rose, 1984. HMI of Schools Report, 'Police Liaison with the Education Service', DES, 1983.

105 Kenneth Newman, 'Policing London post Scarman', Sir George Bean memorial lecture, 30 October 1983.

106 Ibid.

107 *The Guardian*, 17 October 1984.

108 Martin Boddy and Colin Fudge (eds), *Local Socialism*, London, Macmillan, 1984.

109 Michael Ignatieff, 'Law and order in a city of strangers', *New Statesman*, 27 May 1983.

3

The Myth of Black Criminality

Paul Gilroy

> The Police must win... but we must never be seen to win easily. If policemen all loaded down with special equipment went to a demonstration and arrested 1,000 people and no policemen were injured, why the critics would be coming out of the woodwork. It's like a good cricket match: we must thrash the other side, but our public likes us much better if we come from behind to do it.
>
> Deputy Assistant Commissioner George Rushbrook
> Metropolitan Police

The last decade has witnessed 'law and order' moving steadily to the centre of the political stage. As the national crisis has deepened, the extension of police power and the recruitment of law in political conflicts have become commonplace. The rule of law and maintenance of public order have appeared in forms which involve a racist appeal to the 'British Nation'[1] and have become integral to maintaining popular support for the government in crisis conditions. Indeed the recent history of 'law and order' is scarcely separable from the growth of popular racism and nationalism in the period following Enoch Powell's[2] famous intervention. Powell's wide-grinning piccaninnies have grown up, and with the onset of their adulthood, potent imagery of youthful black criminals stalking derelict inner-city streets where the law-abiding are afraid to walk after sunset[3] has been fundamental to the popularization of increasingly repressive criminal justice and welfare state policies.

Because of their capacity to symbolize other relations and conflicts, images of crime and law-breaking have had a special ideological importance since the dawn of capitalism.[4] If the potential for organized political struggle towards social transformation offered by criminality has often been low, images of particular crimes and criminal classes have frequently borne symbolic meanings and even signified powerful threats to the social order. This means that 'crime' can have political implications which extend beyond the political consciousness of criminals. The boundaries of what is considered criminal or illegal are elastic and the limits of the law have been repeatedly altered by intense class conflict. It is often forgotten that the political formation of the working-class movement in this country is saturated with illegality. The relation of politics to 'crime' is therefore complex. These points should be borne in mind if socialists are not to rush into the arms of the right in their bid to 'take crime seriously'.

Black Crime and the Crisis

In contemporary Britain, the disorder signified in popular imagery of crime and criminals, to which law and order is presented as the only antidote, has become expressive of national decline in several ways. At best, a lingering environmentalism makes a causal link between crime and unemployment or the deterioration of the inner cities. At worst, discussion of crime becomes subsumed by the idea that the rule of law, and therefore the Nation itself, is somehow under attack. Here alien criminals[5] take their place alongside subversive enemies within[6] and self-destructive defects in the national culture.[7] Race is, however, always dominant in the way this decline is represented. The left's failure to appreciate how the racism of slump and crisis is different from the racism[8] of boom and commonwealth, has meant that they have not grasped how notions of black criminality have been instrumental in washing the discourse of the nation as white as snow and preparing the way for repatriation. The imagery of alien violence and criminality personified in the 'mugger' and the 'illegal' immigrant has become an important card in the hands of politicians and police officers whose authority is undermined by the political fluctuations of the crisis. For them, as for many working-class Britons, the irresolvable difference between themselves and the undesired immigrants is clearly expressed in the latter's culture of criminality and inbred inability[9] to cope with that highest achievement of civilization – the rule of law.

The centrality of race has been consistently obscured by left writers on police and crime, often too keen to view 'racism' as a matter of individual attitudes adequately dealt with under the headings of prejudice and discrimination, and the struggle against it as an exclusively ideological matter far removed from the world of class politics.

In answer to this tendency, it is our contention that recognition of the contemporary importance of racial politics allows a number of important analytical and strategic issues to take shape. It is not only that a left movement which makes rhetorical commitment to viewing the law as an arena of struggle can profit from careful attention to the methods and organizational forms in which various black communities have won a series of legal victories whilst simultaneously organizing outside the courtroom, though the history of such cases, which span the 12 years between the Mangrove 9[10] and the Bradford 12, does merit careful inspection. It is rather that taking the experience of black communities seriously can transform 'left-wing' orthodoxy on the subject of the police and thereby determine a change in the orientation and composition of the struggle for democratic local control of police services. It is fruitless, for example, to search for programmatic solutions to 'discriminatory police behaviour' in amendments to the training procedure when professional wisdom inside the force emphasizes a racist, pathological view of black familial relations, breeding criminality and deviancy out of cultural disorganization and generational conflict.[11] If this racist theory is enshrined in the very structure of police work, it demands more desperate remedies than merely balancing the unacceptable content against increased 'human relations' training. However, left-wing writers have tended to ignore the well-documented[12] abuse of the black communities by the people which stretches back to the beginnings of post-war settlement in sufficient volume to have made a considerable impact on their critical view of the police. This history not only shows the manner in which police violate the letter and the spirit of the law in their day-to-day dealings with blacks. It is sufficient to prompt the questions about the kind of law which deprives 'illegal' immigrants of their rights of habeas corpus, restricts their rights of appeal, operates retroactively, and bids its special branches to round them up whilst sanctioning vaginal examinations and dangerous X-rays of other would-be settlers.[13]

Lack of attention to other important issues has similarly reduced the value of left analysis of police and crime. The continuing war in the six counties of Northern Ireland has had profound effects on the police service in the rest of the UK. These go beyond the simple but important idea that operational techniques, methods of surveillance and even structures of criminal justice refined in that experience are being progressively implemented in Britain.[14] The appointment of Sir Kenneth Newman to the Metropolitan Commissionership indicates the official premium placed on lessons learned there, but the fact that senior policemen routinely study General Frank Kitson's *Low Intensity Operations*[15] and Colonel Robin Evelegh's *Peace Keeping in a Democratic Society, the Lessons of Northern Ireland*,[16] more accurately conveys the transformation of policing theory which has followed the impact of counter-insurgency planning. It has been argued[17] that theories of 'community policing' most clearly represent the fruits of this relationship, and though we cannot go into this in detail here, several basic points can be made. Counter-insurgency theory not only stresses the need to combat domestic subversion,[18] but also the annexation and synchronization of social and welfare-state institutions under police control. Though all of Kitson's methods are not readily transferable to the current situation on mainland Britain it is clear that his definition of subversion includes activities which are neither illegal nor alien to the political traditions of the working-class movement in this country. 'It [subversion] can involve the use of political and economic pressure, strikes, protest marches, and propaganda.'[19] General Kitson has recently been appointed Chief of Land Forces in the UK. It is also worth pointing out that it is the liberal ex-police chief John Alderson who has been credited with pioneering the study of counter-insurgency theory on the senior command course at Bramshill Police College.[20] Kitson's emphasis on the psychological dimension to law enforcement and peace-keeping operations 'psyops' is echoed in Alderson's stress on the imagery and language of police politics:

> We need a climate to be created in which we [the police] are seen not as potential enemies, but as potential friends and, dare I use the word, brothers. You have to start talking like that. You have to use expressions like that. The rhetoric of leaders and administrators is critical.[21]

If policing by consent is the fundamental principle of the British approach, crisis conditions dictate that policemen have ceased to merely pay lip-service to this idea, they now recognize that consent must be won, maintained and reproduced by careful interventions in popular politics.

It has been suggested that the use of computers in Northern Ireland has made a considerable impact on the British police in its own right. Here too there are lessons which have been learned from maintaining law and order in the six counties.[22]

Popular Politics of Law and Order

Various fractions of the left movement, increasingly marginal to popular concerns, have recently glimpsed in the intensity of feeling around questions of law and order a means to gain proximity to the working class. These theorists[23] take note of the fears of crime and violence which have been amplified by the entry of police chiefs into media politics. But rather than view these fears as themselves produced by a novel situation in which the police have begun to derive their ideological authority from a direct relationship to the police, and their political legitimacy from an increasingly acceptable voice in matters of social policy, this fear is taken as an unproblematic reflection of the reality of crime in working-class communities. There is not the slightest acknowledgement that police are in a good position to mould and even create public fear in such a way as to justify an increase in their powers. This is a serious lapse in view of the fact that they state intellectuals have begun to abandon the idea that detecting and preventing crime can be the principal object of police work, arguing instead, that[24] 'the fear of crime ... is perhaps only marginally related to the objective risk of becoming a victim' and that 'people who feel well policed are well policed'.[25]

One consequence of this is that the public, particularly the black public must be re-educated[26] in more realistic expectations of the police and their capabilities. We shall explore the way in which this shift has transformed the politics of policing below, but it must be immediately related to an understanding of the manner in which chief constables have become media personalities and also to the personalization of their office which has followed Sir Robert Mark's reign at Scotland Yard. It is remarkable that the left has accepted the over-polarization of debate around the contrasting police personalities of James Anderton and John Alderson.[27] Alderson has himself warned that this simplistic view 'obscures more than it reveals'. There is also evidence to suggest that the police in Devon and Cornwall are as capable of the excesses of 'fire-brigade'[28] policing as their brother officers in Manchester. This makes nonsense of the view of community policing as a miraculous cure-all for urban ailments and the symptoms of economic crisis. Alderson's much publicized solutions to the problems of a society 'in which the only permanence is change' appear attractive when contrasted to the crudities of operation 'Swamp 81', but the reality of community policing is rather more complex in theory let alone in practice, than the optimism and enthusiasm of some left commentators would suggest. It is not always appreciated, for example, that 'community policing' is not planned to be an alternative to other 'more dramatic'[29] modes of police work, but rather a 'complementary strategy' designed to 'bring the reactive and preventive roles of the police service into a balance appropriate to long-term aims and objectives'.[30]

A senior officer from the West Midlands, where Alderson's ideas have been put to the acid test of the inner city, dispels the idea that community policing alters the fundamental orientation of aims of the police officers who practise it: 'We are not always the nice guys ... these are good sound operational PCs in uniform doing an operational PC's job, but they are doing it more effectively ... We're not trying to create a force of social workers or make claims we are getting involved in welfare. It's very much policing.'[31]

In his evidence to the Scarman inquiry, Brixton's home-beat policeman, John Brown,[32] provided further insights into the relationship between the 'criminal intelligence' gained in the practice of 'penetrating the community in all its aspects' and the more reactive and aggressive styles of policing. Brown explains that he not only guided the Special Patrol Group round his own beat during their tour of duty in Brixton, but also that in the past he aided officers from a neighbouring district in collecting the names of demonstrators engaged in an entirely lawful and non-violent trade union dispute. When asked if this could be described as intelligence gathering, Brown replied, 'No it is not that'.

Illusions about the nature of policing theory revealed in a naive view of community policing are compounded by an innocent faith in the evenhandedness of police practice on the ground. Ian Taylor, for example, criticizes the left as conspiratorial in their approach to policing issues and 'proves' this by suggesting that the police have been systematically curtailing the military activities of the fascist right, and calling for bans of their marches. That the gun-running activities of the right can be exposed on prime-time television without the police prosecuting the individuals responsible makes nonsense of Taylor's first claim.[33] The nature of blanket bans which restrict all protest, and which cannot therefore be regarded as victories, invalidates his second. On this last point, it is remarkable how little critical comment has greeted Lord Scarman's recommendation that the Public Order Act 1936 be amended so that the police must be notified in advance of any procession or demonstration.[34]

The left's failings in relation to law, police and crime go far beyond poor analysis of the immediate situation or misunderstanding of the Scarman Report. However, discussion of the conflicts of summer 1981 and the political responses to them can illustrate more general failings with great clarity.

In a series of influential articles, John Lea and Jock Young[35] have argued that the source of the summer riots lay, not in matters of police harassment and abuse, but in the political marginalization of inner-city communities. Their analysis is disabled by a startling ignorance of police-community relations. Worse than this, the view of the black communities which they advance shares a great deal with the most conservative explanations of the conflict. They view West Indian life as characterized by pathological family relations and a high degree of generational conflict, but these are not presented as the sole source of black criminality. Discrimination, disadvantage and economic alienation clash with inappropriate aspirations derived from the internalization of 'British values' (sic) and this also generates the 'propensity' to crime. Thus the relation between race and crime is secured, not directly, as in the biological culturalism of Conservative explanations, but at one remove which is equally dangerous, particularly as it prompts speculation as to why it is only the black poor who resolve their frustration in acts of criminality. To present 'black crime' as a primary *cultural problem* whether forged in the economic 'no man's land' between deprivation and restricted opportunity, or secured in a spurious social biology, is a capitulation to the weight of racist logic. This suggests a total discontinuity between the cultures of black and white youth which is inappropriate given the multiracial character of the riots, and becomes openly visible when Lea and Young trace the roots of urban British street crime to a 'minority and deviant sub-culture within the West Indies'.

The emphasis on black culture legitimates the idea that any black, all blacks, are somehow contaminated by the alien predisposition to crime which is reproduced in their distinctive cultures, specifically their family relations. Police theorists have already made the link between supposedly 'Victorian' conceptions of discipline in the West Indian home and the growth of Rastafarian inspired criminality:

> This unfortunate break-up of family association has seen the formation of substantial groups of young blacks leaving home and banding together in numerous squats and communes, unemployed and completely disillusioned with society. Most of them have donned the Mantle of Rastafarianism, or more precisely the criminal sub-cult of the dreadlock fraternity.[36]

Young and Lea do little more than reproduce this pathology in polite social. democratic rhetoric.

Their political solution to police–community conflict is built on the possibility of instituting what they described as 'consensual policing'. This, they explain, is a situation in which 'the policeman is in and with the community'. They refer to the breakdown of this relationship, implying therefore that it existed in the past, yet are unable to cite a single concrete historical instance of where or when this model of social harmony has actually existed. Their related view of the police officer as a friendly or avuncular figure, acceptable to the urban working class bears scant relation to the numerous instances of conflict between working-class communities and the police which appear to have extended well into this century. Their view is also unable to accommodate the practice of forms of social crime in urban working-class communities, particularly by young people,[37] let alone patterns of intra-class struggle which have often involved forms of property crime.[38]

Young and Lea present the militarization of inner-city policing as a straightforward, if undesirable, response to rising levels of 'street crime' in inner areas. There is no acknowledgement of the possibility that broader imperatives of social control and public order have been transformed by crises of political representation and in the economy. The neat scenario which presents rising street crime as the cause and police militarization as the effect, places the blame for this state of affairs squarely on the shoulders of a minority of deviant blacks. It is posited at the expense of engaging with the history of police–community relations, particularly in so far as this relates to the black communities. Supt Lawrence Roach,[39] sometime head of the Met's Community Relations Branch, has revealed how the development of specialist community relations policing has arisen out of the exigencies of policing the blacks; police theorists' views on the functions of communities in police strategy[40] also suggest that techniques devised in policing black areas can provide a new paradigm for policing cities in crisis conditions.

Significantly, prior to their defeat by black youth at the Notting Hill Carnival in 1976, Metropolitan Police evidence to the Commons Select Committee described a situation in London where, during the preceding 12 months, forty incidents 'carrying the potential for large scale disorder' had developed out of police attempts to arrest black youths. The pattern of this conflict dates back to the early 1970s, landmarked by notable cases of police–community conflict in Notting Hill (1970), Brockwell Park (1973),

Stockwell, Cricklewood, Dalston, Hornsey and Brixton (1975). However, London was not unique in the scale of street-level conflict between the police and the black communities. In Birmingham, the massive stop-and-search operation which sealed off the Handsworth area following the murder of a policeman in July 1975 involved the arrest of 600 blacks though only one was charged. (The officer had been stabbed after setting his dog on a young woman outside the Rainbow Room Club.) In Leeds, the bonfire-night confrontations in Chapeltown occurred annually from 1973 to 1975. The summer of 1976 saw well-documented conflict in Manchester, Birmingham and at least four different parts of London.[41]

The combined weight of these 'isolated incidents' is sufficient to transform the picture presented by Young and Lea, restoring in the process a determinancy to the dynamics of police–community conflict which is obscured by their idea of black 'counter-culture' or 'unintegrated ethnic culture'. The systematic application of militaristic and reactive policing to black areas the length and breadth of Britain undermines any view of consensual policing – black streets have never enjoyed the benefits of this police policy. Furthermore, the nature of these police operations is not adequately grasped by reference to 'discrimination' or the 'prejudice' of individual officers. They are systematic and, in police terms, rational, as a complex body of specialized policing theory informs them and legitimates the view of blacks as disproportionately prone to criminality.

Black political organization against police abuses has frequently exhibited a unity between people of Asian and Afro-Caribbean descent,[42] yet most left-wing writers on the subject seem curiously keen to introduce a pernicious contradiction between the interests of the two communities with regard to law and order. Several authors have identified an implicit Asian demand for more rather than less police activity,[43] albeit of a rather different type from that which they have come to expect from the British police. This suggestion, which derives its plausibility from the twin racist stereotypes of the quiescent Asian victim and the criminally inclined West Indian street youth, has been achieved at the expense of historical record. Young and Lea, Taylor and Frith all cite the rioting outside the Hamborough Tavern in Southall, 1981 as an example, and each views this incident as violence of a different order from that experienced elsewhere. Their suggestion that the militant Asian youth did not know what they were doing when they attacked police and skinheads alike is derisory. It is impossible to grasp the meaning of the 1981 riots in Southall without careful attention to previous confrontations there. In 1976, after the death of Gurdip Singh Chaggar, and again in 1979 during the police riot there, Asian youth acquired their own grievances against the local police whose abuse of the black community had been catalogued as early as 1973 by Dr Stanislaus Pullé. It is therefore more plausible to suggest that their assault on the police was not an inarticulate demand for more bobbies on the beat, but a sign of their deep anger, created by years of harassment, and a powerful statement to the effect that like their sisters and brothers in the Afro-Caribbean communities, militant Asians viewed community self-defence as the legitimate answer to racist violence. It is worth recalling that the initial response by officers at a police disco in Hammersmith to the news that rioting had started was to sing 'there ain't no black in the Union Jack'.[44] They were silenced by their senior officers.

The central argument here is that the question of black crime must be approached in a historical fashion, and in a context supplied by the overall pattern of police–community conflict in conditions of deepening crisis. In conclusion, there are several general points about the priorities and structure of police practice which need to be brought into the discussion. There is strong evidence to suggest that emphasis on particular crimes can engineer what appear to be crime waves of these offences, not only because of heightened police sensitivity to these crimes, but also as a result of changes in police practice.[45] It is certainly plausible that 'mugging' has constituted a self-fulfilling prophecy of this type. Blom-Cooper and Drabble[46] have recently shown that the Met's manipulation of the compound categories in which their statistics are recorded can be used to support this view. Young and Lea are not alone on the left in their tendency to take critical crime statistics at their face value.

E.P. Thompson[47] and Ian Taylor, among others, have also been disinclined to question these figures. It is important that the left clarify its views of officially recorded crime rates, particularly as a growing number of police thinkers and right-wing ideologists proceed unimpeded by the idea that they are an accurate reflection of crime actually experienced.

The Police Federation magazine, hardly noted for its radical politics, recently argued: 'no informal person regards the existing criminal statistics as the most reliable indicator of the state of crime'.[48] More significantly, Inspector Peter Finnimore's essay 'How should police effectiveness be assessed', winner of the 1980 Queen's Police Gold Medal Essay Competition, attacked statistics not only as a guide to the level of crime, but also as a measure of police activity: 'It is difficult for experienced police officers to concede that skilful police work has relatively little effect on overall crime levels, but it must be realised that no criticism is implied by such a view.'[49]

In addition to this, the fact that official surveys of the victims of crime have consistently returned findings[50] which are completely at odds with the idea that crime itself rises when 'crime rates are soaring', should draw comment from the left. None of these authors appear to be aware of this. Finnimore is correct to insist that the issue of objective knowledge of crime leads directly to whether it is within the capacity of police to prevent or deter. Most recent left thinkers subscribe to what Home Office researchers have called the 'rational deterrent' model.[51] Young, Lea and Taylor, though they are correct to emphasize that the flow of information from communities is the main source of police knowledge, balance this by the idea that in exchange for the information the police will prevent crime. They are particularly concerned with the everyday forms in which it is experienced by working-class communities. This view of police capability is debatable to say the least, for two distinct, but related reasons. Scrutiny of the history of policing in Britain,[52] particularly its cities, suggests that everyday crimes in which the working class are the victims have never been of major concern to police; and secondly, the proliferation of private scrutiny firms described by Hilary Draper[53] suggests that the police may not even have been very successful in protecting the property of the bourgeoisie. Recognizing these limitations to their capacity, police chiefs and senior Home Office researchers have begun to raise the question of whether police are capable of deterring or preventing criminal activity. Assessing recent British research into the effectiveness of policing, R.V.G. Clarke and K.H. Heal from the Home Officer Research Unit conclude: 'The crime prevention value of a police force rests less on precisely what it does than on the symbolic effect of its presence and public belief in its effectiveness.[54] Sir Robert Mark, who uses these arguments to justify a greater police concern with public order and anti-terrorist crime, puts the same point with characteristic bluntness: 'A great deal of crime is simply not preventable. Even the biggest police force that society could want or afford to pay would be unlikely to have any significant effect on the numbers of thefts, burglaries, or on crimes of violence between people who know each other.[55]

This points to the need for more imaginative and bold initiatives from the left on the issue of law and order. Contemporary 'socialist' thinking on crime and police is dominated by pathological and environmentalist explanations wedded to a practice of progressively greater demands on a criminal justice system in which formal, legal equality sits uneasily on real inequality and relations of power and domination. In crisis conditions, police have increasingly separated the crime detection/prevention side to police activity from its political and ideological requirements.

Afterword

This essay was completed at the end of 1982. It could not be merely updated without wholesale revision and I believe that it has value in its original form which betrays the conflicts and anxieties of the period. Since its completion the danger to which it points in many respects has been realized. Left and right increasingly have come to share a common view not merely of the problem of inner-city crime, but more disturbingly of the issue of race itself in which crime plays a central role. Black law-breaking supplies the historic proof that blacks are incompatible with the standards of decency and civilization which the nation requires of its citizenry.

If the term 'new racism' retains any value as a shorthand it points to the intersection of left and right around common definitions of the meaning of 'race' in terms of culture and identity. This emphasis and the convergence it allows is significant for the degree to which it transcends the otherwise opposed positions of formal politics. Crime in which blacks are involved for left and right alike is intrinsically un-British and alien. More than this, certain categories of crime are now identified not merely as those which blacks are most likely to commit, but as crimes which are somehow expressive of the ethnicity of those who carry them out. For example, in their book *What is to Be Done about Law and Order?*, published under the imprint of the Socialist Society, Lea and Young, writers against whom the original polemic of this article was aimed, have referred to the origins of street crime in the 'residual ethnic factor' in black urban life.[56] Similarly, the riots of autumn 1985 were dismissed by the right as 'a cry for loot rather than a cry for help' and by the parliamentary left as 'barbarous acts of criminality' which betrayed, in Lea and Young's phrase, 'the absence of any *viable* tradition of ethnic politics' (my emphasis). It is not that blacks lack the means to organize themselves politically but that they do so in ways in which are so incongruent with Britishness that they are incapable of sustaining life! Their distance from the required standards of political viability is established by their criminal character. Thus black crime and politics are interlinked. They become aspects of the same fundamental problem – a dissident black population. Street robberies and street protests are elided into a single phenomenon: 'street crime'. This is defined both by its context and by the cultural ties which invest that context with meaning.

The riots of 1985 were 'race riots' not because they were carried out largely, though by no means exclusively, by blacks but because in the folk grammar of contemporary racism, the type of events they were told white Britain something about the nature of 'race' and its problematic relation to authentic substantive Britishness.

The left position on 'race' and crime criticized in the article is, far more than I realized at the time of writing, a symptom of a wider political crisis. These socialist academics think that they are writing the social policies of the next Labour government. The notion of class on which their Labourist dream depends is being experienced by the majority of the population as a contingent and meaningless fact. Class relations are changing profoundly and new antagonisms are being created in urban areas between a pauper-ized, permanently workless layer and the young urban cadres of the professional and managerial class who are colonizing the inner city as gentrifiers. The fear of crime speaks above all to the anxieties of this latter group. It offers a spurious means to connect their experience of vulnera-bility and victimage to the lifeworld of other-city residents with whom they have absolutely nothing in common.

The Labourist politics of law and order is defined by its populist character. The populist potential of the crime issue, as a cynical means to repair Labour's failing relationship with its traditional supporters in the urban areas, has grown and been made concrete in the work of local authorities who, like Roy Hattersley in the run up to the 1983 election, effectively accuse police chiefs like Kenneth Newman of having stolen Labour's policies on crime. Putting 'bobbies back on the beat' has become a shibboleth of this new Labourism. Only the right has had the intellectual honesty to query the facile equation of more police with less crime. Islington in north London has sought to rehabilitate its own image in the popular press as a bastion of the 'loony left' through carefully constructed interventions into law and order politics. These have included a joint drive by the borough and the police to increase black recruitment.

One last issue arises from the article which needs to be identified and dealt with. It concerns the mythical status of black criminality. By calling the article 'The Myth of Black Criminality' I did not intend to suggest that blacks did not or could not commit crimes or to invoke a pastoral definition of the black communities or the inner cities as places where crime did not occur. I sought instead to refer the reader to the images and representations of black criminality which seemed to me to have achieved a mythic status in the lexicon of contemporary race politics.

Asserting the disproportionate involvement of blacks in some categories of crime masks rather than disposes of significant problems in measuring their participation. The validity of official statistics and survey methods in the analysis are not the least of these difficulties. Britain's black population is a poor one and it would be remarkable if their law-breaking was not related in some way to their poverty. Banal formulae which emphasize an untheorized concept of 'marginality' in place of the more familiar notion of deviance simply deprive blacks of the opportunity to be seen as other than reactive monads incapable of considered behaviour in the active mode. Their reduction of politics to mere policy does nothing more than offer Labour's municipal bureaucracies the lazy comfort of simple solutions to their intractable problems. The possibility of a direct relationship between ethnicity, black culture and crime is an altogether different and more complex issue which requires detailed historical investigation and which is likely to end, as previous attempts to quantify crime itself, only in raising further yet more speculative questions.

Acknowledgement
This is an updated version of a paper which was published in *Socialist Register*, 1982.

Notes

1 S. Hall *et al. Policing the Crisis*, London, Macmillan, 1978.
2 Enoch Powell's speech Wolverhampton, April 1968, reprinted in, 'Freedom and reality', London, Paperfront, 1969.
3 *The Sun*, 13 September 1978, is typical of the imagery referred to, there are many other examples.

4 See *Crime and the Law, The Social History of Crime in Western Europe*, V.A.C., Gatrell, B. Lenman and G. Parker (eds), Europa, 1980; especially chapters by Larner, Weisser and Davis.

5 P. Worthsthorne, *Sunday Telegraph*, 29 November 1981.

6 James Anderton, *Manchester Evening News*, 16 March 1982.

7 Alfred Sherman, 'Britain's urge to self-destruction', *Daily Telegraph*, 9 September 1976.

8 Martin Barker's excellent *The New Racism*, London, Junction Books, 1981, is an exception to the left's failures. See also Errol Lawrence, 'The roots of racism' in *The Empire Strikes Back*, London CCCS/Hutchinson, 1982.

9 Sir Kenneth Newman's views on the biological base of West Indian anti-authortarianism can be found in the American *Police* magazine for January 1982 (Vol. 5, No. 1). See also speech by Basil Griffiths, vice-chairman of the Police Federation, reported in *Police Review*, 28 May 1982.

10 See A. Sivanandan *A Different Hunger*, London, Pluto, 1982 (especially his account of Asian and Afro-Caribbean struggles in the chapter *From Resistance to Rebellion*). Also see copies of *Race Today* for the period.

11 Paul Gilroy, 'Police and Thieves' in *The Empire Strikes Back, op. cit.*

12 Derek Humphry, *Police Power and Black People*, London, Pan; 1972, Gus John, *Race and the Inner City*, Runnymede Trust, 1972; Dr S. Pulle, *Police/Community Relations in Ealing*, Runnymede/Ealing CRC, 1973; Joseph Hunte, 'Nigger Hunting in England', West Indian Standing Conference, 1964; Institute of Race Relations, *Police against Black People*, 1978.

13 Paul Gordon, *Passport Raids and Checks*, Runnymede Trust 1981.

14 Paddy Hillyard, 'From Belfast to Britain: Some critical comments on the Royal Commission on Criminal Procedure', *Politics and Power*, 4, 1981; K. Boyle *et al.*, *The Legal Control of Political Violence*, NCCL, 1980.

15 Gilroy, *op. cit.*

16 London, Faber, 1971.

17 C. Hurt, 1978.

18 Kitson, *op. cit.*

19 Kitson, *op. cit.*

20 *Time Out*, 5 September 1976, p. 3; *Searchlight*, November 1976.

21 *Police Review*, 19 March 1982.

22 Duncan Campbell, 'Society under surveillance', in P. Hain (ed.) *Policing the Police*, Vol. 2, London, John Calder, 1980.

23 The tendency referred to is exemplified by the recent works of Jock Young, John Lea and Ian Taylor. Taylor's *Law and Order Arguments for Socialism* is the fullest exposition of this position, Macmillan, 1981. His article in *New Socialist*, 2, November–December 1981 also merits attention. Young and Lea also published in *New Socialist* January–February 1982. See also *Critical Social Policy*, vol. 1, no. 3, and *Marxism Today*, August 1982.

24 R.V.G. Clarke and K.H. Heal, *Police Journal* vol. LII, no. 1, January–March 1979.

25 John Alderson, Chief Constable's Report, 1980.

26 Sir David McNee, Commissioner's Report, 1981.

27 One instance of this is the way in which Alderson was interviewed in *Marxism Today*, April 1982; also M. Kettle, *Marxism Today*, October 1980.

28 The case of David Brooke is particularly interesting, see *The Guardian*, 12 May 1981.

29 See Alderson's evidence to the Scarman Inquiry, 'The case for community policing', p. xii.
30 Supt. David Webb, 'Policing a multi-racial community', unpublished paper, West Midlands Police, 1978.
31 Supt. A. Lievesley, *Police Review*, 7 March 1980.
32 Scarman Inquiry, Day 6, 22 May 1981.
33 'Guns for the Right', *World in Action*, Granada, July 1981; See also *Searchlight*, August 1981.
34 Scarman Report, para. 8.63.
35 See note 23.
36 Webb, *op. cit.*
37 Stephen Humphries, *Hooligans or Rebels, an Oral History of Working Class Childhood*, Oxford, Basil Blackwell, 1981.
38 Jerry White, 'Campbell Bunk, a lumpen community in London between the wars', *History Workshop*, 8, Autumn 1979.
39 Supt. L. Roach, *Police Studies*, vol. 1, no. 3, 1978.
40 John Brown, 'The function of communities in police strategy, *Police Studies*, Spring 1981 and *Police Review*, 31 July 1981.
41 *Race Today* is the best single source of information on these confrontations; for Southall see Campaign Against Racism and Fascism (CARF), *Southall the Birth of a Black Community*, IRR, 1981.
42 The examples of BASH (Blacks Against State Harassment) and Southall's People Unite are the most obvious; Sivanandan cites numerous others in his article *'Resistance to Rebellion'* in *A Different Hunger* op. cit.
43 All those in note 23, plus Simon Frith in *Marxism Today*, November 1981.
44 *Searchlight*, October 1981.
45 E. Schaffer, *Community Policing*, London, Croom Helm, 1980, p. 17.
46 *British Journal of Criminology*, vol. 22, no. 2, April 1982.
47 'The state of the nation', reprinted in *Writing by Candlelight*, London, Merlin, 1979.
48 *Police*, February 1982.
49 *Police Journal*, January–March, 1982, vol. LV, no. 1, March 1982.
50 See Home Office Statistical Bulletin 12 March 1982. R.E. Sparks, M.R. Glenn and D.J. Dodd, *Surveying Victims*, N.Y. Wiley, 1978.
51 Clarke and Heal (eds.), *The Effectiveness of Policing*, Aldershot, Hants, Gower, 1980.
52 For example, David Jones, *Crime, Protest, Community and Police in Nineteenth Century Britain*, London, Routledge & Kegan Paul, 1982.
53. *Private Police*, Brighton, Sussex, Harvester Press, 1978.
54 See note 24.
55 *Police Review*, 12 March 1982.
56 For a more detailed consideration of these issues see my *'There Ain't No Black in The Union Jack': The Cultural Politics of Race and Nation*, London, Hutchinson, 1987.

4

Community Policing: Towards the Local Police State?

Paul Gordon

Few people would deny that the shape of British policing has changed dramatically, if not fundamentally, over the past decade. The structural changes begun in the late 1960s and early 1970s, in particular the development of reactive 'fire-brigade' policing, the emergence of a quasi-military 'third force' concealed inside the ordinary police, the expansion of surveillance, in terms both of technology and the number of subjects, have been consolidated.[1] This consolidation, which grew apace in the aftermath of the urban rebellions of 1980, 1981 and 1985, was all too clear in the policing of the miners strike of 1984 and 1985. At the same time, formal police powers have been considerably enlarged, most notably by the police and Criminal Evidence Act 1984 which came into effect in 1986, and by the Public Order Act 1987. But the concern which has rightly focused on these developments has, in general, ignored what may turn out to be an equally important development, that of 'community policing', now supported by a range of social and political opinion.

Defining 'community policing' is not at all simple. At times, it seems that there are as many definitions as there are people talking about it, or chief constables saying that they are doing it. What it comprehends in practice is virtually everything from putting officers back on foot patrols through programmes of 'community relations', juvenile liaison, community involvement, through the all-embracing theory of John Alderson, until 1982 the chief constable of Devon and Cornwall, to the 'multi-agency' or 'corporate' approach to policing developed by Sir Kenneth Newman after he became Metropolitan Police Commissioner in October 1982. What all these approaches and practices have in common is that they involve attempts by the police to deal with people whose support appears to the police to be weak or non-existent, and which therefore requires to be bolstered or harnessed or even created. In attempting to define community policing it is therefore necessary to examine each of its component parts. Before doing so, however, it is necessary to examine briefly the notion of the consensual basis of British policing, a basis to which much community policing claims to be returning.

The Myth of Consent

It is the accepted wisdom that the consent of the public lies at the heart of the British policing tradition and much of the writing on community policing harks back to a golden age of policing when the police could count on the active support and consent of the British public. It is doubtful whether such a golden age ever existed, as a growing body of historical work shows.

Robert Storch, for example, writing of the 'plague of the blue locusts' – the advent of the new, professional police in the mid nineteenth century – has shown that the imposition of the modern police was widely opposed, often violently, as the police came as 'unwelcome spectators into the very nexus of urban neighbourhood life'.[2] Such resistance continued into the twentieth century and although its form may have changed from the anti-police riots of previous years, its content differed little. Most recently the lack of consent for the police and resistance to policing has been most evident in Britain's black communities. At the start of the 1970s, for example, one writer described police – black relationships in Handsworth, Birmingham as 'one of warfare – and anything but cold'[3] and the 1980, 1981 and 1985 urban rebellions were but the most heightened and most recent of a long series of open clashes between police and black people.

In effect the police and governments had recognized this for some time, however reluctantly they might acknowledge it in public. Community relations work with the black community, which has existed as a separate and distinct concept of police work only since the late 1950s and early 1960s, was nothing other than an attempt to deal with this lack of consent and support. Until this time, a police historian of the subject has said, 'every policeman was a community relations officer, seeking ... to retain and reinforce the goodwill, of the public towards their police force'.[4] What brought about this development was not just post-war changes in attitudes towards authority (now seen as 'something to be questioned rather than respected'), nor increased social mobility within society, but increased mobility 'between cultures'. It was this, the same historian argues, which 'had broken down the homogeneity of the community to the extent that policemen were no longer able to clearly identify with the people they sought to serve'.

In 1958, therefore, the Metropolitan Police appointed a chief superintendent with responsibility for the co-ordination and development of police activity in the field of race, and ten years later a Community Relations Branch was created to co-ordinate the work of the divisional community liaison officers. Outside London a similar picture emerged at the same time. In 1967, a Home Office circular, *'Police and coloured communities'*, was sent to all chief constables and appears to have been influential in the creation of community relations work in a number of forces. Further impetus was provided by the 1970 Home Office working party report on police training in race relations and the Parliamentary Select Committee inquiry into police – immigrant relations in 1970–71, both of which recommended more community relations work. In 1976, 29 out of 43 police forces in England and Wales said they undertook functions in community relations, and 17 had separate community relations departments.[5]

This development of police – community relations work took place at the same time as the state, which had institutionalized racism in its immigration controls, increasingly intervened in race relations, through anti-discrimination laws and community relations organizations. Like those measures, police – community relations was one of the means by which an attempt was made to manage the black population and to mediate its opposition and distrust. But in looking for the reason for this distrust, the police located it in their cultural backgrounds and social structures, rather than in the fact that immigrants from the Caribbean and the Indian subcontinent had first encountered the British police as an occupying force and, quite literally as the article quoted above puts it, 'the enforcement arm of the white establishment'. It was the same colonial policing policy which was adopted in the areas of black settlement *in* Britain. In addition, the development of a specialist concept of community relations work absolved the police in general of any notion that they were accountable to the black community. Instead, that became the work of the specialist officers. Not surprisingly, community relations hardly touched the surface of ordinary, everyday racist policing.

As the history of police–black relations in Britain shows,[6] police–community relations work did nothing to show Britain's black citizens that they had no reason to distrust the police. Rather, it coexisted with practices which have affirmed that distrust and, at the same time, has placed the black community as a group apart from the rest of society, a group requiring its own special liaison measures.

Youth Work

Just as black people were perceived by the state to pose problems and so require special liaison measures, so increasingly in the 1950s and 1960s did young people. Indeed, as Stuart Hall has pointed out, the racist riots of Notting Hill in 1958 which became a focal point for the two issues, have two histories, not one. One was that of the development and emergence of popular racism, the other that of panics about post-war changes generally, 'for which the term "youth" had by then become a vivid social metaphor'.[7]

Police work with juveniles, of course, pre-dates the post-war emergence of 'youth' as a problem: formal cautioning of juveniles had been part of policing since the early twentieth century. But the first attempt to set up a specialist liaison scheme was only made in Liverpool in 1949. The chief constable explained that the main purpose of the scheme was pre-emption and that the police were 'ideally situated to learn of potential delinquents at an early stage and take immediate action to prevent them developing criminal tendencies'.[8] In 1952 a Juvenile Liaison Department was created and other forces were encouraged to follow suit when the Home Office circulated details to all forces in the mid-1950s.

Similar developments had been taking place in Scotland, although they were part of a broader policing strategy which had yet to develop elsewhere. The first juvenile liaison officers were appointed in Greenock on Clydeside in 1956 by David Gray, who was later to become Inspector of Constabulary for Scotland. The appointments involved close liaison with local authority departments and the development of extensive police involvement in youth work generally, including youth clubs and in schools. In this liaison can be seen the early, and very tentative beginnings of modern community policing.

Juvenile liaison was given its greatest impetus by the major changes in the juvenile justice system in the 1960s which marked a shift away from a formal legalistic model towards one increasingly concerned with a welfare approach. In Scotland, the lay children's hearing inevitably involved much closer liaison between the police and social sevice departments to exchange information about juvenile behaviour. In England and Wales, although the mandatory consultation between the police and local authority social services envisaged by the Children and Young Persons Act 1969 never materialized, the Act did provide a framework for a preventive, welfare-oriented approach. The police, while generally opposed to the Act, sought nevertheless to take advantage of it and in 1968, just before it was passed, the Metropolitan Police set up its Juvenile Bureau to collect information about juvenile offenders from various agencies such as schools and social work departments, for carrying out visits to homes, and attending at court to advise magistrates on the disposal of cases. By the time of a 1977 Ditchley conference on preventive policing, some 31 forces in England and Wales had activities specifically directed towards juveniles. In 1978, another Ditchley conference was held specifically on the subject of juveniles and the police, and was attended by chief constables and representatives of the probation service, social services and education service. As a result of the conference, a circular was issued jointly by the Home Office, the Department of Health and Social Security, the Department of Education and Science and the Welsh Office, emphasizing the need for co-operation between agencies and inviting chief constables to take the lead in convening local meetings of the relevant services to discuss liaison and the scope for joint activities.[9]

The momentum of the conference was maintained, the Inspector of Constabulary reported, and 'further efforts were made to break down the barriers . . . between members of the different professions'. Thus in Devon and Cornwall the police had secured one-week attachments of officers to local probation and social services departments, and there was a joint police and social services Juvenile Bureau in Exeter. In North Yorkshire, the police had arranged exchanges with probation officers, and in South Wales a Juveniles Affairs Committee had been set up comprising police, education and social services representatives to promote co-operation between the various agencies.[10]

Police work with juveniles therefore led directly to increased police involvement with other agencies, particularly social services and education departments. Although at this stage such inter-agency co-operation was largely confined to matters affecting juveniles it laid the ground for an expansion of police involvement with other agencies on a range of other subjects and the development of an overall strategy of community policing. Thus, juvenile liaison led to police having direct access to schools. The importance of this has been stressed by many police officers. A Scottish Office report noted that many police forces regarded schools work as 'the corner-stone of the community involvement branch's interests and concerns because the education system provides a ready-made structure in which the police contribution can be accommodated and through which they have comprehensive access to young people'.[11] Similarly, John Alderson, probably the most sophisticated exponent of community policing, has described schools work as no less than the 'sine qua non of all good pro-active systems'.[12]

Although developments in this field have been patchy, many forces have put considerable resources into schools work and this aspect of policing has developed rapidly since the mid-1970s. Although the first schools liaison officers were only appointed in 1966 by Sussex Police with full-time costs being created three years later, by 1975, according to HM Inspector of Constabulary, several other forces had made similar appointments, including South Yorkshire, Leicester and Nottingham which had all seconded officers to work exclusively in schools, while others, such as Cleveland, used the local beat officer for schools work. In Devon and Cornwall a schools scheme was run jointly by the police and the local education authority and in North Wales officers were based at local education offices. In Hampshire in 1980 a police officer was appointed as a full-time counsellor at a 'large and troublesome comprehensive school', an appointment made on the initiative of the local education authority. In 1981, four police officers joined the staff of a comprehensive school in Peterlee, County Durham. The school timetable was even rearranged so that lessons could be given by the police on their role in the community and the social costs of crime and vandalism.[13] In January 1982, the scheme was expanded to take in a further three schools and the police team was said to be concentrating on pupils aged between 11 and 13, since older pupils, they said, were already too hardened in their views. Children were being asked to pass on any information they had about vandalism and theft.[14] Devon and Cornwall Police have gone even further. There, 24 full-time officers cover the 1,000 schools in the area, and the police have jointly funded with the education authority, a full-time 'moral education adviser'.[15]

Such involvement of police in schools has not gone unchallenged. In 1979, Hackney Teachers Association(the local branch of the National Union of Teachers) adopted a policy of non-co-operation with the police. The immediate cause of this was the death at the hands of the police of an east London teacher, Blair Peach, who was killed during an anti-racist demonstration in Southall, in April 1979. But the action also owed much to a growing awareness among teachers of the suspicion and distrust with which the police were regarded by many black pupils and their families.[16] A similar position was taken by the All London Teachers Against Racism and Fascism which sought to prevent the extension of police activities in schools on the grounds not only that classes taken by the police were of dubious educational value but that police work in schools was cosmetic and did not affect policing *outside* schools.

The contention that much if not all of what the police actually do in schools is of dubious educational value has been upheld by what appears to be the only detailed account of police work in schools, a study by Dr G. Vorhaus of the 'schools involvement programme' run by police in the London Borough of Hillingdon.[17] This found a number of factual errors and considerable lack of clarity in the police lessons, little separation of fact and opinion in the content of lessons, and little apparent concern by police teachers of the effects of shocking and upsetting material.

Such criticisms, however, have been largely dismissed by the police and those working in education who support police involvement in schools. For instance, in 1983 HM Inspectorate of Schools published a report describing objections to the presence of police in schools as resulting from 'misunderstandings' which had enabled a small group of teachers 'to capitalize upon the general unease among teachers that a particular incident has generated'.[18] One such particular incident occurred at a north London school in early 1981. The police response to a reported incident involved not just six cars, but a police helicopter as well. Pupils at the school alleged assaults by police on black pupils, as well as racist abuse. Black pupils were called 'black bastards' and one white girl was called a 'fucking nigger lover'. The police response was that such allegations were 'the usual standard sort of propaganda about police going in with big boots on the kids. We did not go in with big boots. We responded as we should have responded . . . the response was excellent.'[19] Not suprisingly, the school decided to abandon the involvement of the police with its senior classes.

The Inspectorate's report did not address itself to such incidents or to the general allegation that police involvement in schools went alongside police harassment of young people. Uncritically accepting police involvement in schools as a good thing, it provided further impetus for such work by recommending the establishment of more formal links between education authorities and the police and the application of this throughout the country.

The report could, in addition, have questioned police involvement in schools on two other points which hold for community policing in general. First, it could have questioned the use made by police of schools work to gather information and intelligence. The Durham Police involved in the scheme mentioned earlier said that they asked children to pass on any information they might have about theft and vandalism, while one officer in the Lothian and Borders Police said they used schools not only to obtain information from the pupils themselves but from the staff about the pupils and their relatives outside the school:

> We go down to the schools a lot. You get a hell of a lot of information from the kids. They get wise to us once they're about seven or eight, but they still like to boast about what their big brothers or their dads have been up to so we get a lot off the teachers.[20]

The ethics of such behaviour – by police and teachers – have gone largely unquestioned.

Second, the Inspectorate could have questioned police involvement in schools as a dubious attempt to engineer and mould consent, particularly where, on the admission of the poilce themselves, such work is aimed at the youngest age-groups who are most easily influenced, in a situation where such attempts cannot be easily questioned or disputed.

The Inspectorate's report opened the way for increased access by the police to schools and in 1986 the main teachers' unions came to an agreement with the police on access to, and involvement in schools. The guidelines[21] state that the objectives of police–school liaison should be to foster positive relationships between schools and the police service, with the aim of developing young people's understanding and respect for the law and the rights and duties of individuals. Despite such statements and numerous qualifications, for instance that the decision whether to invite police into schools for educational purposes is one for headteachers 'in the light of local circumstances, and bearing in mind the needs and sensitivities of the communities served by the school' or that educational visits should not be used for crime investigation, the guidelines marked an important victory for the police. Not only that, but they take it for granted that there is a valid role for the police in education, ignoring both Vorhaus's criticisms of police classes and the more general point about why it is thought that only the police can teach about the law, rights or the danger of drug abuse, or that they are the best people to do so.

From community involvement . . .

The juvenile legislation of the 1960s was essentially based on a pathological view of juvenile crime and delinquency: it was juveniles themselves who were to blame, along with their immediate environment of the family and the community. It was therefore only logical that juvenile liaison be extended to liaison with the broader community from which juveniles came. Such community involvement, as it came to be called, including co-operation between the police and local authority agencies such as the probation and social services, planning departments and others, closely followed the creation of the Greenock juvenile liaison scheme in 1956. There, the chief constable, David Gray, arranged for local residents to meet representatives from schools, churches and the local authority to form a local youth welfare association. The following year, again on the initiative of the police, the local authority adopted a plan to ensure the co-operation of churches, teachers and police in a scheme to improve the local physical environment.

In a sense Gray was ahead of his time for police community involvement activities really only spread in the 1970s. In 1971, for example, the Scottish Office issued a circular encouraging all forces to set up community involvement branches to liaise with social work departments, deal with schools, establish juvenile liaison schemes and promote the special constabulary. By the time of the reorganization of the police in 1975, 19 of the 20 Scottish forces had created community involvement in branches. Similarly in England and Wales police forces had begun to intervene in communities. In 1974, for example, a special project was established in the Kirkby district of Merseyside following a police-initiated meeting of clergy, teachers, councillors, social workers and 'community leaders'. A chief superintendent was seconded to work full-time with the project and in 1979 a wider scheme was launched on Merseyside under the slogan 'Into the Eighties with Pride', its stated purpose being 'to increase the level of community policing by a much greater degree of community involvement'. Similar schemes have been launched on the initiative of the police in other areas. What they illustrate is not just further involvement of the police with other agencies but, as the Kirkby statement shows, the connection between community involvement and the broader idea of 'community policing'.

The ground for police intervention of this kind had been well laid by the development of government urban programmes in the 1960s and 1970s. The Urban Aid Programme, introduced in 1968, was a clear response to Enoch Powell's 'rivers of blood' speech, and was based, as Lee Bridges has said, 'more on the grounds of political expediency than on any well thought-out theory regarding the nature of urban poverty'.[22]

But just as the changes of the period in the juvenile justice system were based on a social pathology approach, so the Urban Aid Programme, and the Community Development Projects, which were introduced in 1969, were based on a pathological approach, locating the problems of the inner cities in the failure of individuals, families and communities.

The Urban Aid Programme and the CDPs were run not by the Department of the Environment but by the Home Office, the Department of 'law and order' and immigration control, internal and external. The social control aspect of urban policy was always implicit but, as Bridges has shown, by late 1973 it had become quite explicit. The then Home Secretary, Robert Carr, announcing the results of a major review of urban policy, made it quite clear that the Home Office's primary function was the maintenance of 'law and order' and social stability. Urban social policy had to be developed in this context.

The police were closely involved in the planning of CDPs and once, established, many individual projects were approached by the local police with offers of assistance and co-operation. North Shields CDP, for example, did not only receive informal visits from the local police, but every month also received specially compiled lists of offences reported in the project area. The lists ceased when the police realized the project was not making use of them. Such attempts by projects to maintain some independence and distance from the police made it difficult for the police to get too involved, but by the mid to late 1970s, this had begun to change.

In Scotland, the police had increasingly established 'special police projects' in urban areas selected by the police on the grounds of extensive 'police problems and anti-social behaviour'. In such projects, police work included co-operation with local authority departments such as housing and social services, as well as running youth clubs, tenants' associations and play schemes. The police frequently say that the purpose of their involvement in such projects is to stimulate self-help on the part of the tenants involved and then to withdraw. In practice matters do not always resolve themselves in this way. In the Easterhouse project in Glasgow for example, the police have been reported as considering that there is such a shortage of 'local leadership' that they have no alternative but to continue to play a leading role, and a community involvement officer continues to work full-time on the project. Similarly in Aberdeen, attempts to have local people run a community project foundered and the community involvement officer now not only runs the youth club, but does so under a police-sponsored committee.

In England and Wales, the police have, according to the Inspector of Constabulary, sought to be associated as closely as possible with schemes set up under the most recent of the urban programmes, the Inner City Partnerships set up in 1978. In Newcastle, this has simply meant something of the nature of carrying out physical crime prevention work, while in Manchester the police, with the support of the Partnership programme, established a police presence in areas where there was high vandalism. In Birmingham, however, the police have gone furthest in the development of policing in association with the Partnership programme. Using Partnership money, the West Midlands Police set up the Lozells Community Policing Project in conjunction with the education, probation and social services departments. The Lozells project in Handsworth is frequently cited as a model of contemporary community policing and is therefore worth considering in some detail.

The project originated in the report, *Shades of Grey*,[23] written by John Brown, a sociologist with a long connection with the police, and published in 1978. Brown had been commissioned to write the report following widespread allegations by local people of police malpractice and police racism. Brown's report did not answer these allegations. Instead he laid the blame for poor relations between the police and black people in the area on 200 or so Rastafarians who, Brown claimed, were largely responsible for terrorizing the local community and the police.

The Lozells Project was set up as a direct result of Brown's report and has received £50,000 (rising to £75,000) of Partnership money each year. A large proportion of this money in the first year of operation, 1979, was distributed by the police to various groups in the community by means of a committee of police and representatives of the various statutory agencies in the area. Since then the money has gone towards the cost of a police-operated community centre and has been less and less available for other groups. Invariably groups which do receive money have to accept some form of police involvement as a price of financial support and there have been allegations that groups which do not take police money and involvement are subjected to harassment such as raids and searches. In addition, in 1982 it was further alleged that a Labour Party Young Socialists conference on black youth scheduled to be held in the area had to be cancelled when police intervened to have a venue booking cancelled.[24]

The significance and importance of the Handsworth scheme for the policing of the future has been candidly spelled out by its architect. In an article for a police journal in 1981 Brown wrote:

> Handsworth in the last three years demonstrates a growing pattern of police community contact and interaction – with education and Youth Services through police contributions to school programmes and to leisure and sports activities for young people; with the Social Services through joint consultation on young offenders, and through training exchanges; with the Probation Service through a victim support scheme; with ethnic minorities through collaboration in dealing with community problems and through encouragement of self-help schemes; with housing authorities through discussions on the control of 'squats'; and with a wide range of other statutory and voluntary bodies.... As a result of this community involvement, police in Handsworth

are now able to act with greater confidence and with greater public backing, and to harness more effectively both community co-operation and community resources in containing crime and disorder.[25]

Police involvement in communities, whether informally through beat policing or more formally through urban programmes and other inner-city projects, have thus placed them in a powerful postion. They have access to areas, communities and information which could otherwise not be available to them. They often control money and the allocation of resources and they inevitably come into close contact with other agencies, statutory and voluntary. This inter-agency relationship is never one of equality for, as the police themselves emphasize, the police are in a unique position to provide leadership and initiative and generally to act as a focal point for joint work. They are therefore in a position to determine priorities, to control the direction of activities and to isolate and marginalize those who disagree or criticize. This role takes on an added significance in the context of the changes in urban policies themselves and, in particular, the increasing concern with the central direction and control of the inner cities and its residents. To this end, the various social agencies of local government have been marshalled and required to resolve the ambiguity in their roles between welfare and control functions, increasingly in favour of control. The alternative is to risk marginalization, cuts and closure.[26] At the pivot of such inter-agency work stand the police who can not only direct, but can draw on the other agencies for their own ends of social control.

... to community policing: Aldersonism

The inter-agency co-operation between the police and other agencies which developed from juvenile liaison to specific projects such as that in Lozells, has so far been essentially limited in scope, either confined to a particular section of society, such as juveniles, or else confined to one particular geographical part of a police force area and, more often than not, regarded as 'experiments'. It was only with the writing and practice of John Alderson, until recently chief constable of Devon and Cornwall, that there began to emerge an all-embracing concept of community policing. Although Alderson has now left the police to pursue a career as a Liberal politician, his work continues to be important both because of the practical and theoretical legacy bequeathed to other police officers, and because of Alderson's continued espousal of community policing in political quarters.

His major work, *Policing Freedom*,[27] was published in 1979. In response to what he saw as the era of the 'technological cops who rarely meet their public outside conflict or crisis', Alderson argued for what he called 'pro-active' policing, as distinct from policing which is reactive (that is merely responding to events) or even that which is merely preventive. Pro-active policing has all the elements of preventive policing but goes beyond it, setting out to 'penetrate the community in a multitude of ways... to reinforce social discipline and mutual trust'.[28]

It envisages a very high degree of co-ordination and co-operation with all other agencies of government from the top administrative level to the bottom working level' in order not just to control the 'bad' but to activate the 'good'. In such activation, the police, by virtue of their 'unrivalled knowledge of crime and social awareness' are 'ideally placed' to provide the necessary leadership.[29]

What this means in practice is that at a local level there are Community Police Councils to receive information about crime and police problems and to represent the public interest, inter-agency co-operation with social services, probation, education, health, youth, planning and housing services, as well as the voluntary sector, and community police constables. In other words, Alderson's community policing represents a merging of the various components of community policing which previously existed only as isolated and one-off projects or activities elsewhere.

At a national level, Alderson has called for the creation of a government Department of Community Affairs jointly sponsored by what he has called the 'Five Ministries of Law and Order' – the Departments of the Environment, Education, Health and Social Security, Employment and the Home Office.

What this system is designed to achieve is that

> real criminal elements can be better isolated from those striving to live orderly lives. The flow of information improves. The negative attitude of a community towards the criminal process turns positive... When in such a setting the police have to use force and to exercise their legal role they are better understood and, in their turn, feel less alienated.[30]

Again the strands in other community policing activities become clear: the flow of information to the police, improved image of the police and law enforcement, and community policing as a means of ensuring support for police activities which might otherwise be unpopular.

In Devon and Cornwall, where Alderson was chief constable from 1973 until 1982, the first step in the implementation of this theory was the creation of a Crime Prevention Support Group which was to examine the selected 'problem areas' with a view to identifying crime and other community problems, to experiment with new ideas in crime prevention initiatives, to direct police resources, and to 'harness and activate participation and support' towards the creation of good citizenship and community awareness and thereby help to control crime'.[31]

A second step was the formation of a Community Policing Consultative group which involved the media, magistrates, churches, trade unions, and the various local authority services. The group provides a forum for considering ways of reducing crime, identifying community needs and formulating possible multi-agency action. It is the linchpin of Alderson's community policing practice.[32]

In his evidence to Scarman, Alderson, in a carefully timed submission, said that legislation was necessary to make community policing a reality at a national level, and that it was 'pie in the sky' to expect it to be brought about voluntarily since neither the understanding nor the will for it existed. Alderson is only partially correct. Although his extensive writing and speeches and statements to the press have been received with scarcely concealed hostility by the hard-liners of the Association of Chief Police Officers, there are few police chiefs who do not want to be seen to be engaged in community policing. At the time of the Scarman inquiry when Alderson accused other police chiefs of being 'unable to grasp the essential need for radical change' and warned that 'one hundred and fifty years of British police heritage could go down the drain', Barry Pain, chief constable of Kent and President of ACPO, announced indignantly, 'I've been employing community policing for years. The difference between me and John Alderson is that I don't go around shouting it from the rooftops.' In a sense this was true but for most police forces, and for much of the public, community policing means no more than putting more police officers back on foot patrols. Thus, in the years following the 1979 Edmund-Davies pay awards to the police, when recruiting increased and many forces reached their authorized levels of personnel for the first time in many years, many forces put a high priority on beat policing. The Inspector of Constabulary noted in his report for 1979 that beat policing was being expanded by several forces and there seemed to be few chief constables who did not want to be seen putting more men and women on the beat. At the same time some police claims have to be treated with some cynicism. In Greater Manchester, for example, James Anderton had been telling his police authority since 1976 that he was convinced that a uniformed presence on the streets was the most effective deterrent to a number of crimes. In 1982, in a speech on police accountability, he said that 'community policing in Greater Manchester has been equally, if not more successful, as it has been in all other police areas in the country'. What Anderton did not say was that despite an increase in recruitment, the police presence on the streets had not increased. The highest increases had been in the ranks of inspectors and above, while the increased number of constables – 259 between 1975 and 1980 – could be accounted for by increases in special forces. Thus, 100 officers had been added to the airport police, 60 to the Tactical Aid Group (a local mobile reserve similar to the Special Patrol Group), 60 to the Community Contact Branch, and 30 to the full-time police band. None of these officers were available for beat patrols.[33]

The reason for this espousal of 'community policing' from the highest ranks of the police was not just that more officers were becoming available but, more crucially, that mobile patrols and reactive policing were increasingly being criticized, from within the police as well as from outside it. The criticism was not just that they were harming the police image, but that they were proving counter-productive. The distance of the police from the public meant not only that police and public met each other increasingly in situations of conflict or confrontation, but that the police did not receive the routine information it needed from the public if it was to carry out its job. Putting officers back on the beat, therefore, improved the police image (as all accounts of such schemes show) and, more important, ensured that the police were better placed to receive intelligence and information. Again, this is a point emphasized by police accounts of beat policing. An account of a 'patch policing' experiment in Milton Keynes defined as one of the objectives, 'to activate community spirit and collaboration with the police'.[34] And John Brown, a sociologist closely involved with the police, has written of the community police officer that:

> Because he has earned acceptance and therefore his place in the locality, he is able to move about with freedom and trust even in places – such as those around the meeting places of black youth – which other, specialist police may well consider akin to No Go areas, only to be approached mob-handed.[35]

The job specification for an 'area constable' in one force makes the intelligence-gathering function quite explicit. It states that the officer should:

a. Secure the services of at least one observer in every street, not a paid professional informant, but someone who knows the inhabitants and is inquisitive enough to find out what is going on and who is willing to pass on such information gained;
b. get to know the habits and all other information about criminals in his/her area;
c. cultivate shopkeepers, tradesmen and garage proprietors who are a good source of information;
d. keep observation in parks, playing fields, schools and other places where children congregate.[36]

In Coventry, the community police officer's brief was put even more bluntly and was said to be, 'Anything that affects people, affects you. Wherever there is a social gathering, there will be a police presence.'[37]

The intelligence and information-gathering role of the beat police officer is therefore particularly important to the police in that it ensures an access to areas and communities which would otherwise be impossible. It is a means of breaking down and penetrating community resistance. Such intelligence-gathering has an increased importance in the context of the development of police collators, that is, sophisticated, sometimes computerized, methods of collating routine information about people which officers pick up in the course of their duties, and which often consists of hearsay and other unverifiable material. This information is often circulated throughout the force in an 'intelligence sheet' and is available to all other parts of the police, including special forces such as the Special Branch and Illegal Immigration Intelligence Unit.

Beat police officers are not therefore separate from reactive policing, but a part of it. The apparent conflict between the two approaches is sometimes noted by the police themselves. One police officer in Coventry, not involved in a community policing scheme, complained that 'We get all the flak when we go down and lock them up... it's not them that get beaten up'.[38]

At least two community policing schemes have tried to take this conflict into account. A 'neighbourhood policing' experiment in London and Surrey, begun in 1981, involved the division of the experiment area into two sectors with alternating police teams providing 'neighbourhood policing' in one sector and response policing in the other. Similarly in Skelmersdale, Lancashire the community policing project operates at two levels. On the one hand are the 'structured patrols' of four area teams, each of nine officers who operate on foot from 8 a.m. to 2 a.m. the following morning. On the other hand is the 'patrol support' of 40 officers which provides 'response' services to the area teams on a normal shift system. As the *Sunday Telegraph* put it, 'half the force are meeting and greeting people, and the rest doing conventional "response" work'.[39] A similar point was made by the *Sunday Times* in respect of a beat policing scheme in Stoke:

> Unlike the old bobby on the beat, these men are part of a pervasive system of intensive policing that is supported by a sophisticated command and control computer system. The beat policemen are supplemented by panda cars (or 'incident response vehicles'), the CID crime squad, a local equivalent of the SPG, and the specialist units such as drug squads.[40]

A graphic example of how this worked in practice was provided in the police raid on the Black and White cafe in St Paul's, Bristol in 1980 which led to street fighting between the police and black people, and the withdrawal of the police from the area. Francis Salandy, a local activist and a member of the Defence Committee, described how the local beat officer was a frequent visitor to the cafe where he would sit and chat with people. 'It now appears', Salandy said later, 'that the police use this local "bobby" approach to gather intelligence among the black community with a view to busting them later.'

The Shape of Things to Come

Alderson retired early from the police in early 1982 but before his departure community policing had received its most important impetus yet, as a result of the 1981 urban rebellions and the Scarman report. Scarman was clearly sympathetic to Alderson's ideas and had, in addition, spent some time during his inquiry with Superintendent David Webb who ran the Lozells project in Birmingham. His report recommended a re-examination by the police of their methods and greater 'community involvement' in the policy and operations of policing. Scarman was not offering the police a soft option. He made it clear that he was not against policing methods such as the use of SPG-type units, or stop-and-search powers on principle and he did not demur at the decision made by the Home Secretary while his inquiry proceeded to make available to the police riot equipment such as plastic bullets, water cannon and CS gas. By means of the involvement of the community with the police, Scarman wanted to ensure that when, for example the SPG was used, the police had the support of at least some sections of the community.

The cornerstone of this involvement was to be a system of consultation between the police and public. Provision for this is now contained in the Police and Criminal Evidence Act 1984 which places a duty on police authorities, in consultation with the chief constable, to make arrangements for 'obtaining the views of people ... about matters concerning the policing of the area and for obtaining their co-operation with the police in preventing crime'. In London, this duty falls to the Metropolitan Police Commissioner who is required to consult the borough councils about the 'arrangements that would be appropriate'.[41] But even before the advent of the Police and Criminal Evidence Act moves to establish consultation arrangements had begun with the issue of a circular to chief constables in June 1982 by the Home Office. This set out guidelines for the new consultation and liaison arrangements and emphasized that the purpose of the new committees was to be consultation only. The independence of the police in enforcing the law would not be affected. The committees are not therefore steps towards greater accountability of the police to the public, as some have viewed them. Rather they have been set up precisely at a time when demands for accountability reached a new height. Scarman was clearly aware of this and openly rejected arguments for control of the police. The Government too is aware of it and has firmly set its face against any increased accountability of the police. Both clearly hope that consultation will divert attention from accountability and will help to co-opt some of those, particularly those in the middle ground of politics, who are genuinely concerned by police malpractices and might otherwise move in the direction of demanding accountability.

The creation of consultative committees, however, is not just a government and police smokescreen or public relations exercise. It is not just *against* accountability – it is *for* the co-option of the community into policing. The arrangements envisage a wide range of bodies being involved and the Home Office guideline suggested MPs and councillors, representatives of government departments such as the health service, the Department of the Environment, and the Department of Education, and representatives of local government departments such as social services. Other suggested bodies include community relations councils, trades councils, chambers of commerce, churches, ethnic minority organizations, and councils for voluntary service.

Just how this co-option will work in practice remains to be seen. Some indication, however, is already available. In Brixton in July 1982, the consultative committee gave its support to a police plan to demolish several houses which had been squatted in and to replace them with a police-sponsored community centre, funded by the Urban Programme. In November, police sealed off the 'Front Line' in Railton Road to allow the local authority to repossess the properties and demolish them immediately even before the promised community centre had been built. The operation had the support of both Labour and Tory councillors and was backed up by 500 police, including the riot-trained Immediate Response Units who dispersed a large protest march and cleared the streets. The sole objection of the consultative committee was that it had not been consulted about the timing of the operation. Both the committee and councillors had allowed themselves to be used by the police to show that they had the support of 'community leaders' in their operations.[42] Given the vast experience of liaison arrangements and the complete lack of powers for the Scarman-style successors, it is difficult to conceive that other consultative committees will have a different experience.

But the committees are important in that they illustrate the early development of a multi-agency approach to the policing of the inner city at a very local level, bringing together councillors, police and representatives of local authority departments and non-statutory bodies such as trades councils and chambers of commerce. And it is worth noting that critics of the consultative arrangements have been severely attacked by the police. Hackney Council in London, for instance, which refused for a long time to be involved in consultative arrangements and instead invited police to attend meetings of a special sub-committee of its own police committee, was accused of being anti-police and of hindering the fight against crime.[43]

Only weeks after the publication of the Home Office guidelines, the Police Staff College at Bramshill was hosting a conference on a multi-agency approach at a much higher level. The conference, entitled 'The Urban Future', was part of the senior command course for future chief constables, assistant chief constables and commanders, and brought together a formidable array of senior police officers (including some from abroad), senior civil servants from various departments, academics, chief executives of local authorities, councillors, and representatives of the media, social services and commercial and financial institutions. The focus of the conference was reports by students of the college (all superintendents and chief superintendents) on visits to inner-city areas in London, Manchester, Birmingham and Glasgow.

On a previous occasion, at a small seminar on police–public relations, the College Commandant, Sir Kenneth Newman, had spoken of police officers being sent to study 'ethnic flashpoints'. (This was March 1981, only weeks before the Brixton riots.) The officers would write a thesis on their visit and would 'follow through in exercises with members of the Commission for Racial Equality and finish off with the production of policy papers which might be of use and benefit to chief constables around the country'.[44]

The term 'ethnic flashpoints' was not used in the conference papers themselves. Instead Newman simply said that the purpose of the officers' visits had been to identify areas where there might be opportunities for policy development, to scrutinize examples of "best practice", and their relevance to the service as a whole, and, most importantly, to identify areas and organizational levels where multi-agency co-operation could be developed'.[45]

The Manchester team reported that the multi-agency dimension in practice was best illustrated in the initiatives taken by police and social services ... to establish common training programmes'. The London team, which had visited the east London borough of Hackney, saw schools as a 'key area for policy development and co-operation between agencies' and stressed the importance of youth centres as another opportunity for agencies to work together. In addition, the team emphasized the police need to become more involved in the Inner City Partnership. In Birmingham 'territorial jealousies, bureaucracy and strong feelings of independence' were all seen to inhibit a coherent multi-agency approach, although the police had established liaison committees at subdivisional level even before the Scarman report. It was in Glasgow, however, that the multi-agency approach had been developed furthest. There the police were an 'essential ingredient in the corporate policy [of the local authority] sitting on a variety of committees and expressing views and opinions given considerable credence by members and officers'.[46]

As Commissioner of the Metropolitan Police, Newman was well placed to put this multi-agency approach to work in practice. Indeed, in a report to the Home Secretary in January 1983, only months after his appointment, he described the 'first-aid measures' he intended to take in reorganizing the police emphasizing the importance of such an approach. He wrote: 'Problems identified locally will be tackled systematically by co-ordinating the contributions of police, public and local agencies. The concept of a corporate strategy is vital.'[47] Newman's plan provides the clearest exposition yet of the place of community policing in an overall policing strategy. It asserts that increasing demands mean that the police are unable to prevent and detect crime and that the public must be involved in crime prevention, thus freeing the police for public order and strategic crime prevention.

Newman does not use the words 'community policing', preferring to speak of a 'multi-agency approach' or 'corporate strategy', but the difference is one of words, not substance. In Newman's strategy for the policing of London, consultative committees are to be used 'as a vehicle for directing the overall strategy' and there is to be 'close contact with other statutory and voluntary agencies to harness their efforts, in crime prevention and reduction. A key component of this has been the development of 'neighbourhood watch' schemes. Such schemes, borrowed from the United States, have now been set up not just in London but all over England and

Wales and generally involve local crime-prevention exercises, such as the police marking of property, and the posting of signs indicating the existence of a 'neighbourhood watch area'. The formal existence of many such schemes says little, however, about what they actually do and achieve. It is clear, for instance, that schemes quickly become moribund and that many exist in name only. In terms of effect, research suggests that the schemes merely have a significant 'displacement' effect, reducing some forms of crime in one small area' only to increase it in other adjacent or nearby areas to which it moves.

It would be a mistake, however, to look at neighbourhood watch simply in terms of crime prevention. Neighbourhood watch is clearly aimed at mobilizing support for the police among the middle class and 'respectable' working class and, at the same time, as a means of gathering low-level intelligence. As one study concluded: 'Neighbourhood watch remains a police-controlled programme with limited community participation which locks into the long-term programme for multi-agency policing'.[48]

In addition to such measures, Newman was also able to learn the lessons of an experiment in 'neighbourhood policing' set up by his predecessor, Sir David McNee, in 1981. In an unpublished paper[49] Inspectors Ian Beckett and James Hart defined the 'problem' as being: 'how far can the community contribute to policing activities and how can a police organization motivate and control their assistance?'. Again, the multi-agency approach is offered as a solution, with officers in charge being instructed to ensure that the day-to-day activities of other agencies such as social services 'fully co-ordinate with the police strategy at the operational level'. Police policy itself should 'acknowledge and influence policy decisions made by all other agencies who provide any kind of service to the communities. Where the policies are incompatible, the police must make forceful attempts to convince the other parties as to the value of a co-ordinated approach. It is also considered that liaison with local political figures will be important at this level.'

The project was scheduled to end in 1983 and was to be evaluated by the Police Foundation, a research institution set up in 1979 to undertake research into the problems facing the police. Its trustees include senior police officers, civil servants, businessmen and at least one ex-Cabinet minister.[50]

But like the other advocates of community policing, Newman had no intention of allowing this approach to stand in the way of reactive policing. Indeed, reactive and community policing were complementary parts of Newman's overall strategy, and community policing was designed both to free police resources for reactive policing and to ensure public co-operation and support for it. Thus Newman listed six main objectives for his policing strategy. The first three of these are: to increase directed foot patrols in 'priority areas', that is those with the highest incidence of street robberies, street disorders and burglaries; to maintain and improve the policing of demonstrations and outbreaks of spontaneous rioting; and to increase the detection of street robbery and burglary by the use of specialist squads such as the Special Patrol Group, and by upgrading the status and quality of information gathering and use.

To these ends, the Newman policing strategy involved the targeting of working-class areas in the inner city, usually those with a significant black population. In his report for 1983, for instance, the commissioner spoke of 'symbolic locations' where black communities, especially young people, 'come to view a particular location with something of a proprietorial attachment resenting intrusion, especially by the police to enforce the law'.[51] Similarly in 1986 it was revealed that the Metropolitan Police had compiled a list of housing estates regarded as having a potential for disorder. One of the criteria used to compile the list was 'a high density of population and ethnic mix'. The targeting of such areas involves, alongside the development of 'multi-agency policing' the deployment of local equivalents of the Special Patrol Groups – District Support Units (DSUs). Such units have, in addition to their public order role, other functions when on stand-by, including anti-burglary patrols, rowdyism patrols, searches, road blocks and observation duties. In carrying out these functions, the DSUs have recourse to the extensive powers of arrest, questioning and stop and search granted to the police under the police and Criminal Evidence Act 1984. Community policing and reactive response policing go hand in hand.

This is as true of other chief constables as it was of Newman. The advent of community policing does not mean that the structural changes which have taken place in British policing since the 1960s and 1970s will be reversed. The Special Patrol Groups, Tactical Aid Units and support groups will not be disbanded; guns, CS gas and plastic bullets will not be dumped; and political surveillance will not be ended. More than one commentator has stressed that community policing is but one part of a *total* policing approach. John Brown has spoken of the 'fundamental police priority' being to bring the 'reactive and preventive roles into a balance appropriate to long-term objectives',[52] and John Alderson himself has said that community policing 'provides a complementary element in a total police strategy'.[53]

Other police chiefs and police writers have made it clear that community policing can only apply to some people and not to others. The Chief Constable of Merseyside, Kenneth Oxford, has written that it is optimistic to think that community policing can cure; 'the sickness of present day society . . . what if the communal values are not supportive of law and order? In this case the police will be obliged to work against that community'. Oxford made it clear which communities the police would have to work against saying that 'the sub-cultures of some communities are such (street crime, drug taking, illegal drinking etc.) that inevitably the police will come into conflict with them'.[54] Similarly, right-wing sociologist, P.A.J. Waddington has asked 'what of community policing if it's a community of criminals?'[55] In other words, community policing can exist, but only alongside other forms of policing which will be used when community policing fails or is thought unlikely to succeed.

But the main problem is not that community policing is not an alternative to reactive policing. More important, community policing is an attempt at the surveillance and control of communities by the police, an attempt which operates under the guise of police offering advice and assistance, and which is all the more dangerous because it not only merges the activities of different agencies of the state, but does so under the control and direction of the police. As Lee Bridges has put it:

> community policing merges at the local level the coercive and consensual functions of government, enabling the police to wield a frightening mixture of repressive powers, on the one hand, and programmes of social intervention, on the other, as mutually reinforcing tools in their efforts to control and contain the political struggles of the black and working class communities.[56]

At the same time, community policing offers no prospect of greater democratic control of the police and policing. Indeed, community policing has come to the fore precisely at the same time as there has been widespread demands for greater public accountability and control of the police. Control of community policing remains firmly in the hands of the police.

Instead we must locate community policing in the context of the increasing disciplining of society by the state, the emergence of the 'strong' disciplinary regime' which, Stuart Hall has argued, is necessary 'if the state is to stop meddling in the fine-tuning of the economy, in order to let 'social market values' rip, while containing the inevitable fall-out, in terms of social conflict and class polarization'.[57]

Such discipline takes many forms – trade union laws, immigration controls, the criminalization of whole sections of society, the use of the family to control children and keep women in the home , urban programmes, and of course, direct repression by the police using a 'new technology of repression' and unprecedented new powers. Community policing recognizes that such open control may be counter-productive and seeks to penetrate communities to break down community resistance, to engineer consent and support for the police, and to reinforce social discipline. It is an aspect of what Stan Cohen, writing of Foucault's 'punitive city', has described as a 'correctional continuum' which involves 'the proliferation of agencies and services, finely calibrated in terms of degree of coerciveness or intension or unpleasantness' and which points to a future 'when it will be impossible to determine who exactly is enmeshed in the social control system – and hence subject to its jurisdiction and surveillance – at any one time'.[58]

Community policing is but one aspect of this continuum of discipline and is all the more dangerous because it appears to offer an alternative to unwelcome police practices and strategies and at the same time to hold out some hope for reducing crime and thereby improving the social conditions of the inhabitants of Britain's inner cities. Hence, we find, that community policing (usually quite undefined) is supported on all parts of the political spectrum,[59] while critical accounts (including this one) are dismissed as pessimistic or unrealistic.[60] What unites all these writers and political spokespeople, however, is a refusal to recognize the political nature of policing in Britain in the 1980s, a refusal to accept that the police have, in Stuart Hall's words undertaken to police 'the social crisis of the cities', and a refusal to see that, as criticism grows not just of the police but of the society they represent, community policing is an increasingly important aspect of this 'policing the crisis'.

Acknowledgement

This is a much revised version of a paper which was published in *Critical Social Policy*, Summer 1983.

Notes

1 See, for example, *Policing the Eighties: the Iron Fist*, State Research, 1981; Phil Scraton, *The State of the Police*, London, Pluto Press, 1985.
2 'The Plague of the Blue Locusts: police reform and popular resistance in Northern England', in Mike Fitzgerald *et al.* (eds), *Crime and Society: Readings in History and Theory*, Open University and Routledge & Kegan Paul, 1981.
3 Gus John, *Race in the Inner City*, Runnymede Trust, 1970.
4 Lawrence Roach, 'The Metropolitan Police Community Relations Branch', *Police Studies*, vol. 1, no. 3, September 1978.
5 David Pope, *Community Relations: the police response*, Runnymede Trust, 1976.
6 See, for example, Institute of Race Relations, *Police Against Black People*, IRR, 1979; and Paul Gordon, *White Law: racism in the police, courts and prisons*, London, Pluto Press, 1983.
7 'Racism and reaction', in Commission for Racial Equality, *Five Views of Multi-Racial Britain*, CRE, 1978.
8 Quoted in Eveyln Schaffer, *Community Policing*, London, Croom Helm, 1980, p. 29.
9 *Report of HM Inspector of Constabulary for 1978*, HMSO, 1979.
10 *Report of HM Inspector of Constabularly for 1980*, HMSO, 1981.
11 N.J. Shanks, *Police Community Involvement in Scotland*, Scottish Office, 1980.
12 *Communal Policing*, Devon and Cornwall Constabulary, 1979, p. 10.
13 *The Guardian*, 13 October 1981.
14 *Sunday Times*, 17 January 1982.
15 *Times Educational Supplement*, 18 September 1981.
16 Hackney NUT, *Police Out of Schools*, 1985.
17 G. Vorhaus, *Police in the Classroom: a study of the schools involvement programme in Hillingdon*, Hillingdon Legal Resource Centre, 1984. See also Advisory Committee on Police in Schools, *Policing Schools*, ACPS, 1986, for a general account of the issues.
18 *Police Liaison with the Education Service*, Department of Education and Science, 1983.

19 *The Guardian* 19 March 1981, *New Stateman*, 27 March 1981.
20 Quoted in Robert Baldwin and Richard Kinsey, *Police Powers and Politics*, London, Quartet, 1982, p. 101.
21 The text of the guidelines can be found in *Police*, June 1986.
22 '"The Ministry of Internal Security": British urban social policy 1968–74', *Race and Class*, vol. XVI, no. 4, April 1975.
23 Cranfield Institute, 1978.
24 *Labour Weekly*, 11 June 1982.
25 'The functions of communities in police strategies', *Police Studies*, Spring 1981.
26 See '"The Ministry of Internal Security": British urban social policy 1968–74', *Race and Class*, vol. XVI, no. 4, April 1975; and 'Keeping the lid on: British urban social policy 1975–81', *Race and Class*, vol. XXIII, nos 2/3, Autumn 1981/Winter 1982.
27 Plymouth, Devon, Macdonald and Evans.
28 Ditchley Conference on preventive policing, 1977.
29 *Communal Policing*, op. cit. p. 46.
30 *Observer*, 28 March 1982.
31 *Communal Policing*, op. cit. p. 31.
32 A full, though uncritical, account of the scheme can be found in Colin Moore and John Brown, *Community versus Crime*, London, Bedford Square Press, 1981.
33 *New Statesman*, 7 April 1982.
34 *Police Review*, 17 August 1981.
35 *Police Review*, 6 July 1979.
36 Quoted in Baldwin and Kinsey, op. cit. p. 288.
37 *Sunday Telegraph*, 27 September 1981.
38 Ibid.
39 Ibid.
40 22 March 1981.
41 Police and Criminal Evidence Act 1984, section 106
42 *Searchlight*, December 1982.
43 *Sunday Times*, 24 November 1985. See also Rod Morgan and Christopher Maggs, *Following Scarman?: a survey of formal police/community consultative arrangements*, Centre for the Analysis of Social Policy, University of Bath, 1984.
44 *Relations between Police and Public*, Sir Halley Stewart Trust, 1981.
45 Unpublished conference papers, 1982.
46 Ibid.
47 Metropolitan Police press release, 24 January 1983.
48 Harry Donnison *et al.*, *Neighbourhood Watch: policing the people*, Libertarian Research and Education Trust, 1985.
49 *Neighbourhood policing: a policing strategy for residential city areas*, 1981.
50 *State Research*, no. 21, December 1980/January 1981.
51 *Report of the Commissioner of Police for the Metropolis for the Year 1983*, HMSO, 1984.
52 *Shades of Grey*, Cranfield Institute, 1977, p. 48.
53 *Policing Together*, Devon and Cornwall Constabulary, 1980.
54 *Police*, June 1982.
55 *Police Review*, 18 January 1982.
56 'Keeping the lid on: British urban social policy 1975–81', *Race and Class*, vol. XXIII, nos 2/3, Autumn 1981/Winter 1982.
57 *Drifting into a Law and Order Society*, Cobden Trust, 1979, p. 4.

58 'The punitive City: notes on the dispersal of social control', *Contemporary Crises*, Vol. 3, No. 4, October 1979. The point is developed in Cohen's *Visions of Social Control*, Cambridge, Polity Press, 1985.

59 See, for instance, the contributions in Peter Bradley (ed.), *A Review of Community Policing*, Centre for Contemporary Studies, 1984.

60 See, for example, Robert Reiner, *The Politics of the Police*, Brighton, Sussex, Wheatsheaf, 1985, p. 211 and David Downes and Tony Ward, *Democratic Policing*, Labour Campaign for Criminal Justice, 1986, p. 44.

5

Unreasonable Force: Policing, Punishment and Marginalization

Phil Scraton

Introduction

Since the late 1960s the economic contradictions inherent within the development of advanced capitalism and their political and social consequences have become sharply evident. The complex class relations derived in the offices and on the shop-floors of multinational companies and within the layers of the central and local state institutions, the sexual divisions of a patriarchy integrated within the structural arrangements of an advanced capitalist political economy and the legacy of racism rooted in the slave and colonial economies of British imperialism have surfaced as workers, women, black people and the unemployed have carried their struggles against economic exploitation and political oppression onto the streets.[1] The arrival and consolidation of unemployment, particularly among young people, as a permanent, growing and structural feature of the British economy in the 1980s has turned industrial action over union representation, pay and conditions[2] into often bitter and long-fought campaigns in defence of essential industries and whole communities.[3] Persistent attempts to control industrial action and to regulate the internal affairs of trade unions, features of both Heath and Thatcher administrations[4] have drawn a direct and physical response from trade unionists typified by the use of 'flying' and 'mass' picketing. Demonstrations and marches, particularly to promote racist ideas and policies or to oppose them, have frequently brought many people onto the streets. From the anti-fascist demonstrations of the 1970s, which culminated in the death of Blair Peach in April

1979,[5] there developed the full-scale uprisings of inner-city black communities in 1980, 1981 and 1985.[6]

During this period media-hyped pressure has mounted also over the 'escalation' or 'spiral' of crime, particularly street crime, which has been identified and widely publicized as the most significant 'social problem' of inner-city life.[7] On the other hand increases in racial harassment and racial attacks[8] together with new evidence of the serious under-reporting of violence against women have revealed the reluctance and inadequacies of the law and its enforcement in the selective response to criminal acts of violence. Yet women have become more visible in terms of the regulation of their collective protests, be they directed towards male violence in 'reclaim the night' or sex-shop protests,[10] or towards peace initiatives such as Greenham.[11] The police have found themselves, often not unwillingly, in the centre of these issues. Stuart Hall clearly identifies the classic dilemma:

> Wherever the law draws the line, the police are required to hold it. Conflicts with the state, with employers, with specific laws and regulations, with policies and conditions, are inevitably displaced onto the police in any serious confrontations. As a society we lay on them the responsibility for discharging what may be mutually irreconcilable responsibilities: they must enforce the law impartially, defending the liberties of the citizen, while maintaining public order and the Queen's Peace.[12]

It is inevitable that in terms of operational policies and practices the priorities and emphases adopted by the police, at both chief constable and police constable levels, will be sources of debate if not dispute. Following a relatively 'quiet period' exemplified in the post-war image of 'Dixon of Dock Green', the issue of how the police discharge their duties in response to the conflicts around crime, public order and industrial conflict have re-emerged as a focus of major political, if not constitutional, controversy.[13] Serious criticisms have been made of the 'strategies' used to police certain areas – particularly black and Irish communities;[14] the handling of industrial pickets and political demonstrations;[15] the use of special squads including Special Patrol Group-type units and Police Support Units;[16] surveillance techniques and intelligence gathering;[17] and an increasing dependence on technology.[18] To a large extent public concern has been fuelled over these issues as the consolidation of the power of chief constables has become evident through their willingness to become involved directly in wider political debates and the rising influence of their national organization – the Association of Chief Police Officers (ACPO). Statements by successive Metropolitan Commissioners on the 'state of the nation', political subversion and industrial conflict[19] and by chief constables such as James Anderton of Greater Manchester on moral responsibility with regard to homosexuality, promiscuity and AIDS have ensured constant media attention. The 'Guardians of the Peace' have become the 'Guardians of the Conscience' of the assumed moral and political majority.

Keepers – or Definers – of the Peace?

It has been this privileged access to the media, well-interpreted much earlier in Becker's reference to 'hierarchies of credibility',[20] which has enabled chief constables to respond aggressively and publicly to the criticisms of their policies, their priorities for law enforcement and their methods. The generalized police view, shared by each of the police organizations, is that much of the criticism of contemporary policing has originated in the career aspirations and ulterior motives of left-wing politicians, civil libertarians and community leaders. In fact, as the well-documented tensions between police authorities and their chief constables over operational policies and practices have shown, the criticisms have a much broader constituency.[21] What began in 1979 on Merseyside as a debate about the accountability of one chief constable[22] soon developed into an issue of the role and responsibilities of police authorities[23] and eventually became a problem of the control of the police within a democratic political process.[24] The levels of hostility and the moral indignation of charge and counter-charge have produced a political climate in which there are real difficulties in establishing an informed, tolerant or constructive debate.

The belief that the 'arm of the law' has become over-extended and what is needed is a 'firm hand on the police' by no means has been confined to radical critics of the police. As a consequence police accountability at all levels – organizational, legal and political – has become a central focus with the fine line between 'control' and 'accountability' often blurred. Senior police officers consistently have reinforced the significance of this distinction in their discussions of police accountability and the law. They argue that in enforcing the law the police are not, and should not be, controlled politically. Rather, in the 'long tradition' of British policing, they should be accountable to the 'community' through its 'consent'. In 1973 Robert Mark, then Metropolitan Commissioner, in his highly publicized BBC Dimbleby Lecture, stated:

> The fact that the British Police are answerable to the Law, that we act on behalf of the community and not under the mantle of Government, makes us the least powerful, the most accountable and therefore the most acceptable police force in the world.[25]

Mark's successor, David McNee, reiterated this position. He considered that the directions of the first Commissioners, Rowan and Mayne, were definitive:

> Their original instructions to the force made it clear that the old tradition of policing from within the community, with the consent of the community, was the guiding principle of the new system.[26]

In 1982 following the opening of the new £9 million police headquarters on Merseyside, a new publicity brochure announced the arrival of the 'most modern and well-equipped police headquarters in the world'.[27] The brochure opened with two quotes

> The police of this country have never been recognized either in law or by tradition as a force distinct from the general body of citizens. The principle remains that a police officer, in view of the common law, is only a person paid to perform, as a matter of duty, acts which, if he were so minded, he might have done voluntarily.[28]

> There are two very important advantages that our police enjoy over most others in the world. Firstly, that it was founded on a tradition of common law – law that evolved naturally to meet the needs of the people – and, secondly, that its officers are drawn from the community, performing their duties on behalf of us all. The job of the police is therefore to uphold our own self-imposed rules.[29]

Thus the police officer is a 'citizen-in-uniform' whose job is merely a formalization of the duties of all socially responsible citizens. The Law, enforced and applied 'as a matter of duty', is 'natural' – rather than socially or politically constructed – and it has emerged over time from identifiable 'needs of the people'. At the heart of this position is the idea of a harmonious society in which there is a generalized consensus on rules for the common good. There is no ambiguity here in the taken-for-granted notion of 'the community' – its acceptance is central in each of the above quotes. The 'Law' is of that community – it is 'ours' – and the rules are 'self-imposed'. The police also 'belong' to us as *our* representatives in the neutral enforcement of 'our' Law. From this is derived the deeply held belief, the police argue that it is a principle, that they are no more than 'citizens-in-uniform' engaged in the democratic process of 'policing by consent'. As upholders of a just and consensual rule of law they respond as neutral arbiters in its enforcement. Consequently in the demanding and recurrent conflicts, which from time to time surface, the police provide the 'thin blue line' which keeps apart the opposing interests or factions. They are the 'keepers of the peace', the 'guardians of consensus'.

Police biographers also reflect the development historically of the 'new police' as one which quickly won the hearts and minds of 'the people'. Critchley, for example, considers the introduction in 1829 of Peel's Metropolitan Police officers as the arrival of a non-political, state-sponsored force which upheld the common good and the neutrality of the state's order. Initially resisted, he concludes that within ten years 'their imperturbability, courage, good humour and sense of fair play won first the admiration of Londoners and then their affection'.[30] Sir Leon Radzinowicz also notes the initial cross-class antagonism towards a systemized form of national policing but considered that within five years the police had 'ceased to be regarded, except in the most radical circles, as a threatening innovation'.[42] Challenging the interpretation of a generalized acceptance of the police during the middle period of the nineteenth century Fitzgerald *et al.* state:

Critchley and Radzinowicz *assume* the historical inevitability of the consolidation of the police. Thus, while they acknowledge opposition to and struggle against the new police, they argue that by the mid-point of the nineteenth century, the police were widely acceptable to, and assured the co-operation of, the majority of the populace.[32]

What more recent work has suggested is that while the nineteenth century was a period in which the police extended their formal presence throughout Britain and consolidated their powers as a civil force, they did not meet with universal or unequivocal co-operation from the communities they served. There was considerable opposition, culminating in anti-police riots, as the police flexed their lawful muscles over public gatherings, public order and recreational practices,[33] and over demonstrations by the poor and industrial actions by workers.[34] Within the cities and towns the poor and the unemployed experienced 'a greater chance of being arrested for "drunkenness", "loitering", "common assault", "vagrancy" or whatever else the duty sergeant decided to write in his big book'.[35] From the outset the police responded to specific individuals and identifiable groups differentially and according to shared assumptions about their perceived reputations. A recent historical account of the history and development of the police in Liverpool demonstrates clearly that the relationship between the police and the policed was one of complexity lacking in predictability rather than one of mutual trust and legitimacy.[36] Cohen concludes that by the end of the century the Metropolitan Police had received 'grudging acceptance' on the streets of the Metropolis[37] and research by Davis on the history of the police in Islington shows that the police had well-established practices of surveillance on 'problem families' and 'potential criminals' by this time.[38]

Thus the portrayal of the police as the 'thin blue line' or neutral arbiters in external, social conflict is a naive and simplistic version of the tradition of British policing. The nineteenth century was a period in which the political function of the police was established and consolidated. In policing civil disorder, strikes and lock-outs and political demonstrations the police operated within parameters set by governments and the rule of law and interpreted with lawful yet permissive discretion by senior officers. On the street officers possessed wide discretionary powers in the negotiation and enforcement of the law. While operational policies and priorities were influenced by governmental directives and public opinion the police were not identified within working-class communities as being neutral either in policy decisions or in their routine practices. As the enforcers of law and order they were engaged in the administration of law and order of a certain kind – one which never possessed the consent, nor reflected the interests, of communities and neighbourhoods in working-class neighbourhoods. This legacy was carried into the twentieth century and hallmarked the inter-war period. For the poor, the unemployed, striking workers and political demonstrators have persistently represented a threat to the established order. Working-class resistance to poverty, unemployment, casual labour –

struggles against the persistence of exploitation and the economic processes of marginalization – has been met directly, on the streets or on picket lines, by the police as the state's civil force of regulation and control. Consequently the police have been regularly pitched against the interests of working-class people. In their enforcement of the law against hunger marchers, political demonstrators, suffragettes and strikers they have been identified clearly with employers and intransigent governments. With the institutionaliza-tion of often aggressive and violent forms of policing, legitimated via the full authority of the state, the organized working class has never accepted the impartiality of the police in strikes or lock-outs.

The portrayal of the police as crime-fighters upholding the established virtues of the rule of law has been somewhat undermined in the post-war period by persistent revelations that many large forces, but especially the Metropolitan Police, have become deeply involved in professional crime.[39] This was of such concern to Robert Mark that on becoming Metropolitan Commissioner in 1972 he identified his main task as the eradication of the 'autonomy' and corrupt practices of the CID – the 'firm within a firm'. There were several hundred dismissals and resignations, the formation of a new internal investigation department (A10), and, eventually, a much publicized investigation of police involvement in organized crime – Operation Coun-tryman. While Mark's reaction to widespread corruption presented the police with a crisis in credibility and a decline in morale it was taken as a clear indication of the willingness and capacity of the police to regulate their own affairs effectively. 'Putting the house in order' was the first step to securing a new climate of professional trust and efficiency which confirmed the legal and organizational accountability of the police.

Subsequent revelations concerning the use and abuse of the supergrass system[40] – whereby criminals provide key information in return for immun-ity from charges – and the significance of the masonic links within the police[41] indicate that such an interpretation of the Mark years might be premature. For substantial discretion operates in the selectivity of 'deals' done with known criminals and the definition of 'legitimate' information. This extends to decisions about who should be prosecuted, the extent of charges and the negotiation, even reconstruction of evidence. It is here that the dual role of the police, as investigators and prosecutors, becomes significant. Allegations made to the Countryman inquiry included the involvement of detectives in 'setting up' robberies, steering inquiries away from positive suspects to innocent people, framing others by planting evidence and verballing.[42] The close association both formal and informal, of the police with known criminals and informants, particularly in relation to supergrass information, indicates that the institutionalized practices revealed by Mark's attempted purge have remained intact and the Countryman investigation failed.

One of the main reasons for the failure of Operation Countryman undoubtedly was the 'wall of silence' and lack of co-operation which the investigating team met with throughout its investigation. This raises a further significant issue concerning the effectiveness of organizational constraints on police malpractice. Pioneering studies of the organizational and social aspects of British police work emphasized the significance of 'police group work' and suggested that in the post-war period the balance of operational control lay with the discretionary practices of lower-ranked officers rather than with senior officers or police authorities.[43] Further to this is the conclusion that it is the occupational, 'mess-room', culture of the rank-and-file officers which occasionally provides the basis for resistance to the objectives of 'managerial professionalism'[44] and to the development of 'community involvement' strategies.[45] Recent in-depth research into city-based police work emphasizes the significance of the 'mental map' of the community, based on shared assumptions about identifiable groups such as professionals, women and blacks, which prevails within the occupational culture of police work in a particular area.[46] It is the reputations of individuals or groups which provide the basis for the differential police responses, the strategies and tactics adopted, in particular situations.

> By one strategy or another, by one tactic or another, the appearance of police control or more precisely, as far as our officers are concerned, the reality of control – is maintained. All strategies and tactics are supported by this fundamental view and by aspects of knowledge about 'prisoners' and figures. The strategies emphasize control, hedonism, action and challenge – constituents of the occupational culture. These cultural strands of policing are woven together as practical skills employed on the streets . . . these strategies distance Hilton's officers from the constraints of legal rules and force directives, from the criticisms of the public that is policed, from the influence of the least powerful groups living and working in Hilton. Hilton's rank-and-file officers are free to police in their own style, with their own assumptions and strategies intact.[47]

This was an issue central to the findings of the Metropolitan Police-commissioned report[48] on police–community relations carried out by the Policy Studies Institute (PSI). In-depth research with beat officers, in patrol cars and at police stations revealed an occupational culture in which the 'mental map' of the community was clearly defined by age, race, class and sex. The researchers found that the climate which prevailed, messroom culture, was one of a 'cult of masculinity' in which aggressive, heavy-drinking and sexist behaviour was the norm. Also deeply institutionalized was a level of racism which constantly permeated conversations and attitudes towards black people.[40]

Clearly these attitudes have serious consequences in practice particularly in the response of the police to women as victims of male violence or to black people as victims of racial attacks or racial harassment. They are attitudes, as indicated by the historical discussion, which penetrate deeply into the social relations of production – be they concerned with 'striking' workers, the 'undeserving' poor, or the 'scrounging' claimants. In the wake of the

1972 miners' strike and the closure of the Saltley Coke depot by 'flying pickets' a survey of rank-and-file police officers showed that only 45% considered that the law was enforced adequately on picket lines. Of the officers surveyed a significant proportion wanted a more rigorous programme of enforcement and 51% demanded tighter overall control of pickets with a substantial majority calling for the total abolition of picketing.[50] An article in *Police Review* written by a well-known author on police matters, Kenneth Sloan, reflected the dominant attitude of police officers towards strikes during the 1978–9 'winter of discontent':

> Members of picket lines are dedicated people who hold strong beliefs in the right of their cause, plus, all too frequently, a few fully paid up members of the 'kick-a-copper' brigade. It is *impossible to reason with either*. As individuals the pickets may be perfectly reasonable, but in groups they are *blinkered and brainwashed* by their union representatives and unwilling to show themselves to have any *human feelings* in front of their colleagues. (Emphasis added.)[51]

What is evident from the preceding discussion is that the range of assumptions concerning the status, powers, impartiality and accountability which are central to the police position as outlined are not upheld by historical and contemporary research. That the police are, in some mystical way, 'above politics' operating outside of the inherent, structural conflicts of classism, racism and sexism is plausible yet illusory. Occasionally the guard drops and what is revealed is a clear picture of intent and circumstance. For example, Robert Mark stated in a foreword to one text: 'The post-war years have seen a gradual change in our role from mere law enforcement to participating in the role of social welfare and even more importantly to that of contributors in the *moulding of public opinion and legislation*' (emphasis added).[52] In response to the policing of the Grunwick dispute in 1975–6 Mark's allegiance was clear when he commented that the owner 'courageously and successfully stood firm against politically motivated violence on the streets'.[53] He considered that the Shrewsbury pickets had 'committed the worst of all crimes, even worse than murder', by their attempt 'to achieve an industrial or political objective by criminal violence'.[54] James Anderton, the Chief Constable of Greater Manchester after a series of confrontations with the police authority argued that 'enthusiastic democrats' were opening the door to 'those whose sole aim is political direction and control of the police and the removal of independence and power from chief constables'.[55] In a longer statement a year later he said:

> I sense in our midst an enemy more dangerous, insidious and ruthless than any faced since the Second World War. I firmly believe that there is a long-term political strategy to destroy the proven structure of the police and turn them into an exclusive agency of a one-party state. I am also convinced that the police service is now a prime target for subversion and demonstration...chief constables must ensure that their forces are not infiltrated by undesirable people who could wreak havoc.[56]

Anderton's position on the involvement of the police, particularly at a senior level, in political interventionism was already well established although his previous comments concerning the fight to protect the foundations of democracy and the traditions of morality had been confined to apparently spontaneous comments in interviews or on television chat shows.[57] In 1986, after a decade of political and religious comment, James Anderton was elected as president of ACPO by his fellow senior officers. He succeeded the equally outspoken Charles McLachlan, Chief Constable of Nottinghamshire, whose views and decisions were central to the policing of the coal dispute in 1984–5. With the Nottinghamshire coalfields enjoying the most advanced technology and secure economic future McLachlan's force area covered the heartland of strike-breaking throughout the dispute. By using road-blocks on motorway intersections and all A roads he stretched police powers to the limits of lawful discretion, turned the county into a virtual island and restricted severely the rights of strikers to picket working pits.[48] Despite the fact that the National Coal Board had taken no civil action to establish the illegality of picketing McLachlan's personal position was unequivocal:

> Supporting the freedom of people who want to prevent people going to work is not supporting freedom, but supporting anarchy, violence, riot, and damage and everything else.[59]

Further, in response to criticism from the Nottinghamshire Police Authority:

> Who am I to serve? Am I to serve the people who are coming in to attack Nottinghamshire people and beat the living daylights out of them if they get a chance, or do I serve the people who are being beaten? I serve the people who are being beaten, and this Committee does too, and don't forget it![60]

If the chief constables established their autonomy from police authorities in terms of operational policy decision, priorities for law enforcement and the strategies and tactics to be employed, over the Merseyside dispute of 1979–81[61] and the urban uprisings of 1980–81,[62] their refusal to consult with their authorities throughout the coal dispute consolidated this position.[63] As one police researcher commented:

> For all the rhetoric about the democratic accountability of the British police they have become virtually impervious to any control by elected political bodies, and are adamant about remaining so.[64]

Thus, to return to Hall's quote used in the opening paragraphs of this chapter the police response to recent conflicts in the inner cities and over industrial action has not been concerned with 'holding the line' which is 'drawn by the law'. Rather it has been one of establishing clear political autonomy over operational policies, priorities and practices and then employing that autonomy, together with lawful discretion, to prioritize and interpret laws selectively towards differential enforcement. As has been shown from the historical evidence the process of differential policing has a well-established tradition in the surveillance, regulation and control of 'target' individuals, groups and communities. What appears to have surprised police authorities is the permissive but correct interpretation of the 1964 Police Act which has enabled chief constables to operate free of effective local democratic accountability.[65] The struggle, and eventual victory, of the chief constables in the political arena has been all the more dynamic and disturbing because of the form and content of their political statements. For not only are the above statements a collective defence of an established order but also they reveal an ingrained and fundamentalist conservatism. They are not reflective of generalized 'British' political and moral values *but* values from within one narrow and intolerant tradition.

Furthermore, the occupational culture of police work can and, as has been shown, in some areas does reflect the worst excesses of this fundamentalism. These tensions have been marked particularly in the inner cities where whole areas, and therefore the people in them, are written off as 'scum', 'niggers' or 'slags'. Despite the mass of evidence, from within and from outside the police, concerning the implications of the collective attitudes which construct the 'mental map' of the force area, there has been a remarkable failure to exorcize forces of their prejudices and bigotry. Rather, senior officers have preferred to turn on their critics as some kind of proto-revolutionaries hell-bent on undermining the morale and credibility of the police in order to subvert the principles of justice and democracy. This line, in keeping with the Thatcher administration's constant referrals to 'the enemy within' and 'the loony left', is plausible and reflects a clear coincidence of interests between the fundamentalist conservatism present within the government, within ACPO and within the police officers' organizations. What is clear is that the police have come out from their political closets and affirmed their autonomy from governmental, local or national, control. This is a far cry from their public position as 'citizens-in-uniform' of the community 'performing their duties on behalf of us all'. In the operational policy decisions taken in camera at suite level to the operational practices carried out publicly at street level the law is not so much in the keeping of the police as in their possession. Before considering the implications of this in case-studies from 1985 it is important to outline, however schematically, the recent extensions of police powers carried through by successive Thatcher administrations amid much controversy.

Back from the 'Abyss'

The Conservatives' defeat in 1974 inevitably was linked to the perceived chaos in industrial relations which included the use of the law to gaol London dockers and Shrewsbury building workers, the three-day week, the power workers' strike and, most symbolically, the miners' victory at Saltley Gates.[66] The latter incident was taken as *the moment* when the predicted breakdown in law and order, the full-blown crisis in industrial relations, had arrived. The face-to-face, hand-to-hand victory of the mass pickets over the massed police symbolized the potential power and political solidarity of the unions and demonstrated beyond doubt that organized collective action on a large scale could close workplaces. Beyond this, however, it showed that the police were ill-equipped, tactically and organizationally to cope with such determined action.

> Many of those in positions of influence looked into the abyss and saw only a few days away the possibility of the country being plunged into a state of chaos not so very far removed from that which might prevail after a minor nuclear attack.... This is the power that existed to hold the country to ransom: it was the fear of that abyss which had an important effect on subsequent policy.[67]

In this account of British economic policy during the Heath period Brendon Sewill, then special assistant to the Chancellor of the Exchequer, explains that the handling of the 1972 miners' strike was left almost entirely to the National Coal Board. His opinion, shared by many of his contemporaries, was that if the Heath administration was to achieve its intended goal of moving towards a free-market economy, and challenge the Butskellite, Keynesian hold of the Macmillan years, inflation controls were essential and their achievement would be wholly dependent on restrictions on union power. The post-war consensus, which had served the Tory challenge to Attlee so well, was in its death throes.

Andrew Gamble's important work on the 1970s as a period of economic decline argues that the 'resistance of the unions' becomes a 'major obstacle to the 'rule of market' once 'the state has been rolled back'.[68] The legacy of industrial conflict and trade union consultation has been presented consistently by the right and its attendant media as one of excessively powerful unions. This is evident in Sewill's use of the populist phrase 'holding the country to ransom'. As Gamble states:

> From the point of view of social market theory trade unions are voluntary associations which have a legitimate purpose in providing insurance and welfare for their members. When, however, they seek to interfere in contracts in the labour market, and to influence attitudes and behaviour of employees at work, they cease to be involuntary associations and become coercive groups and private monopolies.... A minimal state does not mean a weak state. On the contrary, the state has to be strong to ensure the conditions in which a free economy can work. That means confronting and transforming all those institutions that stand in the way.[69]

Alongside the Tories' commitment to a free-market economy, conceived under Heath, was the construction of a 'law and order' platform with one of its central planks being a full-scale attack on 'secondary picketing'. In 1972 Maurice Macmillan, then Secretary of State for Employment, stated:

I hope we might get a code of picketing practice, interpreting the law into practical guidance for members of unions and helping to exclude those people who take part in those troubles who have nothing to do with them, have nothing to do with the unions concerned, have no concern for the good of the work-people and are there only to make trouble.[70]

This position gathered momentum throughout the mid-1970s remaining central to the Conservative opposition's 'law 'n' order' bandwagon and drawing significant support, as we have seen, from the police and also from the judiciary. Challenging the basis of the 'right' to strike, for example, Lord Denning argued that there was no such right in law, 'not at any rate when it is used so as to inflict great harm on innocent bystanders or to bring the country to a halt'.[71] For Denning striking was not an issue of 'rights' but one of 'power'.

As the Conservatives mounted their campaign to win the next election the issue of the 'power of the unions' slotted in neatly alongside the other essential strands: the dependency-creating welfare state and the pervasiveness of 'scrounging';[72] the decline of educational standards and performance due to comprehensive education;[73] the escalation of street crime, crimes of violence and political terrorism;[74] the growth of permissiveness, the decline of morality and the undermining of the 'family unit'.[75] The election of the first Thatcher Government in 1979 assured that each of these issues would be targeted for special attention. Within months Reg Prentice announced the setting up of a Specialist Claims Control Units to combat the 'menace' of the 'undeserving' poor.[76] Apart from this expansion which initially recruited over one thousand new fraud officers to the payroll of the DHSS, the police and the armed forces received exceptionally high pay awards, new legislation to curb union power was rushed on to the statute book, a family policy unit was established to advise the Government, a new police bill was drafted and a full-scale inquiry into public order – with a view to legislation – was instituted. The law 'n' order rhetoric fast became a reality. The many right-wing voluntary pressure groups and advisory organizations set up in the mid-1970s as the political and intellectual backbone of the 'New Right' had found a champion for their causes in Prime Minister Thatcher.[77]

Stuart Hall captured the mood of the period in transition:

We are now in the middle of a deep and decisive movement towards a more disciplinary authoritarian kind of society. This shift has been in progress since the 1960s; but has gathered pace throughout the 1970s and is heading, given the spate of disciplinary legislation now on the parliamentary agenda, towards some sort of interim climax.[78]

For Stuart Hall a 'regression towards stone-age morality' and the 'blind spasm of control' were the twin pillars of 'authoritarian populism' used to justify and rationalize deep political and institutional shift towards a strong authoritarian and coercive state. It was within this context that new law and strategies for its enforcement, on the cards after the confrontations of the early 1970s, were consolidated. The revitalized police forces would play an essential part in the process of consolidation with new and permissive powers guaranteed by the Employment Acts, the Prevention of Terrorism Act and, eventually, the Police and Criminal Evidence Act and the Public Order Act.

While the latter two Acts were being drafted and redrafted as Bills the full extent of the developments in police training and strategies following the inner-city uprisings of 1980–81 became evident in the police response to the coal dispute. It soon emerged that the events of the Heath period would never again be repeated. First, the Civil Contingencies Unit had been established to report to the Cabinet on key industries and the likelihood of industrial action. Second, the National Reporting Centre had been set up at Scotland Yard to be activated in the event of major civil disorder or industrial action. It is run by the current president of ACPO and is intended to provide mutual aid across force boundaries in the form of specially trained Police Support Units (PSUs). Third, a high proportion of officers from each force had received new forms of colonial-style, riot-training using the full range of offensive equipment. Fourth, ACPO had produced a top-secret manual, *Public Order, Tactical Operations*, which included the following extraordinary instruction:

> [Shortshield squads] ... disperse the crowd and incapacitate missile throwers and ringleaders by striking in a controlled manner with batons about the arms and legs and torso so as not to cause injury. To use the show of force to the greatest advantage officers should make a formidable appearance.[70]

This short extract was one of the only parts of the manual to be revealed and its legality was challenged by Gareth Peirce, the solicitor for defendants in the trial of miners prosecuted for serious public order offences at Orgreave.[80] Despite attempts by the Association of Metropolitan Authorities to gain access to the manual its contents remained restricted to members of ACPO.

Taken together the implications of these moves are clear. With the political autonomy of chief constables secured, the capacity of the police to work as a national force established and the paramilitary tactics, training and equipment supported by central government, ACPO had emerged as the single most influential 'law and order' body – in terms of law-making as well as policy decisions – within the state.[81] This authoritarian shift was achieved without consultation with police authorities, without parliamentary debate and without informed public discussion. Consultation had been confined to closed, regular meetings held between the Home Secretary, the Attorney General and ACPO. Given the coincidence of interests at the political level the outcome was hardly surprising. It was soon reinforced on the statute book.

The extension of Police Powers

In January 1986 to 1984 Police and Criminal Evidence Act (PACE) became operational. The highly controversial Bill,[83] drafted and redrafted by successive Thatcher administrations, brought to fruition many of the recommendations made by Sir David McNee – then Metropolitan Commissioner – to the 1980 Royal Commission on Criminal Procedure. This was hardly surprising given that:

> McNee's proposals dominated the public perception of the work of the Royal Commission. They strongly influenced the proposals emerging from the rest of the police... undoubtedly the most influential set of recommendations received by the Commission, and the most detailed manifesto of police intentions in the exercise of their principal task: the enforcement of criminal law.[84]

McNee's evidence to the Royal Commission also noted that certain irregular practices, such as the abuse of Judges' Rules during periods of detention, had become institutionalized.

It was his position that this was necessary to enable officers to be effective in questioning suspects. His conclusion was that powers should be extended in order to meet the demands on police officers. The powers given to the police by the Act certainly place them well beyond the realms of 'citizens-in-uniform'. They have the power to use force in stop-and-search on the street, to enter forcibly the houses of people *not* under suspicion of criminal activity, to take samples and fingerprints forcibly from people detained without charge and to use force in strip and intimate body searches. Police powers of arrest without warrant have been extended to include people suspected of committing any offence if they refuse to give their name; if the name given is believed by the police to be false; if they have not given a 'satisfactory' address; if they might harm themselves or others, damage property, obstruct the highway or cause an 'affront to public decency'; if there is a child or other 'vulnerable' person at risk. A lawful arrest is made as long as the person is told that she or he is under arrest and has been given a reason. In specified circumstances the police can then search the person and the place where the arrest took place.

The Act enables the police to hold a person in custody without charge for up to 24 hours, on the authority of an inspector, in order to secure or 'preserve' evidence or to allow questioning to continue. This period can be extended for up to 60 hours, on the authority of a superintendent, and a further 36 hours on a magistrate's authorization, if a person is suspected of a 'serious arrestable offence'. This category includes murder, rape, kidnapping, firearms and explosives offences, hijacking and hostage-taking. It also includes *any* offence under the Prevention of Terrorism Act (PTA). The most controversial cases here, however, are those which *might* lead to serious harm to state security or public order, serious interference with the administration of justice, serious injury or death to another person, substantial gain or serious financial loss to anybody. This final category is elastic: 'having regard to all circumstances, serious for the person who suffers it'. Each of these categories reaffirms the broad operational discretion made available to police officers in defining 'seriousness' and thus being able to detain people without charge for up to 4 days and nights.

While a detainee has the right to have a friend, relative or other person informed of her/his detention and the right to consult *privately* with a solicitor, *suspicion* of a 'serious arrestable offence' removes these rights. A superintendent can delay access for up to 36 hours or, for PTA charges, for up to 48 hours. Searches for property, including strip searches and intimate body searches (mouth, anus, vagina) are also permitted under the 1984 Act. They can take place without consent and, if necessary, by force. Non-intimate body samples and fingerprints can be taken without consent and 'reasonable force' can be used. The issue of discretion dominates the phrasing of the 1984 Act and continues to be central to the use and abuse of police powers. As discussed earlier, this includes the use of road-blocks to seal off areas and the cordoning-off of neighbourhoods on the grounds that an offence is 'likely' to be committed.[85] This leaves the police free to use road-blocks as they feel appropriate. A further example relates to warrants. For the checks on police powers of search (magistrates' warrants for general searches; judges' warrants for access to confidential records) can be ignored if the police believe that important evidence might be removed or be at risk.

Effectively PACE has institutionalized processes which previously walked the fine line of legitimacy. In defending the Act the police and Conservative politicians argue that there is a new code of practice including a detainee's right to a record of all that happens while in custody, information on rights, access to a solicitor, rest periods and the rights of householders relating to search. The code restricts the police yet the investigation of complaints and sanctions for breaking the code are administered internally. Discretion remains the central issue whether this relates to 'reasonable force', 'reasonable suspicion' or 'serious, arrestable offence'.

In May 1985 Leon Brittan, then Home Secretary, announced the official release of the Conservative Government's White Paper: Review of Public Order Law.[86] His statement to the House of Commons directed the White Paper's proposals towards 'criminal offences committed daily on the picket-line'.[87] With the 1984–5 coal dispute fresh in the minds of the general public Brittan placed the issue of industrial conflict within a more generalized imagery of violence: 'People have the right to protection against being bullied, hurt, intimidated or obstructed, whatever the motive of those responsible may be, whether they are violent demonstrators, rioters, intimidatory mass pickets, or soccer hooligans.'[88] This use of the 'spectrum of violence', so much a central theme of Margaret Thatcher's speeches on law and order, became a feature of the media's response to the White Paper.

Phil Scraton

Whatever the varying quality of the media comment on the White Paper its coverage of the proposals consolidated a well-established commitment to the central themes: that violent civil disorder is on the increase and existing new laws inhibit its regulation and containment; that there exists a spectrum of violence which ranges from acts considered to be intimidatory to serious acts of personal violence and political terrorism; that the majority of people are decent, law-abiding citizens and need to be protected from the excesses of the 'enemy within'.

Thus the White Paper, which provided the basis for the 1986 Public Order Act, was introduced and portrayed as a reasonable and rational response to difficult situations in which the 'right' to demonstrate and protest needs to be balanced against the 'protection' of the 'wider community'. From the outset this assumed that that had been previously understood as constituting fundamental rights, such as political demonstrations and industrial picketing, reflecting interests which *inherently* are opposed to the interests of the wider community. Within a month of the Thatcher Government's 1979 election the then Home Sectretary, William Whitelaw, announced a full review of public order. The eventual Public Order Act drew on four subtantive reports[80] and the 'lessons learnt' from specific events, such as the coal dispute, and general issues, such as animal rights protests, Greenham women's protests and football hooliganism.

The 1986 Public Order Act, therefore, is geared to have the regulation both of 'static demonstrations' and of marches. Also it legislates against newly defined specific offences. Under the Act it is an offence to hold a march or demonstration unless at least 7 days' notice has been given to the police. Marches can be banned by the police if they have reason to believe that they might lead to public disorder. There is a new criminal offence of taking part in a banned march and, accordingly, police officers have the powers to arrest. They have the powers also to regulate marches by insisting on specific conditions which can be extended to new, immediate conditions made by the most senior officer on duty at the time of a march or demonstration. These powers have been extended to the policing of many open air static demonstrations which will be subject to police conditions concerning the number of demonstrators, the precise location of the demonstration and the overall direction of the events. New powers of arrest have been introduced for the offence of 'watching and besetting'.[90]

There are new statutory offences of riot, violent disorder and affray carrying maximum penalties of 10 years', 5 years' and 3 years' imprisonment respectively. Each covers situations in which people are together in a private or public place, using or threatening to use, unlawful violence towards other people or towards property. There has to be established, or 'inferred' from their conduct, that there is a 'common purpose' and that a 'reasonable' person present would fear for their safety. It extends the previous common law offence, which was restricted to the actual use of force or violence, to that of the *threat* to use force or violence. Beyond this 'disorderly words or behaviour' have been introduced as categories for prosecution where 'alarm or distress' is caused. The permissiveness and breadth of this new offence effectively criminalizes any form of 'disorderly' behaviour – real or imagined.

The 1986 Public Order Act, therefore, confirms the absolute operational discretion of chief constables without any requirement for consultation with police authorities. Chief constables have been empowered to ban individual demonstrations, impose conditions on marches and processions, control the size, location and duration of static demonstrations or public meetings. That the police are to be the sole possessors of decision-making over public order, be it in advance preparation and notification or 'on the ground', has been placed beyond doubt by the 1986 Act. As matters of operational policy, encompassing a whole spread of significant local factors in any given situation, it might have been expected that such decisions would have been negotiable with democratically elected members of police authorities. In not one of these decisions, however, will chief constables be accountable to police authorities.

Alongside the general issue of policy decisions is the extension of police powers in terms of the operational policies of individual officers. The enforcement of the newly codified offences of riot, unlawful assembly, affray and disorderly behaviour remains highly discretionary, particularly the inclusion of the subjective category of 'threatening' behaviour. This allows for the criminalization of almost any action, deliberate or otherwise, which might instil fear into another person.[91] Given that the White Paper gave the example of youths 'shouting obscenities' or 'pestering' people, the potential range of the offence is immense. This broad extension of police powers, a consolidation of new powers defined within PACE, will result in many convictions solely on police evidence. Taken together the 1984 PACE and the 1986 Public Order Act have provided a major development in the autonomy of chief constables and their senior officers in the policies and practices of police operations.

1985: 'The Year of Living Dangerously'

> At one end of the spectrum are the terrorist gangs within our borders and the terrorist states which arm them. At the other are the hard left, operating inside our system, conspiring to use union power and the apparatus of local government to break, defy and subvert the laws. Now the mantle has fallen on us to conserve the very principle of parliamentary democracy and the rule of law itself.[92]

This attack by Prime Minister Margaret Thatcher late in 1984 was by far her most virulent against the 'fascist Left'. She generalized picket-line violence during the coal dispute and interpreted this as being symptomatic of the sinister subversion of democracy and the destruction of the rule of law. As with a simultaneous speech by the then Home Secretary, Leon

Brittan, the clear intention was to place the legitimate use of union power and the properly constituted apparatus of local government in the category of the 'hard Left' and to equate this with acts of political terrorism. Democratically elected union officials involved in their lawful duty of organizing pickets at their place of work and democratically elected councils which saw fit to support the strike were moulded together with acts of terrorist violence and presented as the 'enemy within'. The Conservatives in office were cast as the saviours of parliamentary democracy and the rule of law. The law and order ideology, evident in the rhetoric of the Brittan/Thatcher speeches, demonstrated the precise coincidence of interests between the Government and ACPO. It was in this climate that PACE was to be introduced and the Public Order Bill drafted and passed.

In May 1985 when the first details of the Public Order White Paper were leaked to the media the first television news coverage used out-takes of soccer violence, picket-line clashes and Greenham women to announce a 'tough-line on hooliganism, thuggery, militancy and terrorism. The juxtaposition of such widely diverse categories of 'acts of violence' and 'threats to the democracy' became the central ideological construction of the political representation and media portrayal of the 'necessity' for extended police powers. Thatcher's 'spectrum of violence' became the essential material of the media's response to the White Paper. The *Daily Express*, for example, lauded Brittan's proposals in the 'aftermath of race riots, animal rights demos, Greenham, the miners' strike, the Libyan Embassy siege and soccer violence'.[93] The marginalization of protesters as criminals, even terrorists, was evident in Brittan's appeal to decency and respectability and it was a sentiment echoed throughout the tabloid press and the *Daily Telegraph* and *The Times*. Each of the major themes of the authoritarian response to law and order were present: that violent civil disorder is on the increase and existing laws inhibit its containment; that there exists a spectrum of violence which ranges from 'intimidation' to serious acts of personal violence and political terrorism; that the majority of people are decent, law-abiding citizens with a deep sense of moral responsibility who need to be protected from the excesses of the 'enemy within'. Thus in the spring of 1985 the White Paper was introduced and portrayed as a reasonable and rational response to difficult situations in which the right to demonstrate and protest has to be 'balanced' against the protection of the 'wider community'.

By 1985, then, the political position over law and order and the administration of criminal justice had consolidated around a series of policy initiatives and statutory changes which were justified on the basis of the absolute, self-evident necessity of an authoritarian response to crime, civil disorder and industrial conflict. The police had affirmed their autonomy in operational policies, priorities and practices and had adopted widespread paramilitary strategies, training programmes and equipment. The courts were geared to the broad and permissive use of the law and legal powers, such as the imposition of blanket bail conditions, to regulate protest.[94] This climate was also one in which reactionary policies over sentencing, parole and the extension of the use of imprisonment could be brought to fruition.[95] Finally, new law had been codified and was about to be introduced. In that sense the process of criminalization was complete.

The political management and containment of opposition to this authoritarianism had been clear throughout the 1984–5 coal dispute, permeating the thinking and response of the police involved on picket lines and their selective enforcement of the law. It led to unparalleled scenes of police aggression at Orgreave where pickets were charged repeatedly by riot police on horseback and on foot.[96] It brought the cordoning off of Armthorpe and the handing out of arbitrary punishment to those who ventured on to the streets and voiced their concern. It was present in the courts where bail conditions and payments of costs were used as instruments of direct punishment and the control of picketing. It was reinforced daily by an almost universally hostile media and a persistently biased news coverage of the dispute. What the dispute demonstrated was that as part of the process of regulation which contains resistance to the inherent structural inequalities of British society, operational policy remained firmly rooted in the interests of employers and their political representatives and affiliates. This regulation and its forceful application was inherited by other situations in 1985 where people received direct notice that a paramilitary response would be exercised readily by the police as a first option rather than as a last resort.

In 1984 Michael Heseltine was showered with red paint at a student demonstration in Manchester. This was one in a series of such demonstrations against the Government and against 'right-wing' speakers by students during the year. Early in 1985 John Carlisle MP was attacked at Bradford University while defending economic and social links with South Africa. This led to the cancellation of visits to other institutions and much media debate about free speech at institutions of higher education. On 1 March 1985 Leon Brittan, then Home Secretary, was to speak at the University of Manchester Students' Union on 'Law and Order'. There was a substantial but not excessive number of students on the steps of their union awaiting the arrival of Leon Brittan and an appropriate number of police officers there in attendance. Just after 7 p.m., however, a squad of approximately forty officers, following an inspector, descended on the crowd and without warning or instruction forced their way on to the steps punching and kicking the students and throwing them physically down the steps. The accounts of these events in statements to the Students' Union and to a later inquiry[97] alleged violence by the police against peaceful demonstrators of a most serious nature. Students claimed to have been punched, kicked, elbowed, dragged by the hair and thrown down the steps to the concrete pavement. Also they alleged obscene verbal abuse and personal degradation by the police. At no time were the students asked to clear the steps and there were few arrests. What was clear from the allegations and from television and photographic coverage, as well as from eye-witness accounts, was that the police used force arbitrarily and unreasonably, inflicting considerable pain and punishment on the students. Subsequent evidence has shown that the operation was planned carefully and the decision about the operational practices were premeditated and taken at a high level.[98] The Independent Inquiry concluded:

> We believe that the events in Manchester have to be seen in the context of [recent and undemocratic] legal developments and changes in policing. The policing of the demonstration outside the Students' Union at Manchester University on 1 March 1985 involved the unacceptable use of force and abusive language by police officers well-trained in public order policing, against innocent civilians participating in a peaceful demonstration. We can only conclude that this sort of conduct forms part of the training of these officers, and is now considered an acceptable part of this type of policing. We consider this to be wholly unacceptable.[99]

Following the serious complaints made against the Greater Manchester Police, officers from the Avon and Somerset force were brought in to conduct the police inquiry.

Soon after the visit of Leon Brittan the students held a mass meeting to decide on their plan of action. The meeting was concerned particularly over the injuries sustained by a Student Union Council member, Sarah Hollis, who had been thrown down the steps by the police and knocked unconscious. Another student, Steven Shaw, who had contact with the Manchester City Police Monitoring Unit spoke at the meeting and he suggested involving the Unit by submitting witness statements. From that moment both Steven Shaw and Sarah Hollis allege a catalogue of police harassment which included burglary at their homes, anonymous telephone calls, persistent following and stopping, and threatening behaviour. Steven Shaw claimed that on 14 May 1985 he was taken to Bootle Street Police Station to assist with police inquiries into the Home Secretary's visit. He claims that he was strip-searched and one officer assaulted him by inserting his finger in his anus. The following day after giving evidence to the police inquiry Sarah Hollis states that she was stopped by two men and threatened with arrest. Both students went into hiding but on 15 June Sarah Hollis was stopped again by two men who made it known to her that they were aware that she was due to go into hospital for routine checks. They said:

> We have been told that you paid a visit to the Inquiry at the Town Hall today: been telling them some of your little lies have you? Well, you can just go back tomorrow and tell them . . . none of it was true . . . if you don't we'll pay you a little visit in hospital next week . . . we can just walk into the Ward M3 Female and really give the doctors something to sort out . . . or we could sort something out when you get out of hospital. Yeah, how do you fancy getting

fucked by a black man? You would probably enjoy it because a little bitch like you would never get laid any other time.[100]

Steven Shaw was badly beaten up again almost a year after the events. Sarah Hollis withdrew her evidence and refused to discuss the matter further and Steven Shaw fled the country in order to avoid further harassment. In February 1987 following the completion of police inquiries it was announced by the Police Complaints Authority (PCA) that two officers were to be charged with perjury and one with assault relating to the incidents at the students' union and that five officers were to be reminded of the need for 'greater accuracy' when making entries in their notebooks. In the case of eight assaults which they accepted no action would be taken because of the failure to identify officers. The PCA report did not confirm allegations that police officers had removed or hidden their numbers. Of the burglaries the PCA report had nothing to say. Furthermore the PCA report did not comment on the serious allegations of collaboration between officers, particularly on the part of the investigating officers from the Avon and Somerset force. Finally with regard to the serious case of Steven Shaw it was revealed that the DPP was to charge him with an 'attempt to pervert the course of justice'. Nothing was revealed of the complaints made by Sarah Hollis. In March 1987 she stated that she had been bullied by police officers from the Avon and Somerset Police who were investigating her complaints and that given the outcome of the internal inquiry she had no faith in the police complaints procedure.[101]

The style of response adopted by the police in Manchester was taken as being a clear indication that 'ordinary' situations of public protest were to be policed more aggressively using newly developed riot-training such as wedges and snatch squads. In 1985 these developments extended to the unlikely setting of Stonehenge where members of the self-styled 'Peace Convoy' intended to hold their annual celebration of the Summer Solstice. In April the *Daily Telegraph* announced:

> A police task force, using tactics that curbed the violent excesses of the miners' 'flying pickets' during the pit strike, is to go into action in June to protect Stonehenge.[102]

Three weeks prior to the festival road-blocks were put up around Stonehenge and on 1 June the police joined forces with the Ministry of Defence and local childcare departments of the Social Services to disperse the Peace Convoy. Nick Davies, an *Observer* reporter, joined the convoy as the riot police set about wrecking mobile homes and vehicles and arresting their inhabitants. The television coverage of the events bore out his report:

> I witnessed women and children being hit with truncheons, glass from broken vehicle windows showering down on those inside and a mother dragged out of a shattered window with her child and thrown weeping to the ground... windows were smashed by the police and occupants were dragged out through

a storm of truncheons; broken heads, broken teeth, broken spectacles. It was a whirl of destruction. Officers started to climb through windows, lashing out at all sides with their sticks. Reporters screamed at the police to calm down.[103]

Eleven of the convoy children were taken immediately into care and there were 550 arrests. A local landowner, the Earl of Cardigan, who allowed the convoy members to shelter on his land stated:

I shall never forget the screams of one woman who was holding up her little baby in a bus with smashed windows. She screamed and screamed at them to stop, but five seconds later 50 men with truncheons and shields just boiled into that bus. It was mayhem, no other word for it.[104]

Within months all charges of unlawful assembly against 241 of those arrested were dropped. There was no explanation as to why the police officers used excessive levels of force or why 'as part of the contingency plan, a small team of firearms officers was on hand'.[105] Apart from the serious implications for civil liberties[106] the use of a high degree of force, in Manchester and then Wiltshire, in a carefully pre-planned and orchestrated operation again raised major questions about riot-trained police as a 'first-line' response.

Given the 'dual messages' received by communities or groups 'marginalized', and targeted by renewed police responses – on the one hand the message of trust and support promised by community policing on the other the hard-line message of the truncheon and the shield – it was only a matter of time before inner-city black communities responded to the increase in police harassment. On 9 September 1985 in Handsworth, Birmingham youths replied angrily to persistent harassment, threw petrol bombs and looted shops, and two Asians died in a shop fire.

In his report to the Home Secretary Geoffrey Dear, the Chief Constable of West Midlands, directed responsibility for the disturbances away from police–community relations. He stated:

There is firm evidence to suggest that the disorders were at the outset orchestrated by local drug dealers who had become fearful of the demise of their livelihoods... the riots were fuelled and organized by persons who require the supply of drugs to continue their lifestyle.... There is no doubt that the police drug operation against dealers caused a sense of frustration.[107]

There resulted bitter controversy because of the resistance to a public inquiry and the credibility given to an internal police inquiry. This was heightened by the Chief Constable's request to the police committee to lift its ban on plastic bullets as the use of baton rounds 'would have been justified' during the disturbances. A local church-related community group, All Faiths for One Race, wrote an open letter to the Chief Constable stating police strategy was 'playing the interests of one group off against another and ensuring that divisions occur or are exacerbated' and 'should the use of weaponry used by the police give rise to death or injury, the responsibility lies squarely with the police'.[108] In July 1986 Geoffrey Dear defended his new programme of police riot-training on the basis of the increasing incidence of violence faced by the police in public order situations.[109] It was clear that opposition to the development of forceful interventionist strategies including the use of baton rounds had not altered his position.

Soon after the Handsworth conflict serious disturbances erupted in Britain. Following the shooting of Mrs Cherry Groce by a police officer, leaving her paralysed from the waist down, there was immediate anger in the community. For seven officers had broken down the door to her house in a search for her son. The police station was attacked with petrol bombs and the police response was to introduce riot equipment. There was an immediate escalation in the violence on the streets. A Lambeth press release stated:

> A number of tenants reported damage to their homes which they say was caused by the police. The police were seen running along a balcony smashing windows with their truncheons. Doors were kicked in and one police officer allegedly said, 'This is how we treat you niggers' as he smashed a front door.[110]

A *Guardian* sub-editor, Celia Locks, resident in Brixton stated:

> I saw several people hit by truncheons. In Acre Lane a man was lying on his back splayed through a smashed glass window. Bystanders said a policeman had pushed him through the window which had already been broken. I saw an exultant policeman waving his truncheon and shield above his head as though in triumph. The police charged along Acre Lane, vans driving ahead so that people were effectively trapped between squads. Officers aggressively chased people, hitting out with truncheons.... Three officers ran up to four of us walking along. One of them shoved his shield into my back and said, 'You fucking bitch'. My home, about half a mile away, seemed very far ... a few officers, wielding truncheons and shields charged up the road. This time I tried to run out of the way but stopped when an officer came after me. Shoving me into a shop doorway, he pushed a truncheon under my chin and fingered my right breast. When I said I was not doing anything he said, 'What are you doing on the streets then, love? Go home!' It appeared that these streets had become a 'No Go' area for civilians.[111]

A week later the police raided the home of Cynthia Jarrett in Tottenham without a search warrant. She collapsed and died during the raid and there followed a peaceful protest march to Tottenham Police Station. That evening there was a massive confrontation between the police and the people on the Broadwater Farm Estate as riot-clad officers faced barricades and petrol bombs. The police drummed their shields and there was extensive street fighting which culminated in the killing of PC Keith Blakelock. During the evening the Metropolitan Commissioner deployed CS gas and baton rounds. Newman's decision was supported by the following statement:

> I wish to put all people of London on notice that I will not shrink from such a

decision should I believe it a practical option for restoring peace and preventing crime or injury.[112]

Following the killing of the police officer it was inevitable that there would be a high police profile on Broadwater Farm. The estate was put under virtual siege with police officers on every landing of the flats and at all meeting points. Relations remained strained as police officers smashed down doors in pursuit of their investigations. Haringey Council set up an inquiry into the policing of the estate but the police declined to give evidence.[113] Just four days before the independent inquiry published its recommendations the Metropolitan Commissioner published a review on public order. A new paramilitary force, the Territorial Support Group, was announced as the 'first wave' response to public disorder. In the review Newman stated that the 'traditional role of the "British bobby" is no longer compatible with that of an officer engaged in riot control'.[114] The new TSGs, Newman admitted, would 'take us to a point midway to a third force'.[115]

Thus it had become clear towards the end of 1985 that at the level of operational policies and practices the priorities were clearly set for policing the remaining years of the decade and beyond. At a policy level the ACPO manual's objectives, as far as they have been made known, have been consolidated into broader strategies for policing civil disorder. The use of riot equipment and specially trained Territorial Support Groups as a first-line paramilitary option have been formulated throughout Britain's police forces as an effective 'third force'. Well-tried police strategies developed both in Commonwealth countries and, most pertinently, in Northern Ireland have become incorporated into the police response. The overall justification for these developments from the Home office, the chief constables and spokespeople from the police organizations has been the 'rising tide' of street violence and the establishment of 'criminal communities' as 'no-go' areas for the police. In his 1987 speech to the Association of Conservative Lawyers, referred to in the introductory chapter, Newman made it clear that the 'targets' are at the heart of the predominantly black communities.

What 1985 also provided, however, was clear evidence of the extent to which police officers were prepared to go in carrying out this more aggressive policy. Just as the ACPO manual raises questions about the legitimation of unlawful behaviour on the part of the police so the broader implications of more forceful first-line strategies involving the deployment of riot police raise serious doubts over the use of 'reasonable force'. In all the above examples serious allegations have been made consistently concerning the use of unreasonable levels of force. In 1985 this issue was at its sharpest in the events of 1st and 2nd October in Toxteth, Merseyside.

1985: 'Punishment Park'

'There's no question of the police being brutal – they're marked men if they start that business. They're normal family people and I'm the same as them: you react to a situation as it develops. Once a prisoner starts violence he's going to be arrested come what may! And the more force he's going to use, the more force is going to be applied to him. I very rarely see force in excess of need.'[116]

This quote is taken from an interview with a senior police surgeon on Merseyside in the late 1970s. Soon after this, events in the Metropolitan Borough of Knowsley, Merseyside Police's 'K' Division, brought widespread allegations of brutality and intimidation against officers based at the Huyton Police Station. The events took place in the summer of 1979 and culminated in a vote of no confidence in the police being taken by the council, the local MP, Sir Harold Wilson, writing to the Home Secretary and a crisis between the Merseyside Police Committee and the Chief Constable, Kenneth Oxford, coming to a head when he instructed elected members publicly to 'keep out of my force's business'.[117] The details of the course of events[118] and the specific cases, including the death of Jimmy Kelly in police custody,[119] are dealt with in Chapter 7 but it soon became clear that what began with specific questions over certain cases soon escalated into a major issue with national implications over the political accountability of the police. As a direct result of the controversy between the Chief Constable and the police committee the county solicitor was asked to prepare a full and thorough report on the role and responsibilities of the police authority. His report was presented in 1980 and its conclusion was that in terms of operational police decisions and the practices of police officers the police committee effectively had no powers to direct or instruct the chief constable.[120]

No sooner had these events provoked considerable public concern over the policing of Merseyside, in terms of policy decisions and the use of force, than further events, this time in the inner-city area of Toxteth, occurred which reaffirmed this concern. The major civil disturbances of 1980–81 demonstrated nationally that inner-city communities, particularly black people in those communities, had become alienated from the police as a direct result of years of institutionalized racism in the police and the persistent targeting of black communities as 'high crime' areas. While much that has been written on the 'disturbances', 'riots' or 'uprisings' has focused on pluralized versions of black people's experiences of racism – presented either as a problem of individual attitude or as a series of structural problems including unemployment, bad housing, poverty, under-achievement in schools – the centrality of racism in police policy and practices has been underplayed. What is clear from even a brief examination of the relationship between the police and the black communities in Liverpool is that black people have suffered and endured racist abuse and the arbitrary use of excessive force at the hands of the police over a long period of time. This has been the direct result of a well-established programme of differential policing which has sought to target black people as being 'more likely than not' to have been involved in crime and therefore worthy of extra attention as 'suspected persons'.[121]

A Police Committee Working Party was set up during the Toxteth uprising and it reported in October 1981. Of central concern to the working party was the allegation 'expressed most frequently and often' within the Toxteth community: that of police harassment. This included: 'indiscriminate and extensive use of formal stop and search procedures'; 'verbal abuse and physical violence on the part of the police'; 'subsequent arrests on the sole charge of assaulting an officer'; 'overpolicing and/or aggressive policing'. Additionally the working group stated its profound concern over allegations raised with a high degree of consistency: the stereotyping of large sections of the community as potential criminals or second-class citizens; a lack of respect for the area's residents and their rights; a lack of understanding of and sympathy for the life-styles of different ethnic groups; persistent verbal and racist abuse. The group's conclusion was that the 'sheer weight of adverse evidence compels us to recognise that a gulf exists between the police and certain sections of the community in Liverpool 8'.[122]

With Lord Scarman mildly criticizing the police for differential policing initiatives and the Merseyside Police Committee Working Group severe in its response to its findings, the sustained pressure on senior officers to reply to the charges of harassment, brutality and abuse consolidated. On Merseyside, however, the Chief Constable already had available a well-rehearsed justification for his hard-line, differential policing strategy. Writing in 1980 he argued that the Merseyside Police faced a 'frequently hectic, often dangerous task' due to the fact that 'crime and disorder are ever present and always have been so throughout the turbulent history of the city'.[123] In his evidence to Scarman, Kenneth Oxford devoted an entire chapter to arguing that allegations made against the police over harassment, aggressive methods, racial discrimination, the operation of the complaints procedure and inadequate training were unfounded. Juxtaposed to his dismissal of the working group's findings was the claim that Merseyside in general, and Toxteth in particular, had come to be dominated by lawlessness, militancy and violence. For, 'it is a matter of historical fact that Liverpool has been beset by problems of violence and public disorder throughout the centuries'.[124] He described the 'Liverpudlian' as having an 'aggressive nature' with a reputation for being 'proportionately tougher, more violent and more pugnacious' than the inhabitants of other seaports, where drunkenness and violence always have been a way of life.

In Oxford's evidence he left Scarman in no doubt that Liverpool's reputation as a 'tough, violent city' had been fulfilled and he listed a history of 'riots' by strikers and the unemployed in support of this claim. Violence and militancy were seen to be self-evident and were understandable in terms of nature, culture and tradition. The responses of trade unionists and the poor between the wars as resistance to low wages, casual work unemployment and grinding poverty were dismissed as meaningless violence and wanton destruction by the socially inadequate or the pathologically criminal.

Having established the historical roots of Merseyside's violence in general terms Oxford singled out Toxteth, the area which had grown up, ironically, around the traditionally wealthy boulevards of Prince's Park, and its immigrant populations as presenting an added dimension to the problem of violence: that of race. He listed the arrival of Irish immigrants, Welsh rural labourers, numerous 'other foreign nationalities' and then, following the Great War, 'a remarkable increase in the number of coloured immigrants'. Immigration contributed significantly to the 'turbulent character' of the city and Oxford attributed poverty, unemployment and overcrowding specifically to the Irish, 'which then, as now, were the breeding grounds for violence'. He concluded that 'each of these communities brought with them associated problems, disputes and tensions which on occasion spilled over into outbreaks of violence'. In fulfilling 'her [sic] reputation as a tough, violent city' Liverpool could rely on its pathological outsiders. He noted that in the post-war period 'there were violent disturbances involving the presence of United States forces; between Chinese and other coloured residents; anti-Jewish riots; between white and coloured people in the vicinity of Upper Parliament Street'. The history of religious, race, class and feminist struggles in Liverpool was collapsed into portrayals and explanations of violence which provided a convenient synthesis of pathological aggression and cultural transmission.

In dealing with the contemporary situation Oxford quoted extensively from the Chief Constable's Reports from 1975 onwards. His predecessor 'referred to a decline in standards of self-discipline, which is reflected among young people, some of whom have no respect for the law and no sense of responsibility to society, a decline which is manifested in the ever spiralling increase in crime of all classifications and particularly crimes of violence'. This spiral was specified in terms of 'criminals who set out to rob quite deliberately armed with firearms, axes, wooden clubs . . ., or those who drag old ladies off their feet to steal the modest contents of their handbags'. In this analysis clearly appalling acts of violence were generalized throughout 'young people'. Consequently the acts of a few became the criteria by which whole communities were to be judged. Oxford relentlessly pursued this line. In 1976 it was 'crimes of material violence . . . which intrude so much upon everyday life' and also 'the increase in offences of violence in which females are the attackers'. Violence, said Oxford, was 'a disease of national and international proportions'. With crime caused by 'greed, selfishness and violence' he argued that 'either the thieves and vandals will take control, or, restrictive legislation will be introduced to curtail their freedom and inevitably that of decent society'. According to Oxford, the distance between the decent and the criminal was 'fundamental'.

Working with the same logic which he applied to his historical analysis it comes as no surprise to find that Oxford located the crime problem particularly within the pathology of immigrant communities. In his chapter on crime he stated that there had been a 74% increase in crimes of violence against the person throughout Merseyside since 1979. Most of this crime he situated in Toxteth, 'where large numbers of ethnic minorities, including blacks, live'. As presented, the selected, and selective, statistics centred Merseyside's violent crime spiral on Toxteth. Theft from the person was shown to be five times greater and robbery ten times greater than the national average. According to Oxford the Toxteth area has become the 'natural homing ground for immigrants', the base for 'so-called mugging' and the place where 'street prostitution is customary and there is a flourishing drug traffic'. Taken together the escalation in crime and violence and the long history of violence and militancy provide the backcloth to Oxford's policy initiatives. He concluded that this range of evidence demonstrated that crime and violence 'foreshadow the recent events in Toxteth and indicate some of the problems with which the Merseyside Police has had to contend since its formation in 1974'.

The juxtaposition of general assertions about the apparent genetic, or at least culturally learnt, violent characteristics of the 'Liverpudlian' and the racist environmentalism delivers an inevitability of violence and a conscious disregard for *all* law. Immigrants are shown as bringing with them only associated tensions and cultural inadequacies. Presumably young blacks are caught both ways: born as Liverpudlians into an inherently violent community. The portrayal of endemic violence is not new, it merely reinforces Liverpool's reputation as a 'tough city'. Through this reputation is offered a whole range of easy explanations: the hard-bitten humour, the close camaraderie, the infamous militancy, the street crime and lawlessness, the disregard for authority, the tragedy at Heysel Stadium; the story goes on. Specifically, Oxford's neat dovetail of genetic characteristics and social contagion provides him with an obvious explanation for Toxteth's high rates of crime. This is the focus of the country's 'worst law and order' problem. It enables him to remain within the community not only in his search for explanations but also in his application of policy. For no one escapes the inner-city web of violence, except the consensual, white, semi-detached, professional classes to whom this lawlessness is a constant threat.

Coming, as it did, from a chief constable the broad use of reputations of crime and violence as a justification for police strategies and practices – an operational police orientation which prioritized and consolidated the well-established tradition of differential policing – provides a clear basis to an understanding of police work. For it is through the reputation that the hard-line police responses, at both policy and practice levels, come to be justified not only to politicians or the media but also throughout the force. A tough, rough people require a tough, rough police response. Specified neighbour-hoods become 'war zones' – places where the imagery is reflected not only in the attitudes and practices of the police officers 'on the ground' but also where it forms the very foundations of operational policy. It is an imagery which is deeply institutionalized and underpins differential policing policies, strategies and practices. It was used by Oxford to explain and justify the use of saturation policing and aggressive tactics. It presented the public response to the Toxteth uprising in 1981 as the necessary use of violence in response to violence – a public order problem so massive, yet so indigenous that out-siders could not grasp it. It explains Merseyside's militant reputation, its strikes, its hooliganism, its street crime and, especially, its urban riots.

Following a series of incidents in Toxteth during 1985 a number of allegations were made to the Police Committee and to its chairperson, Councillor Margaret Simey, concerning insensitive policing and also police harassment of black people in the community. A series of meetings was held in the community in June at which a range of problems were raised by community representatives. These included: the deployment of the Operational Support Division (OSD) in Toxteth using unmarked vehicles; aggressive and racist policing against black people in the city centre; the use of unreasonable force in evicting black demonstrators from a City Council meeting; selective searches of 'black only' properties following a bank raid; a raid on the Toxteth Sports Centre; the stereotyping of black people as criminals despite Scarman initiatives in training; the inadequacy of the police complaints system and the 'reality' of police reprisals against complainants.[125] These allegations were repeated in September 1985 at a meeting of the Granby Police/Community Liaison Forum, attended by the Deputy Chief Constable, when the picture portrayed by many black people was one of being contained within Toxteth by hostile and racist policing in the city centre and by the 'heavy presence of police on the perimeter of the Toxteth section with vehicles operating sirens and containing numbers of police officers... causing disturbance and concern to some residents'.[126]

Overall Margaret Simey noted her concern about the number and consistency of allegations which claimed a deterioration in the relations between the police and the Toxteth community particularly after the measure of success of a community policing programme under Superin-tendent Jim O'Hara. On 1 October 1985, however, matters took a serious turn for the worse. Following a well-publicized court case at the City Magistrates' Court, which involved four men appearing before the court over the death of a London man in Toxteth two months earlier, a crowd returned to Toxteth. A window at the local police station was broken and several vehicles and people were attacked. A few of the vehicles were set alight and traffic was halted. This happened between 5 p.m. and 6 p.m. and the police dispersed groups of youths during that period. At this point operational command was under Superintendent O'Hara but apparently without warning and certainly without O'Hara's knowledge or consent a

Police Support Unit (PSU) and other mobile units from the OSD were deployed into area. It was O'Hara's opinion that the use of OSD contributed to the unrest on the streets.[127]

One of the people to witness the deployment was the Archbishop of Liverpool, The Most Revd Derek Worlock. He stated:

> At first there was an explosion of frustration after events at the Magistrates' Court. By 7.30 p.m. it was evident that it was under control. At 9.00 I found a lot of anger – black and white – about the intensity of the police reaction. Then the police suddenly appeared in riot helmets and shields. They were told that if they would go, we would clear up and get everybody off to bed. I do not want to make judgments, but I did see things that were regrettable. Police communications had broken down – vehicles were moving around very fast and on pavements. That is dangerous.[128]

In a joint letter to Margaret Simey, the Archbishop and the Bishop of Liverpool, The Right Revd David Sheppard, it was noted that the police 'cordoned off the area and sent in a large number of riot police and armoured [sic] vehicles . . . and there seems to have been mounting anger at this show of force . . . the price seems to have been high in damage to good relations built up through community policing in recent years'.[129] From the moment that the OSD was deployed into Toxteth it became virtually impossible for people to move in or out of the area. At the height of the OSD intervention Transit vans and Land Rovers were being driven at fast speed on pavements and stopping to deploy riot officers, truncheons drawn, onto the streets. People were 'targets' for these officers simply by being there and at one point the Archbishop of Liverpool was pinned to a wall. A letter from one of his priests, Revd Peter Morgan, to Margaret Simey stated:

> I saw half a dozen officers leap on a man while I was shouting 'He's drunk'. One after another they leapt at him with truncheons, almost fighting with each other to find part of the man to hit.[130]

An off-duty fireman from Toxteth witnessed this incident. He went to help 'Father Peter' pick up the drunken man. He stated that he was convinced 'that the only reason that they did not attack us at that stage was because the priest was with us'.[131] The drunken man then jumped onto a police van at which point the police 'came swarming around Tommy and began to beat him hard'. The fireman continued:

> suddenly a group of police officers turned on me. I could estimate that about thirty of them paid special attention to me and there was absolutely nothing I could do to defend myself. I cowered against the wall and ducked my head down in the hope of protecting myself. I offered no resistance at all but in spite of that blows were rained on my head, back, shoulders and kicks to my body. I was badly gashed on the back of my head and had to receive medical treatment. I had four or five stitches in my head.

The mass of statements made by civilian eye-witnesses agree on the level of police racism, hostility and brutality on the night. The use of vehicles driven at high speed to disperse crowds is a tactic well established in the colonies and in Ireland's six northern counties. In his response to the police committee in 1981 the Merseyside Chief Constable informed members that he had taken a decision to use vehicles in that way. Claims at a meeting of residents in November 1985 was consistent: vehicles had been deployed in a haphazard and dangerous manner, at high revs and with screeching brakes, along pavements and directly at onlookers'. It was generally felt at the meeting that the police action was deliberately provocative and it had 'frightened and angered people and was thought to have precipitated the much worse civil disorder which followed'.[132] A black community organization worker stated:

> They were driving at greater speeds this time than they had been earlier. The engines were revved up and a great deal of noise was made. Vehicles would turn off into side streets and do U-turns and go round and back again. Vehicles were going up and down the streets scattering people . . . they were intent on clearing us and others like us who were simply watching quietly to see what would happen next.

Apart from the the tactics employed to disperse the crowd, the other major complaint was the level of violence directed towards black people in the community. The meetings held in Toxteth after the events received many complaints and accounts of police racism. As the police officers were deployed from their vehicles they moved into side streets in large numbers, 'banging their shields and shouting "Come on you black bastards"'. The local residents were 'called "nigger", "coon", "whore", "slag", and various other derogatory names by these officers'.[133]   One community worker stated:

> There must have been several dozen police officers all in riot gear and they were walking along the street in rows that filled the whole street. They were banging their truncheons on their shields . . . and seemed to be trying to work themselves up into a frenzy . . . the shout that went out was 'Come on you black bastards'. They were shouting and screaming as they broke into a run. . . . I was disgusted and distressed by their organised, frenzied shrieking.

A black woman stated:

> They were all in full riot gear and they approached us. In particular one of them grabbed me by the arms. He said 'Get home!' and then, 'Fuck off, you slag'. I replied in anger 'Don't tell me to fuck off. And I am not a slag. Look, I live here.' Quite a few of the policemen then took up the cry of 'Slag'. They began shouting it at me and I began to walk away. One of them in particular shouted after me 'We got it right first time, you are a slag'.

What shocked so many of the witnesses to the police operation was the use of indiscriminate violence against anyone who happened to be on the streets. One statement reads:

There was another young lad about 16/17 standing by a shop. A police officer jumped out of the back of the van and went towards him. He grabbed the lad and started beating him with his baton. Another officer joined the officer who had hold of the lad and started punching him and hitting him with their batons... they sandwiched him between two vehicles. They started hitting him with their batons, booting him and punching him and one of the officers shouted 'Gary, lay off him'. The police put the lad into one of the vehicles and drove off.... The other vehicle with the officer 'Gary' in it went towards Princes Road and Princes Avenue and stopped at the lights there. An officer jumped out and threw a baton at the first car that went past. His fellow officers shouted 'Gary, what have we told you, get back in the van'... At about 10.30 p.m. we were standing on the estate of Granby Street where a landrover was parked.... An officer jumped out of the back, got hold of a young woman, hit her in the face with a baton, pushed her to the floor. Someone shouted 'Unit 3 get back in the van'. He didn't get back in the van he just kept hitting the woman. The CO shouted again, 'Gary I have told you to get back in the van and control your temper'.

Clearly the above range of statements, taken from members of the community, church dignatories and community workers, represents a body of evidence which raises serious questions about the incidents which occurred in Toxteth on 1 and 2 October 1985. Given the apparent post-Scarman commitment to community policing initiatives, and the formal complaint made by Superintendent O'Hara to his senior officers over the handling of the October events,[134] the main issue was that of operational policy and organizational control of the OSD. It appears, however, that an early decision had been taken to transfer command from Superintendent O'Hara. In his report to the police committee the Chief Constable stated:

At 6.05 p.m. the control of the incident, which until this stage had been exercised by the Divisional Chief Superintendent from his Divisional Command Post, was transferred to the Incident Control Room at Force Headquarters under the direct command of the Assistant Chief Constable (Operations) in order that the deployment of manpower and resources could be fully co-ordinated.[135]

The meetings held in Toxteth after the events presented the Deputy Chief constable who attended with a range of accounts which alleged that the OSD had been 'out of control'. His reply was that each unit was under the direct control of an inspector. What was not clear from the meetings was whether the problems of communication between the local commander, the OSD and other Police Support Units was due to 'different divisions operating on different radio channels or whether it reflected a more fundamental question of "who's in charge"'.[136] What the evidence shows, and this is supported by the answers given to the Toxteth meetings, is that once deployed the OSD operates largely on its own unit-based discretion. As in most other policing situations the bottom line is the lawful discretion of each individual officer. With specialized units, however, the problem becomes more acute as each group of officers responds as a unit and by the very nature of their training and equipment they are in possession of a high level of collective force. 'Reasonable force' in such circumstances is not going to be defined solely in terms of isolated arrests but that which is considered necessary to respond to a 'riot'.

The use of racist abuse and the beating of riot shields were issues raised with the Deputy Chief Constable. While he assured the meetings 'that he did not condone the use of such language', he pointed out 'the stress which officers in such situations operated'.[137] Members of the Police Committee were invited to consider whether 'shields are beaten in such situations in order to raise morale of officers or to frighten onlookers'. The final cause for concern raised by the meetings was that officers were not identifiable, either by rank or number, and this brought problems both in attempting to speak to those in command and in identifying officers against whom people wanted to make complaints. Some witnesses claimed that numbers had been removed from officers' clothing. The Deputy Constable stated to the meetings that had this been the case when it would not happen again. The Report of the County Solicitor and Secretary to the Police Committee listed the serious issues which arose from the Toxteth incidents: the use of the OSD and the nature of the police operation as being possibly 'unnecessary and provocative; the use of vehicles and the accepted requirement for the use of minimum force; the allegations of racist abuse and random violence by the police; the level and quality of operational control'.

Following the Toxteth incidents of 1985 the Liverpool 8 Law Centre experienced some difficulty in persuading people that the police complaints procedure offered a channel which could and would deal effectively with their grievances. Eventually several official complaints were made and were duly investigated. The outside police investigation was overseen by senior members of the Police Complaints Board. Clearly the complainants, Police Committee members, Law Centre workers and the Community Relations Council were concerned both with the issue of overall command and control and also with the lack of discipline and arbitrary violence which marked the OSD operation.

In August 1986 the response from the Police Complaints Board was that in view of the lack of identification of specific officers no further action would be taken over allegations of assault or abuse. One complainant was told that a senior police officer explained the drumming of shields and the uttering of war cries as 'approved practice'. Thus the broader issue of how the OSD behaved was not addressed. The ACPO manual referred to earlier instructs units to 'use the show of force to the greatest advantage' officers should 'make a formidable appearance'. Certainly on the night of 1 October 1985 the OSD made a 'formidable appearance' on the streets of Toxteth and one which was a long way from the senior police surgeon's reassurances about police brutality. The evidence is consistent in its message that serious assaults and abuse by the police took place and the community had no effective means of redress. The use of force by the OSD went unchallenged and thus defines new levels of acceptability. Effectively the ACPO manual has provided the new base-line for the use of 'reasonable force'. Margaret Simey stated:

> I am appalled that providing they can't be identified the police can do anything they want to the extent of jostling an Archbishop. It's not just the individual police officer but the police itself. There is a yawning void where real grievances are lost from sight. In this case there exists no accountability for the general police in operation on the night. The complaints system is geared to the defence of the profession when it ought to be geared to the defence of people's liberties.[138]

Conclusion

From the discussion so far in this chapter it is evident that 1985 was an important year in the recent development and consolidation of police strategies and initiatives. Following the confrontations of the 1980–81 inner-city uprisings directed against the police and the 1984–5 coal dispute the shift towards authoritarian responses in public order situations sharpened. It was the year in which police forces nationally trained their officers in the new powers under PACE ready for introduction on the streets in January 1986. It was also the year in which the long-awaited White Paper on Public Order was announced which promised the police a whole range of new powers to deal with the 'rising tide of lawlessness'. For this was the period when the new public order training initiatives were developing and the existence of ACPO's manual on public order was revealed. In considering the above case studies it becomes clear that the full implications of paramilitary training within the British police, so long a feature of policing in Ireland's northern counties, can be assessed. Following on from notable events such as Orgreave and Armthorpe in 1984 the range of incidents considered here show the use of offensive tactics and paramilitary equipment within a carefully prepared and organized framework as a first-line response rather than a last-line defence.

What these case studies show is that the police are willing to use unreasonable and excessive force on a mass scale. There is here substantial evidence of abuse, racism, assault and brutality among units of specially selected, riot-trained officers using colonial strategies of public order control. Despite an array of civilian and media evidence, including television film of these events, officers have not been charged with offences which they committed. In every case the Police Complaints Authority has informed complainants that charges could not be brought as it was not possible to identify individual officers. This was the same explanation given to the family of Blair Peach following his killing by a member of the Special

Patrol Group in Southall in 1979. Given that over twenty suspects had been identified from thousands on film at the time of the Heysel Stadium tragedy in Brussels the questions of thoroughness and partiality of the police investigations must be raised in the above cases.

The issue of individual responsibility and subsequent prosecution is important at the level of the operational practices of the police. For it is with the use of lawful discretion in the use of 'reasonable force' that the public comes into direct contact with the police. As has been seen in a range of recent cases, reasonable force is a central concept upon which many cases turn. Under the Criminal Law Act the police can use 'such force as is reasonable in the circumstances' either in the prevention of a crime or in the making of an arrest. In recent cases involving the police use of firearms: the shooting and pistol-whipping of Steven Waldorf in rush-hour traffic; the shooting and paralysing of Cherry Groce in her home; the killing of a young child, John Shorthouse, in his bed; the police defence maintained that these were innocent victims of the necessary armed search for 'violent' persons. The use of ultimate force – shooting – was justified on the grounds that had these innocent bystanders been the 'right' person then the police could have 'reasonably' expected a violent response. The fact that they were not the 'right' people and they did not respond violently cut no ice. While it is difficult to conclude what constitutes 'reasonable' levels of force after the event and in the detached environment of a courtroom the regularity with which police officers escape prosecution or conviction is exceptional by comparison to civilians who are suspected of serious crimes.

The generalized and persistent use of unreasonable force and the apparent reluctance of the police to deal with the problem, for it is they who are entrusted with the formal investigation of complaints, suggests that aggressive policing has become accepted, if not institutionalized, throughout the British police. With the ACPO guidelines, laid down in the *Public Order, Tactical Operations* manual, to 'incapacitate ringleaders' extended beyond the picket lines of the 1984–5 coal dispute, the normalization of the strategies adopted by the Royal Ulster Constabulary has begun to develop a sharp reality on British streets. This permissive framework of operations within which the police respond has provided police officers with the confidence that if they use unreasonable force against targeted individuals or groups they will not be disciplined or prosecuted.

Much of the discussion in this chapter has focused on the operational responses of the police in terms of broad policy decisions, strategies for handling certain kinds of events and the practices of police officers, either individually or in groups, in situations where their authority is challenged. The series of controversies around police powers and accountability which has become a regular feature of the period since 1979 and the first Merseyside confrontation has raised the fundamental question of the political location of the police institutionally within the contemporary state. At the heart of the 'official discourse' on the relationships between the economy, industrial relations, public order and the rule of law is the assumed principle that state institutions and the legal process stand free of the influence of specific economic interests. The 'will of the people' rises through the electoral process and delivers a government whose power extends to legislation as part of its formal rule. Liberal-democracy, then, is implicitly 'consensual' and the legitimacy of government is derived in some notion of a universal 'general will'. Conflict generated within that consensus is recognized and accepted as being the healthy and open pursuit of power, be it economic or political, by competing interests. Within this broad framework the rule of law operates – in its codification, interpretation, enforcement and application – as a set of guarantees against injustices. Liberal-democratic theory assumes consensus around the law and claims for it a form of autonomy and impartiality which enables its enforcers and arbiters to respond with fairness at all times. This structural location is embedded in the doctrine of the separation of powers. The executive, administrative and judicial separation diversifies the formal application of power, each with a countervailing function over the others. Yet in terms of the coercive function and the direct use of the law, what Weber referred to as the state's monopoly on legitimate violence, the powers embodied in the state have received legitimation through the democratic process. It is within this interpretation of liberal-democracy that society is 'policed by consent', the police are the 'thin blue line' between the competing factions and the courts are the 'neutral arbiters' geared to the settlement of aberrant conflict in an otherwise smooth-running system.

Within the framework of liberal-democratic constructions of the rule of law the controversy over the autonomy of the police has been addressed as the conflict between political accountability and operational independence. The police and their spokespeople remain entrenched in a position which they argue is a fundamental principle, as illustrated by the following reflection on Scarman by a senior officer and commentator on the constitutional position of the police:

> The real issue under discussion was the relationship between operational independence and political independence. To the majority of police officers the issue presents little difficulty since they are aware that they are prevented by regulations from taking any active part in politics. The basis for this regulation is that the police must remain impartial. They are the servants of the law and not of governments.[139]

That this 'guiding principle' has become so generalized in its definition and acceptance, that it presents 'little difficulty' for police officers or for their superiors, is a matter of serious concern. As discussed in the introduction to this chapter, it assumes that the law is consistent and unambiguous in both its form and its content. It presents the rule of law as being ahistorical, apolitical and free from the broad range of social and material conflicts and divisions within society. This position, however, is not a product of ignorance or lack of understanding of the structural relations of British society. The police do not require telling that changes in the law or priorities for law enforcement are related directly to the levels and specifics of social, political and economic conflict. In fact what senior officers and their organization, ACPO, have achieved since the 1970s is the 'depoliticization' of the rule of law and the police role as law enforcers. Their plausible argument has been to elevate the law to a 'natural' status above the partisan preferences of party-political debate and to locate their primary responsibility as legal servants rather than political puppets. What this sleight of hand has produced is a political autonomy for chief constables and their officers unrivalled in any other state institution or public service with the possible exception of the military.

By using the phrase 'operational independence' to cover all aspects of policy, priorities and practices the police have guaranteed their political independence. Their claim is to uphold the principles of democracy, which includes government by elected representatives of the people at both national and local levels, yet they possess a unique freedom from formal state control. In that sense they define themselves 'in' or 'out' of democracy as it pleases them. By invoking the principle of the primacy of the rule of law not only do the police purposefully disguise the permissiveness of lawful discretion in the application of their considerable powers but also they deny the right of people in a democratic society to a legitimate say in the function of the police as it affects them and the communities in which they live.

Critical theories of the state, the process of legitimacy and the rule of law within advanced capitalist society locate social and political conflict and the coercive responses of the police, the criminal justice process and the military within historical contexts quite different from those proposed by the pluralist approaches of liberal-democratic analysis. These theories emphasize the fundamental significance of relations embodied in the unequal political and economic structures of production and reproduction. Relations of class, race and gender, therefore, are derived in the historical and material development of systems of power: capitalism; slavery and colonization; patriarchy. These form the central relations of conflict and confrontation out of which advanced capitalism and the infrastructure of the state have grown and developed. The struggles around class, race and gender are not aberrations, rather they form permanent and inevitable antagonisms. The rule of law provides the site upon which these conflicts and antagonisms can be regulated and contained: it reinforces power relations and seeks to maintain established forms of legal and political order. Thus the police, like the courts, operate primarily to defend and service existing social relations (of patriarchy, of advanced capitalism, of neo-colonialism) and established property rights and to manage conflict by force when it cannot be contained through the formalized political and ideological procedures of negotiation.

The consolidation of chief constables' autonomy in operational policy decisions and the extension of police powers on the ground have been achieved emphatically under the Thatcher governments. A clear coincidence of interests between ACPO, successive Conservative governments and senior Home Office officials has guaranteed the operational independence of the police. The gradual normalization of previously defined 'special powers' reflects a united front which extends from the definers in government and Whitehall, through the enforcers on the streets to the interpreters in the courts. This unity of purpose, an ideological as well as political expression, is not unique to the 1980s but is an inherent feature of the development of the rule of law and its criminal justice system. It has been informed and characterized by a rhetoric of law and order which identifies all opposition to the established order as a 'threat' to the state. The objective is clear: to take acts of political opposition, redefine them as attacks on 'freedom' and place them outside the law.

Through this process of criminalization – the direct, political use of the law – the control functions of the state have emerged strongly and have been justified in their severity. Folk-devils such as soccer hooligans, race rioters, black muggers, Greenham women, animal rights protestors, Scargill's army and Irish terrorists have been summoned and conflated (this litany of the 'lawless' was presented in the introduction to the 1985 White Paper on Public Order) and used as evidence that the 'Kingdom's unity' is threatened by a broad alliance of 'enemies within'. The symbolism of the 'spiral of lawlessness', including contraventions of the moral as well as legal codes, has been mobilized by politicans of all parties and by the media to deflect attention from the inherent structural conflict within Britain. The ideological containment of class conflict, exemplified by the state's response to the coal dispute, owes much to the collapsing of the distinction between 'normal' crime and 'political' opposition.

The hardline, punitive reaction of the police is one based on the proposition that state violence has legitimation when it is applied to criminal acts and to criminality as a social/personal condition. This was clear in Oxford's portrayal of crime and criminality in Toxteth. It has been as part of this process – the criminalization of economically and politically marginalized neighbourhoods and identifiable groups – that the police have responded selectively and differentially. The process of criminalization also justifies the regulation, containment and use of unreasonable force, thus emphasizing the structural relations of marginalization and invoking popular approval and legitimacy – the manufacture of consent – in support of the state. Redefining 'political' action as 'criminal' acts appeals to the deeply held, common-sense assumptions of the law and order lobby. For marginalization is not only a structural location within the social relations of production and reproduction it also reflects profound ideological divisions. The use of excessive force by the police, therefore, is justified legally as fighting violence with violence but also in moral terms as applying a 'just measure of pain'.

Thus the chief constables and their senior officers portray themselves as moral crusaders as well as law enforcers. In keeping the peace they also guard the conscience of the nation. They are free of political control and claim the divine rights bestowed by the rule of law. Their definitions of reality, however, are not value-free for they reflect the institutionalized classism, sexism and racism inherent in the relations of the advanced capitalist patriarchy which is Britain in the 1980s. The often vicious treatment of ordinary people by the police on the streets and in cells is one end of a continuum. At the other is the apparent reluctance of their senior officers to construct and operate a code of discipline which would give those people effective redress for their suffering.

Acknowledgements

Many thanks to Leonie Nash, Margaret Simey and those people who have talked about their experiences of the police on Merseyside. Also to Paul Gordon, Catherine Little, Susan O'Malley, Sheila Scraton, Joe Sim for their support and critical contributions. Finally, to many of my students who have contributed much to my work through undergraduate and post-graduate workshops.

An earlier version of this paper was first presented to the XIV Conference of the European Group for the Study of Deviance and Social Control at the University of Madrid, September 1986.

Notes

1 See A. Friend and A. Metcalf, *Slump City: The Politics of Mass Unemployment*, London, Pluto, 1981.

2 The series of events referred to here, from the 1966 seamen's strike up to the 1975–6 Grunwick dispute, are well covered in S. Hall *et al.*, *Policing the Crisis*, London, Macmillan, 1978. A detailed account of Grunwick is contained in J. Dromey and G. Taylor, *Grunwick: The Workers' Story*, and the police response to the dispute is documented by S. Weir, 'A picket's eye view', *New Society*, 30 June 1977.

3 A good example of this issue is in M. Dickinson, *To Break a Union*, London Booklist, 1984, on the *Warrington Messenger* dispute. See also H. Beynon, (ed.), *Digging Deeper: Issues in the Miners' Strike*, London, Verso, 1985; WCCPL/NUM, *Striking Back*, WCCPL, 1985; R. Samuel *et al.*, *The Enemy Within*, London, Routledge & Kegan Paul, 1986.

4 The Heath Government's 1971 Industrial Relations Act was a significant use of the law to regulate the unions. The 1875 Conspiracy and Protection of Property Act was used against the Shrewsbury pickets in 1972; see J. Arnison, *The Shrewsbury Three*, London, Lawrence & Wishart, 1974; D. Warren, *The Key to my Cell*, London, New Park Publications, 1982. There followed two major pieces of legislation under Thatcher; the 1980 and 1982 Employment Acts.

5 See UCE Supplementary Report, *The Death of Blair Peach*, NCCL, 1980; D. Ransom, *Licence to Kill*, Friends of Blair Peach Committee, 1980.

6 See 'From resistance to rebellion', *Race and Class*, Special Issue, vol. XXIII, 2/3, 1982.

7 While S. Hall *et al.*, op. cit. provided a thorough critique of these developments other work has defended the focus on street crime: for example, M. Pratt, *Mugging: A Social Problem*, London, Routledge & Kegan Paul, 1980.

8 P. Gordon, *Racial Violence and Harassment*, Runnymede Trust, 1986.

9 See J. Hanmer and S. Saunders, *Well-Founded Fear*, London, Hutchinson, 1985; R. Hall, *Ask Any Woman*, Bristol, Falling Wall Press, 1985.

10 See H. Kanter *et al.*, *Sweeping Statements*, London, The Women's Press, 1984; London Rape Crisis Centre, *Sexual Violence*, London, The Women's Press, 1984, Section 9.

11 See C. Blackwood, *On the Perimeter*, London, Flamingo, 1984; A. Cook and G. Kirk, *Greenham Women Everywhere*, London, Pluto 1983. B. Whisker *et al.*, (eds), *Breaching the Peace*, Bristol, Only Women's Press, 1983; M.J. Fletcher, 'Greenham Women: The Criminalisation of Political Protest', unpublished thesis, 1985.

12 S. Hall, *Drifting into a Law and Order Society*, Cobden Trust, 1980, p. 12.

13 The long history of controversy over police–community relations is well documented in T. Bunyan, *The Political Police in Britain*, London, Quartet, 1977; P. Scraton, *Policing Society, Policing Crime*, Milton Keynes, Bucks, Open University Press, 1982; and *The State of the Police*, London, Pluto, 1985, ch. 2.

14 IRR, *Police against Black People, Race and Class* Pamphlet No. 6, 1978; *Blood on the Streets*, Bethnal Green and Stepney Council, 1978; P. Gordon, *White Law*, London, Pluto, 1983; Policy Studies Institute (PSI) *Police and People in London*, Vols I–IV, PSI, 1983.

15 See J. Coulter *et al.*, *State of Siege*, London Canary Press, 1985; WCCPL/NUM, op. cit.; B. Fine and R. Millar, (eds), *Policing and Miners' Strike*, London, Lawrence & Wishart, 1985; S. Spencer, *Police Authorities during the Miners' Strike*, Cobden Trust, 1985.

16 J. Rollo, 'The Special Control Group', in P. Hain, (ed.), *Policing the Police*, Vol. II, London, John Calder; M. Kettle and T. Bunyan, 'The police force of the future is now here', *New Society*, 21 August 1980.

17 Technical Authors' Group, *Police Use of Computers*, TAG Scotland, 1982; C. Pounder, *Police Computers and the Metropolitan Police*, GLC, 1985.

18 S. Manwaring-White, *The Policing Revolution*, Brighton, Sussex, Harvester, 1983; BSSRS Technology of Political Control Group, *Techno-cop: New Police Technologies*, London Free Association Books, 1985.

19 See R. Mark, *In the Office of Constable*, London, Collins, 1979; Sir D. McNee, *McNee's Law*, London, Collins, 1985.

20 H. Becker, 'Whose side are we on?', *Social Problems*, vol. 14, 1967.

21 This can be seen over a range of controversial issues in those local authorities where the authority of the chief constable has been challenged. In Greater Manchester this led to the Manchester Council setting up its own Police Monitoring Unit.

22 For full accounts of this debate see B. Loveday, *The Role of Effectiveness of the Merseyside Police Committee*, Merseyside County Council, 1985; P. Scraton, op. cit.; S. Spencer, op. cit.

23 See S. Spencer, *Called to Account*, Cobden Trust, 1985; S. Spencer, 'The eclipse of the police authority', in B. Fine and R. Millar, op. cit. 1985.

24 R. Reiner, *The Politics of the Police*, Brighton, Sussex, Wheatsheaf, 1985; J. Baxter and L. Kaffman, (eds), *Police: The Constitution and the Community*, London Professional Books, 1986; L. Lustgarten, *The Governance of the Police*, London, Sweet & Maxwell, 1987.
25 R. Mark, *In the Office of Constable*, London, Fontana/Collins, 1979, p. 157.
26 D. McNee, 'Quo vadis?', *Police Journal*, January 1980, p. 10.
27 Merseyside Police, *Computerised Command and Control System*, Merseyside Police, 1985.
28 Report of the Royal Commissioners on Police Activities and Procedures, 1929.
29 Merseyside Police publicity brochure, 1984.
30 T.A. Critchley, *A History of Police in England and Wales* (2nd edn), London, Constable, 1978, p. 55.
31 L. Radzinowicz, *A History of Criminal Law and its Administration from 1750*, Vol. 4, London, Stevens, 1968, p. 190.
32 M. Fitzgerald, *et al.*, *Intervention, Regulation and Surveillance*, Milton Keynes, Bucks, Open University Press, 1982, p. 104.
33 See R. Storch, 'The plague of blue locusts', *International Review of Social History*, 20, 1975, and 'The policeman as domestic missionary', *Journal of Social History*, 9, 1975/6. Also: D. Jones, *Crime, Protest, Community and the Police in Nineteenth Century Britain*, London, Routledge & Kegan Paul, 1982.
34 See R. Geary, *Policing Industrial Disputes 1893 to 1985*, London, Methuen, 1985, which considers the twentieth-century inheritance of the consequences of industrial conflict for police–community relations.
35 M. Ignatieff, 'Police and the people: the birth of Mr Peel's "blue locusts"', *New Society*, 30 August 1979.
36 See M. Brogden, *The Police: Autonomy and Consent*, London Academic Press, 1982.
37 P. Cohen, 'Policing the working-class city', in NDC/CSE, *Capitalism and the Rule of Law*, London, Hutchinson, 1979.
38 Taken from a lecture given by Jennifer Davis at the Open University in January 1983.
39 B. Cox *et al.*, *The Fall of Scotland Yard*, Harmondsworth, Middx, Penguin, 1977.
40 See J. Saward, 'Paper trials: Michael Morris and the evidence of supergrasses', in P. Scraton and P. Gordon (eds), *Causes for Concern*, Harmondsworth, Middx, Penguin, 1984; M. O'Mahoney, *King Squealer*, London, Sphere, 1981.
41 See S. Knight, *The Brotherhood*, London, Panther, 1985.
42 P. Chippindale, 'The story of Operation Countryman', *New Statesman*, 18 January 1980.
43 See M. Banton, *The Policeman in the Community*, London, Tavistock, 1964; M. Cain, *Society and the Policeman's Role*, London, Routledge & Kegan Paul, 1973.
44 S. Holdaway, 'Changes in urban policing', *British Journal of Sociology*, vol. 28, no. 2, 1977, pp. 119–37.
45 E.B. Schaffer, *Community Policing*, London, Croom Helm, 1980.
46 S. Holdaway, *Inside the British Police*, Oxford, Basil Blackwell, 1983. A similar conclusion can be drawn from J. McLure, *Spike Island: Portrait of a Police Division*, London, Macmillan, 1980.
47 S. Holdaway, op. cit. pp. 100–1.
48 D.J. Smith and J. Gray, *Police and People in London: IV The Police in Action*, Policy Studies Institute, 1983.
49 See also R. Gordon, *White Law*, London, Pluto, 1983.

50 Quoted in R. Reiner, 'Police and picketing', *New Society*, 7 July 1977.

51 K. Sloan, *Police Review*, 9 February 1979.

52 R. Mark in the Foreword to T.A. Critchley, *A History of the Police in England and Wales* (2nd edn) London, Constable, 1978, p. xiii.

53 R. Mark, *In the Office of Constable,* op. cit. p. 317.

54 Ibid. p. 150.

55 *The Guardian*, 10 January 1981.

56 *The Guardian*, 17 March 1982.

57 Note particularly his comments on the 'threat to democracy' made on BBC *Question Time* in 1979 and 'the enemy in our midst', 'subversion' and 'infiltration' made in a public speech in March 1982.

58 See N. Blake, 'Picketing, justice and the law' and R. East and P. Thomas, 'Roadblocks: the experience in Wales', in B. Fine and R. Millar, *Policing the Miners' Strike*, London, Lawrence & Wishart, 1985; R. East *et al.*, 'The death of mass picketing' and other papers in P. Scraton and P. Thomas, *The State v. The People: Lessons from the Coal Dispute*, Oxford, Basil Blackwell, 1985.

59 Charles McLachlan in a television interview, 1984.

60 Charles McLachlan reported in *The Guardian* 23 June 1984.

61 See P. Scraton, 'Accountable to No One: Policing Merseyside 1979–81', in P. Scraton and P. Gordon, *Causes for Concern*, Harmondsworth, Middx, Penguin, 1984; B. Loveday, *The Role and Effectiveness of the Merseyside Police Committee*, Merseyside County Council, 1985.

62 See D. Cowell *et al.*, *Policing the Riots,* London, Junction Books, 1983; S. Spencer, *Called to Account*, London, Cobden Trust, 1985; T. Jefferson and R. Grimshaw, *Controlling the Constable*, Cobden/Muller, 1985.

63 See S. Spencer, 'The eclipse of the police authority', in B. Fine and R. Millar, op. cit.; P. Scraton, *The State of the Police*, London, Pluto, 1985, ch. 7.

64 R. Reiner, *The Politics of the Police*, Brighton, Sussex, Wheatsheaf, 1985, p. 192.

65 See C. Bateman, 'The dictatorship of the 43 chief constables', *The Guardian*, 11 August 1984.

66 For a full account of these events see S. Hall *et al.*, *Policing the Crisis*, London, Macmillan, 1978; and for a detailed account of the impact of the Saltley Gates incident see T. Bunyan, 'From Saltley to Orgreave via Brixton', in P. Scraton and P. Thomas, op. cit.

67 B. Sewill in R. Harris and B. Sewill, *British Economic Policy 1970—74: Two Views,* Institute of Economic Affairs, 1975, p. 50.

68 A. Gamble, *Britain in Decline*, London, Macmillan, 1981, p. 159.

69 Ibid. pp. 160–2.

70 Quoted in P. Warren, *Shrewsbury: Whose Conspiracy?*, London, New Park Publications, 1980, p. 10.

71 Speech at the University of Birmingham, quoted in *State Research*, no. 5, April–May 1978.

72 See A. Deacon, 'The Scrounging Controversy: public attitudes towards the unemployed in contemporary Britain', *Social and Economic Administration*, vol. 12, no. 2, 1978; P. Golding and S. Middleton, *Images of Welfare*, Oxford, Basil Blackwell and Martin Robertson, 1982; A. Clarke 'Prejudice, ignorance and panic! Popular politics in a land fit for scroungers', in M. Loney *et al.*, (eds), *Social Policy and Social Welfare*, Milton Keynes, Bucks, Open University Press, 1983.

73 See CCCS, *Unpopular Education*, London, Hutchinson, 1981.

74 See S. Hall and M. Jacques, *The Politics of Thatcherism*, London, Lawrence & Wishart, 1983.

75 See M. Barrett and M. McIntosh, *The Anti-social Family*, London Verso 1982, ch. 1; T. Fitzgerald, 'The New Right and the Family', in M. Loney *et al.*, op. cit.

76 See P. Scraton and N. South, 'In the shadow of the welfare police', *Bulletin of Social Policy*, Summer 1983; R. Franey, *Poor Law*, NCCL/CHAR, 1983.

77 For a thorough analysis of these developments see the early chapters of P. Gordon and F. Klug, *New Right, New Racism*, Birmingham, Searchlight Publications, 1986.

78 S. Hall, *Drifting into a Law and Order Society*, London, Cobden Trust 1980, p. 3.

79 Reported in *The Guardian*, 23 July 1985.

80 G. Peirce, 'How they rewrote the law at Orgreave', 'Guardian Agenda' in *The Guardian*, 12 August 1985.

81 This was a position noted much earlier by E.P. Thompson in his book *Writing by Candlelight*, London, Merlin, 1980.

82 After it was revealed that in February 1984 a secret meeting had been held to develop a strategy to police the coal dispute and attended by chief constables, the Attorney General and the Home Secretary, John Alderson – the former Chief Constable of Devon and Cornwall – disclosed that such meetings had been a regular feature of the Thatcher administrations.

83 See L. Christian, *Policing by Coercion*, GLC/Pluto Press, 1983.

84 M. Kettle, 'The politics of policing and the policing of politics', in P. Hain, (ed.), *Policing the Police Vol II*, London, John Calder, 1980.

85 It is worth nothing that the NCCL Unofficial Inquiry, *Southall 1979*, NCCL, 1980, criticized strongly the police strategy of cordoning off the centre of Southall to enable to National Front to demonstrate.

86 *Review of Public Order Law*, White Paper, Cmnd 9510, 15 May 1985, HMSO.

87 Hansard, 16 May 1985.

88 Ibid.

89 *Review of the Public Order Act, 1936 and Related Legislation*, Green Paper, Cmnd 7891, 1980, HMSO; *The Law Relating to Public Order*, House of Commons Select Committee on Home Affairs, HC756, I and II, August 1980; *Offences Relating to Public Order*, HC85, Law Commission No. 123; *The Scarman Report*, Cmnd 8427, 1981, HMSO.

90 'Watching and besetting' is an offence under Sec. 7 of the 1875 Conspiracy and Protection of Property Act and was 'brought to life' during the coal dispute resulting in over 270 prosecutions.

91 See P. Scraton, 'If you want a riot, change the law', in P. Scraton and P. Thomas, op. cit. 1985.

92 Prime Minister, Margaret Thatcher in a speech on 25 November 1986; *The Guardian*, 26 November 1986.

93 *Daily Express*, 17 May, 1985.

94 See J. Percy-Smith and P. Hillyard, 'Miners in the arms of the law: a statistical analysis', in P. Scraton and P. Thomas. op. cit. 1985; also their *The Coercive State*, London, Fontana, 1987.

95 See M. Ryan and J. Sim, 'Decoding Leon Brittan', *The Abolitionist*, no. 16, 1984.

96 J. Coulter *et al.*, *State of Siege*, London Canary Press, 1984; WCCPL/NUM, *Striking Back*, Welsh Council for Civil and Political Liberties, 1985; B. Jackson and T. Wardle, *The Battle for Orgreave*, London, Vanson Wardle, 1986.

188 *Phil Scraton*

97 Report of the Independent Inquiry Panel; *Leon Brittan's visit to Manchester University Students' union: 1st March 1985*, Manchester City Council, November 1985.

98 See 'A fair degree of force', *Brass Tacks*, BBC2, 31 October 1985.

99 Report of the Independent Inquiry Panel, op. cit. p. 59.

100 Ibid. pp. 54–5; see also David Pallister, 'The Manchester Dossier', *The Guardian*, 24 March 1986; M. Walker, *With Extreme Prejudice: An Investigation into Police Vigilantism in Manchester*, London, Canary Press, 1986. These investigative reports give a detailed account of the events and their aftermath.

101 Sarah Hollis was interviewed on *Out of Court*, BBC2, 3 March 1987.

102 *Daily Telegraph*, 1 April 1985.

103 Nick Davies, *The Observer*, 2 June 1985.

104 Earl of Cardigan, quoted in NCCL, *Stonehenge: A report into the civil liberties implications of the events relating to the convoys of Summer 1985 and 1986*, NCCL, 1986, p. 5.

105 Written reply by Home Office Minister Giles Shaw to Clive Soley, Labour MP, reported in *The Observer*, 28 July 1985.

106 For a full discussion of these see NCCL, 1986 op. cit.

107 Report by Geoffrey Dear, Chief Constable of West Midlands, to the Home Secretary on the Handsworth Disturbances, 19 November 1985.

108 *Policing London*, vol. 21, 1986, p. 113.

109 *Brass Tacks*, BBC, 12 July 1986.

110 *Policing London*, vol. 20, 1985, p. 82.

111 Personal account by Celia Locks, sub-editor, *The Guardian*, 30 September 1985.

112 *London Standard*, 7 October 1985.

113 *The Broadwater Farm Inquiry*, Chaired by Lord Gifford, QC, 1986.

114 *Public Order Review – Civil Disturbances 1981–85*, Metropolitan Police, 1986.

115 *Sir Kenneth Newman*, quoted in *The Guardian*, 3 July 1986.

116 Quoted in J. McLure, *Spike Island: Portrait of a Police Division*, London, Macmillan, 1980, p. 77.

117 These events are detailed in P. Scraton, *The State of the Police*, London, Pluto, 1985; and in B. Loveday, op. cit.

118 See P. Scraton, 'Accountable to no-one: policing Merseyside 1979–81', in P. Scraton and P. Gordon (eds), *Causes for Concern*, Harmondsworth, Middx, Penguin, 1984.

119 See P. Scraton, 'The Coroner's Tale: the death of Jimmy Kelly' in P. Scraton and P. Gordon, op. cit.; P. Scraton and K. Chadwick, *In the Arms of the Law: Coroners' Inquests and Deaths in Custody*, London, Pluto, 1987.

120 *The Role and Responsibilities of the Police Authority*, County Solicitor's Report, January 1980, Merseyside MC.

121 See P. Scraton, 'Policing and institutionalised racism on Merseyside', in D. Cowell, *et al.*, (eds), *Policing the Riots*, London, Junction Books, 1983.

122 Working Party into Police–Community Relations, Merseyside Police Committee, October 1981.

123 Kenneth Oxford, Chief Constable of Merseyside writing in the foreword to J. McLure, op. cit.

124 Kenneth Oxford, *Evidence to the Scarman Inquiry*, Merseyside Police, 1981.

125 Report of the County Solicitor and Secretary, *Informal Meetings of the Community Liaison Sub-Committee*, (CSS/184/85), 26 June 1985, Merseyside County Council.

126 Notes of the meeting of Granby Police/Community Liaison Forum, 24

September 1985, Merseyside County Council.
127 *The Observer*, 7 October 1985.
128 Ibid.
129 Letter dated 11 November 1985.
130 Letter dated 28 October 1985.
131 This statement, and all others following – except where stated – were made by members of the community at the Liverpool Law Centre following the events.
132 Notes of meeting, 4 November 1985.
133 Notes of meeting, 28 October 1985.
134 Reported by Jonathan Foster in *The Observer*, 7 October 1985.
135 Chief Constable's Report to the Police Committee, 15 October 1985, para. 3.
136 Report of the County Solicitor and Secretary, 20 November 1985, op. cit. para. 24.
137 Ibid. para. 21.
138 Personal interview, September 1986.
139 M. S. Pike, *The Principles of Policing*, London, Macmillan, 1985, p. 174, 1985, para. 3.

6

Working for the Clampdown: Prisons and Politics in England and Wales

Joe Sim

Our only hope lies in the people's endeavour to hear our protest and support our cause. Building more and better prisons is not the solution – build a thousand prisons, arrest and lock up tens of thousands of people; all will be to no avail. This will not arrest poverty, oppression and the other ills of this unjust social order.

(John Clutchette: one of Soledad Brothers quoted in 1971)

Introduction

In August 1985, the average daily prison population in England and Wales reached the record level of 48,165. This was a rise of 5,400 from September 1984 and 8,000 more than the system was designed to handle. During the first six months of the year the population had been rising by 235 a week.[1] For those on remand, the rise had been even steeper. In the year ending February 1985, the remand population rose by 16% which was four times the rate of increase for prisoners as a whole.[2] Overall, the rate of imprisonment in the country had risen to 96 per 100,000 of the population as compared to 29 per 100,000 in 1923 and 32 per 100,000 in the 1930s.[3]

The juvenile prison population was also expanding at a faster rate. The latest figures available indicated that the population was 21% higher in the first half of 1983.[4] Within that category young women were coming in for particular attention from the courts. In the first year of the operation of the 1982 Criminal Justice Act, the number aged between 15 and 20 sent to penal establishments rose by 20%.[5]

Expenditure on the prisons also had continued its inexorable rise. In the financial year 1985/6, the budget for the penal system was £638 million, a rise of 36% in real terms (156% in cash terms) since the 1978–79 financial year. Overtime pay for prison officers alone rose by 137% in the years between 1979 and 1985.[6] By 1985, it was costing on average £11,000 per annum to keep an individual incarcerated.[7] This increase in expenditure was matched by an increase in the number of prison officers. By January 1984, there were 24,137 officers and civilian staff working in the service.[8] At the same time the ratio of staff to prisoners had been consistently increasing over the years. In 1971 there were 3.58 prisoners to each uniformed prison officer. By 1984 this had been cut to 2.54 prisoners per officer despite the fact that 'there are nowadays also many more non-uniformed specialist staff working alongside prison officers'.[9]

These developments were themselves underpinned by a major prison building programme which the government had proudly proclaimed to be the biggest undertaken this century. The programme was indeed impressive with 16 new prisons being planned, 14 of which would be opened by 1991. In addition there were major developments or refurbishing schemes taking place at 100 prisons. Altogether the programme would provide an extra 11,700 prison places by the early 1990s.[10] The cost of these plans was estimated (at 1983 prices) to be around £500 million with 5,500 new staff being recruited to support this extension in prison places.[11]

By late 1985, therefore, the prison system in England and Wales was on a major expansionist course. The government was providing the resources necessary to further extend the number of places available to the courts for the sentencing of offenders. The reasons for this extension are complex and sometimes contradictory but require situating the prison system both within developments in the wider criminal justice process and also within the political and economic system itself. It is also important, however, in order to have a fuller understanding of this often complex process to grasp the nature, extent and depth of the crisis which was affecting the prison system in 1985, a crisis which had its roots much further back in history and which had been the subject of major debates and analyses in the 1970s and early 1980s.[12]

The Crisis Inside

The most obvious manifestation of the crisis in the prisons was that of overcrowding. By 1985, living and working conditions for the imprisoned, especially those in the short-term and remand prisons were appalling. This situation, clearly, was not new as throughout the 1970s and 1980s report after report, both official and unofficial condemned the conditions inside as 'an affront to a civilized society',[13] and as 'spartan, gloomy and stagnant'.[14] For prisoners, such rhetoric provided little comfort, especially for those locked up 23 hours a day, two or three to a cell, in a space which measured 12

feet by 8 feet with only a bucket for sanitation. By 1984, 16,000 prisoners
were living in such conditions.[15] The 1984 *Report of the Chief Inspector of Prisons*,
for the fourth year running drew attention to the overcrowding in the
prisons and was scathing about the sanitary arrangements:

> The stench of urine and excrement pervades the prison [Norwich]. So awful is
> this procedure that many prisoners become constipated – others prefer to use
> their pants, hurling them and their contents out of the window when morning
> comes.[16]

Conditions, the report concluded, were likely to get worse and that
overcrowding itself which the chief inspector felt was a fundamental cause
of bad conditions and 'many other evils' seemed at least in the short term
more likely to get worse than better'.[17]

While media, political and public comment concentrated on debating and
highlighting these conditions, other dimensions of the crisis came in for less
scrutiny but were no less important in contributing to the instability of the
prison system in the 1970s and 1980s. One of these dimensions was the
continuing militancy of rank-and-file prison officers who throughout the
previous decade had been in constant conflict with the Home Office, prison
governors, social workers, probation officers and teachers, with members
of their own union executive, the Prison Officers' Association and with
prisoners themselves. This 'crisis of authority'[18] showed no signs of abating
in 1985 as prison officers in different prisons took action over a number of
issues including the perennial one concerning the excessive amount of
overtime which they worked. Any attempt to curtail it was met with fierce
resistance. In 1985 the officers took action at, amongst other prisons,
Bedford, Parkhurst and Wormwood Scrubs in support of different
demands. In May of the same year the then Home Secretary, Leon Brittan
was barracked and booed at the annual conference of the Prison Officers'
Association despite the fact that he had pointed out to those present that 'the
number of prison officers has increased by one fifth since 1979. The budget
for the Service has gone up 85%. Annual expenditure on prison building,
development and repair has gone up nearly 400%'[19]

Serious conflict was also reported to be occurring between staff and
prisoners in a number of prisons. In the three months between April and
June 1985, for example, 316 prison officers and 135 prisoners were
injured.[20] In June, there was a large demonstration by 43 women in
Holloway Prison protesting about brutality inflicted upon a fellow prisoner
who was said to have been dragged into a cell by 8 prison officers, forcibly
stripped and was later refused permission to see a doctor.[21] In April,
probation officers at Aldington near Ashford reported that young offenders
were being punched for forgetting to say 'Sir', for not knowing their
number even though they had not been given any and for not running
quickly enough.[22] Finally, in November 1984, serious violence was also
reported to have occurred at Wandsworth Prison in London, a prison with

the reputation of being one of the hardest in Britain. One prisoner was said to have been dragged from his cell by 12 prison officers, punched and kicked, then carried face downwards from the landing downstairs to the ground floor.[23]

This conflict between staff and prisoners was compounded by continuing disturbances in the long-term maximum security, dispersal prisons. In April 1985, there was a sit-in protest by 25 prisoners at Gartree in Leicestershire, in June there was another at Parkhurst on the Isle of Wight.[24] Finally, in September, staff at Albany maximum security prison voted to restrict the movement of prisoners on the grounds that discipline had broken down. Prisoners were to be allowed out of their cells for 30 minutes instead of the normal 12 hours. The clampdown followed a confrontation between staff and 70 prisoners after a fight between prisoners.[25]

Such protests and disturbances only highlighted the fragile and unstable nature of long-term prisons. There had been major problems of control since the dispersal system was introduced in the late 1960s.[26] Between October 1969 and June 1983 there had been at least ten major disturbances involving five out of the eight dispersal prisons.[27]

The stability and control of the system was also threatened by prisoners engaging in other forms of direct action in an attempt to redress the balance of power inside. In particular, prisoners were increasingly turning to the law both to challenge existing penal policies and the new policies initiated in 1983 by the Home Secretary which effectively abolished parole for whole categories of offenders.[28] While they lost the latter case after a series of convoluted court hearings, prisoners, with the assistance of the European Commission for Human Rights, finally won the right to be legally represented at prison disciplinary hearings. Although this judgement still only applies to serious breaches of the prison rules such as mutiny, and is at the discretion of the Prison Board of Visitors, none the less the latest figures suggest that 1 in 20 prisoners are being represented with some success in terms of the verdicts returned.[29] Prisoners were being supported in their endeavours by a number of groups and lawyers outside the prison walls including Radical Alternatives to Prison (RAP), the National Prisoners' Movement (PROP), Women in Prison, Inquest and the Prison Reform Trust all of which in their different ways were providing alternative sources of information which challenged official explanations and descriptions of events and incidents inside. In that sense, prisons were increasingly becoming much less invisible as the monopoly on information which the prison authorities controlled was severely undermined,[30] a process which had started with the formation of the National Prisoners' Movement (PROP) in 1972.[31]

The continuing crisis in the prisons also meant that the very legitimacy of the system itself was increasingly being called into question. These questions came from different sources but had a common theme, namely that the prisons were not working. From the point of view of state servants, however, this itself was underpinned by a belief that if the prisons were failing then somehow the social order itself was in danger. The former Home Secretary, William Whitelaw had indicated in December 1981 that the appalling conditions inside were 'a continued threat to law and order'.[32] In March 1982, the Lord Chief Justice, Lord Lane, while pointing out that 'prison never did anyone any good' nevertheless warned that if the prison system were to break down then 'all of us – judges, your Lordships and the rest of the population – would inevitably suffer catastrophe'[33]. In 1984, the right-wing think-tank, the Adam Smith Institute, in arguing for the privatization of prisons because of their ineffectiveness complained about the escalating cost of keeping individuals incarcerated at 'three times the most expensive public school fees'.[34] Added to these peals of criticism were the figures supplied by various reform groups, and the government's own research department in the Home Office which pointed out that overall 60% of male offenders and 41% of females were re-convicted within two years of release. For young prisoners the rates were even higher at 69% and 54% respectively.[35]

The crisis of legitimacy in particular, and the prison crisis in general has raised some profound questions about the role of the prisons in England and Wales. These questions bring into sharp focus not only the relationship between prisons and the prevention of crime but also the more fundamental issue of the interconnection between prisons and the maintenance of the social order itself. As has been pointed out:

> The crisis of the British prison system reflects not simply a concern about the state of the prisons but a more widespread belief that the prisons of the state are not making an effective contribution to the maintenance of social order.[36]

The next section of this chapter examines the connection between these two levels: first by looking at the response to the crisis by the state as a way of highlighting and exploring the issues behind the escalation and expansion of the system and second by situating these issues and developments within the broader context of the changes occurring at the complex interface of the criminal justice process, the state and the political economy. It is at this latter level that the politics of the prison system become manifest.

Responding to the Crisis

The state's response to the crisis of overcrowding has been classical and predictable. More prisons are to be built and more alternatives are to be sought. As indicated above, 16 new prisons are to be built in England and Wales, and others are to be refurbished at a total cost of £500 million. The reasoning behind this move was that new prisons would relieve overcrowding, a rationalization which is contradicted by much of the sociological and criminological literature on the subject. Put simply, more prisons equals more prisoners.[37] Even before the latest building plans were announced, between 1970 and 1982, 6,000 new prison places were provided in England and Wales but overcrowding has remained an integral feature of prison life.[38]

In a similar way, the argument for alternatives to custody has been based on the principle that such alternatives would produce a reduction in the prison population by allowing the courts to divert offenders away from custody. In England and Wales these alternatives have included fines, suspended sentences, partly suspended sentences, suggestions for weekend imprisonment and, in 1973, the introduction of Community Service Orders. The idea behind this scheme was that offenders would pay for their crime by working in the community for between 40 and 240 hours. From 1973 until the end of 1982, 135,000 individuals were given Community Service Orders by the courts,[30] but as Ken Pease has indicated, the orders have not been used as an alternative to custody – the majority of those sentenced would not have been sent to prison anyway but would have been dealt with by some other non-custodial punishment.[40] More generally, as Stan Cohen has pointed out, the introduction and use of such alternatives has been to increase rather than decrease the total number of offenders who are pulled into the system in the first instance: 'in other words, "alternatives" become not alternatives at all but new programmes which supplement the existing system or else expand the system by attracting new populations – the net of social control is widened.'[41]

It is also worth noting that the parole threshold for short-term prisoners has been reduced. The Home Office has extended the eligibility of those available for parole from sentences of 18 months down to those serving 9 months. In July 1984, when it was introduced the prison population dropped by 2,000 and it was estimated that around 8,000 extra prisoners would receive parole each year under this procedure.[42] However, while detailed figures are as yet unavailable, the steep rise in the population in 1985 would appear to confound the hope that it would reduce the population. It has also been intimated by a serving member of a Local Review Committee of a prison which is responsible for recommending parole to these kinds of offenders that the objective is to keep the system moving, that individuals are being granted parole 'on the nod' which clearly would lead to a greater increase in the use of the prison system as more offenders pass through it for shorter periods of time.[43]

This response to the overcrowding crisis has been supplemented by other suggestions and programmes for alternatives. In Leeds, unemployed people, former schoolteachers and ex-police officers have been employed as 'trackers' to monitor the movements and activities of offenders. Each are paid £2.50 per hour for a 16-hour week to check three times a day on the whereabouts of the offender for whom they are responsible.[44] It has also been suggested, following their introduction in New Mexico, that offenders could be fitted with electronic bracelets which would send a signal to police if the bearer moved out of a specific 'cell' area which would be determined by the court, or if the tag was removed. It has been argued that the introduction of such a scheme would cut the jail population by 10,000 and save £100 million a year in prison costs and it was welcomed by a former prison governor as holding 'the key to a major reform in penology and for a Christian and humanitarian must be given serious consideration and trial'.[45]

The state's response to the crisis of containment[46] has been equally important in extending and expanding both old and new methods of control inside. It is important to note that this crisis has taken place against a background of a major increase in the number of long-term prisoners in England and Wales. As Stan Cohen and Laurie Taylor have pointed out:

> It does not really matter which sets of statistics are used – the overall numbers or proportion of the long-term population; average sentences served by lifers, etc. – all document the rise in the long-term prison population and the continuing predilection of English judges to hand out longer and longer sentences.[47]

By 1984, the number of adult male prisoners serving sentences of over 5 years was about 4,000. In 1983 alone there were 820 new receptions into the prisons serving sentences of this length.[48] This tendency has been exacerbated by the introduction in October 1983 of restrictions on parole for certain categories of long-term prisoners. These restrictions included: no life-sentence prisoners being released from custody except by the Home Secretary, life was in certain cases, to mean life; those who murdered police officers, prison officers, or children, terrorists and those who carry firearms in the course of a robbery would serve a minimum of 20 years; the maximum sentence for carrying firearms in the furtherance of theft was increased from 14 years to life; no one sentenced to more than 5 years imprisonment for a crime of violence or for drug trafficking was to be released on parole except for a few months before the end of their sentence.[49] The Home Office itself recognized that the introduction of these measures 'will increase the number of long-term prisoners and [significantly] will reduce the range of incentives which bear on their behaviour'.[50] In 1984, as figures became available, it was possible to see this increase happening. In the first six months of that year only 13 offenders sentenced to more than 5 years for drug-trafficking or crimes of violence received parole before their final review compared to 113 in the same period in the previous year.[51]

In this context, and in the wake of the disturbances and demonstrations already referred to, the prison authorities have introduced and utilized a number of techniques in order to maintain stability and control. The basis on which these programmes have been implemented has been the idea that it is a few 'bad apples'[52] who manipulate an otherwise quiescent prison population into confrontation, disturbance and demonstration. At a general level, the authorities have continually reinforced and consolidated prison security measures through the extension of new technology and electronic equipment.[53] Added to this, as with the rest of the criminal justice process in England and Wales,[54, 55] the prisons are also being affected by what is happening in the North of Ireland. The Chief Inspector of Prisons pointed out in his annual report for 1983, for example, that the lessons to be learnt from the escape of 38 prisoners from the Maze Prison that year, apply as much to the prison system in England and Wales as to Northern Ireland when considering the custody and control of dangerous prisoners'.[56]

More specifically, the authorities have introduced and extended various techniques aimed at controlling, neutralizing and isolating those individuals who are regarded as difficult, recalcitrant or subversive. The use of psychotropic drugs to control the behaviour of prisoners has been a major area of controversy in British prisons in recent years,[57] as has been a number of cases of prisoners who have died in custody either through violence or through lack of care by the prison authorities.[58,59]. The introduction of a special squad of prison officers trained in techniques of riot control – the Minimum Use of Force Tactical Intervention Squad (MUFTI) – has further consolidated this drive towards maintaining order and control inside. It has been intimated recently that all prison officers are trained in the techniques of riot control.[60] The prison authorities have also used various forms of segregation in the form of solitary confinement, segregation units and control units[61] to isolate those regarded as difficult. The Prison Reform Trust has recently pointed to a 'significant rise'[62] in the use of special cells in the prisons which require no medical authorization for their use. In particular, the trust points out that women's prisons make a quite disproportionate use of segregation in these cells. They indicate that in 1982 'women in the remand centres were 31 times as likely to be subject to restraint as men in similar prisons'[63]

More recently, a Home Office working party, recognizing that there have been major problems of control in the long-term prisons, and arguing that there was a 'disruptive population ... of the order of 150–250',[64] have called for the introduction of five or six 'long-term prisoner units' to cater for a range of prisoners who present control problems ranging from the highly disturbed to the 'calculatedly subversive'.[65] In addition to units for the 'highly disturbed and highly dangerous',[66] the Home Office proposed a further three or four units should be established for prisoners who present control problems of other kinds.'[67] These units would not be places of last resort, nor according to the proposals would they be punitive in purpose. In addition, the authors of the report believe that they should be run on professional lines. As they point out:

> it is essential that the different units should complement each other and should not simply be an *ad hoc* collection of aims and regimes ... it is also crucially important that the operation and effectiveness of the various units should be centrally monitored and evaluated. We think that only a properly structured

and assessed programme of this kind can provide us with the firm data that we
currently lack in planning for control.[68]

Finally, the report also recommends that 'new generation' prisons should be
introduced which would provide an alternative to the existing policy of
dispersal. These new generation prisons, already introduced in the USA, are
made up of self-contained units which hold between 50 and 100 prisoners,
and where architecturally cells open on to a central area so that staff can
observe all of the cells, in true Benthamite fashion, without having to move
about 'in a consciously patrolling manner'.[60] The authors conclude that:

> the requirement for very high security accommodation is unlikely to be more
> than 300–400 and it would appear that if 'new generation' prison designs are
> indeed successful, this number could be held in two small prisons of the new
> kind without incurring the disadvantages that we have noted as being
> inherent in dispersal policy. We therefore recommend that these possibilities
> are urgently examined.[70]

In November 1984, at a meeting of prison governors, the Home Secretary
expressed the 'greatest interest' in the proposals: 'I am sure that we are now
going in the right direction'.[71] Evidence from the United States suggests
that these new generation prisons may not after all be the panacea for the
problems of the long-term prison system in England and Wales.[72]
Nonetheless, the first step to implementing the new policies was taken with
the announcement in September 1985 that two special units for 'disruptive'
long-term prisoners would open in a year at Parkhurst and Lincoln prisons.
The new Home Secretary, Douglas Hurd, said that these units would be
an effective means of managing prisoners who jeapardize the safety of staff
and other inmates'.[73]

Thus both in terms of short-term and long-term prisoners, the prison
system is expanding in England and Wales. According to Andrew Rutherford
the expanding prison system is performing a dualistic role, namely to

> incapacitate very serious offenders for long periods but also to provide brief
> and salutary prison sentences for minor offenders. With regard to both
> groups there is considerable elasticity, and under conditions of expansion the
> incapacitation net is stretched to include persons other than those convicted of
> serious offences. Habitual property offenders and institutional trouble-
> makers become likely candidates for inclusion. At the same time, the custodial
> threshold is lowered to include persons who earlier would have been fined or
> dealt with by some other non-custodial means.[74]

While Rutherford rightly points to the implications of these expansionist
policies in the prisons for both petty and serious offenders, and *how* they
occur, he does not question *why* they are happening at this historical
moment. The answer to this question is complex but some of the issues
which the question raises provide the focus for the final section of this
chapter.

Facing the Future: The Politics of the Prisons

When Leon Brittan announced the major prison-building programme and the changes in the parole system at the Conservative Party Conference in October 1983, he justified the programme, and tougher law and order policies, on the grounds that crime, particularly violent crime, was out of control. He told the party faithful that while

> tackling lawlessness and disorder is, of course, my top priority . . . it is more than just *my* top priority. In our first term of office the fight against the evil of inflation was the Government's most fundamental task. I believe that in our second term the fight against crime is the key task of all.
>
> There is today a great wave of anger against the wanton violence which disfigures our society. That anger is not confined to this Conference and this Party. It is real, it is genuine. I share it to the full.[75]

In the speech the Home Secretary carefully utilized the populist notion that certain crimes of violence – police murders, child murders and terrorist murders – were escalating and therefore should be responded to by tougher sentencing and penal policies. In raising the spectre of such crimes, Brittan conveniently ignored their uniqueness in proportion to the overall number of crimes recorded in England and Wales. In 1982 over 95% were 'offences against property and many of these were comparatively trivial'.[76] Ideologically and symbolically the violent crimes which he highlighted became crucial for his general argument. A society which allowed such things to happen needed to be disciplined and a sense of order, respect for authority and appreciation of stability restored. Particular images of criminality once again proved to be fundamental for the mobilization and consolidation of law and order policies. As Paul Gilroy has pointed out, 'because of their capacity to symbolize other relations and conflicts such images of crime and law-breaking have had a special ideological importance since the dawn of capitalism'.[77]

In the mid-1970s, as a number of radical criminological analyses indicated, it is also necessary to move beyond these important connections between discussions of crime and the increase in penal sanctions. This move involves situating the prisons in a wider social, political and economic context. The work of Thomas Mathiesen, Mike Fitzgerald and Frank Pearce in Europe[78] and Ivan Jankovic, Chuck Reasons and Russel Kaplan in North America[79] raised questions about the role that the prisons played in controlling surplus populations and maintaining order itself. More recent work in England and Wales by Steven Box and Chris Hale[80] has developed some of the issues raised by these earlier theorists. Box and Hale argue that

> the growth of unemployment which is itself a reflection of deepening economic crises, is accompanied by an increase in the range and severity of state coercion, including the rate and length of imprisonment. This increased use of imprisonment is not a direct response to any rise in crime but is an

ideologically motivated response to the perceived threat of crime posed by the swelling population of economically marginalized persons.[81]

The authors point out that for every 1,000 increase in youth unemployment, 23 additional young males are sent to prison. This process occurs after the effects of crime rates and court workload have been controlled for. Prisoners are getting both younger and blacker and are caught in a situation where sentencing policies and law and order campaigns

> are not that concerned to control serious crime. Rather they are more concerned to instil discipline, directly and indirectly, on those people who are no longer controlled by the soft-discipline machine of work and who might become growingly resentful that they are being made to pay the price of economic recession.[82]

A further aspect to the relationship between prisons and the maintenance of order is contained in the *Police Manual of Home Defence* which describes the procedures to be followed in the build-up to a nuclear war including measures to 'maintain internal security, especially the detention of "subversive" or potentially subversive people'.[83] Around 20,000 alleged subversives are thought to be on MI5's arrest list. The Special Branch would be directed by MI5 to arrest alleged subversives.

> Exact internment sites are not known, but under emergency powers legislation almost all the normal peacetime prison population would be released – leaving only the most dangerous prisoners. Whether the children of dissenting parents would be similarly detained or whether families would be forcibly split up is not clear.[84]

In considering the role that the prisons might play with regard to the maintenance of order, it is also important to situate the changes in penal policy and expansion of the system within the more general context of the changes which have occurred in the criminal justice process itself since Margaret Thatcher came to power in the spring of 1979. Since that time there have appeared and been enacted an impressive array of Acts and Bills which in a number of areas have augmented the power of the state. In addition the government has made money available to strengthen the police and prison services where in other areas spending has declined quite dramatically in real terms since 1979. A list of these developments is worth considering in order to grasp their range and scope. In the area of finance, for example, the budget for the police rose to £2.5 billion in 1983/4. By 1985, this budget had risen by 40% in real terms since 1979. Overall, as Table 1[85] indicates there has been a shift in resources towards law, order and defence expenditure and away from other public services.

In the general area of legislation a number of Bills have been introduced and Acts passed which have strengthened the power of the state in a range of areas: a Juvenile Justice Act passed in 1982 which has resulted in a major increase in the numbers of young people sent to prison; three Employment

Table 1 *Public Spending in Real Terms* (millions)

Increase between 1979/80 and 1985/86		79/80	85/86
Law and Order	+27%	3,746	4,767
Defence	+23%	13,405	16,499
Housing	−68%	6,569	2,921
Industry, energy, trade and employment	−26%	5,822	4,338
Other environmental services	−18%	3,833	3,153

Acts designed to regulate and control the activities of organized labour; a Contempt of Court Act which restricts the ability of the media to report court proceedings at the discretion of the judiciary; a new Prevention of Terrorism Act which extends the already draconian powers available to the police under the old Act; a Juries Disqualification Act which increased the number of individuals who could be debarred from jury service; a new Police Act which extends police powers including stop and search, arrest and detention; 10,400 new police officers have been employed; a White Paper reforming the law governing public order has been published which amongst other things will give the police new powers to control the size, location and duration of static demonstrations as well as imposing conditions on marches and processions. There has been an increase and extension in the use of technology such as riot equipment and computers. There has also been an increase in the number and activities of the security services, whose budget for 1986/7 increased to £1,000 million (ten times the sum publicly acknowledged); this increase has itself been reflected in a widening of the definition of subversion to include activities by those individuals, whose real aim is to harm our democracy but who for tactical or other reasons choose to keep (either in the long or short-term) within the letter of the law in what they do'.[86] This has allowed the security services to engage in surveillance activities and infiltrate groups such as the Campaign for Nuclear Disarmament (CND), trade unions, anti-racist groups and the National Council for Civil Liberties. Margaret Thatcher herself has spoken of an 'enemy within', of the 'Hard Left operating inside our system conspiring to use union power and the apparatus of local government to break, defy and subvert the laws.[87] This area of surveillance has been reinforced by the formation in May 1985 of a Central Intelligence Unit at Scotland Yard to be run by their Public Order Branch. The unit was to rely on 24 London district intelligence officers to pass on information about industrial disputes, meetings and community tension. These reports are then used to plan the deployment of the riot-trained Police Support Units.

Such surveillance techniques and the concern with subversion can also be

seen in the context of military exercises such as Wintex '85 which took place
between 26 February and 16 March 1985. According to the MP Dafyd Elis
Thomas, this exercise tested plans for 'crisis management' at a time of war
but has now more to do with fighting the enemy within than any external
threat:

> The experience of the miners' strike has shown that Wintex '85 is not a
> hypothetical exercise. The integration of police forces, the organization of
> supply convoys, the blocking of roads, the tapping of telephones and the
> harassing of activists show that Wintex '85 is not so much about what the state
> would do in the event of war but the sinister game the state is already playing,
> co-ordinating repression in the coalfields.[88]

Finally, following major disturbances in Birmingham, Leicester, and
Brixton and Tottenham in London, in the autumn of 1985, the Prime
Minister offered what *The Times* called a 'blank cheque' to the police for more
personnel and riot equipment. She told the Conservative Party Conference
that if the police 'need more men, more equipment, different equipment
they shall have them'.[89] Sir Kenneth Newman had already warned
Londoners that they were being put 'on notice' that he would not shrink
from using plastic bullets and tear gas to restore order 'should I believe it a
practical option for restoring peace and preventing crime and injury'.[90] The
process had already started with the press reporting that work was being
rushed through on a £100,000 training centre at Hounslow in London
which would ensure that all 26,000 uniformed police officers in the capital
could train there at least four times a year in a situation which 'includes
exact replicas of streets and housing estates in London'.[91] As significantly, it
was also reported that from mid-October the Special Patrol Group's
armoured personnel carriers would be permanently equipped with plastic
bullets and CS gas and would immediately begin 'emergency training in
handling the riot deterrents this week . . . Police forces in other major cities
are expected to follow London's lead by the end of the year.'[92] Finally, in a
speech to the London branch of the Police Federation, Newman announced
that not only would there be a new style of training for special squads
involving the regular use of plastic bullets and CS gas but 'senior police
officers who do not normally take part in riot training would be specially
instructed'.[93] Newman told the assembled audience that many more police
were to be trained to use plastic bullets and that 'A new centre is ready for
intense training of all ranks to a standard to meet the new level of
viciousness and violence with which we are now faced'.[94]

   This further escalation in the power of the police to mobilize in response
to public order situations came at the end of the year-long coal dispute
where their role in managing and controlling picket lines and mining
communities was seen by many in the communities as violent and
ruthless.[95] Both during and after the dispute the police had been involved in
other public order situations where their response had also been ruthless. In

December 1984, Thames Valley police broke up a picket of students in Oxford, arresting 35 people and allegedly turning the demonstration into a melee. In February 1985, Metropolitan police officers used wedge formations and horses to prevent demonstrators entering Trafalgar Square to a miners' rally. One person suffered a broken leg and others were injured. In March, the Greater Manchester force drove a wedge through students demonstrating against the attendance of the Home Secretary at the university. One observer claimed that hundreds of police appeared without warning and charged with full force at the students, several of whom were injured as they were pushed and thrown by their hair down a flight of stairs. In June 1985, members of the 'Peace Convoy' met the full force of police tactics on the road to Stonehenge:

> I witnessed women and children being hit with truncheons, glass from broken vehicle windows showering down on those inside and a mother dragged out of a shattered window with her child and thrown weeping to the ground ... windows were smashed by the police and occupants were dragged out through a storm of truncheons; broken heads, broken teeth, broken spectacles. It was a whirl of destruction. Officers started to climb through the broken windows, lashing out at all sides with their sticks. Reporters screamed at the police to calm down.[96]

Finally, in October, a demonstration by more than 2,000 people outside the South African Embassy in London was met by police who after severely-restricting the movement of the demonstrators, arrested 320 of them. Officers were seen to be using techniques of arrest such as wrist-bending based on Japanese martial arts. One black Anti Apartheid member described how:

> They grabbed my leg and I fell over. Then police piled in. I was grabbed away with my wrists bent back. They lifted me clear off the ground so that all my weight was on my bent wrists. I was screaming with pain. They called me 'nigger' and 'cunt'.[97]

During the arrests other women complained that their clothing was deliberately pulled in such a way that it amounted to sexual harassment while a blind black man was seen being forced to the ground.[98] This kind of police response towards demonstrators is also underpinned by a secret manual drawn up by the Association of Chief Police Officers for 'riot' situations which has abandoned the notion of reasonable force 'in arresting *offenders* and instead instructs riot squads how to set about "incapacitating" *demonstrators*'.[99]

In England and Wales there has been an important political debate about the precise nature of these changes in terms of their relationship to the politics of the Conservative Party under Margaret Thatcher and the emergence and consolidation of a new right authoritarianism in the society which itself is underpinned by the adherence to a monetarist economic policy and support for a free-market economy.

In the autumn of 1983, contributors to the journal *Critical Social Policy* outlined what they saw as the increasing authoritarianism in a whole range of state provision and services including social security, the law, housing, the National Health Service, education, the personal social services and social policies affecting women and black people.[100] These changes have been supported by the proposed abolition of the structure of local government in the main metropolitan areas of the country, the placing of individuals supportive of the monetarist thrust in key posts in industry and the civil service, the banning of trade unions in certain areas of government work and centralization of government decision-making within the inner sanction of the Thatcher Cabinet. While the importance of this shift has been stressed, some have pointed to the necessity of considering these changes in a much longer historical perspective. This is to stress the fact that

> the centralization and militarization of policing and the growth of repressive legal regulation have longer histories than most advocates of the Thatcherism concept would like to admit. This is principally because they are histories in which the Labour Party at every level has been extensively and intimately involved.[101]

In a number of influential articles Stuart Hall[102] has also pointed to some of the features to be considered in the analyses of Thatcherism and the emergence of a law and order society. Opening his 1979 Cobden Trust lecture, Hall argued that 'we are now in the middle of a deep decisive movement towards a more disciplinary, authoritarian kind of society'.[103] In developing his ideas, Hall has built upon Poulantzas's concept of 'authoritarian statism' (intensified state control over every sphere of socio-economic life) but has shifted the characterization of the conjuncture to 'authoritarian populism'. In doing so he hoped to 'encapsulate the contradictory features of the emerging conjuncture; a movement towards a dominative and "authoritarian" form of democratic class politics paradoxically, apparently rooted in the "transformism" . . . of populist discontents'.[104]

Paddy Hillyard, again building on the concept of 'authoritarian statism' developed by Poulantzas, has pointed to significant changes in the criminal justice process in the North of Ireland which can be seen to be influencing the changes and developments in the rest of the United Kingdom. Hillyard argues that

> while neither the army nor a paramilitary police patrol the streets, the movement towards the new form of a repressive apparatus is unmistakable. Over recent years in Britain there has been an enormous growth in the technology of control and the military capabilities of the police have been greatly expanded. Moreover, there have been moves to reform the criminal justice system along similar lines as the changes introduced into Northern Ireland in the early seventies.[105]

He outlines a number of strands in this process including a shift from policing offences to policing areas, the decline in the power of the legislature in the development of law and order policies with a concomitant increase in the influence of the police and army and an increasingly bureaucratized and more formal system of administering the criminal law. Hillyard's principal conclusion is that the form of repressive strategy adopted, 'far from being exceptional and a product of the unique circumstances of the political violence in Northern Ireland is, on the contrary, the form which many modern capitalist states are evolving'.[106]

Finally, the contributors to *The Empire Strikes Back*[107] have also demonstrated this rightward shift in state practices, particularly in relation to its articulation through the issues of race and racism. The authors argue that what has happened in Britain through the 1970s is not

a simple extension of repression but a recomposition of relations of power at all levels of society. Although the more overt forms of 'social control' are orchestrated by the police, it is important to note that the whole of society is constituted as a field of social relations structured in dominance. What were once tendencies have taken institutional form during the last few years.[108]

Conclusion

It is within this framework of analyses that the expansion of the prison system can best be understood. It is an analysis which situates initiatives in penal policies and practices within developments in the wider criminal justice process while simultaneously acknowledging the influence of changes within the political economy itself. It is also important to acknowledge that these developments in penal policies and criminal justice practices could be seen as indicative of the government's desire to establish a much more integrated and less informal process of justice in England and Wales which would approach problems of crime and public order in a manner which is rational, professional and ultimately ruthless.[109] The problems of the late twentieth century require such a response, especially in the light of the major disturbances in England and Wales in the summer of 1981 which found the police, in particular, unprepared for the scale and fury of the demonstrations. These events provided a salutary lesson to state servants such as the then Deputy Assistant Commissioner of the Metropolitan Police, Geoffrey Dear who has argued that the disturbances of 1981 'shook the apathy out of the system'.[110] Leon Brittan's short spell at the Home Office and the appointment of Kenneth Newman, the ex-head of the Royal Ulster Constabulary as Commissioner of Police for London were important moments in the move towards a more professional criminal justice system. Newman has since published a 60-page booklet on police ethics and professionalism called *The Principles of Policing and Guidance for Professional Behaviour* and makes clear that where a conflict arises between maintaining order and enforcing the law 'in the last resort the maintenance of public order will be given priority'[111] Leon Brittan himself was also quite clear in what he wanted when he went to the Home Office:

> on taking office I decided that we needed a strategy which would enable us to pursue our priorities and objectives in a deliberate and coherent way. Such a strategy is now in place. It covers all the main areas of the Department's work, both general policies and specific legislative or administrative objectives. We shall be reviewing it regularly. Our principal preoccupation is, and I believe ought to be the criminal justice system which incidently I wish to see treated in all that we do as a system.[112]

With regard to the prisons, Brittan and his successor Douglas Hurd, in true monetarist fashion, have demanded that they start to give value for money. Each prison therefore has been given its own individual budget whose limits it has to work within. Furthermore, some of the most hallowed work practices of the prison officers, especially those relating to overtime will be scrutinized and perhaps abandoned. This, needless to say, has been greeted with antagonism and hostility by the Prison Officers' Association. In demanding these changes Brittan also maintained however that the Prison Service must not be asked:

> to accommodate too many changes too quickly. It has a vital task to perform and must be left to get on with it. At the same time there is much to be done if the Service is to be properly trained and equipped to face successfully the challenges of the last decades of the twentieth century.[113]

In recognizing the significance, extent and impact of the changes in penal policies and the political and economic context within which they are taking place, it is clearly important not to adopt a purely instrumentalist view of the state and state power. There is no straight 'fit' between economy, class and state. As has been pointed out:

> The substantial transformations of the state during the seventies are not simply an outcome of the changes in the economy. To say this would be to confuse long-term tendencies with the immediate causes of change within the state. So it is important to see that the crisis which Britain faced during the seventies, and faces today, is a crisis of hegemony, an 'organic' crisis to use Gramsci's terminology. Its content is not reducible to a cyclic economic crisis in the traditional sense, or a 'crisis of the political system' in the narrow sense. It consists rather of profound changes in the balances of forces, in the class struggle and in the configuration of the class alliances.[114]

Equally it is also important to recognize that much of the process of rationalization and professionalization is fragmentary and incomplete, is contradictory in parts and is not wholeheartedly supported by different groups of state servants. The ongoing disputes between the Prison Officers' Association and the Home Office, the hostility between the Association of Chief Police Officers and the rank-and-file Police Federation and the Federation's resistance to Kenneth Newman's plans for the Metropolitan

Police provide evidence of this conflict. As importantly, the struggle of prisoners inside also provides a challenge and resistance to these changes. Allied to this, the struggle of groups outside of the walls such as the women at Greenham Common, black and mining communities and rank-and-file trade unionists highlight the difficulties that the government faces in its attempts to manage an increasingly fragile social order beset by economic decline, industrial stagnation and political conflict against a background of what Colin Leys has called 'the first instance of the threatened *absolute* decline of a fully capitalist social formation'.[115]

None the less, these developments pose a major threat to the very limited notions of justice and rights which citizens have had in England and Wales. The prisons are part of that process. It is a process in which they are performing a central and increasingly unambiguous role in the maintenance of order. In considering this position it is worth remembering a point made by Michael Ignatieff concerning the reform of the prison system in England and Wales in the 1840s. This thrust of his argument is significant for the situation today:

> The persistent support for the penitentiary is inexplicable so long as we assume that its appeal rested on its functional capacity to control crime. Instead its support rested on a larger social need. It had appeal because the reformers succeeded in presenting it as a response, not merely to crime, but to the whole social crisis of a period, and as part of a larger strategy of political, social, and legal reform designed to re-establish order on a new foundation. As a result, while criticized for its functional shortcomings, the penitentiary continued to command support because it was seen as an element of a larger vision of order that by the 1840s commanded the reflexive assent of the propertied and powerful.[116]

It is that 'larger vision of order' which has to be appreciated if the politics of the prisons in England and Wales are to be clearly understood, and responded to, in the last quarter of the twentieth century.

Acknowledgements

Thanks to all of those who attended my session at the European Conference in Hamburg. The discussion and comments were very helpful in clarifying my thoughts. Special thanks to Anette Ballinger and to Rusty for their support.

Finally thanks to The Clash for providing the first part of the title to this chapter.

Notes

1 See *The Guardian*, 29 July 1985, 9 August 1985, 10 August 1985, 20 August 1985, 3 September 1985.

2 *The Guardian*, 18 April 1985.

3 *The Guardian*, 10 August 1985. It is also worth noting that figures compiled by the National Association for the Care and Resettlement of Offenders (NACRO) at the same time showed that in 1982 (the last year when figures were available) the United Kingdom as a whole imprisoned, both in absolute numbers and in proportion to the population more people than other comparable nations of Western Europe. 274 men and women were imprisoned per 100,000 of the population in that year. NACRO, *The Use of Imprisonment: Some Facts and Figures*, p. 1.

4 *The Guardian*, 10 December 1984.

5 *The Guardian*, 15 August 1985.

6 *The Guardian*, 21 May 1985; *The Guardian* 6 June 1985; Home Office, *Criminal Justice: A Working Paper* Home Office, 1986, p. 34.

7 *The Guardian*, 10 August 1985.

8 Home Office, *Criminal Justice: A Working Paper*, Home Office, 1984, p. 24.

9 Geoff Coggan cited in *The Guardian*, 14 June 1985.

10 Speech by the Home Secretary to the Prison Officers' Association's National Conference, 21 May 1985, p. 3.

11 *Prison Service News*, 1983; *The Standard*, 21 November 1983.

12 M. Fitzgerald and J. Sim, *British Prisons*, Oxford, Basil Blackwell, 1982; M. Fitzgerald and J. Sim, 'Legitimating the prison crisis: a critical review of the May Report', *The Howard Journal*, vol. XIX, 1980, pp. 73–84.

13 *Report of the Work of the Prison Department England and Wales 1980*, HMSO, Cmnd 8228, p. 4.

14 Ibid. p. 18.

15 Home Office, op. cit. p. 22.

16 *Report of Her Majesty's Chief Inspector of Prisons 1984*, HMSO, cited in *The Guardian*, 25 October 1985.

17 Ibid.

18 Fitzgerald and Sim, op. cit. p. 11.

19 Speech by the Home Secretary, op. cit. pp. 6–7.

20 *The Guardian*, 10 August 1985.

21 *The Guardian*, 21 June 1985.

22 *The Guardian*, 26 April 1985.

23 *New Statesman*, 25 November 1984.

24 *The Sun*, 23 April 1985; *The Guardian*, 7 June 1985.

25 *The Guardian*, 21 September 1985.

26 Fitzgerald and Sim, op. cit. ch. 4.

27 Home Office, *Managing the Long-Term Prison System. The Report of the Control Review Committee*, Home Office, 1984. In Scotland similiar events were happening in Peterhead, Scotland's only maximum security prison. See J. Boyle, *A Sense of Freedom*, London, Pan, 1977.

28 M. Ryan and J. Sim, 'Decoding Leon Brittan', *The Abolitionist*, no. 16, 1984.

29 P.M. Quinn, 'Help for prisoners at adjudication: second thoughts', *British Journal of Criminology*, vol. 24, no. 4, 1984, p. 396.

30 Fitzgerald and Sim, op. cit. p. 6.

31 M. Fitzgerald, *Prisoners in Revolt*, Harmondsworth, Middx, Penguin, 1977.

32 Cited in *Report of her Majesty's Chief Inspector of Prisons*, op. cit. p. 17.

33 Hansard, 24 March 1982, col. 987.

34 Adam Smith Institute, *Justice Policy*, Adam Smith Institute, 1984, p. 61.

35 NACRO, op. cit. p. 2.

36 Fitzgerald and Sim, op. cit. pp. 23–4.

37 A. Rutherford, *Prisons and the Process of Justice*, London, Heinemann, 1983.

38 *The Guardian*, 14 June 1985.

39 Hansard, 24 January 1984.

40 K. Pease, 'Community service and prison: are they alternatives?', in K. Pease and W. McWilliams (eds), *Community Service by Order*, Edinburgh, Scottish Academic Press, 1980.

41 S. Cohen, *Crime and Punishment: Some Thoughts on Theories and Policies*, Radical Alternatives to Prison, 1979. See also S. Cohen, *Visions of Social Control*, Cambridge, Polity Press, 1985.

42 *The Guardian*, 14 March 1985.

43 Personal communication with a parole board member.

44 *Daily Telegraph*, 15 October 1984; *The Times*, 15 October 1984.

45 *Daily Telegraph*, 5 May 1983.

46 Fitzgerald and Sim, op. cit. p. 20.

47 S. Cohen and L. Taylor, *Psychological Survival*, 2nd edn, Harmondsworth, Middx, Penguin, 1981, p. 10.

48 Home Office, op. cit. p. 13.

49 Ryan and Sim, op. cit. p. 6.

50 Home Office, op. cit. p. 1.

51 *The Guardian*, 14 March 1985.

52 Fitzgerald and Sim, op. cit. p. 93.

53 Ibid. pp. 98–100.

54 P. Hillyard, 'From Belfast to Britain: some critical comments on the Royal Commission on Criminal Procedure', in D. Adam *et al.*, *Politics and Power* Vol. IV, London, Routledge & Kegan Paul, 1981.

55 P. Hillyard, 'Lessons from Ireland', in B. Fine and R. Millar *Policing the Miners' Strike*, London, Lawrence & Wishart, 1985.

56 Home Office, *Report of Her Majesty's Chief Inspector of Prisons*, HMSO, 1983, p. 11.

57 T. Owen and J. Sim, 'Drugs discipline and prison medicine: the case of George Wilkinson', in P. Scraton and P. Gordon, (eds), *Causes for Concern*, Harmondsworth, Middx, Penguin, 1984.

58 G. Coggan and M. Walker, *Frightened for My Life*, London, Fontana, 1982.

59 P. Scraton and K. Chadwick, *In the Arms of the Law*, London, Pluto Press, 1987.

60 Personal communication with a serving prison officer.

61 Fitzgerald, op. cit. pp. 40–1.

62 Prison Reform Trust, *Beyond Restraint*, The Prison Reform Trust, 1984, p. 2.

63 Ibid. p. 7.

64 Home Office, op. cit. p. 15.

65 Ibid. p. 17.

66 Ibid. p. 21.

67 Ibid.

68 Ibid. p. 22.

69 Ibid. p. 7.

70 Ibid. p. 8.

71 *The Listener*, 18 April 1985.

72 See ibid.

73 *The Guardian*, 18 September 1985.

74 Rutherford, op. cit. p. 58.

75 Conservative Party News Service, *Extract from Leon Brittan's Speech to the Conservative Party Conference*, 11 October 1983, p. 2 (emphasis in original).

76 *Criminal Statistics England and Wales*, Cmnd 9048, London, HMSO, 1982, p. 32.

77 P. Gilroy, 'The myth of black criminality' in M. Eve and D. Musson (eds), *The Socialist Register*, London, Merlin, 1982, p. 47; reprinted as Chapter 5 of the present volume. See also S. Hall *et al.*, *Policing the Crisis*, London, Macmillan, 1978.

78 T. Mathiesen, *The Politics of Abolition*, London, Martin Robertson, 1974; M. Fitzgerald, op. cit.; F. Pearce 'Crime, corporations and the American social order', in I. Taylor and L. Taylor (eds), *Politics and Deviance*, Harmondsworth, Middx., Penguin, 1973, pp. 13–41.

79 I. Jankovic, 'Labour market and imprisonment', *Crime and Social Justice*, vol. 8, 1978, pp. 17–34; C. Reasons and R. Kaplan, 'Tear down the walls? Some functions of prisons', *Crime and Delinquency*, vol. 21, 1975, pp. 260–72.

80 S. Box and C. Hale, 'Economic crisis and the rising prisoner population in England and Wales', *Crime and Social Justice*, 17, September 1982, pp. 20–35.

81 Ibid. p. 22.

82 S. Box, *Power, Crime and Mystification*, London, Tavistock, 1983, p. 22.

83 *The Guardian*, 19 March 1985.

84 Ibid.

85 *The Guardian*, 23 January 1985.

86 *The Guardian*, 29 January 1985.

87 Conservative Party News Service, 'Why democracy will last', *The Second Carlton Lecture by Margaret Thatcher*, 26 November 1984, p. 10.

88 *The Guardian*, 10 February 1985.

89 *The Times*, 12 October 1985.

90 *The Observer*, 13 October 1985.

91 *News of the World*, 13 October 1985.

92 *The Mail on Sunday*, 13 October 1985.

93 *Daily Express*, 17 October 1985.

94 *Daily Mail*, 17 October 1985.

95 Welsh Campaign for Civil and Political Liberties and National Union of Mineworkers, *Striking Back*, WCCPL/NUM 1985; J. Coulter, S. Miller and M. Walker, *State of Siege*, London, Canary Press, 1984; M. Jones, *Killed on the Picket Line 1984: The story of David Gareth Jones*, London, New Park Publications, 1985; P. Scraton, *The State of the Police*, London, Pluto, 1985.

96 *The Observer*, 2 June 1985.

97 *New Statesman*, 25 October 1985, p. 5.

98 Ibid.

99 O. Hansen, 'The armlock of the law', *New Statesman*, 25 October 1985, p. 11.

100 *Critical Social Policy*, Issue 8, Autumn 1983. See also T. Mainwaring and N. Sigler, *Breaking the Nation: A Guide to Thatcher's Britain* Pluto Press and New Socialist, 1985.

101 P. Gilroy and J. Sim, 'Law, order and the state of the left', *Capital and Class*, no. 25, Spring 1985, p. 18.

102 See, in particular, S. Hall, 'The great moving right show', *Marxism Today*, January 1979, pp. 14–19; S. Hall, 'Authoritarian populism: a reply', *New Left Review*, no. 151, May/June 1985, pp. 115–24.

103 S. Hall, *Drifting into a Law and Order Society*, Cobden Trust, 1980, p. 3.

104 S. Hall, 'Authoritarian populism: a reply to Jessop *et al.*', *New Left Review*, no. 151, May/June 1985, p. 118.

105 P. Hillyard, 'Law and Order', in J. Darby, (ed.), *Northern Ireland: Background to the Conflict*, Belfast, Appletree Press, 1983, p. 60.

106 Ibid.

107 Centre for Contemporary Cultural Studies, *The Empire Strikes Back*, London, Hutchinson, 1982; see also P. Gordon, *Whitelaw*, London, Pluto, 1983.

108 Ibid. p. 21.

109 Thanks to Paul Gilroy and Paddy Hillyard for discussing this point with me.

110 Cited in Gilroy and Sim, op. cit. p. 49.

111 Cited in *Policing London*, no. 19, August/September 1985, p. 67.

112 Leon Brittan. Evidence to the House of Commons Home Affairs Select Committee, 23 January 1984, cited in *Criminal Justice: A Working Paper*, Home Office, May 1984, Foreword.

113 Leon Brittan. Speech to the Prison Officer's Association op. cit. p. 13. A similar theme of rationalizing crime control in terms of strategic policing, private security and volunteer patrols for the USA is discussed in J. Wilson, (ed.), *Crime and Public Policy*, Institute for Contemporary Studies Press, 1983.

114 Centre for Contemporary Cultural Studies, op. cit. p. 19.

115 C. Leys, 'Thatcherism and British manufacturing: a question of hegemony', *New Left Review*, No. 151, May/June 1985, p. 5 (emphasis in original).

116 M. Ignatieff, *A Just Measure of Pain*, London. Macmillan, 1978, p. 120.

7

'Speaking Ill of the Dead': Institutionalized Responses to Deaths in Custody

Phil Scraton and Kathryn Chadwick

Introduction

In 1980, following the controversy which surrounded the deaths of Jimmy Kelly and Blair Peach at the hands of the police, the Deaths in Custody project was founded. The main purpose of the project was to monitor specific cases of custody deaths – involving the police, prisons and secure institutions – and cases in which negligence or brutality were alleged. It is one of a series of projects which have their origin in the debates which have emerged from writings in and around critical criminology during the late 1970s.[1] Central to these debates was the relationship between what Wright termed the 'world at the level of appearances'[2] and the broader political and economic frameworks which provide determining contexts within which individuals interact and react. Important to these developments was the exhaustive analysis by Hall *et al.*[3] of mugging as a moral panic within the contexts of the political-economic crisis of advanced capitalism and the ideological construction of law and order issues. Furthermore there has been a real attempt, particularly in feminist analyses,[4] to examine critically the rule and practice of the law and the state in terms of people's own accounts of how they experience and receive the state's interventions and to contrast these experiences against official accounts and appreciable shifts in the definition, enforcement and application of the law. What this direction in research embodies is the objective of establishing a synthesis between experiences manifest at the personal, social and structural levels. It responds to E.P. Thompson's call to root analyses of the rule of law and authoritarian shifts in the state and their operational consequences within a systematic examination of case histories.[5] Further to this is Sivanandan's priority of 'turning cases into issues'.[6] Taken together these directions have created an initiative in critical research which has provided close monitoring of the police, prisons, mental institutions and courts. Inevitably, given its explicitly critical nature, much of this work has been carried out without the formal cooperation of the state agencies but findings from those projects which have gained such access have underlined the significance of critical work.[7]

Much of this work is concerned with how 'official' definitions of class, race and gender – for example – are combined with images, assumptions and reputations of criminality and deviance. It is the institutionalization of such images which, over time, become ideologies. The systematic, institutionalized transmission of these ideological constructs provides the basis for the political management of crime, 'social problems' and a whole range of social policy and criminal justice responses. As Stedman-Jones has shown most clearly the classification of people in terms of a 'rough-respectable' continuum and in terms of their perceived collective 'dangerousness' or moral degeneration was well established in the administration of Victorian values of justice.[8] The disciplining and regulation of the masses in the late nineteenth century used the ideology of the genuine or deserving poor as a means of condemning many to harsh regimes in prisons, asylums and workhouses.[9] These continua, relating to respectability, conformity and genuineness, have remained as integral components in the administration of contemporary welfare and justice. They are visible in the social construction of the 'mugger', the 'inadequate' and the 'mad'. They extend to images of the 'psychopath' and the 'terrorist' and their consequences go beyond the common-sense assumptions of daily encounter. They are the stock-in-trade of the tabloid press, reinforcing fears and igniting prejudice. They are not merely analytical constructs but are powerful definitions present in the discretionary use of state power by the police, Department of Health and Social Security officials, magistrates, judges and prison officers.

Sexism, racism and classism are ideologies deeply institutionalized in the British state. They provide the ready justification for the marginalization of identifiable groups. The process of marginalization, particularly the enforced unemployment of a relative surplus population to stabilize the long recessions of capitalism, is rooted at the economic level but its interpretation, in terms of class fractions, is necessary at the political and ideological levels. In that sense the intervention of the state's institutions – its very political management – reflects, transmits and reinforces the ideological construction of identities and reputations. It is this *range* of responses – economic, political and ideological – which cuts into people's daily lives and which, taken together, forms the process of marginalization. Consequently just as sections of the working class become marginalized, so their identities or reputations become criminalized. Stop and search, employed universally in inner cities by police against black people, is one obvious example of the effective consequences of the process of marginalization. What the 'official' connection between blacks and street crime has achieved is the daily, hourly harassment of black people by police and other state agencies merely because they are black.[10]

The politics of marginalization, then, has become an integral part of the operation of criminal justice. The continua related to this process – rough/ respectable, dangerous/conforming, undeserving/deserving – are employed to construct identities which then justify harsh and differential responses in the enforcement and application of the rule of law. It is in this way, reinforced by class, race and patriarchal prejudices of the British state tradition, that the continua become embedded in official discourse. Thus a man who violently raped a woman can be given a £2,000 fine because the judge considered that the woman was guilty of 'contributory negligence' in accepting the rapist's offer of a lift.[11] A man can be given a suspended sentence for the murder of his wife because it was considered that by having occasional relationships with other men she was guilty of provocation.[12] These two examples are typical of many similar judgements made by the police, magistrates and judges in their enforcement and application of the law.[13] They reflect the ease with which sexist assumptions about women's ascribed sexuality can be employed to dismiss the brutality of oppression experienced regularly by women in patriarchal society.[14] Their institution-alization reveals the serious consequences of sexist ideologies.

Thus the concern of critical analyses of the state and the rule of law has been to trace the connections between the political management of marginalized groups within state policy – as forms of regulation and control – and the real consequences for people in their daily negotiation with state agencies. Where people are placed on the appropriate continua (that is, the subjective judgement of their 'worthiness', 'reliability', 'genuineness', and so on) is the effective construction of identity and reputation. It is only through an analysis of the use of negative reputation that a broader understanding of the significance of the coroner's court, in the cases of deaths in custody or in other related, controversial circumstances, can be reached.[15]

In an earlier important paper which focused on the death of James Davey in police custody the Warwick Inquest Group provided a critical and imaginative analysis of the procedures of referral, investigation and examination which contextualize the coroner's inquest. As the group stated, 'the state has adopted the inquest, rather than the criminal prosecution and trial, as the forum for the public examination of those deaths where the police are suspected of bearing some responsibility'.[16] We extend that assertion to include prison custody where often the only witnesses to the death are the custodians themselves. Inevitably, then, friends and relatives of the deceased attend the inquest in the expectation that the issue of liability is on the agenda. Repeatedly they are disappointed and frustrated in their attempts to gain access to the relevant investigative documents. Beyond that, as this chapter will show, they become disillusioned and embittered by a procedure which relies on the effective building of negative reputations of the deceased in often unsubtle attempts to justify acts of negligence or brutality. This work is an added dimension to our longer-term project and we have relied heavily on attending inquests, the appropriate transcripts and interviews with families and friends of the deceased in order to establish a broader structural analysis of the procedures and influences typically present in controversial cases.

Controversial Deaths and Official Discourse

> Liddle told his doctors, family and friends that what he got outside the Key Club was nothing to what he got later inside the police station. He revealed how five police took their jackets off and kicked and beat him until he pleaded with them to stop. Liddle was let out of the police station the next morning. He was so ill and badly injured he could hardly move.[17]

Liddle Towers was a 39-year-old electrician who was arrested outside a Gateshead club early in 1976. Civilian eye-witnesses alleged that the eight arresting officers gave him a severe beating. He never recovered from the injuries that he sustained and in February 1976, just three weeks after his arrest, he died. Following the police investigation into a complaint made by his family no police officers were prosecuted with his assault nor was there considered to have been any breach of force discipline. An inquest was held into his death during October 1976 and the jury returned a verdict of justifiable homicide. The verdict confirmed that, *whatever the reason*, the police had killed Liddle Towers. Given that eight officers arrested and handcuffed him it seemed inconceivable that his killing could be justified. The family felt that effectively the inquest verdict legitimated an unlawful killing. Undoubtedly the verdict was a major embarrassment to the authorities – if Liddle Towers was killed by the police then the issue of liability should have been pursued and settled in the criminal courts. The Attorney General made a rare step and applied to the Queen's Bench Divisional Court and the Lord Chief Justice quashed the inquest verdict.[18] It was the Lord Chief Justice's opinion that a verdict consistent with the evidence would have been accidental death, the fatal injury being sustained when an officer had 'accidentally fallen onto Towers'.

The coroner at the second inquest interpreted this ruling by the following instruction to the jury:

> If you think that the force used was reasonable in the circumstances then you would return a verdict of death by misadventure even if you thought that, in

the course of it, there were *some acts which went beyond the bounds of proper conduct* on the part of the police officers if you are not satisfied that *these acts caused the death*. (emphasis added)[19]

The jury's unanimous verdict following this unambiguous direction was 'death by misadventure' and was consistent with the earlier ruling of the Lord Chief Justice.

The coroner's instruction, however, revealed serious inconsistencies over liability. Acts *might contribute* to a death but the coroner directed that the jury needed to be satisfied that they *caused* the death. Further, he introduced the issue of 'reasonable force'. It was the jury's assessment of 'reasonable' in the circumstances which was central to the eventual verdict. On this subjective and distant assessment, flying in the face of eye-witness allegations of police brutality, the verdict of misadventure was reached. The confusion and contradictions of the two inquests created widespread concern. This focused particularly on the issue of personal liability and the adequacy of the inquest procedure for handling deaths in police custody or deaths which involved allegations of police brutality or negligence. The confusion over liability was compounded further in the press. Typical of this was the following headline: 'POLICE ARE CLEARED OVER LIDDLE TOWERS'.[20]

A coroner's inquest, however, is not a court in which people are on trial. It is an inquiry and its procedure is inquisitorial and not adversarial, as in other courts. In that sense 'guilt' is not at issue and no one is accused. Should liability, civil or criminal, be raised then the inquest should be adjourned and the issue of liability resolved in the appropriate court. The coroner's discretion is permissive and exceptional. He or she (there are only two women coroners) is solely responsible for the holding of an inquest; for the conduct of the inquest including the selection, calling and examination of witnesses; for summing up their evidence and for directing the jury, in cases where a jury is used; and for the naming of 'possible' verdicts. The purpose of the inquest is limited to arriving at a verdict consistent with the physical cause of death. Inevitably the circumstances in which the death occurred must play a part in weighting the evidence before the inquest. The circumstances are important to the pathologist in writing her or his medical report on the death, to the coroner's investigation, to the selection and examination of witnesses and, ultimately, to the coroner's direction of the jury. Clearly in situations where deaths occur in controversial circumstances, liability is the central issue as far as families of the deceased are concerned. Further, as the Liddle Towers case revealed, when complainants are denied access to the internal police investigations the inquest provides the only forum in which the evidence can be heard, albeit in part, and cross-examined. It has been this sequence of events which has contributed significantly to the elevation of the issue of liability to one of primary concern.   In April 1979, with the Liddle Towers controversy still continuing, Blair Peach was clubbed to death by a member of the Metropolitan Police Special Patrol Group.[21] He was returning from an anti-fascist demonstration against the National Front in Southall when he was caught up in a police charge. Two months later Jimmy Kelly died, drunk and beaten, in police custody on Merseyside.[22] In both situations civilians claimed to have witnessed acts of police brutality. These cases heightened the concern over the death of Liddle Towers. With complaints in both cases not upheld the inquests again became the sites of controversy over criminal liability. This inappropriate pressure on the coroner's court was increased further when the Home Secretary, William Whitelaw, refused demands for public inquiries until the inquest verdicts has been reached.

This series of cases developed into a major political row in Parliament. In 1979 and 1980 two MPs, Michael Meacher and Stan Newens, used parliamentary questions to gain information on the extent of deaths in custody. The figures were obtained with surprising difficulty. There was no central record of deaths in police custody or related deaths and the figures had to be collected from each chief constable. The first official figure provided for England and Wales,and covering the period 1970 to 1979, was 245 but this was later revised to 274: 138 in police cells and 138 in hospital while still technically in custody. There were no figures provided for related deaths; that is, as a result of injuries sustained while in police custody (such as Liddle Towers) or as a result of an act of police brutality outside custody (such as Blair Peach).

It was the climate of public concern generated by the specific deaths, the lack of precise records on deaths in police custody or in related circumstances, and the emerging confusion over the coroner's procedures for referral, investigation and examination of controversial deaths which led, in 1980, to a Home Affairs Committee (HAC) inquiry into deaths in police custody. The HAC inquiry took evidence from eleven sources which included: five police-related bodies (the Police Federation, Association of Chief Police Officers, Metropolitan Police, Police Superintendents' Association, Association of Police Surgeons); three government agencies (Home Office, Director of Public Prosecutions, Solicitor General for Scotland); and the two professional bodies directly involved (the Coroners' Society, the British Association for Forensic Medicine). Michael Meacher was the only individual to submit evidence yet there existed a whole range of campaign groups and several civil liberties organizations which had developed important work around specific cases and their broader implications. This material was not sought out by the inquiry.

What was claimed as a thorough HAC inquiry, then, was by the very constitution of the evidence little more than a summary of 'official discourse'. This is a significant criticism of the thoroughness claimed for the inquiry as there is a clear coincidence of interests between the ten organizations listed above, for they share a well-established and deeply rooted commitment to the formal structures as they exist and a close ideological association on law and order issues. Thus it was no surprise that the report dismissed 'generalized accusations of police brutality to those in custody', while stating that 'the limits of our investigation do not permit us to form any view about individual allegations'.[23] It is difficult to establish just what the committee was driving at in this statement as there is no evidence to suggest that generalized accusations of police brutality had ever been made. The controversy had arisen out of specific cases and their handling by various state agencies and, taken together, they indicated that there were serious problems over the procedures of investigation and examination covering deaths in police custody. Yet no informed evidence specific to these cases was taken by the HAC. Quite wrongly the HAC statement was taken by the media as a generalized exoneration of the police and as a reaffirmation of the adequacy of the coroner's inquest in relation to the specific cases. The issues raised by the cases were not identified, let alone discussed, by the HAC inquiry.

Following the outcry over the cases of Liddle Towers, Blair Peach and Jimmy Kelly the issue of deaths in other forms of custody, particularly prison, added further important dimensions to the controversy. Since 1979 there has been a range of material published on deaths in custody or deaths in controversial circumstances. This has taken the form of accounts of specific cases;[24] of unofficial inquiries;[25] of analyses of deaths in prison,[26] and the setting up of a range of campaign groups.[27] In 1980 our research project was funded to critically examine the relationship between the coroners' procedures and deaths in custody or in related circumstances. The project has examined the controversial tradition of the coroner's court, the contemporary structure and application of the procedures, a whole range of specific cases and the broader implication of the cases.[28]

This chapter introduces a relatively new development in the work. Following criticisms of the investigation and inquest procedures which emerged out of the controversial cases the police, the coroners and the Home Office repeatedly stated that families had voiced few complaints. The implication of such official comment was that politicians and campaigners were using cases as political currency in the debates over police powers and accountability. One coroner, interviewed early in the project, voiced a typical reaction:

> The Meachers of this world have isolated deaths in police custody as being of political interest ... they're not interested in the individual cases... it's anti-establishment, anti-police, anti-prison... trying to get a kick in... you start agitation, you start demonstration,... rent a crowd.[29]

In a centre-page spread, the day after the three-week inquest into the death of Jimmy Kelly had ended, the *Daily Mail* headline read: 'JIMMY KELLY'S LAST FAILURE'. The article commented that Jimmy Kelly's life was one of persistent failure. It portrayed a man to be pitied, someone who had 'failed' at everything that he had attempted. The 'last failure' referred to in the headline was the failure of the case to become a 'cause celebre'. It concluded:

> It was used by politically-motivated people, who jumped on a local bandwagon

of reasonable concern to stir up his ghost to harass and haunt police and authority as a whole...Whatever he did in his life he did not deserve the Workers' Revolutionary Party taking over his death.[30]

The paper's editorial mockingly referred to Jimmy Kelly as 'THE CORPSE THAT BECAME TRENDY'. Apart from causing Jimmy Kelly's family further distress and anger, the article reflected, once again, a theme which recurred in the 'official' commentaries on the cases. This was the assumption, without any evidence, that the cases and their associated campaigns had been hijacked and then manipulated by groups on the 'extreme left' in order to discredit the police and the courts. Kenneth Oxford, the Chief Constable of Merseyside, complained bitterly that the Kelly case was used to mount an 'almost neurotic attack on the police service generally'. He continued:

> The tragic Kelly case was further cited to illustrate my reluctance to inform my police authority of matters pertinent to their responsibility: again completely unfounded and untrue, but seized upon by those who question the accountability of chief police officers.[31]

In his annual report for 1979, as in other statements, the Chief Constable attacked members of the county council and members of the police committee for 'vituperative, misinformed comment'.

The Tory chairman of the police committee at the time of the inquest stated that the Kelly family was being used by 'insidious people who are bent on destroying law and order'.[32] The chairman of the Police Federation, Jim Jardine, described the campaign as 'the usual ragbag of people who spend their time sniping at the police service'. He told Federation members on Merseyside that the cases amounted to a 'campaign of abuse' which represented a concerted effort to 'denigrate the whole police service'.[33] More seriously, the former Metropolitan Police Commissioner, Sir Robert Mark, used the cases to warn of 'the danger of subversion of the operational independence and thus the impartiality of the police'.[34] Mark's successor, Sir David McNee, argued that it was not just a case of 'obvious extremists' but people of apparent good intent – church leaders and local politicians – who were 'undermining our authority and seeking to destroy our tradition of policing by consent'[35] He warned such people to 'get off our backs'.

In this almost neurotic response to the serious allegations concerning acts of police and prison brutality and to the considerable doubts concerning the adequacy of the coroner's inquest, the families' responses to their own cases were lost. Clearly many deaths in custody do not bring complaints from friends or relatives of the deceased. There are a considerable number of deaths the circumstances of which are uncontested. However, it is difficult to assess how many deaths would be contested if people had the information and resources upon which to base their cases. People tend to have a deep sense of trust in the fairness and impartiality of the criminal justice process. There is an implicit trust in the police and in the thoroughness and rigour of the police complaints procedure. Coroners, like pathologists, are viewed, almost universally, as being state officials independent of the police, the prisons and the criminal courts. In that sense, as the official account of the procedures claims, the police investigation of complaints and the coroner's investigation represent thorough, impartial and independent inquiries. In the latter case, the inquest is portrayed as a 'public inquiry'[36]

While there is an apparent acceptance and confidence in the thoroughness and impartiality of the investigation of deaths in custody or in cases involving allegations of brutality or negligence the depth of such official claims has to be considered in terms of particular cases and the people caught up in their investigation. What has become clear is that with so much tension surrounding the cases, with the police, the coroners and the Home Office so apparently 'threatened' by challenges over state powers and accountability in custody situations, the inquests into these controversial deaths have become legal battlegrounds over criminal liability. In these cases counsel representing state interests (that is, police officers, prison officers, chief constables) set out to establish reputations of individuals which suggest, in some way, that the deaths could be legitimated. The ease with which 'reputations' can be used to justify deaths in custody and to minimize the seriousness of allegations is evident from a comment made by Dr Johnson of the British Association of Forensic Medicine. In answer to a question about whether he thought there was any real concern about the numbers of people who die in police custody he replied:

> No, I do not, frankly. The people who die in custody, are, for the most part, people, if I may say so, at risk; they are alcoholics, drug addicts, people wandering at large, vagrants, the underprivileged, let us call them. I think that they are at risk anyway.[37]

This position on the 'type' of people who die in custody has serious implications at two associated levels. First, it typifies an attitude that the deaths of such people in custody remain non-controversial. It assumes that people who choke on their own vomit, hang themselves in a distressed state, or die unattended in a police cell are not controversial so long as they are checked every half-hour. The easy processing of such cases through the coroner's court as though they represent a kind of 'normal' or 'acceptable' death in custody is a practice of real concern.[38] The second implication of this position is that the authorities marginalize the people concerned. A negative reputation is established and developed which suggests that *they* – the people who have died – are the problem. It is as if their actions have contributed to their deaths. What is clear from those cases which have become controversial is that where people could not be located in such 'obvious' categories then attempts were made to establish negative reputations which complied with the responses of the police or prison officers and which, if accepted, provided justification for brutality.

Images of Violence

From the early 1970s the law and order platform now closely associated with the politics of Thatcherism has been constructed successfully on an appeal to 'common sense'–that 'society is more violent'. The folk-devils have been mobilized with care and connected to each other as if to illustrate that the moral fabric, as well as the political-economic base, is trapped in the process of universal degeneration. The United Kingdom is in the grip of the mugger, the hooligan, the urban guerilla, the militant trade unionist, the ultra-left politician, the political terrorist and, incredibly, the woman protester. In November 1984 at the height of the coal dispute the Prime Minister and the Home Secretary made simultaneous speeches which focused on the 'spectrum of violence' and 'the enemy within'. Margaret Thatcher made the unqualified equation between democratically elected politicians/union officials and political terrorists. Her statement was the end of a long road, built on the bitter memory of the defeat of the Heath government by the consolidated efforts of the unions, and it represented the end of what Stuart Hall termed the 'drift' into a law and order society.[39] The authoritarianism promised in the 1979 Conservative Party Manifesto had been brought to life with harsh policies (for example, clampdown on welfare claimants, and the 'short, sharp, shock') and new laws (for example, three Employment Acts, the Police and Criminal Evidence Act, and the Public Order Act). In case there was any doubt left in the public's mind the announcement, in May 1985, of the White Paper on Public Order was prefaced by listing the full range of folk-devils referred to above.

Within this climate harsh responses by and within the state have been justified as being reasonable in the circumstances. Just as 'reasonable force' has to be justified by the police in the arrest and restraint of individuals so this notion has been applied generally throughout the last twenty years to justify general policy and law-making responses of a repressive nature be it in Ireland's six northern counties, on the picket lines or on the streets of Brixton, Toxteth and Handsworth. Clearly in situations where forceful policing or strongarm practices have led to serious injury or death the imagery of violence and lawlessness has been purposefully developed in building public reputations of individuals or neighbourhoods. It is as if they as individuals–or their immediate environment–contributed to the circumstances of their injuries or death.

In the cases which form the basis of our research two images of violence have emerged as significant influences on the outcome of inquests. The first is the portrayal of individuals as being pathologically violent or of their neighbourhoods as being lawless or anti-police. The second is the equation between political protest and violent disorder. Examples of the first category begin with the portrayal of Liddle Towers as being a violent and wild man, under the influence of drink, who took a good deal of physical force (eight officers) to restrain him. At the inquest much was made of the fact that Liddle Towers had been a boxing coach and that he had a criminal record. He was cast in the mould of a violent, aggressive criminal. Yet his criminal record related to petty offences and his 'aggression' was judged solely on the basis of his background in boxing. It was difficult for lawyers for the family to contest the undercurrent of his reputation because they had no prior knowledge of the case put by lawyers representing the police officers or the chief constable. As only one police officer out of the eight appeared at the inquest it was impossible to cross-examine the police officers on their statements. Yet eye-witnesses, and Liddle Towers himself, alleged that the police used excessive force in his arrest and detention. It was clear to his family that a reputation had been constructed of Liddle Towers as a violent man and that this influenced the coroner and the jury in their consideration of whether the police used 'reasonable' force. It was this issue which led directly to a verdict of misadventure. Yet according to his friends and relatives the person described to the court was not the person that they knew.

Much the same imagery was used at the inquest into the death of Jimmy Kelly. He was described as having a well-established criminal record, as being a man who would fight if provoked, and as someone who was regularly drunk. The 54-year-old man who had a weak heart and had difficulty in going up stairs was depicted as being wild and fighting drunk on the night he was arrested. This transformation had produced such aggression that an officer gripped his testicles to force him into the back of a patrol car; he somersaulted out of the car and onto the ground where, in order to restrain him, an officer sat astride him and delivered several blows either to his face or his chest (Jimmy Kelly sustained a double fracture of the jaw); he was handcuffed with his hands behind his back; he was carried to a personnel carrier and transported to the police station on the floor of the vehicle; he was dropped on his head on arrival at the station; he was laid out, on his back, on the charge-room floor where he wet himself and died. This is the police version of the events.

Eye-witnesses claimed that he was severely beaten. Throughout the inquest the force used and admitted to by the police was justified by a carefully constructed reputation of criminal violence. This reputation was seized upon by the popular newspapers presenting Jimmy Kelly as a thug with a deep hatred of police officers. The imagery did not end there. Witnesses who testified that they had seen taking place an act of police brutality were systematically discredited by references to their personal biographies and to the local neighbourhood's reputation of violence and police-baiting. One witness jumped to his feet and shouted 'who's on trial here?' and another witness had suggestive unqualified references made to her school past. In each case these were deliberate acts of intimidation geared to discrediting the reliability of their testimony. Each gloved allegation had been carefully researched and was delivered to the inquest at the point of maximum effect.

Jimmy Kelly's character portrayal and the intimidation of witnesses by lawyers representing the Chief Constable brought this response from his family:

> That wasn't our Jimmy in there ... that was someone they created for their own purposes ... They slandered good people. It was a travesty.[11]
> Call that justice? You could see what they were doin' were doing ... complete fabrication. They have it their own way, makin' people out to be criminals.

Throughout the inquest a picture was drawn which portrayed the Huyton people, within the broader context of Merseyside – infamous for militancy and violence – as being inherently lawless. At the height of the inquest a young boy was called as a witness who claimed that the police had reacted calmly in their arrest of Jimmy Kelly. His evidence was a direct contradiction of all other civilian evidence and, in fact, of the police evidence of the use of force. The Chief Constable's counsel used his evidence to claim that a systematic campaign of intimidation and threats was being mounted in the community to silence pro-police evidence. Suddenly and dramatically it was revealed that one of those responsible for this public campaign was sitting in the public gallery. At this point a youth, later headlined as a 'THUG' in the popular press, was led from the court. He was never charged with any offence nor was any explanation given by the coroner for this extraordinary event. Yet the effect had been achieved with this apparently stage-managed event. The jury had been given sight of the living proof of intimidation.

The Kelly family were distraught at this continuing sequence of events. They wrote to their MP, Sir Harold Wilson, and implored him to intervene by contacting the Home Secretary. They listed the bullying and intimidation of witnesses under cross-examination, the apparent reluctance of the coroner to intervene to prevent such an abuse of the procedure and the depiction of Jimmy Kelly as a criminal and their community as anti-police, as major flaws in the adequacy of the inquest as a forum in which to examine, thoroughly and impartially, the circumstances of Jimmy Kelly's death. Despite Harold Wilson's representations on their behalf, the inquest continued in the same vein and the long and unequivocal summing up by the coroner directed the jury towards a misadventure verdict.

The inquest into the death of James Davey, following a brief period on a hospital life-support machine, paralleled many of the events of the inquests of Liddle Towers and Jimmy Kelly. In March 1983 he had been arrested in connection with the death of another man. He was held in Coventry but was to be taken to London for further questioning. It was in the attempt by several police officers to remove him from his cell that James Davey received the serious injuries from which he later died. There were no witnesses, other than police officers, to the events that killed him but it was clear from the state of his body that he had been subjected to a high level of violence during his struggle with the police officers. There was a clear admission in the police evidence that force had been used including a sergeant's

statement that he had held James Davey in a 'neckhold'. Much of the
questioning at the inquest turned on the strength of this arm-lock to the
neck and whether or not its force was reasonable in the circumstances. The
jury was asked to consider whether the 'intent' of the arm-lock was one of
restraint or excessive violence. Both issues – 'reasonable force' and
'intent' – are inherently subjective categories yet jury members were asked
to make objective assessments having only police evidence upon which to
base their judgements.

Inevitably the jury's assessment of the related issues of force and intent
was influenced by the depiction of James Davey's character and past. As
with all other controversial inquests the family's solicitor, Gareth Peirce,
did not receive copies of the police officers' statements to the internal police
inquiry. Consequently she was unprepared for the serious allegations made
against him and the implications that were drawn from his previous
criminal activities. Unlike Jimmy Kelly and Liddle Towers, James Davey did
have a criminal record which included serious crimes. As in the other cases,
however, his reputation was used at every opportunity to remind the jury of
James Davey's contempt for the law and the police. It was stated that traces
of cannabis had been found at his parents' home and a police officer told the
court how 20 years previously he had broken Davey's nose in an attempt to
arrest him. 'It was a case of him or me', he stated – making it clear that
excessive violence had to be met with severe force. This evidence to the
court took the family's solicitor by surprise and the withholding of
statements which had been made to the police investigation led the family's
barrister, Michael Mansfield, to comment that he was having to conduct the
case 'with my hands tied behind my back'. As in the other inquests, this
statement cut no ice with the coroner.

In his long summing up to the jury the coroner reminded the jury how the
police, in their own words, had knocked James Davey's legs from under him
and how the Sergeant had lain on top of him, using a neckhold, while
several other officers restrained their prisoner with two sets of handcuffs, a
rope and a belt. After two or three minutes, because James Davey was
'banging his head up and down', the neckhold was released and he turned
blue. His last days were spent on a life-support machine. One coroner's
direction on 'reasonable' force hinged on the question of the 'intent' of the
use of force by the police. In itself such a definition is contentious. For while
the police might not have *intended* to use the level of force which killed him, in
actuality that was what happened. The family's contention was that at best
the issue was one of negligence in terms of James Davey's welfare and could
have led to a verdict of 'lack of care'. At worst it was one of extreme brutality
which could have resulted in a verdict of 'unlawful killing'. It was Michael
Mansfield's argument that 'lack of care' was an important verdict which the
coroner failed to offer the jury and that it would be an appropriate verdict as
the police had acted in a 'grossly negligent way'. The verdict was not offered.
After four hours the jury told the coroner that a majority verdict had been

reached. The coroner instructed that the cause of death was the pressure which had been applied to the neck. The following, extraordinary statement was then read by the jury foreman:

> The only verdict we can reach is one of accidental death but *we feel that an unreasonable amount of force was used.* [emphasis added]

This contradictory statement was rejected by the coroner and he sent back the jury to decide between accidental death (reasonable force) and unlawful killing (unreasonable force). The verdict drew a most unsatisfactory end to a highly controversial inquest: 'As the law stands we can give no other verdict than accidental death.' Clearly the reputation constructed of James Davey influenced the entire climate of the direction of the jury and the reaching of the jury's verdict. It was also clear that the jury was unhappy with the choice of verdict. James Davey's family were angry with the verdict and the way in which it had been reached. His brother responded:

> We are shocked and disgusted. The jury was pressured into making a decision after they had clearly stated that the police officer had used unreasonable force. We don't feel that the verdict has in any way vindicated the police.

The 'criminal violence' or 'aggressive behaviour' of individuals extends to cases where people are controlled in prisons and mental institutions. In the case of George Wilkinson, for example, his isolation in successive prisons and the heavy use of drugs were each justified by his depiction as a 'control problem'.[40] His death, in HM Prison, Liverpool, brought an eventual verdict of misadventure. Yet it was clear from the evidence to the inquest that George Wilkinson had endured the worst aspects of the British prison system. The structural question, over containment of 'difficult' prisoners, over the use of drugs as a form of control, over the adequacy of prison hospitals to handle serious cases, were lost as George Wilkinson's reputation as a violent man was used consistently to justify the levels of control which were adopted. This issue has been central to a range of other cases of deaths in prison.[41]

Reputations of violence, however, are not restricted to criminal acts. In the case of Blair Peach the entire inquest turned on the issue of political violence. For Blair Peach was killed by a police charge, which came at the end of a massive anti-fascist demonstration in Southall. 'Reasonable force' in this context took on an extended and unique meaning at the inquest into his death. All civilian eye-witnesses stated that the demonstration had ended and the crowds were dispersing. Blair Peach and his friends were walking home when the police charge came at them from behind. The police position, however, was that a 'riot' was in progress and that they were using the force appropriate in the circumstances. The coroner reflected this when he stated, 'we have to remember that there was a riot going on – reasonable force would be that necessary in the circumstances to quell a riot'. He added which he could not cope' (Derek Harris). This focus on the relative to the imagery of political violence by introducing an extraordinary camparison. He stated that there were 'two extreme theories'. First, that Blair Peach had been killed by 'his own side' in order to produce a martyr for its cause. Second, that he had been killed by the Metropolitan Police. This played to the imagery of political extremism in which the Anti-Nazi League, of which Blair Peach was a member, was represented as an extreme, revolutionary group which was an 'outsider' to the Southall community. The verdict, despite the Police Complaints Board eventual finding that a member of the Special Patrol Group had killed him, was that Blair Peach's death was by misadventure. To some extent, by being there as a political demonstrator, Blair Peach had contributed to his own death. The following statements were made by family and friends:

> Blair was a fine person. He was involved in political campaigns throughout his time in London. He always went to demonstrations but essentially he was a pacifist – he did not believe in achieving ends through violence. The picture built of him and accepted by Burton [the coroner] was of a militant, violent extremist. Nothing was further from the truth.

> We saw it happen. We know who murdered him – it was the SPG. Our evidence was systematically torn to shreds by the association with extremist, even terrorist causes.

Images of Inadequacy

In the earlier quote, taken from his evidence to the Home Affairs Committee, Dr Johnson asserted that most people who die in custody 'are at risk anyway'. His categories – alcoholics, drug addicts, people wandering at large, vagrants, the underprivileged – represent a kind of litany of 'the inadequates'. Many of the inquests into deaths in prison, particularly suicides, which we have researched focus on the 'individual' in terms of personality, background and ability to 'cope'. It is assumed that people take their own lives not out of any rational response to brutal regimes, harsh conditions or round-the-clock isolation but through a personal defect in character or background which renders them as individuals inadequate in meeting the reasonable demands of essentially fair regimes. Of all the recent cases where this line of analysis has been evident, both at the inquests and in a subsequent government inquiry, the eight deaths of young men at the Glenochil Youth Custody Complex in Scotland provide the most harrowing examples of national concern.[42]

The 'Glenochil Complex' was founded in 1966 as a Detention Centre and was extended in 1976 to include a Young Offenders' Institution. It combines these functions, each with its own regime, and draws its population from throughout Scotland. The Detention Centre receives male young offenders, aged between 16 and 21 who have been given sentences between 4 weeks and 4 months. Its regime is punitive, determined by the

Conservative Government's 'short, sharp, shock' initiative. In 1984, 1,037 inmates passed through the Detention Centre and the average number in residence was 156, each allocated to single-cell rooms. The 'trainees', as they are termed, live under a token-system of rewards for good behaviour, have minimal recreation time, receive restricted visits, are marched between all bases with commands shouted military-style, and endure their days in total silence. The Young Offenders' Institution regime is quite different. It receives inmates whose sentences are over 9 months who are housed in purpose-built, high-security cell blocks. Glenochil's reputation is that of being 'the end of the line' for the young 'hardmen' of the Scottish prison system. The average daily population of the Young Offenders' Institution in 1985 was 275. There is much more association than in the Detention Centre and there is a strong, well-established hierarchy among inmates based on violence and intimidation. This hierarchy is recognized and endorsed by the regime. As we have stated elsewhere:

> Glenochil Young Offenders' Institution . . . exemplifies the institutionalization of male violence. On the blocks the physically or mentally handicapped, the unassertive, the weak, the sex offenders and the loners are subjected to a relentless barrage of physical torment and mental torture. They are extorted, verbally harassed, physically beaten and constantly threatened. On exercise or alone at night in their cells they undergo a constant hail of abuse including direct incitement to 'top themselves'.

These two regimes, then, are formally and informally punitive. For an inmate 'success' in coping with his sentence is achieved by facing up to the aggression and violence – both institutionalized and cultural – without 'bottling out'. Fear has to be hidden and privatized both from other inmates and from staff. It was within this climate of institutionalized male violence that between 1981 and 1986, 8 inmates committed suicide and 25 inmates made 'serious suicide attempts'.[44] Further, in 1984 alone 75 inmates in the Detention Centre and 89 inmates in the Young Offenders' Institution were kept in strip-cells and isolation on 'strict, suicide observation'. Following recommendations given at successive Fatal Accidents Inquiries (the Scottish equivalent of the inquest) a Scottish Office inquiry was set up (the Chiswick Report).

What has become clear from the Fatal Accident Inquiries into the tragic events at Glenochil, and this was endorsed by the Chiswick Report, is that the main response of state officials in their investigation of the cases is that the focus is almost exclusively on the individuals concerned and their personalities rather than on the institutions and their regimes. The sheriff's determination at successive Fatal Accident Inquiries has provided statements such as: 'an unhealthy interest . . . to see what hanging felt like' (Robert King); 'an attempt to draw attention to himself, get sympathy or special treatment' (William McDonald); suffering 'mental illness' (Angus Boyd); 'an outburst of despair at the situations which confronted him, with 'adequacy' of the individuals to cope with essentially fair and rational regimes was prominent throughout the Chiswick Report.

In the report 'para-suicide' was defined as a release of tension, personal indifference towards life or a means of signalling distress. Without providing any evidence, but clearly reflecting opinions given by psychiatrists at the Fatal Accident Inquiries, the report stated: 'In the context of Glenochil, the motivations *not* concerned with the intention to die are more apparent.'[45] In other words, most of the deaths were not intentional. The report then proposed a form of 'contagion theory' to explain the development of a 'pattern of suicidal behaviour' at Glenochil. 'Suicide', the report stated, 'was in the air.' While the report rejected the notion of 'suicidal type' it adopted clear indicators of risk. Following the classical positions around individual pathology and personality disorder the indicators were listed: 'early history of parental loss and separation during early childhood, frequently followed by unsatisfactory upbringing'; 'alienation from society, of repeated rule-breaking and of poor personal relationships'; 'isolated individuals'; 'changes in mood'; 'away from home, friends and family'.[46]

The Chiswick Report, despite its 63 recommendations, left no ambiguity as to the major factors central to the emergence of a pattern of suicide: 'risk' was in the minds and past histories of individuals – they are the vulnerable minority; reacting to their own inadequacies to cope they 'attempt' suicide and a few unintentionally succeed; acts of para-suicide become contagious and 'used' by inmates as a threat to authority; 'suicide is in the air'. Nowhere was the daily routine of punishment and brutalization examined or analysed. Rare acts of 'physical sanctions' were noted and the archaic torture of the treatment 'programme' for strict-suicide observation was criticized. The regimes at Glenochil and those entrusted with the 'care' of the inmates in fact drew praise from the inquiry, endorsing previous statements at successive Fatal Accident Inquiries. The Chiswick Report recognized 'the difficult and unrewarding task to which the great majority of staff at Glenochil show a high level of commitment', and it was 'impressed by the dedicated efforts that have been made by the Governor and his staff to review practices and procedures'.[47] With regard to the broader allegations made against the Glenochil regimes, by many former inmates and families of inmates,[48] which focused on institutionalized brutality, fear and intimidation, the report – like the Fatal Accident Inquiries – remained silent.

As one mother stated:

We fought for a public inquiry ... and what was it we got? A group of so-called experts, three of them from Glenochil itself, who told us that the kids were depressed or mentally ill. My son went in there as normal as you or me ... now he's dead ... he deserved to be sent away for what he did but he didn't deserve to die. They've got away with it, they'll always get away with it. They just close ranks ... he was just an ordinary kid.

Images of Women

Until recently the issue of women's experiences of the criminal justice process has been neglected within criminology and academic work around the law. This is no surprise as it reflects a strong patriarchal tradition within the social sciences in general with women's history, experiences, politics, culture, writing – the list is endless – being peripheral to 'real issues'.

The relatively small proportion of women in prison compared to men is one of the reasons for the apparent 'invisibility' of women in research studies or official accounts.[49] A major Home Office study of adult prisons and prisoners covering the period 1970–82 devoted only 2 out of its 74 pages to women in prison.[50] Women's imprisonment, as with women in the criminal justice process, has been neglected as an issue in its own right by successive governments, criminal justice agencies and their officers, and by researchers, teachers and authors in criminology. In the early 1980s, reflecting the emerging strength of women's campaigns and organizations, there has emerged significant new research, publications and case material on the experiences of women in custody, and the nature of the regimes they endure.[51] A combination of research and campaigns, particularly the work of the Women in Prison group, has revealed institutionalized problems including: repressive regimes with programmes of severe punishment and rigid discipline; the systematic neglect of women's health; massive use of drugs for 'treatment and control'; self-mutilation and, ultimately, deaths of women in prison.

Home Office statistics on the number of women who have died in custody are limited to the post-1974 period. The statistics record 13 deaths between 1974 and 1982,[52] but there has been a recent acceleration in the number of custody or custody-related deaths. As to the details of the cases there remain some unanswered questions – for example, five women died in prison between 1975 and 1977 but the Home Office has given no information on their names, where or how they died. These cases include: two women dying in Holloway from a 'mystery virus'; a woman setting fire to her cell on an observation block; cases of inadequate medical treatment including, in January 1986, a woman not being given prescribed drugs; self-mutilation, head-bashing and, eventually, suicide; and a woman who committed suicide following her release from Holloway's C1 psychiatric wing.[53]

The death of Christine Scott in 1982 is typical of a series of subsequent cases of self-mutilation or death. She had been sentenced to 6 months' imprisonment for breaking a window and died of a subdural haemorrhage. She had a history of suicide attempts and was placed, in isolation, in an observation cell at Holloway. Other prisoners reported that 'she was attempting suicide for three days, repeatedly throwing herself from the radiator to the floor'.[54] She was discovered by a prison officer who stated that there was not a single part of her body without a bruise'[55] The inquest jury rejected a verdict of suicide and returned one of death by misadventure.

Dr Berry, Medical Officer at Holloway, stated at the inquest that Mrs Scott had reacted disastrously to this sentence'.[56] He had recommended at her trial that she should be given hospital treatment as she would be unable to cope in a prison setting. For she had been 'screaming, agitated and disturbed' while on remand. Her prison sentence was justified by the magistrate on the grounds that the public needed protection from her. Clearly it was inappropriate, indeed it proved fatal, to send Christine Scott to prison. In Holloway it appears that her mental condition was neglected and there are serious doubts about the adequacy of single-cell allocation and regular supervision. Her previous history plus the medical opinion of Dr Berry should have been sufficient to have had her accommodated in a place where she could receive proper medical care and 24-hour supervision. Since 1981 at Holloway women have set fire to themselves, attempted to gouge out eyes (one woman succeeded), constantly bashed their heads against walls and radiators, and in one case, attempted to cut off a breast using a smashed light-bulb.[57] Many of these incidents have taken place in Holloway's psychiatric C1 wing and occur most frequently when women are locked up in isolation for 23 hours per day.

These incidents are not isolated. In 1984 the *Observer* disclosed that there were 24 incidents of attempted suicide or self-mutilation over a 20-day period.[58] In October 1985 a further 15 incidents were reported.[59] C1 wing, known to the inmates as 'The Muppet House', holds 40 women, each of whom is categorized 'disturbed' by the prison authorities. The official explanations of the extraordinary level of self-mutilation, attempted suicide and suicide focus solely on explanations of individuals being pathologically disturbed. Yet the frequency and intensity of the incidents raises serious doubts again about the institution, its regime and its practices. Central to this are the broader contexts of discipline, punishment and regulation experienced by women in prison.

As in men's prisons, on which there is an extensive literature, women's imprisonment produces many of the same repressive, organizational features: personal and social deprivation, personal indignities, loss of civil rights, racism, inhuman conditions, bullying and staff abuse. Beyond this, however, women experience institutionalized sexism which is all-pervasive in and out of prison. The regime of the total institution, however, allows no escape from the enforcement of the ideology of womanhood and its central foci of sexuality, femininity, domesticity and submissiveness. For the prevailing ideology of womanhood – the caring, nurturing, serving, passive individual – together with the social and ideological construction of women's criminality are central to the treatment meted out to women by the police, the courts and the prisons. Whereas men's criminality is portrayed as 'normal' – an extension of their inherent masculinity – but 'bad' and requiring 'punishment'; women's criminality is seen to be 'abnormal' – in opposition to their inherent femininity – and explained as an 'illness' or a 'deficiency' in need of treatment. It is in this way that Pat Carlen argues that women criminals have been given the status of 'other': 'other than real women, other than real criminals, other than real prisoners'.[60] Thus women in prison are seen as being irrational in their criminality, as being deficient in their womanhood and as being in need of rehabilitation or reform not in terms of their previous acts but in terms of their status as women. According to Pat Carlen the custodial penalty is given to 'those who have failed as mothers', to 'appease the public's obsession'. For, 'in rebelling against marital tyranny she has also stepped outside domesticity and motherhood'.[61]

At the time of sentencing, then, a woman's sexuality, moral conduct, femininity and commitment to motherhood and domesticity are significant considerations in the type and length of sentence given. These issues are significant in cases where women are not on trial, as in the controversial inquest into the death of Helen Smith at a high-society illegal drinks party in Jeddah.[62] In prison women are subjected to policies and practices, geared to their 'rehabilitation', based on femininity, domesticity and motherhood. Emphasis, then, is on the need to restore and preserve family life by promoting motherhood and housewifery – which, in terms of prison-work, means domestic chores.

The categorization of 'criminal' women as 'sick', 'mad' or 'disturbed' leads to the medicalization of women in prison. 1983 Home Office statistics showed that the total dosage rate of central nervous system-related drugs in Holloway was 247 doses per woman. Yet the highest male prison was Wakefield with 183 doses per man.[63] This high level of drug use, both as a form of treatment and control, reflects a well-established tradition in patriarchal medical care that women's health and behaviour is dictated primarily by their psychology as women. In prison, coupled with isolation and pressures to conform to a stereotype of 'womanhood', the consequences are severe. Regimes run on these lines lead to increased isolation, internalized tensions and personal suffering. This leads to closer surveillance, stronger controls and the use of disciplinary procedures – a NACRO report in January 1986 found that women prisoners are punished for disciplinary offences twice as often as men.[64] The most frequent offence is 'disobedience or disrespect'. It is this sequence of events, and not individual pathologies, which has major implications for the state of women's health, both mental and physical, the horrific consequences of which have been so clearly illustrated by women's experiences of Holloway C1:

> It's sheer desperation. As if you've become a non-entity. You're nothing. Then you want to do anything to get feeling. You want to rip yourself to bits to feel something. It's dead in those cells. You can tell they want to cut you off from all the good things in life. You want to feel pain: anything to feel some experience. You feel this strong urge to cut yourself up. I've reached that

point. I've started banging my head, again and again, harder and harder, against the concrete wall.[65]

You just sit there. You do nothing. All you've got is a mattress on the floor and a potty. All your possessions are left outside the door. People just sit there. They howl or they scream or sit there and bang their heads against the wall. I felt that I was going off my head when I was in there: everyone is screaming and banging so in the end you start banging yourself.[66]

When she went there on remand she was agitated but OK. They put her in C1 for 13 days and it had a tremendous effect on her. The woman in the next cell was quite close to her and eventually killed herself. On the anniversary of her time in Holloway she went to the top of a multi-storey car-park and threw herself off. I thought she was better but her time inside had left its mark. We can never prove it, but I know it.[67]

Conclusion

In 1986 and again in 1987, the British state sent more people to prison proportionate to head of population than any other West European state.[68] Under successive Conservative administrations sentences have been lengthened, parole made more difficult, 20 years minimum detention for certain offences enacted, the prison-building programme extended and internal regimes – such as 'short, sharp, shock' – introduced. In terms of law enforcement the coal dispute has ensured that an operationally autonomous, paramilitary form of national policing has been consolidated.[69] The introduction of the Police and Criminal Evidence Act in January 1986 and the Public Order Act in 1987 each have extended substantially police discretion over arrest and detention. With these developments the treatment that people receive – or fail to receive – while in custody becomes a major issue of public concern. The authoritarian shift within the state has legitimated more punitive and regulatory regimes and associated practices in prison and police custody.

Our work establishes that at all levels state institutions are reluctant to operate mechanisms which make their regimes and practices properly accountable. Operational policies and practices are dictated by institutionalized ideologies which are deeply entrenched in the formal and informal structures of the police and prison services. The images covered here, of violence (both criminal and political), of personal inadequacy and of women, provide clear examples of the political management of identities. Racism is another most significant ideology institutionalized and rooted in the agencies of law enforcement and imprisonment.[70] From the cases we have discussed here and from the many others we have considered the lasting impression is that in order to protect the operational policies and practices which obtain in custodial situations the authorities effectively marginalize those people who self-mutilate, attempt suicide or die through suicide, neglect or acts of brutality.

In terms of the cases we have studied the convenient labels, Dr Johnson's 'litany of the deviants', cannot be applied. They remain typical of the kind of dismissive explanations too readily employed by the police, the prison authorities, legal counsel and coroners. They are the stock-in-trade of a sensationalist media more concerned with 'who shot J.R.' than with who murdered Blair Peach. It is a process of categorization which suggests that to some extent the 'violent', the 'dangerous', the 'political extremist', the 'inadequate', the 'mentally ill', contribute directly to their own deaths either by their personal condition or their personal choice. Further, the marginalization of categories suggests that these people not only suffer from diminished responsibility but consequently have diminished civil rights. Thus their deaths, and the responsibility for them, are of lesser significance. Barry Prosser died at Winson Green Hospital Wing in a cell for which there was only one key. He had 'been attended' by a group of prison officers and his injuries were horrendous. The inquest verdict was that while in the safe and protective custody of a prison hospital he was unlawfully killed. Yet, it appears, no one was responsible.

Acknowledgements

Many thanks to Jimmy Boyle, Sarah Boyle, Sally Channon, Paul Gordon, Sheila Scraton and Joe Sim for their invaluable support and critical comment.

Notes

1 The other, associated projects have been on police powers and accountability; the DHSS and the policing of welfare fraud; the papers contained in P. Scraton, and P. Gordon, (eds) *Causes for Concern*, Harmondsworth, Middx, Penguin, 1984. For a more theoretical overview of the debates see S. Hall and P. Scraton, 'Law, class and control', in M. Fitzgerald, *et al.*, *Crime and Society: Readings in History and Theory*, London, Routledge & Kegan Paul, 1981.

2 E.O. Wright, *Class, Crisis and the State*, London, New Left Books, 1978.

3 S. Hall, *et al.*, *Policing the Crisis*, London Macmillan, 1978.

4 Carol Smart's work has been definitive here: see *Women, Crime and Criminology*, 1977; *The Ties that Bind*, 1984; and, with C. Brophy, *Women-in-Law*, 1985; all published in London by Routledge & Kegan Paul.

5 See P. Scraton and P. Gordon, op. cit.

6 A. Sivanandan, 'Challenging racism: strategies for the eighties', *Race and Class*, vol. XXV, no. 2.

7 See, for example, the Metropolitan Police commissioned study: *Police and People in London*, vols I to IV, Policy Studies Institute, 1983, vol. IV, in particular, provides corroboration for the well-established allegations of institutionalized sexism

and racism in the Metropolitan Police.

 8 G. Stedman-Jones, *Outcast London*, Harmondsworth, Middx, Peregrine, 1978.

 9 See M. Fitzgerald *et al.*, *Surveillance, Regulation and Control*, OU Course D335, Crime and Society, Block 2, Open University Press.

10 See A. Sivanandan, *A Different Hunger*, London, Pluto, 1982; P. Gordon, *White Law*, London, Pluto, 1983; P. Gilroy, 'The myth of black criminality', in *Socialist Register 1982*, London, Merlin, 1983.

11 S. Jeffreys and J. Radford. 'Contributory negligence or being a woman? The car-rapist case', in P. Scraton and P. Gordon, op. cit.

12 J. Radford, 'Womanslaughter: a licence to kill? The killing of Jane Asher', in P. Scraton and P. Gordon, op. cit.

13. See B. Toner, *The Facts of Rape* (2nd edn) London, Arrow, 1982; P. Pattullo, *Judging Women*, NCCL, 1984.

14 See E. A. Stanko, *Intimate Intrusions; Women's Experiences of Male Violence*, London, Routledge & Kegan Paul, 1985; R.E. Hall, *Ask Any Woman*, Bristol, Falling Wall Press, 1985.

15 See P. Scraton and K. Chadwick, *In the Arms of the Law: Coroners' Courts and Deaths in Custody*, London, Pluto, 1987.

16 Warwick Inquest Group, 'The inquest as a theatre for police tragedy; the Davey case', *Journal of Law and Society, vol. 12, no. 1, Spring 1985.*

17 'The police, coroners and the Liddle Towers case' unpublished paper from JAIL Conference 'Whose Law and Order?', London, 1979; see also J. Mapplebeck, 'The strange death of Liddle Towers', *New Statesman*, 29 July 1977; *Sunday Times* Insight Investigation, 8 October 1978.

18 *Regina v. Coroner for Durham County ex parte Attorney General*, 28 June 1978.

19 *The Times*, 18 October 1978.

20 Ibid.

21 The Police Complaints Board, in a written reply to Celia Stubbs, stated that they could not prosecute any individual officer in this case as it was not possible to identify which of the six officers under investigation struck the fatal blow which killed Blair Peach.

22 P. Scraton, 'The Coroner's Tale: the death of Jimmy Kelly', in P. Scraton and P. Gordon, op. cit.

23 Home Affairs Committee Report: *Deaths in Police Custody*, [H.A.C. Inquiry] HMSO, 1980, p. v, para. 4.

24 Liddle Towers Committee, *Killing No Murder*, 1976; D. Ransom, *Licence to Kill*, Friends of Blair Peach Committee, 1980; P. Scraton, 'The Coroner's Tale: the death of Jimmy Kelly', op. cit.

25 Unofficial Committee of Inquiry Supplementary Report, *The Death of Blair Peach*, NCCL, 1980.

26 R. Geary, Deaths in Prison, *NCCL Briefing Paper*, 1980; G. Coggan and M. Walker, *Frightened for my Life*, London, Fontana, 1982; T. Owen and J. Sim, 'Drugs, discipline and prison medicine', in P. Scraton, and P. Gordon, op. cit.

27 The campaigns which formed around the deaths of Blair Peach, Jimmy Kelly and, in prison, Barry Prosser and Mathew O'Hara, formed together a national organization, Inquest, in 1981. There are now many other campaigns associated with Inquest and it publishes a regular bulletin in *The Abolitionist.*

28 P. Scraton and K. Chadwick, op. cit.

29 A coroner in the North-West of England interviewed as part of the main project

in 1981.

30 *Daily Mail*, 17 April 1980.

31 The Chief Constable of Merseyside, *Annual Report for 1979*.

32 *Liverpool Echo*, 17 April 1980.

33 *Police*, December 1980.

34 *Police Review*, 14 November 1980.

35 Sir D. McNee, 'Quo vadis?', *Police Journal*, January 1980.

36 The most detailed account of these official claims, particularly the claim that the inquest provides a 'fail-safe' system, can be found in the evidence of the Coroners' Society to the HAC inquiry, op. cit.

37 Evidence to the HAC inquiry, op. cit. p. 54.

38 In the research project we found it usual in such cases for the coroner to take evidence solely from the custodians and from a pathologist and to instruct the jury to return a verdict immediately and without leaving the jury time to deliberate.

39 S. Hall, *Drifting into a Law and Order Society*, London, Cobden Trust, 1980.

40 T. Owen and J. Sim, 'Drugs, Discipline and Prison Medicine: The Case of George Wilkinson' in P. Scraton, and P. Gordon, op. cit.

41 See G. Coggan and M. Walker, op. cit.

42 See P. Scraton, and K. Chadwick, 'The experiment that went wrong: The crisis of deaths in youth custody at the Glenochil Complex', *The Abolitionist*, no. 2, 1985, also in B. Rolston and M. Tomlinson, *The Expansion of European Prison Systems*, European Group for Studies in Deviance and Social Control, 1987. The inquiry referred to is *Report of the Review of Suicide Precautions at HM Detention Centre and HM Young Offenders' Institution, Glenochil*, Scottish Home and Health Department, HMSO, Edinburgh, 1985 [The Chiswick Report] op. cit.

43 P. Scraton and K. Chadwick, 1985, op cit.

44 *Scottish Daily Mail*, 2 June 1985.

45 The Chiswick Report, op. cit. para. 2.3.1.

46 Ibid. paras 2.5.2, 2.5.3.

47 Ibid. para. 6.2.1.

48 Many of these allegations were made publicly during the summer of 1985 by people attending mass meetings, held in Edinburgh and Glasgow, organized by the Gateway Exchange entitled: 'Glenochil; Dare to Care'.

49 Figures for 1983: 42,072 men in prison and 1,390 women. *Report on the Work of the Prison Department*, HMSO, 1983, p. 7. In August 1985 the total prison population was over 48,000.

50 Mott, J. *Adult Prisons and Prisoners in England and Wales, 1970–82*, HMSO, 1985, pp. 48–50.

51 P. Carlen, *Women's Imprisonment*, London, Routledge & Kegan Paul, 1983; P. Carlen *et al.*, *Criminal Women*, Cambridge, Polity Press, 1985.

52 *The Abolitionist*, no. 15, 1983, p. 15.

53 The cases are covered in detail in P. Scraton and K. Chadwick, 1987, op. cit.

54 Inquest Annual Report 1982–83.

55 *Eastern Daily News*, 13 October 1982.

56 Ibid.

57 see Polly Toynbee's *Guardian* article on 'Deranged and disturbed women in prison', 15 October 1984.

58 N. Davis, 'Violence of jail women', *The Observer*, 25 November 1984.

59 N. Davis, 'Mentally ill "on trial" at Holloway', *The Observer*, 10 November 1985.
60 P. Carlen *et al.*, op. cit.
61 P. Carlen, 1983, op. cit.
62 See P. Scraton and K. Chadwick, 1987, op. cit. Much of the this case centred on Helen Smith's sexual and moral conduct yet it bore no relevance to the circumstances of her death.
63 P. Solomons, 'Drugs in prison', *The Abolitionist*, no. 2, 1984, p. 36.
64 NACRO, *Offences Against Prison Discipline in Women's Prisons*, NACRO, 1986.
65 Pauline Thomas, recounting her experiences of Holloway C1 wing in C. Moorehead, 'The strange events at Holloway', *New Society*, 11 April 1984.
66 Josie O'Dwyer recounting her experiences of Holloway C1 wing in N. Davis, 'Muppet house of horror at Holloway', *The Observer*, 16 September 1984.
67 The father of a young woman who committed suicide. The inquest had not been held at the time of writing.
68 See the European Group for Studies in Deviance and Social Control Report 1986; K. Chadwick, 'Gaol fever', in *State Watch*, *New Socialist*, October 1986.
69 See P. Scraton, *The State of the Police*, London, Pluto, 1985.
70 See P. Gordon, 1983, op. cit.

8

The Problem of Men: Feminist Perspectives on Sexual Violence

Liz Kelly and Jill Radford

Critical criminology emerged to challenge both traditional criminology and interactionist perspectives in the early 1970s. As Frances Heidensohn[1] has pointed out, like all brands of criminology before it, it failed to ask questions about women's relationship to, and experience of, crime. Fifteen years later, the 'newest' criminology, Lea and Young's 'realism', offers only a tokenistic nod to the questions feminists have raised.[2] This chapter is not a review of feminist perspectives on crime and deviance, it is limited to examining how some of the questions raised by critical criminology are reflected in or challenged by recent feminist work on sexual violence. We will, however, highlight how an understanding of men's sexual violence as a form of control of women can provide insight into criminological concerns (that is, why so few women, compared to men, are targeted for control by official state agencies).

Feminist work on sexual violence has been done predominantly by radical/revolutionary feminists. The issues it raises are problematic not only for malestream socialists, sociologists and criminologists (be they 'critical', 'Marxist' or 'realist') but also for socialist feminists.

The basic premise of critical criminology was that an analysis of crime must begin with the structures of power within particular societies at particular times. Within this framework specific attention was drawn to the following: definitions of crime are political, socially constructed by powerful groups through political processes and popularized by a blend of ideology and coercion; criminal acts can be rational acts and, in some circumstances, forms of resistance to oppressive social relationships; official statistics reflect particular definitions and decisions about the enforcement of law; the causes and, therefore, solutions to crime must be examined from a structural rather than individualistic perspective.

Whilst feminist anger, action and research around sexual violence takes up these issues – and more – we do so from a position different from many of the early critical criminologists. We were, and are, not middle-class academics campaigning on behalf of 'disadvantaged groups'. Feminist concerns have emerged directly from our individual and shared experiences. Our activism, theorizing and research on sexual violence, for example, highlighted or amplified issues we were aware of as women having to live our daily lives with the threat and reality of sexual violence.[3] All feminist work on sexual violence, from working in refuges and rape crisis centres, to organizing demonstrations and campaigns, to designing research methodology, to theorizing, has roots in personal experience.

But Which Structural Starting Point?

Critical criminology has its root in Marxism. Feminist perspectives on sexual violence have their roots in an analysis of women's oppression which draws on the concept of patriarchy.

The crime that concerns us here is men's violence to women which cuts across other divisions such as class and race. Feminists in many different countries have set up refuges for battered women, support services for women and girls who have been abused and are challenging particular cultural forms of sexual violence. Historical evidence and evidence from a range of cultures and societies suggests that sexual violence occurs in most societies and that certain forms of sexual violence occur in the majority of human societies, particularly rape and violence to wives.[4] Feminists are unlikely, therefore, to accept the premise of much critical criminology to date that the 'causes' of crime are to be found only in the structure of capitalist social relations.

We see patriarchy as a systematic set of social relationships through which men maintain power over women and children. The forms these social relationships take in any particular society vary. Patriarchal societies may also include hierarchies constructed on the basis of class, race and sexuality which divide men and women. One of the forms of control common to patriarchal societies is the use of sexual violence. Again, the particular forms and frequency of sexual violence in any particular society may vary, as may its interaction with other power systems in that society. The presence of sexual violence is, however, one of the defining features of a patriarchal society. It is used by men, and often condoned by the state, for a number of specific purposes:

> to punish women who are seen to be resisting male control; to police women, make them behave or not behave in particular ways; to claim rights of sexual,

emotional and domestic servicing; and through all of these maintain the relations of patriarchy, male dominance and female subordination.

Patriarchal oppression like all forms of imperialism/oppression/exploitation is ultimately based on violence.[5]

While critical criminology of the 1970s named and drew attention to crimes of the powerful, it defined power solely in terms of capitalist social relationships, thereby failing to address other systems of power. This analysis allowed no space for other oppressors to be identified and their actions defined as 'crimes of the powerful'. If sexism and racism and class domination are seen as analytically separate but coexistent systems[6] within capitalist societies the analysis of power and control becomes much more complex. Specific groups may be systematically disadvantaged in all three systems – black, working-class women – but other groups which have little power in one system may be powerful in others. Sexual violence as a means of control and/or expression of power can be used by men regardless of their class or race. Racism can be used by white people regardless of their class or gender.

In raising questions about the structural bases of power within societies feminists have addressed the behaviour of all men within their society. The fact that groups of men are exploited and oppressed in particular ways is not seen as either an explanation of, or an excuse for, violence towards women and children.

> *Any* form of male violence damages. Be it from the police, *or* the males of the community. . . . At all times all women do well to remember that the rapists of one race or group are as culpable as the rapists of another. Neither oppression or privilege exonerates the crime of rape.[7]

While recognizing that women's liberation requires fundamental changes in the structures of all patriarchal societies, feminists have demanded that sexual violence be taken seriously in the present. This both involves public agencies making violent men accountable for their behaviour and all men questioning and challenging the patriarchal construction of masculinity. The latter challenge requires men to take responsibility for their sexual practice: to, for example, critically examine their use of force, coercion or pressure in heterosexual relations and how use of pornography affects their attitudes to, and behaviour in relationships with, women.

Romanticizing Offenders and Forgetting the 'Victims'

The initial concern of feminists working around sexual violence was to challenge the trivialization of, and selective attention paid to, sexual violence. This took place on a number of levels:

taking the right to name and define men's sexual violence from the perspective of women's experience;

developing alternative feminist services like rape crisis lines, refuges for
battered women and support groups for incest survivors;
campaigning around particular cases, law reform and the general issue of
women's safety;
documenting women's experience of sexual violence;
developing critiques of previous research in the area;
defining ourselves [women] as survivors rather than victims of men's
sexual violence, thus rejecting the premise of 'victimology' and populist
thinking that women are passive, inadequate and blameworthy victims.

While from malestream sociology Cohen[8] has challenged the 'depersona-
lized, dehumanized' picture of the deviant and stressed the importance of
understanding the rationality in acts defined as criminal, feminists noted
something more in relation to sexual violence. It was precisely men's
rationalizations for their actions that had been elevated into theories and
explanations for their violence towards women. Amir's[9] notion of 'victim
precipitated rape' and the victim-blaming evident in many of the pre-1975
articles and studies of sexual abuse and 'domestic' violence[10] reflected
commonly held male assumptions about sexual violence. In a number of
these studies it is clear that the male authors identified with the male
offender's perspectives and, in so doing, they failed to take into account the
abused woman's experience. Feminists also noted the regularity with which
these understandings were reflected in media reporting of sexual violence
and in the response of social agencies and the law.[11]

In the 1970s, as in earlier campaigns in the nineteenth and early twentieth
century,[12] feminist writing and actions around sexual violence were fuelled
by anger at the neglect of women's experiences and at the general
acceptability of men's justifications for their acts.

The initial response of the left to feminist demands that sexual violence be
both taken seriously and viewed from the perspective of the victimized
woman was muted, to say the least. There were a few isolated attempts,
mainly at meetings and in internal documents, to suggest that violence from
working-class men was a reflection of their powerlessness in capitalist
societies, but these were the exception rather than the rule. The rule was a
deafening silence.

While today many radicals feel that they have to refer to the reality of
sexual violence, few have re-examined their perspective in the light of the
feminist critique. Few have seen gender, and the construction of masculinity, as a basis from which to examine deviance and criminality. Where,
for example, are the reflections on riots and street violence that explain the
fact that it is predominantly young males who are involved?[13] Faith Evans[14]
is very much the exception in looking at gangs from this perspective. He
argues, from his own experience, that disputes about territory are also
concerned with rights of sexual access to young women within the area the
gang controls.

There has been some criticism within the left[15] of unquestioning sympathy for those defined as criminal, but this critique draws on Marx's own writings and is not addressed to sexual violence. What a feminist perspective demands is a recognition of the complexity of power relations and, through this, open discussion of the variety of forms of criminality. Attention must be paid to the impact of crime on those who are victimized and certain forms of criminal behaviour must be defined as unacceptable within any type of society.

Official Statistics v. Feminist Statistics

In running feminist services and talking to other women, feminists quickly realized that official statistics revealed little about the reality of sexual violence. The incidence and prevalence of all forms of sexual violence were vastly under-reported. US federal-funded victimization studies had already suggested that only between 1 in 2 and 1 in 4 rapes were reported to the police.

One of the impacts of feminist campaigning has been an increase in incidence research, particularly in the United States (sexual violence is one of the biggest growth areas in US research in sociology, criminology and psychology), but increasingly also in the UK.

Diana Russell conducted the first random sample survey which included a range of forms of sexual violence in San Francisco in the late 1970s.[16] Her methodology was adopted by Jalna Hanmer and Sheila Saunders for their Leeds study and by Jill Radford for a study on Wandsworth London.[17] Both these studies limited their enquiries to the previous year. Both studies found alarming incidence figures for the previous year: 59% of the women in Leeds had had at least one experience of sexual violence, 76% of the women in Wandsworth. Liz Kelly[18] asked women about a range of possible forms of sexual violence they might have experience during their lifetime. Almost 80% of her smaller sample had experience six or more forms of sexual violence.

A number of studies have focused on the incidence of particular forms of sexual violence. Diana Russell estimated that between 1 in 2 and 1 in 3 US women experienced rape or attempted rape in their lifetime.[19] Ruth Hall's[20] UK survey found an incidence rate of 21% for rape and 20% for attempted rape. Studies of sexual harassment at work in the USA and the UK have recorded incidence rates ranging from 45% to 90% of women.[21] Studies of the incidence of sexual abuse of children and incest suggest that between 1 in 6 and 1 in 3 women have been sexually abused in childhood.[22,23] Sandra McNeill[24] found that 63% of the women she interviewed had been flashed at. As yet, no incidence studies of 'domestic' violence have been done in the UK, but US incidence studies estimate that violence occurs in between 1 in 6 and 1 in 3 relationships.[25] More recently attention in the USA has been paid to 'courtship violence' and similar incidence estimates have emerged as in 'domestic' violence research.[26]

What all these studies, and the many others not referred to here, demonstrate is that sexual violence is a characteristic feature of women's lives and that many women experience a number of forms of sexual violence, possibly on repeated occasions, during their lifetime. This reality is not reflected in either official statistics or large-scale victimization studies. It is a reality which must lead to a questioning of any theory which refers to 'victim precipitation' or 'victim proneness' or which attempts to argue that certain forms of sexual violence are located within specific social groups. The new research on incidence demonstrates that all women are vulnerable to sexual violence.

As Betsy Stanko[27] has argued, incidence figures from recent research suggest that women's fear of crime is far from 'irrational'. A number of writers, drawing on the incidence in official statistics of rape, have suggested that women's fear of rape is disproportionate to the likelihood of ever experiencing it. If the incidence of rape is taken from feminist studies the picture is somewhat different. It is even more different if we take into account the fact that women's fear of all forms of sexual violence may be articulated around the issue of rape, as this is seen as a legitimate fear. Many women feel they will not be taken seriously if they say they fear being flashed at or harassed on the street.[28] It is important to note that at the time women are being followed/flashed at/harassed they do not know how the event will end. It is only in retrospect that such events can be defined as 'minor'.[29] Women do not experience sexual violence as a number of discrete events. What in law and criminology would be defined as 'minor' may, because of its place in a cumulative experience, have major impacts on women's subsequent feelings and behaviour.[30]

The alarming findings from many of these studies arise partly because feminism has created the climate in which researchers have seen sexual violence as an important area for study. There are also issues concerning methodology which affect the research findings. Where the research has been done by feminists there has been an awareness of the difficulty for women to discuss these experiences alongside an under-standing of the complexity of the issue of definitions. Many feminist researchers have also questioned the model of distanced, objective research methods. In research design, therefore, attention has been paid to how questions are formulated and how interviews are conducted in order to encourage and enable women to discuss what are often painful memories. Various methods of supporting women after taking part in research on sexual violence, such as a referral to other groups, setting up self-help groups and organizing community meetings, have been an integral part of research methodology.[31]

A Feminist Definition

The Schwendingers[32] challenged legalistic state definitions of crime and suggested an alternative which draws on ethics and the concepts of 'social inquiry', 'public wrong' and 'anti-social' behaviour. Through this, they argued, it becomes possible to define institutional behaviour that denies human rights as criminal. Their logic permits defining imperialism, racism, sexism and poverty as criminal. Like most structural approaches attention is directed to the institutional level and away from individual behaviour. By implication progressive change must occur at the structural/institutional level.

Feminist definitions have, by contrast, emerged from understanding and documenting women's experience. The development of feminist research and discussion over the past 15 years can in a very real sense be seen in terms of ever-widening definitions and naming of sexual violence in general and of particular forms. A few examples will illustrate this point.

Early feminist discussions of rape, while taking issue to some extent with legal definitions of rape, focused on the use of explicit violence and force. One aspect of this was the suggestion that rape should not be defined as a sexual crime, but as a form of violent assault.[33] As feminists increasingly questioned the construction of heterosexuality, the commonness of forced and coerced sex emerged. This has shifted the terms of the debate back into the area of sexuality and Catherine MacKinnon is amongst the many feminists who argue that the definition of rape should not be separated from the critique of heterosexuality.

> The male point of view defines them by distinction. What women experience does not so clearly distinguish the normal, everyday things from which those abuses have been defined by distinction.... What we are saying is that sexuality in exactly these normal forms often does violate us. So long as we say those things are abuses or violent, not sex, we fail to criticize what has been made of sex.[34]

Sexual harassment was initially defined in the context of paid work and authority relations. As research on sexual harassment at work developed it became clear that women were often harassed by co-workers, and Benson[35] has documented the harassment of a woman professor by a male student, illustrating that gender rather than authority relations are the key factor. Liz Kelly[36] suggests that women's work roles are more or less sexualized and that this affects the frequency, form and severity of harassment – the most extreme form being experienced by women who work in the sex industry.

Discussing sexual harassment with women has also highlighted that it occurs in a range of settings and across a number of relationships. The term, for example, is increasingly being used to describe some aspects of girls' experience in mixed schools.[37] Attention has also been directed to street

harassment and forms of sexism present in women's day-to-day encounters
with men.

The shift in understanding of 'domestic' violence is another example of
this process of extending definitions. When feminists set up refuges they
also named the violence experienced by the women using them as
battering – a name which focuses on physical violence. As more women
came to refuges and talked about their experience of abuse it became clear
that physical violence was one aspect of 'domestic' violence; women also
described forced sex and a range of mental and psychological abuse.

Ruth Hall[38] introduced the term 'racist sexual violence' to describe the
fact that for black women racism and sexism may be inseparable. 'Racial
assault" is kept separate from "sexual assault" in many people's minds – one
is a "race issue" and one is a "women's issue". Black women can make no
such separation.'

As feminists paid attention to what women experienced as abusive the
definitions they began with expanded and new words were developed with
which to name previously unnamed abuse. At the same time we shifted
from seeing various forms of male violence as separate phenomena to
viewing them as part of a more general phenomenon – sexual violence. Liz
Kelly[39] has used the term 'continuum' to reflect the range within the
general term 'sexual violence' and within each of the particular forms of
sexual violence. Feminist definitions of forms of sexual violence will
continue to develop as we learn more about abuse as women experience and
understand it.

Patriarchal Institutions

One of the most important contributions of critical criminology has been to
explore the role of law and policing in relation to state control. Yet again
feminist work on sexual violence has asked a somewhat different question –
why has sexual violence not been controlled by the law or other state
agencies? The issue has not been too much control, but rather too little.

While accepting that the law in capitalist societies is constructed with a
framework that protects certain interests and that enforcement decisions
are linked to these interests, feminists like Catherine MacKinnon[40] have
insisted that a feminist analysis of the state is essential to our understanding
of these processes in relation to sexual violence.

> As a beginning, I propose that the state is male in the feminist sense. The law
> sees and treats women the way men see and treat women. The liberal state
> coercively and authoritatively constitutes the social order in the interest of
> men as a gender, through its legitimizing norms, relation to society, and
> substantive policies. It achieves this through embodying and ensuring male
> control over women's sexuality at every level, occasionally cushioning,

qualifying, or *de jure* prohibiting its excesses when necessary to its normalization... the state, in part through law, institutionalizes male power.

Through her complex analysis of the patriarchal structure of the state it becomes possible to understand the systematic failure of the criminal justice system and other social control agencies to protect women from sexual violence. Also it explains why it is only when feminists campaign around these issues that any changes in the interests of women and girls take place.[41] In the rest of this section we will look in greater detail at the failure to take sexual violence seriously, at feminist campaigns to afford women greater protection, and at recent attempts to co-opt feminist perspectives.

Studies on the institutional response to rape have, for the most part, concentrated on the criminal justice system, and while using a variety of methods and a range of samples reach similar conclusions. At each stage of the process cases are 'screened out', decisions hinge on common-sense assumptions about what rape is, which type of women are raped, and which type of men rape. The justifications for decisions are articulated around the likelihood of successful prosecution.[42] One US study[43] estimates that less than 15% of reported rapes reach trial and that 1% result in a conviction for rape.

Research on 'domestic' violence has addressed a wider range of institutional responses and reveals a consistent failure to define the man's behaviour as violent and/or criminal resulting in a failure to provide women with support and/or protection.[44] Police refusal to arrest and prosecute, even where the woman has an injunction, is marked. They rely on a crisis-management and 'keeping-the-peace' approach rather than enforcing the criminal law. A recent controlled field experiment in the United States has demonstrated that arrest was the most effective strategy in preventing further violence.[45] Studies in the USA and the UK[46] suggest that charges are reduced, where 'domestic' violence is prosecuted, so that cases can be tried in lower courts. This results, in cases where sentence is passed, in the majority of violent men being fined or put on probation despite evidence of serious violence and use of weapons. Allowing a violent man his liberty means that the women's safety is further jeopardized. Many women, knowing their attacker will not be sent down, realistically fear that seeking police protection and/or pressing charges will only result in further violence.

Studies of social-work and medical response to 'domestic' violence show that professionals often fail to detect/record or take seriously the fact that women are experiencing abuse,[47] thus making their responses inappropriate. There is also evidence that professionals have stereotyped views of 'domestic' violence, which often result in them seeing the woman as, at least in part, responsible for the violence.[48] Evan Stark and Ann Flitcraft, through their study of a hospital emergency room, maintain that it is this failure to act by professionals which traps many women in violent relationships:

The social services, broadly construed to include education, religion and recreation as well as medicine, law, police and welfare, function today as a reconstituted or extended patriarchy, defending the family form 'by any means necessary', including violence, against both its internal contradictions and women's struggles.[49]

A similar picture of failure to detect and act has emerged more recently in terms of sexual abuse and incest. Whilst little in-depth research has been done on current agency practice, the plethora of articles in vocational journals, the setting up of in-service training and the urgency with which new response models are being discussed all suggest dissatisfaction with previous forms of response. David Finkelhor[50] argues that despite an enormous amount of discussion and change in this area in the USA over the past five years responses to reported sexual abuse are still essentially arbitrary, being dependent on the varying practice of the agency first approached.

What the studies mentioned here, and many others not referred to, document is a failure to name sexual violence, and where abuse is acknowledged a failure to meet women's needs. Across the studies of a variety of institutions several key themes emerge: failure to take the extent, severity and impact of violence seriously; a focus of attention on the woman's behaviour; unless criminal prosecution is taking place a failure to confront the man about his violence.

Feminists responded to the failure of professionals in relation to sexual violence in two ways. First, they set up their own services to support/protect women, ranging from refuges and crisis lines through to self-defence classes and women's transport schemes. All of these services attempted to meet specific needs that the failure of other social agencies highlighted. Second, feminists have campaigned to change the attitudes and practice of professionals towards abused women and girls. The changes in police practice in a number of countries and the involvement of feminists in the training of a range of professionals is one result of this campaigning.

While there is no doubt that feminist campaigning has had some impact on perceptions and practice around sexual violence, the form of the response has not been necessarily one all feminists would welcome. There is an ongoing discussion in the United States about the extent to which refuges and rape crisis lines have been institutionalized via funding and professionalization.[51] Feminists are also critical of a number of changes that are taking place in official agency practice.

The recent announcements by the Metropolitan Poice about the changes in how women reporting rape will be treated, and the introduction of examination suites, have been seen in the context of the police shooting of Cherry Groce and the inherent sexism and racism of the British police force.[52] To many feminists these changes are window-dressing, masking the fact that the fundamental changes that are needed have not taken place.[53]

Diversion programmes are increasingly being used in the USA (and to some extent in the UK) to keep men charged with assault of their partner or incest out of the criminal justice system. These 'alternative' methods have the same result as the old method of not taking sexual violence seriously – men's violence to women and girls they know is not treated in the same way as violence to women or men they do not know. Such programmes also tend to require that the woman or girl takes part in a treatment programme. On completion of the programme the man is deemed to be 'cured' and all charges are dropped. These programmes are being adopted with great rapidity, yet there is little evaluation taking place and almost no evidence to suggest they are effective in changing men's behaviour.[54]

We are concerned that in the rush to 'do something' about the apparent dramatic increase in incidence of sexual violence ways of seeing and dealing with abused women and girls that are not informed by a feminist perspective are developing. The difference in approach is best summarized by the use of the terms 'victim' and 'survivor'. Non-feminist responses defined abused women/girls as victims, who need help and sympathy (and in many cases treatment). This approach also tends to be based on an individualistic model which, while it may not make women responsible for their past experiences of violence, certainly implies that they are responsible for preventing further violence.

While women are victimized on a regular and recurring basis, the term victim implies a passive response to the events themselves and their aftermath. Feminists are now increasingly using the term survivor in relation to sexual violence. This term draws attention to the many ways women resist violence and to the coping strategies they use in dealing with the effects of sexual violence on them over time. When working with women who have been abused feminists seek to validate, and encourage women to build on, the strength they have demonstrated in resisting and coping. In understanding that sexual violence is part of the structure of patriarchal relations feminists are aware that there are limits to the protective strategies women might adopt. At the present time no woman can ensure her own safety. A future free of the threat and reality of sexual violence requires nothing less than the total transformation of patriarchal relations.

One of the problems with the legal response is that it is based on male (expert) definitions of crime. In relation to rape, for example, the male definition of 'real' rape focuses on stranger attacks on 'innocent' women – the Bad Wolf attacking Little Red Ridinghood. Assaults which fit this stereotype are those which the police and legal system are beginning to address in terms of 'reforms' in sentencing and police interrogation.[55] One foreseeable consequence of this is that the majority of rapes, which fall outside this definition will be deemed as not 'real' rape, and will either be no-crimed by the police or result in not-guilty verdicts following a humiliating (for the raped woman) trial. Reforms based on malestream definitions will benefit only a minority of abused women, and may in fact make things more difficult for the majority. This is just one example of the problematic nature of legal and institutional reform.

The Law and Order Debate

Sexual violence has not been subject to the same forms of social control as many other forms of crime. Many feminists have pointed out that not holding individual violent men accountable for their behaviour amounts to condoning sexual violence. The insistence by feminists that male violence be treated in the same way as other forms of violence has led some people to argue that feminists are playing into the right-wing lobby on the issue of law and order.

Feminist campaigns have not focused on giving the police or state more coercive power, but on highlighting a double-standard in the enforcement of already existing laws. Where campaigns have focused on changing the law, it has been to change definitions (the Rape in Marriage Campaign) or to afford women protection (the Domestic Violence Act 1976 and the Housing (Homeless Persons) Act 1977). Very few feminists have given unquestioning support to legislation which extends police powers and offers no clear and direct benefits to women (for example, the Police and Criminal Evidence Act 1984 and the Janet Fookes' Sexual Offences Act 1986).

To refuse to acknowledge that there is a real problem with the enforcement of already existing legislation denies women the protection they need and condones the behaviour of individual violent men. As we stated earlier, feminists do not accept that men's exploitation as workers, or oppression as blacks, justifies or excuses violence towards women. The fact that working-class women and black women do report rape, sexual abuse and domestic violence shows that they do not accept or condone men's violence and that many of them look to the law to sanction abusive men.

> While it remains critical that black people continue actively struggling against racism and discrimination, it must not be done at the physical and psychological expense of black women. We have paid our dues and black men must be held responsible for every injury they cause.[56]

Some black feminists have argued that alternative methods for protecting black women need to be explored while the police and courts remain racist institutions. The success of such alternatives are, as Beth Ritchie points out, dependent on black communities taking a strong stand against sexual violence. In the meantime many black women will continue to use the police and courts and it is the responsibility of all anti-racists to challenge racist practices in these institutions.

Feminists are aware that the other side of the classism and racism of law enforcement is that white middle-class men are far less likely to be prosecuted for sexual violence. It has been central to much feminist research to point out that white middle-class men are as implicated in sexual violence as any other group of men and to demand that all abusive men are made accountable for their behaviour.

Focusing on male sexual violence as a primary form of social control highlights the ways in which women's lives, at home, at work, and in the public arena are controlled by men. At the same time, we know that women are far less likely to be targeted for control by formal state agencies – the police, the courts and the penal system.[57] Women who do find themselves 'up before the law' are those who have or appear to have broken out of control by individual men. The women prisoners in Pat Carlen's[58] study of Cornton Vale in Scotland were disproportionately 'outwith domesticity' (that is, beyond the control of individual men in the family). Maggie Casburn[59] argues that it is young women who are deemed by the state to be 'at risk', 'in moral danger' or 'beyond parental control' who receive custodial sentences. They are women outside the control of their families – read fathers – who are sentenced 'for their own good'. Similarly, in relation to public order issues, it is women who have achieved or who are struggling for autonomy from male control – be they the suffragists of the early century, or Greenham women, or open lesbians, who are targeted for state control. Prostitute women, who are also outside traditional male control, are not only denied protection from the male violence they encounter in their working lives, but are also targeted as a group for criminalization by the state.

Although this may read as a reductionist argument these are some of the consequences for women of a patriarchal social order in which state agencies of control play a last-resort role, drawn on only when the first line of control, by individual men, is threatened. As the Women's Liberation Movement has long recognized, women face inequality and oppression on a range of levels including the ideological. It is here that certain behaviours by individual, or groups of, women are constructed as 'deviant' and, therefore, within the province of state control agencies.

Viewing sexual violence as a primary form of male control can explain not only why the law operates selectively in the protection it affords women but also why women as a gender class are rarely targeted for state policing. As Andrea Dworkin[60] has pointed out, women are subject to two levels of policing: by individual men and by the state. The success of male sexual violence as a form of control or policing, its legitimation by the state via the failure to treat sexual violence as 'real' crime results in state agencies seldom having to intervene in the control of women. This analysis of sexual violence as a structured part of patriarchal social relations also suggests that where reforms are introduced they are likely to be partial and have little impact on women's experience of sexual violence.

Notes

1 F. Heidensohn, *Women and Crime*, London, Macmillan, 1985.
2 See J. Lea: and J. Young, *What Is to be Done about Law and Order*, Harmondsworth, Middx. Penguin, 1984; and R. Kinsey, J. Lea and J. Young, *Losing the Fight against Crime*, Oxford, Basil Blackwell, 1986.
3 L. Kelly, 'Sharing a particular pain', *Trouble and Strife*, 3, 1984, pp. 516–20. J. Radford, 'Womanslaughter and the criminal law', in P. Scraton and P. Gordon (eds), *Causes for Concern*, Harmondsworth, Middx, Penguin 1984.
4 L. Leghorn and K. Parker, *Women's Worth: Sexual Economics and the World of Women*, Boston, Routledge & Kegan Paul, 1981. P. Reeves Sanday, 'The Socio-cultural context of rape: a cross-cultural study', *Journal of Social Issues*, Vol. 37, no. 4, 1981, pp. 5–27.
5 J. Hanmer, 'Male violence and the social control of women', in G. Littlejohn, B. Smart, J. Wakeford and N. Yural Davies (eds), *Power and the State*, London, Croom Helm. Kate Millett *Sexual Politics*, London, Hart-Davis, 1970.
6 For an excellent discussion of the debate around the concept of patriarchy, and a defence of its usage and a discussion of the independence of structures of oppression, see S. Walby, *Patriarchy at Work*, Cambridge, Polity Press, 1987.
7 A.J. Hearne, 'Racism, rape and riot', *Trouble and Strife*, 9, 1986, pp. 8–13.
8 A.K. Cohen, 'The sociology of the deviant act: anomie theory and beyond', *American Sociological Review*, 30, 1965, pp. 5–12.
9 M. Amir, *Patterns in Forcible Rape*, Chicago, University of Chicago Press, 1971.
10 E. Ward, *Father–Daughter Rape*, London, The Women's Press, 1984. E. Wilson *The existing research into battered women*, London, National Women's Aid, 1975.
11 S. Jeffreys and J. Radford, 'Contributory Negligence – being a woman', in P. Scraton and P. Gordon (eds), *Causes for Concern*, Harmondsworth, Middx, Penguin, 1984.
12 S. Jeffreys, *The Spinster and her Enemies: Feminism and Sexuality 1880–1930*, London, Pandora, 1985.
13 See A.J. Hearn op. cit. for a discussion of these issues. She writes not from the perspective of a radical criminologist but from her experience as a black woman living in Brixton.
14 Off Our Backs, April 1986. Between Ourselves: Reproductive Freedom in the Black Community. p. 4.
15 P.Q. Hirst, 'Marx and Engels on law, crime and criminality', *Economy and Society*, 1, 1972, 28–56.
16 D. Russell, *Rape in Marriage*, New York, Macmillan, 1982. D. Russell, *Sexual Exploitation*, Beverley Hills, Calif, Sage, 1984.
17 J. Hanmer and S. Saunders, *Well-Founded Fear*, London, Hutchinson, 1984. J. Radford, 'Policing male violence – policing women', in J. Hanmer and M. Maynard (eds), *Women, Violence and Social Control*, London, Macmillan, 1987.
18 L. Kelly, *Surviving Sexual Violence*, Cambridge, Polity Press, forthcoming.
19 D. Russell, 1984, op. cit.
20 R. Hall, *Ask Any Woman*, Bristol, Falling Wall Press, 1985.
21 See, for example C. Cooper and M. Davidson, 1982, *High Pressure: Working Lives of*

Woman Managers, London, Fontana. NALGO, Sexual Harassment at Work, unpublished mimeograph, 1981. C. Safran, 'Survey on sexual harassment', *Redbook Magazine*, November 1976, pp. 216–20.

22 T. Baker, 'Readers' survey on sexual abuse', *19 magazine*, September 1983, pp. 34–6, 48–52. D. Finkelhor, *Sexually Victimized Children*, New York, Free Press, 1979.

23 D. Russell, 'The incidence and prevalence of intrafamilial and extrafamilial sexual abuse of female children', *Child Abuse and Neglect*, 7, 1983, pp. 133–46.

24 S. McNeill, 'Flashing – its affect on women', in J. Hanmer and M. Maynard, op. cit.

25 M.A. Schulman, *A survey of spousal abuse against women in Kentucky, Washington DC*, US Department of Justice, 1979. M.A. Straus, M.J. Gelles and S.K. Steinmetz, *Behind Closed Doors*, New York, Anchor Books, 1980.

26 J.M. Makepeace, 'Courtship violence among college students', *Family Relations*, vol. 30, no. 1, 1981, pp. 97–102. M. Riege Larner and J. Thompson, 'Abuse and aggression in courting couples', *Deviant Behaviour*, 3, 1982, pp. 229–44.

27 E. Stanko, 'Typical violence, normal precautions: men, women and interpersonal violence', J. Hanmer and M. Maynard, op. cit.

28 L. Kelly, 'Women's experiences of sexual violence', PhD thesis, Essex University, 1986. S. McNeill, op. cit.

29 J. Hanmer and S. Saunders, op. cit., S. McNeill, op. cit.

30 L. Kelly, 'Effects or survival strategies? The long-term consequences of experiences of sexual violence', in D. Finkelhor and G. Hotaling (eds), Beverley *Papers from The Second International Family Violence Conference*, Beverley Hills, Calif., Sage, in press.

31 See, for example, J. Hanmer and S. Saunders, op. cit., L. Kelly, 1986, op. cit., D. Russell, 1984, op. cit.

32 H. Schwendinger and J. Schwendinger, 'Defenders of order or guardians of human rights?', *Issues in Criminology*, 5, 1970, pp. 123–57.

33 L. Clark and D. Lewis, *Rape: The Price of Coercive Sexuality*, Toronto, Womens Press, 1977.

34 C. MacKinnon, 'Violence against women – a perspective', *Aegis*, 33, 1982, p. 52.

35 K.A. Benson, 'Comment on Crocker's "An analysis of university definitions of sexual harassment"', *Signs*, vol. 9, no. 3, 1984, pp. 516–19.

36 L. Kelly, forthcoming, op. cit.

37 See, for example, C. Jones, 'Sexual tyranny: male violence in a mixed secondary school', in G. Weiner (ed.), *Just a Bunch of Girls*, Milton Keynes, Bucks, Open University Press, 1985; P. Mahony, *Schools for Boys? Co-education Reassessed*, London, Hutchinson, 1984. D. Spender, *Invisible Women: the Schooling Scandal*. London, Writers and Readers, 1982; S.J. Scraton, 'Ideologies of the physical and the politics of sexuality: girls' physical education considered' in S. Walker and L. Barton (eds), *Changing Policy, Changing Teachers* Milton Keynes, Open University Press, 1987.

38 R. Hall, 1985, op. cit. p. 48.

39 L. Kelly, 'Sexual violence as a continuum', in J. Hanmer and M. Maynard, op. cit.

40 C. MacKinnon, 'Feminism, marxism, method and the state: an agenda for theory', *Signs*, vol. 7, no. 3, 1983, pp. 644–5.

42 G. Chambers and A. Millar, *Investigating Sexual Assault*, Edinburgh, HMSO, 1983.

L. Holmstrom and A. Burgess, *The Victims of Rape: Institutional Reaction*, New York, Wiley, 1978. G. La Free, 'Variables affecting guilty pleas and convictions in rape cases: toward a social theory of rape processing', *Social Forces*, vol. 58, no. 3, 1980, pp. 833–50. T.W. McCahill, S. Meyer and L. Fischman, *The Aftermath of Rape*, Lexington, Mass., Lexington Books, 1979.

43 V. McNickle Rose and S.C. Randall, 'Where have all the rapists gone?', in J.A. Inciardi and S. Pottieger (eds), *Violent Crime: Historical and Contemporary Issues*, Beverley Hills, Calif., Sage, 1978, pp. 75–89.

44 V. Binney, G. Harkell and J. Nixon, *Leaving Violent Men*, Leeds, National Women's Aid Federation, NWAF, 1981. M. Homer, A. Leanardi and M. Taylor, *Private Violence, Public Shame*, Middlesborough, CRAWC, 1984.

45 L.W. Sherman and R.A. Berk, 'The specific deterrent effects of arrest for domestic violence', *American Sociological Review*, vol. 49, no. 2, 1984, pp. 261–72.

46 A.T. Laszlo and T. McKean, 1978, 'Court diversion: an alternative for spousal abuse cases', in *Battered Women: Issues of Public Policy*, Washington DC, US Commission on Civil Rights, 1978, 327–56. F. Wassoff, 'Legal protection from wife-beating: the processing of domestic assaults by Scottish prosecutors and criminal courts', *International Journal of Sociology of Law*, 10, 1982, pp. 187–204.

47 M. Maynard, 1985, 'Response of social workers to battered women', in J. Pahl (ed), *Private Violence and Public Policy*, London, Routledge & Kegan Paul, 1985, pp. 125–41. E. Stark and A. Flitcraft, 'Social knowledge, social policy and the abuse of women: the case against patriarchal benevolence, in D. Finkelhor, R.J. Gelles, G.T. Hotaling and M.A. Straus (eds), *The Dark Side of Families: Current Family Violence Research*, Beverley Hills, Calif., Sage, 1983, pp. 330–48.

48 M. Borkowski, M. Murch and V. Walker, *Marital Violence: The Community Response*, London, Tavistock, 1983. J. Pahl, 'The general practitioner and the problems of battered women', *Journal of Medical Ethics*, vol. 5, no. 3, 1979, pp. 11–17.

49 E. Stark and A. Flitcraft, op. cit. p. 464.

50 D. Finkelhor, *Child Sexual Abuse: New Theory and Research*, New York, Free Press, 1984.

51 E. O'Sullivan, 'What has happened to rape crisis centres? A look at their structures, members and fundings', *Victimology* vol. 3, nos. 1–2, 1979, pp. 45–62. S. Schecter, *Women and Male Violence: The Visions and Struggles of the Battered Women's Movement*, London, Pluto, 1982.

52 H. Brown, 'A day in the city', *Trouble and Strife*, 8, 1986, pp. 5–10.

53 L. Alderson and L. Kelly, 'Interview with London Rape Crisis', *Trouble and Strife*, 10, 1987, pp. 48–56.

54 J. Conte, 1984, 'Progress in treating sexual abuse of children', *Social Work*, vol. 29, no. 3, 1984, pp. 19:3, 258–63. M.J. Eddy and T. Myers, 'Helping men who batter: a profile of programs in the US', paper at the Second International Conference of Family Violence Researchers, August, 1984, University of New Hampshire.

55 J. Radford, 'Thanks for nothing, Lord Lane', unpublished paper from the European Conference on Critical Legal Studies, London, April 1986.

56 B. Ritchie, 'Battered Black women: a challenge for the community', *The Black Scholar*, March–April 1985.

57 F. Heidensohn, op. cit.; C. Smart, *Women, Crime and Criminology: a Feminist Critique*, London, Routledge & Kegan Paul, 1976.

58 P. Carlen, *Women's Imprisonment: A Study in Social Control*, London, Routledge & Kegan Paul, 1983.

59 M. Casburn, *Girls Will Be Girls*, Women's Research and Resources Centre, London, 1979.
60 Andrea Dworkin, *In conversation with Alison Hennegan*, ICA, London, May 1986.

9

The Criminalization of Women

Kathryn Chadwick and Catherine Little

Introduction

In 1976, Carol Smart's *Women, Crime and Criminology* was published; this was the first real attempt to put forward a feminist perspective of female criminality. Smart realized that her first task was to develop a critique of the existing studies from a feminist perspective. She stated: 'The majority of these studies refer to women in terms of their biological impulses and hormonal balance or in terms of their domesticity, maternal instinct and passivity.'[1] Her work opened the door to the development of further feminist critiques of criminology and over the past ten years the literature in this area has grown and the importance of a feminist criminology has been established.

Both traditional and early critical criminology failed to look at the contrasting social worlds and experiences of women and men. They did not address, let alone provide answers as to why, first, women's criminal careers are different to those of men, and second, why women are treated differently within the criminal justice process. Discussions and analysis traditionally have focused on male behaviour and male criminality. Theoretical criminology has largely been about, for, and written by men.

To some extent the relatively small number of women who experience the criminal justice process as offenders explain their apparent 'invisibility'. However, the vast number of women who experience the criminal justice process as 'victims', many being victims of serious crime, suggests that the invisibility of women is less to do with relatively small numbers but, rather, it reflects a patriarchal society in which women's experiences systematically have been ignored. Furthermore, the invisibility of women within academic criminology merely reflects a strong patriarchal tradition within the social sciences in general with women's history, experiences, culture, and politics being peripheral to the 'real issues' prioritized for research, teaching and publication.

In this chapter a feminist analysis is used to consider critically the processes by which women in contemporary society come to be criminalized. Pat Carlen[2] states that one of the failures of traditional criminology and some feminist criminology, is the 'failure to distinguish analytically' between law-breaking and criminalization. Law-breaking refers to a violation of established legislation, for example, exceeding the speed limit. Criminalization refers to behaviour seen to be deviant, but not necessarily law-breaking, which then becomes criminalized, for example the women's peace protest at Greenham Common.

It is the criminalization of women's behaviour, and in particular the perceived sexuality of women, which will be our focus. Although, our overall analysis will be from a feminist perspective the analysis incorporates themes first developed within the labelling perspective, in terms of the defining of behaviour and criminalization, and from within earlier critical criminology, in terms of the significance of social, political, economic and ideological contexts and constructions. Through the feminist critique we challenge the traditional academic and common-sense biological assumptions about the natural role of women as mothers and carers. Dorothy Smith[3] and Carol Smart[4] refer to this as the 'reconstruction of patriarchal ideologies' around women. A negative picture, very often related to their biologies, has always been painted of women, and feminist criminology sets out to replace these negative patriarchal ideologies with research that locates the issues into a wider structural context. This means considering women not only in relation to the family, but also in relation to the state and criminal justice process. This raises further the issue of the impact of patriarchal ideologies, and their institutionalized presence within the criminal justice process, on women's lives.

Following on from a theoretical analysis of the process of criminalization, beginning with the work of labelling theorists through to more recent debates within critical criminology, we consider how the social control of women leads to state control,[5] thus consolidating the process by which women are criminalized. Also, it is important to consider the position of women in relation to the nuclear family and the relationship between women's paid and unpaid work and the function of domestic work in the home, as the economic marginalization of women is also central to criminalization. Our first example of criminalization focuses on the position of women in relation to welfare and the policing of welfare claimants. By looking specifically at cohabitation, we show how the behaviour of women becomes criminalized. Prostitution, our second example, is a clear example of the social and state controls of women's sexuality and behaviour which leads to criminalization. Our third example concentrates on women who are protesting against state policy; here we focus specifically on the women's peace camp at the United States air base at Greenham Common. Although this has been a peaceful, non-violent protest the women at Greenham have found themselves up against the law and the criminal justice process. Finally, we look at the implications of recent legislation, particularly the Public Order Act of 1986, in realtion to the activities of women. This suggests that the criminalization of women will continue as the policies and practices of the police become consolidated by legislation.

The Process of Criminalization

Hall and Scraton[6] define the process of criminalization as 'the application of the criminal label to a particular social category'. Derived from the work of social interactionists such as Becker and Lemert,[7] an act is not perceived as a crime until it has been defined as such. The significant areas of debate within this process focus on: how certain acts are labelled, who has the power to label, and how police and judicial control is legitimated as the application of justice within the criminal justice process. Where the analysis has moved beyond the formative work of social interactionists is in its critical and rigorous examination of the construction and significance of the 'power of the definers'.[8] It has achieved this objective by locating political, economic and patriarchal relations as central to an analysis of the rule of law and the process by which certain behaviours become criminalized.

Theoretically, then, the process of criminalization has its roots in the labelling perspective which focused on the social construction of crime as a means of 'social control'. In contrast critical criminologists have adopted the concept of 'state control',[9] suggesting that criminal labels were applied not only to activities perceived as illegal by the majority but, more importantly, to activities which are identified as being threatening to the political stability and established order of the state.

The criminalization of specific acts, then, not only legitimates the control of such activities within the criminal justice process, but also captures the consent of the people who are more likely to support state action against political or social movements linked to criminal activities. Evidence to support this can be found in three recent examples. First, the criminalization of those involved in recent industrial disputes such as the 1984–5 coal dispute and the 1986–7 print workers' dispute at Wapping, both of which have been portrayed as constituting a violent threat to democracy and the maintenance of law and order.[10] Secondly, in June 1985, the police response to the Peace Convoy which was perceived as a threat to established family life and conventional forms of living.[11] Finally the Greenham women are portrayed as having stepped outside and rejected the role ascribed to all women: the 'natural' role in which domesticity, femininity, sexuality, housewifery and caring are central.[12] Like so many groups of women in similar situations, asserting their independence from male control threatens the established order of patriarchal relations within society.[13]

As Hall and Scraton[14] state:

> Some criminal groups have sometimes been singled out by the media and treated repressively for social and political reasons. Though it is their crimes which appear to attract attention, they may in fact, be the victims of wider attitudes of social hostility, which find a conveniently displaced expression through the focusing on the criminal aspect.

What recent critical research in criminology has shown is that the process of criminalization, a process by which political acts can be redefined as unlawful, is used to protect and reinforce the interests of an established order be they primarily political or economic. The process is intricate as not only does it demand state institutional responses from the police, the courts, the mental institutions and the prisons, it also relies on the winning of popular consent for state policies and legal shifts which are essentially authoritarian.[15] The role of the media in the creation of social and political concern, the most extreme form being that of 'moral panics',[16] is central to this process. Criminalization is a political response to political and social protest – a political response which uses the legal form to regulate and put down social and political unrest. The derivation of this response often lies within inherent economic contradictions, be they related to the processes of advanced capitalism or patriarchy. The state institutional response, however, relies heavily on winning 'hearts and minds' by establishing ideological appeals to popular consent.[17] Political, economic and ideological forces, then, work together to facilitate the criminalization process. It is in relation to popular ideologies of sexism that we prioritize women and social welfare. Using the examples of women who cohabit rather than marry, women who work as prostitutes, and women involved in political protest, we examine the proposal that through sexist ideology the criminalization of women is different to that of men.

The Social and State Control of Women

In order to understand why certain acts are criminalized and, specifically, the way in which women are treated and regulated by state power, it is important to consider the broader contexts in which women and women's behaviour is socially defined and controlled. Recent feminist research shows overwhelmingly that gender divisions and women's regulation begin with the process of primary socialization in the family and, secondly, socialization in the peer groups, school and the media.[18] Socialization acts to

> reinforce the ways of acting, thinking and feeling 'characteristic' of the female

role, femininity and womanhood, to the more formal processes of institutional intervention through legislation by the state, the implementation of the law, the penal system and the criminal process.[19]

Smart and Smart state that social control takes many different forms and is evident in both 'public' and 'private' domains. It is acknowledged that certain dimensions of social control relate only to women. These include the reproductive cycle, a double standard of morality, a subordinate and legal status in the family, and the separation of 'home' and 'work' coupled with the ideology of women's place.[20]

It is 'in their place' – in the home with the family – that Jill Radford suggests women are most closely controlled. She states: 'The prime agency for the controlling, watching, supervising, segregating and changing the behaviour of women is the family.'[21] Within the privacy of the traditional nuclear family in patriarchal societies, the authority, dominance and responsibility for this regulation lies with men. Women who move outside 'their place' – into the public sphere – are met with controls and policies. Controls in the public sphere work at two different levels: in the workplace women are constrained and controlled by the types of work available to them and by sexual harassment.[22] Second, women are controlled by their lack of access to social space and recreation, such as in pubs and on the streets.[23] Women's rational fear of abuse, attack and sexual assault controls access to all forms of social space.[24] Likewise, fear of loss of status and reputation relating to respectability and sexuality[25] controls women's responses and opportunities.

This range of controls on women's social and personal lives within and outside the family has many consequences. Clearly it creates isolation, with little confidence and self-esteem. As Mary Eaton suggests,[26] women are so 'effectively controlled by their socialization and the conditions of their existence', that this must be seen as a major factor in explaining why so few women become involved in criminal activities. The regulation and surveillance of young girls' and women's behaviour and movements gives them little opportunity to indulge in criminal activities.[27]

What, however, happens to those women who do not conform to these processes of regulation – women who cohabit rather than enter into the marriage contract; women who are forced into prostitution in order to make a living; women who do not fit into the neat category of white, middle-class respectable heterosexuality; women who exert their independence to fight social and political issues – women who do not fit into the image or the acceptable way of behaviour? Invariably women who do not subscribe to living within the nuclear family or who attempt to exercise control over their own lives are labelled and treated as deviant. In short, they have stepped outside their prescribed role and have challenged 'their' definers, thereby challenging established 'power relations'.

In this chapter we are concerned with the criminalization of those women who exert control over their own sexual activities and/or their own sexuality. There is a connection between the marginalization of women through their economic dependence and the control of women's sexuality. Before concentrating on specific groups of women, however, it is necessary to look at the processes by which women are economically marginalized.

Women, the Family and Work

Given the strength of biological explanations and expectations around sexuality, motherhood and childbirth, the family role and functions prescribed for women not only form a strong economic and ideological construction but permeate throughout state institutions and create the foundations upon which the political management and regulation of women is institutionalized. In advanced capitalist societies, as with other patriarchal societies, the family has developed as an oppressive and constraining institution for women.[28] Women's fundamental function within the family is to reproduce and care for the paid workforce and the future wage-labourers. Beveridge demonstrated that this primary role should be reinforced by the Welfare State. He stated:

> Maternity is the principle object of marriage. The attitude of the housewife to gainful employment outside the home is not and should not be the same as that of a single woman. She has other duties.[29]

Elizabeth Wilson[30] suggests that the Welfare State maintains the regulation of women by creating ideologies of the 'natural'. If women established independence through paid work in the labour market they are inhibited from meeting the demands and expectations of the established nuclear family.[31]

In the justification of these social arrangements a biological determinist argument is inevitable. This ensures that women remain literally housewives. The post-war period provided clear evidence of this position in the policy of returning women back to the home following their brief period in paid employment as part of the 'war effort'. Bowlby's work on maternal deprivation,[32] which reinforced the ideology of women as 'natural' carers because of their reproductive capacity and thus suiting them to domestic duties,[33] was particularly significant at this time. It is important to emphasize the persistence of the notion of 'naturalness'. For it is women's genetic constitution, the existence of the womb, which makes them better carers. That this role might be learned through years of preparation as girls and young women was not part of the appeal to 'common sense'. This position constructs the family as an alternative location to full state welfare provision. It assumes that women as 'natural' carers will look after the aged, the sick and the disabled under the laudable banner of 'community care'.

Because women are defined in terms of unpaid domestic work within the family they are made financially dependent on men in that the male wage is constructed as a 'family wage'. The principle inherent in social welfare policy is that the man's wage is a family wage and is sufficient to support 'his' wife and 'his' children. Michelle Barrett and Mary McIntosh[34] trace the historical development of the 'family wage' and consider that as capitalism developed women became 'marginalized' in the labour market and children excluded. This forced women to become dependent on men and the 'family wage'. However, a 'family wage' system never operated effectively in Britain because, with few exceptions, working-class wages have never been adequate in providing for a family. Consequently women have been forced into badly paid, part-time and unprotected work in order to establish a minimum standard of living. It can be seen from a cursory glance at the nineteenth-century provision of poor relief that this societal commitment to the 'male breadwinner' has a long history in the practice and principle of state policy.

The 'family wage' system is based on the 'average typical household' of two parents and two children; yet there are few so-called 'average' households.[35] Further, this system does not account for households in which married women work, or where there is a single woman heading the family. Hilary Land[36] examines this 'myth of the male breadwinner'. She quotes a Minister of State for the Department of Health and Social Security as saying: 'The widespread view is that a husband who is capable of work has a duty to society, as well as to his wife, to provide the primary support for his family.'[37] She indicates that this views the 'wife's' wages as of secondary importance or, as widely described, as 'pin money'. The woman's primary responsibility remains that of domestic work, caring for children, the elderly and disabled. This idea is clearly inherent in welfare policy, where women are seen to be economically inactive.

Clearly, then, the implications for women of state policy and practices is the perpetuation of their financial dependence on men and, consequently, the structural inequalities of patriarchal relations. Despite the 1975 Equal Pay Act and the 1975 Sex Discrimination Act little has been done effectively to challenge these inequalities.[38]

This is not to argue that women do not participate in the labour market, but clearly women's paid work is considered secondary to that of men. Women are not classed as part of the 'core' work-force because the historical nature of their work has been predominantly part-time, unskilled, manual, casual and non-unionized.[39] Jenny Somerville[40] argues that women are central to the labour market not only as workers, but as reproducers of the labour force. Women reproduce, care for and turn out the past, present and future paid and unpaid labour force. Significant here is Marx's theory of the 'industrial reserve army of labour', of which women have constituted a significant part. According to Marx, the reserve army of labour is central to the development of the accumulation of capital. In times of periodic crises, structurally inherent in capitalist growth, an easily disposable work-force is necessary to protect and maintain 'core' jobs. Women have continued to provide capital with such a work-force. The 'peripheral' status of women's paid labour together with restricted opportunities in paid employment have served to emphasize women's dependence on the 'male breadwinner'. Collectively women have remained an easily exploitable reserve ever adaptable to the ebb and flow of capital accumulation. The ideological construction of women's role justifies this secondary role in the labour market. In order that female labour can be disposed easily the ideology of women's 'natural' place in the home is used to remove women from the labour market and to 'return' them to the home. Moral panics are created over 'latchkey kids',[41] and it is seen to be desirable for women to devote their entire time to their children and domestic duties. That, however, is not to say that when women are active in the labour market their domestic duties are alleviated, rather they still hold full responsibility for the organization and management of the household.

The structure of the capitalist-patriarchy in its advanced political-economic form leaves women with restricted choices. If they are to gain some degree of independent status by necessity they must make choices that will benefit them.

The Policing of Welfare Claimants: The Criminalization of Women within the DHSS

The legal and financial dependence of women on men has important implications for social policy initiatives concerned with women in relation to welfare provision, particularly social security and the claims for income maintenance. As is documented elsewhere,[42] married women receive an unfair deal from the social security system, but also this applies to women who cohabit because of the application of the 'cohabitation rule'.

This rule was established under the Ministry of Social Security Act 1966 and it applies to a woman and man living together as 'husband and wife'. It is assumed, as in a marriage relationship, that the man is supporting the woman. As there is no official definition, however, this has presented problems for the DHSS Fraud Section. Certain questions are asked by the DHSS to establish whether a couple are cohabiting. These include: whether the couple are living in the same household, whether the relationship is stable, what financial arrangements are made, whether there is a sexual relationship, whether the couple have any children, how they 'appear' in public. Clearly these are criteria which are difficult for the DHSS to establish.

The cohabitation rule exists so that the traditional nuclear family, dependent on the 'family wage' and essential to capitalism, is not threatened. Thus it applies the same rules to a non-married couple as to a married couple. This ensures that there is no alternative to the nuclear family unit.

For whatever reasons those women who step outside the traditional nuclear family can ensure the severe consequences of the DHSS Fraud Section and its application of the cohabitation rule. This is true particularly for single mothers. Throughout the early 1980s there was growing concern over the way in which single mothers were treated by the DHSS and this led to media interest. For many women claiming Supplementary Benefit is their only source of income. Delays in receiving benefit means that they can be left penniless and without state support. A case reported in *The Times*[43] raises this issue. Mrs Petra Barrett telephoned the local DHSS office to be told repeatedly that her cheque would be posted. During a subsequent telephone call she asked if she could call at the office and collect the cheque. The man at the DHSS office asked her to wait while he consulted a senior colleague. She overheard the man explaining the situation to a woman who would not allow Mrs Barrett to be treated differently from other claimants. The man was quoted as saying, 'for heaven's sake, she's got three children, she's a single parent', to which Mrs Barrett distinctly heard the woman reply, 'come on, none of them are single parents. They're all living with some fella'. Eventually, Mrs Barrett was told she could go into the office and collect her cheque. Understandably she was upset and angered. However, Mrs Barrett only received this publicity because her case was considered by the press to be 'respectable' and 'deserving'. This reflected her social standing in the local community, where she was a member of the tenant's association and a potential Labour candidate for the local council. For many women, who are seen to be 'undeserving', there is no way out of such a situation. This is shown in the case of Kay.

Kay had been claiming Supplementary Benefit for 3½ years. Her husband had left her when her son was 3 months old. After 2 years she qualified for long-term benefit, but she decided just before the due date that she would live with her boyfriend. She informed the DHSS and he claimed for them as partners. This lasted only a few weeks as Kay's boyfriend spent their benefit on alcohol and cigarettes and, therefore, did not provide for her. Following this Kay was denied benefit for 17 weeks. At the tribunal Kay was presented as a 'deserving' woman. The tribunal obviously did not consider this to be the case, however, and, she was refused long-term benefit. She was considered to be 'undeserving' because she was a single parent, who had allowed a man to live with her and had 'got pregnant by him'.[44]

The majority of cases investigated by the DHSS in which a woman is considered to be cohabiting follow a similar pattern. Many of these cases are reported by relatives and neighbours and the DHSS investigators keep watch on women in an attempt to establish whether they are cohabiting. This often involves surprise visits to the claimant's home where the investigator 'sex snoops', by checking the bedroom and bathroom for evidence of a male living there. In 1982 the *Daily Mirror*[45] reported that a woman had her benefit withdrawn because her DHSS investigator found a pair of man's shoes in the claimant's home. She was wrongly accused of cohabiting.

When making a claim for benefit single mothers regularly are asked detailed questions about their sex lives by DHSS officers. The DHSS has issued confidential guidelines to officers as to what questions they should ask – for example, claimant's have been asked when they last had sexual intercourse, the time of their last period, and about their use of contraceptives. The press has also reported the use of 'Gestapo' tactics and the use of sex spies to uncover social security 'scroungers'.[46]

In 1980, Reg Prentice announced that there was going to be a 'clampdown' on welfare scroungers. The Tory administration suggested that with an effective fraud squad the DHSS could save up to £50 million per year. At an overall cost of £7 million per year and with 1,050 extra staff Specialist Claims Control Units were established. These units were to move into regional offices and investigate target populations of claimants, independently of the local fraud officers. It was the 'Gestapo' tactics of these units which captured the headlines, particularly in the case of single women. The case of Jane is not an isolated incident[47] Jane lived in a rented house in the West Midlands with her two children. Her only source of income was that she received from the DHSS. One morning Jane was visited by two men from the newly formed Specialist Claims Control Unit who claimed that Jane was being financially supported by a man and that she had been under surveillance for 2 weeks. Following an interview at home, Jane was taken to the local office for a further interview. For several hours, behind locked doors, Jane was subjected to an intense interrogation. Although, Jane knew the allegations against her were false she agreed to sign away her benefit claim. Her claim was taken up by the local welfare rights centre and after 3 months her claim was reinstated. No disciplinary action was taken against the investigators. In periods of increasing hardship, women particularly are forced into a position of structured oppression. They are expected to provide care for their dependants and, in the case of single mothers, they are expected to provide financial support. In some cases people are left with little alternative than to work and claim benefit at the same time. This latter point is raised by South and Scraton,[48] in their work on the 'hidden economy'. They point out that the concern over the 'hidden economy' should be considered in its wider context, for example in the 'social' and 'economic' policy-making spheres. Within the workplace it is expected, and to a certain extent it is taken into account, that people will fiddle and pilfer. When this extends to the area of welfare, however, no such allowance is made. The policing of welfare claimants is also a regulation of the economy in that it is hoped that people will be deterred from supplementing their benefit by 'working on the side'.[49] South and Scraton consider the 'hidden economy' in terms of welfare claimants claiming benefit and receiving extra money from some form of work.

Clearly then, the tactics of the DHSS Fraud Squad and Specialist Claims Control Units are used to deter people from welfare fraud. However, they also deter people from claiming the benefits to which they are entitled or force people to withdraw their claims following a non-prosecution interview, similar to that experienced by Jane. The welfare claimant is stigmatized and marginalized by his/her claimant status. As mentioned previously, however, women suffer dual marginalization as they experience restricted choices in other fields, such as employment opportunities. Women who do not enter into the traditional nuclear family unit or who have been left by men, or been forced to leave them, are further stigmatized and marginalized because they do not conform to the norm whether by choice or not. Thus in attempting to gain some control over their own lives by not living within a nuclear family, they are labelled as deviant and if they contravene regulations, their behaviour is criminalized. It is important to emphasize that it is more acceptable for a man to cohabit, but it is the woman who is portrayed as immoral. In keeping with the legacy of Bowlby it is 'welfare mothers' who bear the blame and the guilt for 'broken homes', 'latchkey kids' and the 'breakdown of morality'. Thus in the 1970s Keith Joseph raised the solution of 'sterilization' and this was echoed in the aftermath of the 1980–81 uprisings by Lord Goodman in a speech to the House of Lords. The ideological construction of 'morality' is neatly and inextricably linked to those categories of 'respectability' and 'deserving'.

The 'Fallen Woman': The Criminalization of the Prostitute

The popular image of the prostitute is that of a 'fallen woman'. The prostitute is seen to be the ultimate example of the unchaste woman for she has deviated from the dominant images and stereotypes of women as passive, submissive and feminine. Women's respectability is judged largely by their sexuality and, placed along a continuum, women are either 'good' or 'bad', virgins or whores. The ideological construction of the prostitute serves to divide and separate women into different categories. Sheila Jeffreys[50] considers some of the reasons for this separation:

> It is in the interests of men that women are divided into groups whose interests are apparently opposed. 'Good' women have been encouraged to turn their anxiety at their precarious position into anger at prostitutes who can appear to threaten the married woman's security and home, to undermine her efforts to control her man and his sexual demands. Or we are told that prostitution is necessary to protect the married woman's security. Neither is true ... It is vital to male supremacy that women be divided into the 'pure' and the 'fallen' so we may not pool our knowledge and engage in the fight against male sexuality as the social control of women.

This division of women into 'good' and 'bad' can be linked also to the 'deserving' and 'undeserving' categories of women claimants discussed in the previous section. These divisions serve to undermine any shared class or gender interests and lay the foundations for the process of criminalization.

Traditional explanations for the occurrence of prostitution invariably are biological and focus on the abnormal sexuality of women. In these portrayals women are seen to lack any moral fibre; they are promiscuous, sex-crazed or simply men-haters who wish to use prostitution to exercise their power over men. Coupled with this they are seen to be lazy and in search of easy work, hence easy money. They are predators on men's sexual needs. The Wolfenden Committee was instructed to inquire into both homosexuality and prostitution, a revealing juxtaposition, and in its 1957 report emphasized these points very clearly:

> Whatever may have been the case in the past, in these days, in this country at any rate, economic factors cannot account for it to any large or decisive extent. Economic pressure is no doubt a factor in some individual cases. So, in others, is a bad upbringing, seduction at an early age, or a broken marriage. But many women surmount such disasters without turning to a life of prostitution. It seems to us more likely that these are precipitating factors rather than determining causes, and that there must be some additional psychological element in the personality of the individual woman who becomes a prostitute. Our impression is that the great majority of prostitutes are women whose psychological make-up is such that they choose this life because they find in it a style of living which is to them easier, freer, and more profitable than would be provided by any other occupation.[51]

In reality prostitution is far from easy work or a comfortable style of living. Prostitutes are alienated from the rest of society, they are subjected to personal degradation and social stigma, they work long and unsociable hours, and run the constant risks of attacks or murder. Many women, as a result of the processes of the labour market discussed earlier, find themselves economically marginalized, so that prostitution becomes an economic necessity. Poverty and a lack of real employment opportunities often leaves many women with little choice. The commonly held assumption that prostitutes choose this form of employment because they 'like it' is strongly rejected by prostitutes.[52]

The law relating to prostitution highlights clearly the 'double standard of morality' which is central to the enforcement of legislation and the administration of criminal justice. Kate Millett[53] comments: 'Prostitution is really the only crime in the penal laws where two people are doing a thing mutually agreed upon and yet only one, the female partner, is subject to arrest.'

A woman prostitute is likely to be prosecuted for activities relating to prostitution but her male client, who creates the demand, is not. Men and male sexuality are not seen to be the problem. The law does not serve to protect women from exploitation and abuse, rather it punishes their behaviour. This double standard of morality suggests that prostitutes' sexuality is a problem, that it is abnormal and outside the realms of 'normal' sexuality and femininity. Further, it affirms that male sexuality is not an issue, merely that a male client is fulfilling his 'natural' sexual needs. It is a double standard with a well-established tradition.[54] The infamous Contagious Diseases Acts institutionalized these double standards of morality in the nineteenth century. In an attempt to control venereal disease the Acts placed special controls on prostitutes, but not on their clients. Women were regarded as solely responsible for transmitting the disease and this justified their control by the state.

In Britain prostitution is not an offence. Rather it is the activities which are associated with it which are illegal, namely: loitering, soliciting, advertising, keeping a brothel, living off the immoral earnings of a prostitute. Although the law recognizes the existence of male prostitutes the category relating to prostitution in the Official Statistics refers only to women. The label 'common prostitute' relates solely to the activities of women and is applied after three police cautions for soliciting. Once the category has been ascribed she may be brought before the court for sentence. The category is used in court to establish that a woman is a prostitute before she has been tried. In effect she is guilty before she even enters the court room. Consequently the principle of 'innocent until proven guilty' which guides procedure in all criminal cases is undermined.

Prior to the Wolfenden Report, which had been commissioned to prevent prostitution as being a public nuisance, the law had allowed prostitutes to solicit custom in the streets. In order to charge a woman with soliciting, a police officer required a witness to give evidence that the woman was causing a nuisance or annoyance to people passing by. Under the present law no evidence is required except that of a police officer's suspicion. Prostitution is one example where formal policing methods have been used to control the behaviour of women. Jill Radford[55] suggests that it is only when women have broken out of men's control, within the traditional nuclear family, and their defined sexuality, that they are seen to be worthy of state policing.

It is important to note the relevance of class relations within prostitution. Those who work on the streets tend to be working-class women, while 'escort' or 'agency' workers are not only involved at a different economic level,[56] but also are less likely to come into contact with the law. The 'street-walkers' are the most vulnerable and exposed of all prostitutes and they are likely to come into most regular contact with the police. They are constantly harassed and cautioned by the police but receive little protection from them. Prostitutes are often beaten up, dumped without payment, raped or murdered. However, these are seen by the police as 'risks of the job'. Kate Millett[57] refers to this as the 'social construction of promiscuity' – by making themselves so accessible prostitutes receive their 'just deserts' and cannot expect to be protected.

The case of the Yorkshire Ripper, Peter Sutcliffe, clearly emphasizes Kate Millett's point. The media and the police consistently made the distinction between Sutcliffe's 'innocent', 'respectable' victims and the 'others'– the 'unrespectable', the 'guilty prostitutes'. 'Real' concern was shown only after the murder of Jayne McDonald, classified as the first 'innocent' or non-prostitute victim.

The now well-quoted statements from the police and judiciary are particularly relevant. West Yorkshire's Acting Assistant Chief Constable, at the time, Jim Hobson,[58] stated:

He [referring to the Ripper] has made it clear that he hates prostitutes. Many people do. We as a police force, will continue to arrest prostitutes. But the Ripper is now killing innocent girls... You have made your point. Give yourself up before another innocent woman dies.

And the infamous quote made by the Attorney General, Sir Michael Havers:[59]

Some were prostitutes, some were women of easy virtue, but the last six attacks involved victims whose reputations were totally unblemished. Some were prostitutes, but perhaps the saddest part of the case is that some were not.

This distinction, between prostitutes and respectable women victims, shows coldly that the prostitutes' lives, by the very nature of their job, are worth less and that Sutcliffe's mission in wiping them out was in some way justifiable.

In terms of women's sexuality the criminalization of prostitutes underlines the significance of patriarchy. Consequently the prostitute is defined as deviant and in need of punishment; she is unprotected, stigmatized and criminalized. The male client, however, is defined as 'normal' and not in need of treatment, regulation or punishment.[60]

Policing at the 'Margins'

Women's experience of policing is less formal and less frequent than that of men. When women do encounter the police, however, they often face sexist practices and harassment deeply entrenched in the police as an institution.[61] This is well documented in cases where women are the victims of male violence.[62] In this final section we examine the policing of women who assert their status and independence, and women engaged in political activity. We will concentrate on the criminalization of Greenham women[63] and finally look at the implications of the 1986 Public Order Act for women and women's protest.

The Criminalization of Greenham Women

In February 1982, Greenham Common peace camp became exclusively a women's peace camp. The camp was established as a response to the siting of United States Cruise missiles at Greenham Common and Cruise and Pershing II in other European countries. Initially the camp was mixed, but it was decided that a 'women-only' camp was desirable. It was hoped that women would be able to develop a strategy of non-violent direct action and build on their collective strength. Throughout the protest the women have faced fierce opposition both from local residents and from the law in its enforcement and application. A combination of civil and criminal laws have been used to criminalize the women's activities and to diminish the effectiveness and development of the political protest.

Fletcher[64] suggests that the criminalization of Greenham women has involved three legal responses: Newbury District Council using its civil powers of eviction, the police using their powers of arrest, and the use of prosecution through the courts. She states: 'Every aspect of the Greenham Women's protest has been defined as illegal... from the claiming of their basic squatter rights to entering the base and dancing on the silos on lst January 1983.'[65]

The influence of the media has made a considerable contribution to this process. Little attempt has been made to explain adequately the motivations behind the peace camp. The tabloid press has been content to focus on the sexuality of women, in particular lesbianism; on the 'deplorable actions' of women who have left and 'neglected' their husbands and children; on the squalid conditions under which the women have been forced to live – although this usually focuses on the general cleanliness of the women; on the impending threats of eviction, the evictions and the subsequent legal action.

Greenham Common air base is policed not only by the civil police but also by the Ministry of Defence police who operate inside the base. Unlike many other recent political demonstrations, the protest at Greenham has been subject to 'soft-line policing'. Arrests have been mainly for criminal damage, obstruction of the highway, obstruction of the police and breach of the peace – the latter being quite an anomaly given the women's strategy of non-violent direct action! Even under a policy of soft-line policing, there have been many arrests and brutality.[66]

> No sooner had I put my hands on the bonnet when a huge bobby sprang forward, punched me on the breast, and sent me flying onto the edge of the pavement... On October 2nd I was taken to a hospital and told I had a dislocated shoulder and bruised ribs.[67]

Cook and Kirk[68] document the incidents which occurred in February 1983, when eleven women were arrested for lying down in Downing Street. Although only charged with the minor offence of obstruction the women were kept in police custody overnight, harassed and moved to another police station during the night where they were left with blankets smeared with dried faeces. Placing these incidents within the wider context of women and policing generally, a relationship which fails to protect women adequately from male violence,[69] it is hardly surprising that such incidents occur.

As Fletcher[70] has documented, Newbury District Council has played a significant role in criminalizing women at Greenham. As owners of the land outside the base, the council has used its civil right of action to evict, and since May 1982 has evicted the camp under the civil law of trespass.[71] In 1984 it was decided that the council should have private ownership of the land, which resulted in an update of the by-laws and daily evictions of camps around the base. Throughout evictions police were present and arrested women for obstruction. Under an amendment introduced late in the passing of the Public Order Act the police will now be able to arrest for trespass.

The majority of Greenham cases have been heard at Newbury Magistrates' Court and this has led to women arguing that they are not receiving fair trials due to the local standing of the magistrates. It is suggested frequently that British Courts administer justice equally to all; that they are politically neutral, operate independently from other state institutions and government and do not function in the interests of a particular social class.[72] However, both the judiciary and the magistracy have been criticized on each of these points. The magistracy is predominantly white, middle-class, middle-aged, Conservative males who are selected for the bench by a secret committee. King[73] states that magistrates have been criticized for their lack of training and knowledge, the contradictory nature of their decisions and their class and racial exclusivity which gives them no experience of the living conditions and lives of those on whom they pass judgement. With regard to Greenham women, Jones[74] states that the Newbury magistrates are local ratepayers, some of whom serve on the police authority and are more than likely to have political views opposed to the women, and this is a severe inhibition on the impartiality of the justice they administer.

Most of the women sentenced at Newbury Magistrates' Court received fines and those women who refused payment were given prison sentences. In handling these cases the courts have operated considerable discretion in dealing with their charges. As Fletcher[75] states:

> On occasions they have given lesser sentences to prevent publicity and thereby reduce resulting support. And on the majority of occasions when the women would have the right to trial by jury, the charges have been dropped or reduced.

It is clear that magistrates at Newbury have exercised political decisions and not administered the principles of justice and equality.

As with other examples used in this paper, one of the reasons that Greenham women have been labelled as deviant is due to their deviation from their 'normal', 'natural' position within the family as wives and mothers. The Greenham women have been so labelled because they pose a threat to patriarchal relations and the control enjoyed by men. This threat and the concentration on the sexuality of Greenham women have been at the centre of local hostility. Newbury residents formed a pressure group, Ratepayers Against Greenham Encampments (RAGE), in order to try to expel the women from the base. Like the local vigilante group[76] the RAGE campaign has shown a deep hostility towards the women using extreme posters and cartoons which portray the women not only as a nuisance but as lesbian, feminist women who are abnormal.

As was discussed earlier, criminalization occurs not because certain activities are inherently criminal, but also because they are perceived as politically threatening. This is particularly true in the case of Greenham women where a combination of social reaction from local people and groups, media coverage, and the institutionalized reaction of the criminal justice process have created a moral panic and a climate in which criminalization is not only inevitable but gains substantial popular support. Again it is the questioning of the sexuality, femininity and domesticity of Greenham women which is mobilized in order to win that support.

The Implications of Recent Legislation

From the evidence put forward it is valid to suggest that the policies and practices adopted by the police and the courts are used to curb social and political threats to the maintenance of the established order.[77] The policies and practices of the police are legitimated by legislation. The 1984 Police and Criminal Evidence Act gave the police new and wide-ranging powers[78] to detain and search people and this has now been consolidated by the Public Order Act of 1986. This legislation has consequences for men and women but it is important to establish briefly the significant issues in relation to women.

Women involved in a wide range of public activity on the streets, whether peaceful or violent, will be affected by the new public order law which not only gives police a wide range of new powers but also provides a permissive crowd control function. Primarily the Public Order Act gives the police extensive powers to control protest and demonstrations – see Chapter 5. Marches and demonstrations will be illegal if the police are not informed 7 days in advance. Thus women will be unable to demonstrate spontaneously, for example after an attack on a woman in a particular location. Two recent examples are the shooting of Cherry Groce in Brixton and the death of Cynthia Jarrett on Broadwater Farm Estate, Tottenham. The police will be able to dictate where and when demonstrations or marches will take place, how many people can attend, limit the duration of the march and make any last minute changes to the route. Also they have the discretion to halt and disband a march. Therefore women may be prevented from demonstrating outside the focus of their anger, for example, porn shops or cinemas, Cruise missile bases or their own workplace during industrial action.

Clearly, at a time when more women are making their voices heard, in many cases by protesting on the streets or in public places, this new legislation poses a major threat to their right to demonstrate and, ultimately, a major threat to their safety. *Policing London* concludes:

> The proposed new police powers will affect all women who take part in political and trade union protest (e.g. Greenham), and in actions in the community (e.g. South London Women's Hospital occupation). It will lead to greater harassment, conflict and even further deterioration of existing relations with the police.[79]

With these extended police powers granted by the 1984 Police and Criminal Evidence Act and the 1986 Public Order Act the processes of marginalization and criminalization have been further legitimized and consolidated in legislation.

Conclusion

We have argued that criminalization is a power relation in which certain individuals or groups are labelled and their activities outlawed by those with access to power. Criminalization, then, is inherently a structural, political process. Marginalization is specifically economic – as has been shown both in the cases of women claiming state benefits and in prostitution. The political and ideological relations of patriarchy serve to maximize and justify the dimensions of marginalization. As we have seen women are on the margins of employment;[80] they are peripheral to the main paid work-force and many suffer from structured and long-term unemployment. Black women are not only subjected by their gender and, often, class, but owing to their position in a white racist society experience an added dimension to their oppression.[81] Politically, women endure discrimination on the grounds of sex in many of the institutions they encounter; the family, work and state agencies. In experiencing the administration of criminal justice women are subjected to discrimination as a consequence of the patriarchal relations within the police and the courts. Institutionalized attitudes and responses effectively serve to politically marginalize women. Reputations and stereotyped images are not only constructed but also are transmitted through patriarchal ideologies. This provides a consistency and permanence at a structural institutional level which is beyond the potential of small-scale reforms or legal adjustment. Through the transmission and perpetuation of common-sense images and ideologies women learn the role, the place and the acceptable forms of behavour to which they must adhere in order to gain status, respectability and protection. The strength of ideology is that it becomes internalized and, therefore, manifested in and through the daily lives of the people it categorizes.

When women react to this control and regulation of their sexuality, which is central to the criminalization of women, they are defined as deviant. When women protest against the control and regulation of their lives, for example in protests against violence against women,[82] they are perceived as a real threat and are treated as such. In addition to this women increasingly are perceived as a threat to the established order and this has been most evident in the media and state response to the women's protest at Greenham Common. While the social and state control of women is powerful women have established strategies of resistance both in direct and in personal ways. Historically the suffragettes organized at a grass-roots level by forming the Women's Freedom League which campaigned to provide alternative political structures to those dominated by men. The suffragettes' struggle was not confined to the gaining of fundamental rights for women but also was concerned with changing existing structures, particularly the male-dominated criminal justice system. Their campaigns also focused on the issue of male violence as a means of maintaining control over women.[83] The strategies adopted by the suffragettes included 'court-watching', demonstrations and the damaging of property. Some of these strategies have been used by women in recent years in their campaigns involving male violence, pornography, sex shops and American bases.

While women's struggles over male violence have never waned, collective campaigns have emerged strongly during the 1970s and 1980s with the consolidation of organized women's groups. Groups such as Rape Crisis and Women's Aid have ensured that the related issues of rape, domestic violence, prostitution and pornography have remained on the political agenda. Also they have provided essential support and practical assistance to women in the community. Other groups organized at the grass-roots level have also been instrumental in raising women's consciousness and reaching out to groups of women historically peripheral to the pre-dominantly white, middle-class women's movement. Groups such as Lesbian Line, Incest Survivors' Line, women's education groups, black women's groups, Women in Prison and even the mainly middle-class Well Women's clinics have provided the platforms from which women could make their voices heard and thus pursue practical reforms at a policy level.

Also there has been an increase in the use of direct action by women including both violent and non-violent strategies. As discussed above, the protests of Greenham women is a clear example of non-violent direct action. The persistence of women's protest, at pickets, on demonstrations and through organized collectives has demanded a political response at more formal political levels. Local authorities, particularly those labour-controlled with active women's caucuses within, have been compelled to provide resources and opportuntiies for the benefit of women throughout local communities.[84] This pressure has resulted in the establishment of Women's Committees and Women's Units such as those in London, Leeds, Bradford, Manchester, Sheffield, Stirling, Edinburgh and Nottingham. Much of the work of these units challenge liberal-feminist constructions of reform - such as equal pay and sex discrimination legislation – which have remained central to the work of the Equal Opportunities Commission. For the evidence is clear that these strategies of legal reform have had a minimal qualitative impact on the lives of women.[85]

The work of Women's Committees and Women's Units represents a response to demands at a grass-roots level (although some of those set up outside London have been initiated by professional women already working within local authority structures). Their function has been to monitor and challenge those policies and practices which discriminate against women and other marginalized groups such as black people, gay men and lesbians and the disabled. They have been essential to the allocation of resources via grant-aided schemes for specified groups to set up their own projects, for example, the Lesbian and Policing project which has been established in one of the London boroughs.

The local authority response, therefore, has been established on a broader basis in the mid-1980s and has been central to the provision and dissemination of information for the formulation of policy aimed at constructing effective alternatives to meet the demands and needs of all women. The success of such committees and units, however, should not be over-stressed as resistance to change in the well-established formal structures has been formidable. Further to this, as Liz Kelly and Jill Radford warn in their paper, is the problem faced by previously 'independent' groups becoming dependent financially and, ultimately, incorporated within the structural arrangements of the local state. Also there has been a marked resistance to women's campaigns within the trade union movement and throughout many branches of the Labour Party.

Thus it is ironic that in so-called 'progressive' circles the struggles of women remain marginalized. Despite the response of some local authorities the needs of many women remain unmet not only on the grounds of sex but also with regard to class and race. In this chapter we have shown how ideologies of sexism rooted in the political and economic relations of capitalist-patriarchy are central to the criminalization of women. As socialist feminists our analysis combines the economic, political and ideological frameworks established by contemporary critical criminology and the location of women's experiences within the state and its structural relations. Not only is this dialectic central to the development of a feminist analysis within criminology but also it has to be a central dimension in the building of a critical criminology.

Acknowledgements

We want to thank our families and friends who gave us support while we worked on this paper. Also thanks to Sally Channon for typing the paper.

Special thanks to Phil Scraton who worked through ideas with us in the early stages and commented on our drafts. We are indebted to his unique insight and support which goes far beyond that of an editor.

Notes

1 C. Smart, *Women, Crime and Criminology*, London, Routledge & Kegan Paul, 1976, xiv.
2 P. Carlen, *Criminal Women*, Cambridge, Polity Press, 1985, p. 7.
3 D. Smith, 'An analysis of ideological structures and how women are excluded', *Canadian Review of Sociology and Anthropology*, 12 (4), Part 1, 1975.
4 C. Smart, op. cit.
5 See C. Smart and B. Smart (eds), *Women, Sexuality and Social Control*, London, Routledge & Kegan Paul, 1978.
6 S. Hall and P. Scraton, 'Law, class and control', in M. Fitzgerald *et al.*, *Crime and Society*, Milton Keynes, Bucks, Open University Press, 1981, p. 488.
7 H.S. Becker, *Outsiders*, New York, Free Press, 1963; H.S. Becker, 'Whose side are we on?', in *Social Problems*, 1967, Vol. 14.; E. Lemert, *Social Pathology*, New York, McGraw-Hill, 1951; E. Lemert, *Human Deviance, Social Problems and Social Control*, Englewood Cliffs, NJ, Prentice-Hall, 1967.
8 H.S. Becker, 1967, op. cit.
9 See the discussion of the contribution of N. Poulantzas in S. Hall and P. Scraton, 1981, op. cit.
10 See E. Wade, 'The miners and the media: themes of newspaper reporting', in P. Scraton and P. Thomas (eds), *'The State v The People: Lessons from the Coal Dispute'*, Oxford, Basil Blackwell, 1985.
11 See P. Hillyard, in *Working Papers in European Criminology*, No. 8. (1987) European Group for the Study of Deviance and Social Control.
12 For further discussion of these ascribed roles see P. Carlen, *Women's Imprisonment*, London, Routledge & Kegan Paul, 1983; F. Heidensohn, *Women and Crime*, London, Macmillan, 1985.
13 Patriarchy refers to a structure of societal and social reproduction based on the material and cultural dominance of men over women. For further discussions of patriarchy see V. Beechey, 'On patriarchy', *Feminist Review*, No. 3, 1979; S. Rowbotham, *Dreams and Dilemmas*, London, Virago, 1983, Section 5 on Patriarchy.
14 S. Hall and P. Scraton, op. cit., p. 487.
15 See S. Hall, *Culture, Media, Language*, CCCS, 1980; S. Hall, *Drifting into a Law and Order Society*, Cobden Trust, 1982.
16 See S. Hall, *et al.*, *Policing the Crisis: Mugging, The State and Law and Order*, London Macmillan, 1978; S. Cohen, *Folk Devils and Moral Panics*, (2nd edn) Oxford, Martin Robertson, 1980; P. Golding, and S. Middleton, *Images of Welfare*, Oxford, Martin Robertson, 1982; L. Curtis, *Ireland: The Propaganda War*, London, Pluto, 1984.
17 Popular ideologies exist around crime, criminality, family life, nationalism,

patriotism, race and gender. See the work of S. Hall, 1980 and 1982, op. cit.

18 See A. McRobbie and J. Garber, 'Girls and subcultures: an exploration,' in S. Hall and T. Jefferson (eds), *Resistance Through Rituals*, London, Hutchinson, 1977; A. Oakley, *Sex, Gender and Society* (revised), Aldershot, Hants., Gower, 1985; Sharpe, S. *Just like a Girl: How Girls Learn to be Women*, Harmondsworth, Middx, Penguin, 1976.

19 C. Smart and B. Smart (eds), *Women, Sexuality and Social Control*, London, Routledge & Kegan Paul, 1978, p. 2.

20 See H. Roberts (eds.), *Women, Health and Reproduction*, London, Routledge & Kegan Paul, 1981; C. Smart, *Women, Crime and Criminology*, London, Routledge & Kegan Paul, 1976; C. Smart and J. Brophy, *Women-in-Law*, London, Routledge & Kegan Paul, 1985; A. Oakley, *The Sociology of Housework*, London, Martin Robertson, 1974; A. Oakley, *Housewife*, Harmondsworth, Middx, Penguin, 1976; A. Oakley, *Women Confined*, Oxford, Martin Robertson, 1980; A. Oakley, *Subject Women*, Oxford, Martin Robertson, 1982.

21 J. Radford, *Women, Crime and Criminology*, unpublished, Open University, 1983, p. 79.

22 See M. Benn *et al.*, *Sexual Harassment*, NCCL, 1982.

23 See V. Hey, *Pubs and Patriarchy*, Milton Keynes, Bucks, Open University Press, 1986; R. Deem, *All Work and No Play: The Sociology of Women and Leisure*, Milton Keynes, Bucks, Open University Press, 1986.

24 See R. Hall *et al.*, *Ask Any Woman*. Bristol, Falling Wall Press, 1985; J. Radford, 'Policing male violence – policing women, unpublished paper, 1985.

25 Women who step out of line are frequently defined as whores and slags. See J. Radford and S. Jeffreys, 'Contributory negligence of being a woman?', in P. Scraton and P. Gordon (eds), *Causes for Concern*, Harmondsworth, Middx, Penguin, 1984; P. Pattullo, *Judging Women*, NCCL, 1983.

26 Eaton, M. *Women, Criminology and Social Control*, Milton Keynes, Open University Press 1986, D310 Block 4.

27 Women's opportunities to commit crime is often seen to be related to their powerlessness. Young girls and women are socialized into accepting a passive role and this is often suggested as a partial explanation for their lack of criminal activity. See E. Leonard, *Women, Crime and Society*, London, Longman, 1982; S. Box, *Power, Crime and Mystification*, London, Tavistock, 1983; F. Heidensohn, *Women and Crime*, London Macmillan, 1985.

28 See M. Barrett and M. McIntosh, *The Anti Social Family*, London, Verso, 1982; E. Zaretsky, *Capitalism, The Family and Personal Life*, London, Pluto, 1976.

29 W. Beveridge, *Social Insurance and Allied Services*, HMSO, 1942.

30 E. Wilson, *Women and the Welfare State*, London, Tavistock, 1977.

31 See J. Somerville, 'Women: a reserve army of labour', in *MF*, No. 7, 1982; V. Beechey, Some notes on female wage labour in capitalist production', in M. Evans, *The Woman Question: Readings on the Subordination of Women*, London, Fontana, 1982.

32 J. Bowlby, *Child Care and the Growth of Love* (2nd edn), Harmondsworth, Middx, Penguin, 1965.

33 See A. Oakley, *The Sociology of Housework*, London, Martin Robertson, 1974.

34 M. Barrett and M. McIntosh, 'The family wage', in E. Whitelegg, *The Changing Experience of Women*, Open University Press and Martin Robertson, 1982.

35 It has been estimated that there are only 20% of households which fit into this category. See J. Root, *Pictures of Women: Sexuality*, London, Pandora, 1984.

36 H. Land, 'The myth of the male breadwinner', *New Society*, October 1975; H. Land, 'The family wage', *Feminist Review*, No. 6, 1980.

37 H. Land, 1980, op. cit. p. 71.

38 For an examination of the effectiveness of the Equal Pay and Sex Discrimination Acts see J. Lewis, *Women's Welfare, Women's Rights*, London, Croom Helm, 1983; S. Atkins and B. Hoggett, *Women and the Law*, Oxford, Basil Blackwell, 1984.

39 See J. Beale, *Getting it Together: Women as Trade Unionists*, London, Pluto, 1982.

40 J. Somerville, op. cit.

41 J. Bowlby, op. cit.

42 See B. Abel-Smith, 'Sex Equality and Social Security', in J. Lewis, op. cit.; Equal Opportunities Commission, *Behind Closed Doors*, EOC Publication, 1981; V. Hall-Smith and C. Hoskyns, *Women's Rights and the EEC*, Rights of Women, Europe, 1983.
    A leaflet published by the GLC Women's Committee and the Child Poverty Group, in 1985, summarizes the inequalities:
    1 Women in married or unmarried couples are barred from claiming Invalid Care Allowance – a benefit paid to people looking after invalids. [This no longer applies due to a defeat for the British Government in the European Court, 1987.]
    2 A married man on retirement pension can claim extra for his wife simply because she lives with him, whereas a married woman can only claim extra retirement pension for her husband in very limited circumstances.
    3 In the case of a married man on retirement pension, his wife can earn up to £45 per week without the extra benefit he gets for her being effected. But a married woman loses the extra retirement pension for her husband if he earns over £20.55.
    4 A woman is more likely to be the partner in a couple who stays at home to look after children. It is a rule that partners who have been looking after children full time for over six months do not qualify to claim SB on behalf of a couple. This rule means that many women are denied the chance to have the family's benefit in their name.
    5 Women's lower earnings and childcare responsibilities can make it more difficult for them to pay the contributions necessary for national insurance benefits altogether. For example, for many disabled women in couples, there is no benefit they can claim.
    6 A woman is less likely to end up getting extra national insurance benefits from her partner and children than the man is, because his earnings are more likely to be high enough to disqualify her.

43 'What single parents must endure to get their money', *The Times*, 12 August 1981.

44 A. Briggs, 'Social Security: playing to win', *Spare Rib*, May 1980, Issue 94.

45 *Daily Mirror*, 'Accused: the snoopers', 1982 (date unknown).

46 See 'curb on questions put to unmarried mothers', *The Times* 13 August 1981; 'DHSS resumes sex checks on single mothers claiming benefit', *The Guardian*, 10 June 1982; 'Gestapo sex spies claim', *The Daily Star*, 6 June 1981.

47 P. Scraton, 'Guilty until proved innocent', *Left Out*, 1983, Issue No. 7; See also P. Scraton and N. South, 'In the shadow of the welfare police', *Bulletin of Social*

Policy, Spring 1983.

48 N. South and P. Scraton, *Capitalist Discipline, Private Justice and the Hidden Economy*, Middlesex Polytechnic Occasioned Paper, July 1981.

49 Ibid. See also A. Deacon, 'Scrounger bashing', *New Society*, 17 October 77; A. Deacon, 'The scrounging controversy: public attitudes towards the unemployed in contemporary Britain', *Social and Economic Administration*, Summer 1978, Vol. 12, No. 2; A. Deacon, 'Spivs, drones and other scroungers', *New Society*, 28 February 1980.

50 S. Jeffreys, 1980, cited in J. Radford, 1983, op. cit.

51 Home Office, *Report of the Committee on Homosexual Offences and Prostitution*, HMSO, 1957.

52 For accounts of prositutes' own stories see C. Jaget (ed.), *Prostitutes: Our Life*, Bristol, Falling Wall Press, 1980; E. McLeod, *Women Working: Prostitution Now*, London, Croom Helm, 1982; K. Millett, *The Prostitution Papers*, London, Paladin, 1975.

53 K. Millett, *Sexual Politics*, London, Sphere, 1971, p. 146.

54 See L. Bland, '"Guardians of the Race" or "Vampires Upon the Nation's Health"?' in E. Whitelegg, *et al.*, *The Changing Experience of Women*, Milton Keynes, Open University Press, 1982; Gordon, L. Duboid and E. Duboid, 'Seeking ecstasy on the battlefield: damage and pleasure in nineteenth century feminist sexual thought', *Feminist Review*, 1983, No. 13; J. Walkowitz, *Prostitution and Victorian Society*, Cambridge, Cambridge University Press, 1980.

55 J. Radford, op. cit.

56 Escort or agency workers are usually involved in 'high-class' prostitution, in rooms rather than on the streets, with affluent clients.

57 K. Millett, *The Prostitution Papers*, London, Paladin, 1971.

58 Cited in L. Bland, 'The Case of the Yorkshire Ripper: mad, bad, beast or male?', in P. Scraton and P. Gordon (eds), *Causes for Concern*, Harmondsworth, Middx, Penguin, 1984.

59 Cited in P. Pattullo, 1983, op. cit.

60 In July 1985, the Sexual Offences Bill, which makes kerb-crawling a criminal offence, successfully completed its passage through Parliament. 'The Bill outlaws kerb-crawling if it can be shown that the motorist was persistent in soliciting prostitutes, or that sexual approaches to other women were made in such a way as to cause "annoyance or nuisance"'. However, the Director of Public Prosecutions is to 'advise lawyers that only in exceptional circumstances should evidence rest simply on the word of a police officer". Source: *The Guardian*, 6 July 1985.

61 See J. Radford, 1985, op. cit.; 'Women up against the law', GLC Conference Papers, 1985; D.J. Smith and J. Gray, *Police and People in London. Vols I-IV*, Policy Studies Insitute, 1983.

62 J. Box-Grainger, *Sentencing Rapists*, RAP, 1983; S. Jeffreys and J. Radford, 'Contributory negligence or being a woman?', in P. Scraton and P. Gordon (eds), *Causes for Concern*, op. cit.; H. Kimble, 'Cry rape and let loose the dogs of law', *Spare Rib*, 1982, Issue 123, October; P. Pattullo, *Judging Women*, NCCL, 1983; E. Wilson, *What Is to Be Done about Violence against Women?*, Harmondsworth, Middx, Penguin, 1983; J. Hanmer and S. Saunders, *Well Founded Fear*, London Hutchinson, 1984.

63 Although we realize the paramount importance of other groups of women

engaged in political activity: particularly black women, Irish women and lesbian women, we felt that we could not do justice to each of them in the words available to us. We did not want to further marginalize these groups of women by only mentioning them in passing, but felt that some acknowledgement of their protests should be made. See 'Women up against the law' conference papers, op. cit.; 'Women and policing in London' in *Policing London*, Issues 1, 2, 3, 1985 and Issues 4, 5, 1986.

64 M. Fletcher, *'Greenham Women: the criminalisation of political protest'*, unpublished dissertation, Edge Hill College of Higher Education, 1985.

65 Ibid. p. 27.

66 See A. Cook and G. Kirk, *Greenham Women Everywhere*, London Pluto, 1983.

67 Letter from a Greenham woman: *The Guardian* 10 October 1984.

68 A. Cook and G. Kirk, op. cit. pp. 47-8.

69 See note 17.

70 M. Fletcher, op. cit.

71 The council were able to do this, after going to the High Court in London where they were granted a possession order, which gave the bailiffs power to evict the camp under the civil law of trespass.

72 For a critique of this, see J.A.G. Griffiths, *The Politics of the Judiciary*, London, Fontana, 1977; S. Hall, *The Politics of the Court: Judicial Impartiality in Question*, Open University, 1982, D335. 5.

73 M. King, *The Framework of Criminal Justice*, London, Croom Helm, 1981. See also P. Carlen, *Magistrates' Justice* London, Routledge & Kegan Paul, 1976.

74 *New Statesman*, 2 March 1984.

75 M. Fletcher, op. cit. pp. 44-5.

76 The vigilante groups are made up of local, usually male residents who harass and attack the women. See B. Harford and S. Hopkens (eds), *Greenham Common: Women at the Wire*, London, The Women's Press, 1984.

77 For example, the recent coal dispute, public order, Greenham women and the inner city uprisings.

78 See GLC Police Committee, *The Police Act 1984: A Critical Guide*, GLC, 1985.

79 *Public Order Plans* – The Threat to Democratic Rights: A Critical Guide GLC Policing London 1985 p. 41.

80 See J. Somerville, 1982, op. cit.

81 See H. Carby, 'White woman listen! Black feminism and the boundaries of sisterhood' in CCCS, *The Empire Strikes Back*, London, Hutchinson, 1982; B. Bryan et al., *The Heart of the Race*, London, Virago, 1985; A. Davis, *Women, Race and Class* New York, Random House, 1982; B. Hooks, *Ain't I a Woman?*, London, Pluto, 1982.

82 For example, Reclaim the Night marches, and protests against pornography and sex shops.

83 See J. Radford, 'Policing women: contradictions old and new', unpublished paper; 1986.

84 'Making waves: a roundtable discussion', *Marxism Today*, July 1986.

85 For further accounts of this point see J. Lewis, *Women's Welfare, Women's Rights*, Croom Helm, 1983; S. Atkins and B. Hoggett, *Women and the Law*, Oxford, Basil Blackwell, 1984; P. Kahn, 'Unequal opportunities: women, employment and the law', in S. Edwards (ed.), *Gender, Sex and the Law*, London, Croom Helm, 1985.

10

The Normalization of Special Powers: from Northern Ireland to Britain

Paddy Hillyard

The aim of this chapter is to describe the different strategies which the authorities have used to deal with political violence in Northern Ireland since 1969. The analysis will attempt to draw out some of the more important features which have tended to be overlooked in those accounts which have been more concerned to highlight the sectarian aspects of the strategies. The principal conclusion of the analysis is that the form of the repressive strategy adopted since 1975, far from being exceptional and a product of the unique circumstances of the political violence in Northern Ireland is, on the contrary, the form which many modern capitalist states are evolving.

No understanding of the various strategies adopted since 1969 is possible without a discussion of law and order in the period from the setting up of the regional government and parliament in the six counties by the Government of Ireland Act 1920.

1920–1969: Special Powers Extraordinary

By mid-summer 1920 the British government had to contend with two law and order problems in the six counties. Both were to remain a feature until the present day. On the one hand, it had to deal with attacks by the IRA and on the other it had to cope with the sectarian attacks, which were mainly carried out on Catholics. It had two forces at its disposal: the Royal Irish Constabulary (RIC), which was controlled by a divisional commissioner outside Belfast and a city commissioner within the city; and various military units stationed in the North.[1] At the time the British government was hard-pressed in the south and west of Ireland and no more troops could be sent north. Indeed, there was in fact pressure for troops from the North to be sent south.[2] In October 1920, the British government announced the establishment of the Ulster Special Constabulary (USC).[3] It was based upon the Ulster Volunteer Force (UVF) – a totally Protestant paramilitary force – which had been reorganized a few months earlier with the tacit approval of the British government. Hence, the USC was from the outset exclusively Protestant. It was divided into three classes. Class 'A' was for those willing to do full-time duty and be posted anywhere within Northern Ireland; Class 'B' was for those willing to do part-time duty in their own locality; and Class 'C' was for those willing to go on reserve and who could be called upon in an emergency. This last class was vaguely defined and became little more than a device to give gun licences to loyalists and refuse them to Catholics.[4] By August 1922 there were 7,000 'A' Specials, 20,000 'B' Specials and 17,000 in a reconstituted 'C' Class. There were also 1,200 full-time members of the newly formed Royal Ulster Constabulary (RUC) which had replaced the RIC in May of the same year.

The Specials played the central role in the establishment of the authority of the new government in Northern Ireland. From the outset their activities were controversial. They were undisciplined and partisan and were regarded by Catholics with a bitterness exceeding that which the Black and Tans inspired in the South.

Their sectarian conduct, as Farrell points out,[5] contributed to the peculiarly intense hatred with which the RUC has been regarded ever since by the Catholic population in the North. Not only were the two forces linked together in the public mind, but also half the initial recruits for the RUC came from the 'A' Specials.

While Farrell emphasizes the role of the British government in the creation of the USC, Bew, Gibbon and Patterson draw attention to the changes which were taking place within the Protestant class bloc.[6] They argue that, in order to challenge Republicanism independently of the British, the Unionist leadership had to give up some of its power to the Orange section of the Protestant working class. The form of the Unionist state apparatus can therefore be seen as a product of the class relations within the Unionist bloc coupled with British approval and support. In other words, they argue that the form of the Unionist state apparatus was not exclusively a product of external politics.

Another central element of the Unionist repressive state apparatus was the Civil Authorities (Special Powers) Act. This was passed in 1922 and gave the Minister of Home Affairs power 'to take all such steps . . . as may be necessary for preserving peace and maintaining order'. It conferred wide powers of arrest, questioning, search, detention and internment on the police and other agents of the Ministry of Home Affairs. It constituted an effective abrogation of the rule of law in the sense that the forces of law and order had the power to arrest and detain anyone they pleased without having to give any justification and without fear of being called to account in respect of any decisions later shown to be unjustified. Northern Ireland from the outset was therefore a state with extraordinary powers.

The Civil Authorities (Special Powers) Act was renewed annually until 1928 when it was extended for 5 years. At the end of 1933 it was made permanent. It was extensively criticized in the late 1930s by NCCL.

The law and order strategy of successive Unionist governments was unequivocal. A constant watch was maintained on Catholic communities and, whenever the state appeared to be under threat – for example, during the IRA campaigns of 1921–2, 1938–9 and 1956–62 – the government introduced internment under the Civil Authorities (Special Powers) Act. It was also used on other occasions, as for instance when Republican politicians were interned for a week during a royal visit in 1951. The main point to emphasize about internment was its wholly executive nature. The formal power provided for in the Civil Authorities (Special Powers) Act permitted the arrest and detention of anyone who was acting, had acted or was about to act 'in a manner prejudicial to the preservation of the peace and maintenance of order'. The responsibility for making the internment order after arrest lay with the minister who was also personally responsible for ordering the release of internees. While there was provision for the appointment of an advisory committee to review the cases, the minister was not bound to accept the recommendations. Internment was therefore a wholly executive measure. Its use highlighted the executive's direct involvement in suppressing political opposition. It was not surprising that the Cameron Commission found that its presence on the statute book, and the continuance in force of regulations made under it, had caused widespread resentment among Catholics.[7] It had after all been used almost exclusively against them to suppress all political opposition to the Northern Ireland regime.

As well as the lack of confidence in the forces of law and order and the festering grievance of the Civil Authorities (Special Powers) Act, Catholics also had little confidence in the courts in Northern Ireland. This stemmed principally from the composition of both the judiciary and juries. The Northern Ireland judiciary throughout its history had been mainly composed of people who had been openly associated with the Unionist Party. Of the 20 high court judges appointed since 1922, 15 had been openly associated with the Unionist Party and 14 of the county court appointments had similar associations. Resident magistrates had also been drawn from the same source. While it does not follow that the decisions of judges and magistrates would be partisan, the composition of both the magistracy and the judiciary did little to inspire the confidence of Catholics in the administration of justice.

The composition of juries further exacerbated the problem of confidence in the administration of justice. Partly as a result of property qualification and partly as a result of the rules concerning the right to stand by or challenge jurors, the composition of juries was mainly Protestant. The qualification for jury service was based upon the ownership of property and as Catholics owned less property, this ensured that the majority on the jury list were Protestants. At this stage, the prosecution was entitled to stand by any number of jurors and the defence might challenge up to twelve without giving any reason, and might object to others for good cause. The end result was that most juries, particularly in Belfast, were Protestant. The risk of bias against Catholics was therefore always present.

It can be seen from this brief analysis of the law and order strategy adopted by successive Unionist governments that it was highly repressive, sectarian and centralized. Moreover, throughout the period, no attempt was made to disguise the political nature of the struggle nor of the response. It was successful in so far as it maintained the regime in power for fifty years. But from the outset it continually alienated the minority community from both the law and the state.

1969–1971: Reform and Repression

The response of the British government, after deploying troops in Northern Ireland in August 1969, was to pressurize the government at Stormont to introduce a series of reforms which, in essence, were aimed to establish a series of institutions to guarantee equality of treatment and freedom from discrimination for the Catholic community.

The principal reforms in the area of policing followed closely the recommendations of the Hunt Committee.[8] The object of the reform was to neutralize the political control of the police and to establish a wholly civilian and non-armed police force. Consequently, the 'B' Specials were disbanded and a new force, the Ulster Defence Regiment, was established under the control of the British army. In addition, the RUC was disarmed and made accountable to a police authority. The continuing violence, however, soon led to the rearming of the police.

The Hunt Committee also recommended the introduction of an independent prosecutor on the Scottish model. But the Unionist government delayed in the implementation of this reform by establishing a committee to consider the proposals.[9]

It was not until after Direct Rule in 1972 that a new office of a Director of Public Prosecutions was set up with full responsibility for the selection and prosecution of all serious criminal charges.

At the same time as the police was being reformed the Unionist government brought in tougher legislation under the Criminal Justice (Temporary Provision) Act 1970 to deal with rioters.[10] The Act provided a 6 months minimum mandatory gaol sentence for anyone convicted of 'riotous behaviour', 'disorderly behaviour' or 'behaviour likely to cause a breach of the peace'. The new law immediately gave rise to numerous allegations of the partisan way in which the legislation was being enforced.

Outside the area of the administration of justice, other reforms were taking place. The discriminatory practices of local government were dealt with by extending local government franchise but at the same time denuding local authorities of considerable powers. A new centralized housing authority was established and administrative units were set up to manage education, planning, and health and social services.[11]

While all these legislative changes were taking place, the situation on the streets was deteriorating. The relations between the army and the Catholic community were rapidly declining as the army took a tougher line against rioters. In 1970, a routine house search precipitated a large-scale riot and the army introduced a curfew.[12]

The conflict was slowly escalating into a guerilla war between the army and the IRA.

In summary, in this period the strategy of the British government was not to define the problem in terms of law and order but to deal with it at a number of different levels. On the one hand, there was a very real attempt to correct the arbitrary and inequitable administration of criminal laws and to establish institutions which would deal with the widespread problem of discrimination. Liberal notions such as the separation of powers, the rule of law, the impartiality and objectivity of judges, and democratic institutions to check the exercise of power were mobilized in support of the reforms but no attempt was made to ensure that the notions were realized in practice. The creation of new institutions and the dispersal of power has meant that the various bodies, which are relatively autonomous, have established their own *modus operandi;* they have structured their own targets and objectives. The dominant feature has been their tendency to reconstitute practical and legal problems as technical matters. On the other hand, the increasing violence on the streets, coupled with the demands of the Protestant community for tougher measures, led to the development of a more coercive strategy to deal with the problem of violence.

1971–1975: Internment and Military Security

The strategy in this period was dominated by the use of internment and the development by the army either through encouragement or by default of its own military security policy. This involved the introduction of a series of techniques which have been used in colonial emergencies in the past and developed by Brigadier Kitson.[13] The combined aim of these techniques was to collect as much information on the IRA in particular and the Catholic community in general. I will deal with each component in turn.

Internment and Detention

Internment was introduced with the agreement of the British government on 9 August 1971. The army and police arrested 342 men on the initial sweep. Within six months 2,357 persons had been arrested and 1,600 released after interrogation. The introduction, impact and subsequent use of internment has been extensively documented and the details need not concern us here.[14] The main point to emphasize is that its use provided an example of unfettered ministerial discretion and highlighted the political nature of the struggle. The state's involvement in suppressing political opposition was clear and unequivocal.

After internment, the level of violence increased rapidly. Many Catholics holding public appointments withdrew from these offices and a rent and rates strike was begun. In January 1972 the army killed 13 civilians during a civil rights march in Derry. An official inquiry by the Lord Chief Justice only inflamed the situation as his report exonerated those responsible.[15]

After Direct Rule was imposed in March 1972, a slight shift took place in the internment strategy. Following the breakdown of discussions between the IRA and the government, a new system of detention without trial was introduced. The principal development was to replace the executive authority of the minister under the Special Powers Act by a new system of judicial determination. All cases now came before an independent judicial Commissioner.[16] The aim was to distance the executive from the day-to-day administration of the emergency powers in an attempt to depoliticize the nature of the response in order to gain the confidence of the minority community in the system. It represented the beginning of a strategy which was to find its ultimate and most sustained and strongest expression in the criminalization policies which were introduced in 1975. The operation of these new procedures received widespread criticisms.[17] The whole system of detention appeared to be dominated by the policies of the security forces and the quasi-judicial hearings were farcical. The new scheme did little to gain the confidence of Catholics. When the government began detaining Protestants in February 1973 the opposition to detention became more widespread.

The last point to note about detention is that those who were detained were not treated like other convicted persons. They were placed in compounds and accommodated in huts rather than cells and were permitted considerable autonomy within the compounds. They were also granted the same rights as prisoners on remand. This meant that they could wear their own clothes and have more visits, letters and parcels than convicted persons. Similar rights were also extended in June 1972 to those who had been convicted in the courts and who claimed to have been politically motivated. These concessions amounted to what was called 'Special Category Status'.

Further changes were made to the detention procedures after the review of measures to deal with terrorism by a committee chaired by Lord Gardiner.[18] These changes were incorporated in the Northern Ireland (Emergency Provisions) Act of 1975 and involved a slight move back towards a system of executive detention. But they were of little importance as the use of detention without trial was suspended in February 1975 and a totally new strategy for dealing with those involved in political violence was introduced. During the period in which internment and detention had been in operation a total of 2,158 orders were issued.

Diplock Commission

At this point it is useful to consider the Diplock Commission[19] because it strongly influenced the way in which the police and army operated in this period. It was also responsible for the form of the strategy adopted in the period 1975 onwards, which will be dealt with later.

The first point concerns the composition of the commission. The members of the commission were Lord Diplock, Lord Rupert Cross, Sir Kenneth Younger, a former Intelligence Corps major, and George Woodcock, a former General Secretary of the TUC. The late Lord Cross was a Professor of Criminal Law and had been a member of the Criminal Law Revision Committee which recommended the abolition of the right to silence.[20]

The second point concerns the type of evidence the commission collected. The commission did not go to Northern Ireland. Only Lord Diplock visited the Province and then only on two occasions. The bulk of the evidence was oral and was taken from people with responsibility for the administration of justice in Northern Ireland, and from representatives of the civil and armed services.

The third and most important point is that the report was produced for the authorities responsible for law and order and not for the people of Northern Ireland as a whole. The underlying problem of the political struggle between opposing groups of very different aspirations was totally ignored and the sole focus was upon the maintenance of public order. In this context, civil rights in general and the rights of suspects in particular, appear as exceptional, anachronistic and even subversive. Long-established common law principles were reconstituted as 'technical rules'. For example, the principle concerning the admissibility of statements, which is fundamental in an adversarial system of criminal justice, was described in a number of places as a 'technical rule'. Burton and Carlin appear to make a similar point, regrettably in jargon-laden and absurdly complex language, when they describe the Diplock report in the following way:

> Its intra-discursive logic is as incoherent as its epistemological justification. Though argued in terms of essentialized justice, relocated within legal evolution, the changes in the technical guarantees of objectivity remain but a part of the syntagmatic strategy which orders the paradigms of the common law mode towards a unity of its discursive object: the discursive appropriation of an official word whose otherness is beyond recognition.[21]

Most of the commission's recommendations were included in the Northern Ireland (Emergency Provisions) Act which came into force in August 1973. The army was provided with the power to stop and detain a suspect for up to 4 hours, and both the army and police were also given the further power to stop and question any person as to his or her identity and knowledge of terrorist incidents. In addition, the police were given the power to arrest anyone they suspected of being a terrorist and detain them for up to 72 hours. No grounds of reasonableness were required. This particular provision, it should be noted, was introduced to enable the administrative procedures required by the Detention of Terrorist Order to be carried out. The Act also provided extensive powers of search. Finally, the Act abolished juries and introduced far-reaching changes in the rules of evidence.

The Northern Ireland (Emergency Provisions) Act, like the Special Powers Act, constituted an effective abrogation of the rule of law.

Military Security
The Act provided ample opportunities for the army to extend its military security policy, which it had been developing throughout 1970. This involved among other things the creation and maintenance of as complete a dossier as was practicable on all inhabitants in Republican areas. The military strategists referred to this as 'contact information'.[22] The principal methods involved interrogation in depth, frequent arrest for screening, regular house searches and head counts.

Internment provided the first opportunity for interrogation in depth to be used by the army. A group of internees were selected and interrogated in depth using a selection of techniques based upon the psychology of sensory deprivation.[23] The impact and effect of these techniques were considerable.[24] While subsequently there was a committee of enquiry set up under the chairpersonship of Sir Edmund Compton to consider the allegations of torture and brutality during interrogation, the principal issue as to who authorized the techniques was never investigated.[25] As it was, the Compton Committee produced a most unsatisfactory conclusion that while the techniques used did constitute physical ill-treatment they did not amount to brutality. A further inquiry was later established under the chairpersonship of Lord Parker to consider whether interrogation in depth should be permitted to be continued.[26]

In the meantime, the Irish Republic filed an application before the European Commission of Human Rights. The case eventually went to the European Court where it was held that the techniques, contrary to the findings of the European Commission, did not constitute a practice of torture but of inhuman and degrading treatment.[27] The British government undertook that the techniques would never be reintroduced. The government subsequently paid out £188,250 in damages to the persons involved.

The other methods of army intelligence-gathering included the use of foot patrols to build up a detailed picture of the area and its inhabitants, house searches, and frequent arrests for questioning. While these methods were used extensively under the Special Powers Act, their use was increased after the introduction of the recommendations of the Diplock Commission in the Northern Ireland (Emergency Provisions) Act.

No figures are available on the number of people stopped and questioned on the street. Nor are any figures available on the number of persons arrested and detained up to 4 hours. But it is known that these methods were used very widely. On occasion large-scale arrest operations were initiated and people arrested at random for apparently no other reason other than to collect more information on the local-community.[28]

Figures are, however, available for the number of house searches and these provide some indication of the extent of the army's intelligence-gathering operations and how they expanded over the period after the introduction of the Northern Ireland (Emergency Provisions) Act. In 1971, there were 17,262 house searches. By 1973, this had risen to 75,000, one-fifth of all houses in Northern Ireland.[29]

Many of the intelligence-gathering activities carried out by the army were of dubious legality. It is very doubtful whether large-scale house searches or the extensive screening was justified under the Act.

In 1974, the powers of arrest and detention were extended still further under the Prevention of Terrorism Act. This was introduced for the whole of the United Kingdom in the wake of the Birmingham bombings. It provided the power of arrest upon reasonable suspicion and 48 hours' detention in the first instance, which could be extended by up to a further 5 days by the Secretary of State. In practice, this was another form of executive detention, admittedly for only a 3-day period.[30]

As the conflict between the army and the IRA intensified the army resorted to a variety of other techniques in order to attempt to defeat the IRA. There is considerable evidence to suggest that the army used *agents provocateurs*, a variety of undercover techniques and assassination squads.[31] In addition, it developed new technologies. These included new methods of crowd control, new surveillance apparatus and the computerization of all its intelligence information.[32]

The RUC during this period took a subordinate role. It was largely excluded from policing the main Catholic areas. There was thus a very clear difference in the deployment patterns of the security forces, with the police mainly controlling Protestant areas where they used an approach closer to the traditional police approach and the army operating principally in Republican areas where it used the methods described above. This differential deployment served only to alienate further the Catholic community.

One response of the RUC to the crisis of confidence within the Catholic community was to concentrate on developing community relations work. A community relations branch was established in October 1970 and the chief inspector in charge of the branch was dispatched to London to study the methods used by the Metropolitan Police in both youth and community relations. The branch worked mainly with young people organizing discos, rambles, adventure holidays and football matches. In addition, the RUC has made strenuous efforts to establish working relationships with all the local politicians.

From a broader perspective, it can be seen that the strategy in this period had three dominant features. In the first place, the strategy openly acknowledged the political dimensions of the struggle. Detainees were treated like 'prisoners of war' and the politics of those convicted in the courts was recognized in the granting of 'special category status'. Secondly, the strategy gave the army considerable autonomy. There was little attempt to control its operations and practices, many of which were of dubious legality. The third feature of the strategy was the extensive use which was made of judges. They were not only used to provide a veneer of respectability to detention, but were also used to chair inquiries. Up to the end of 1975 seven inquiries had been chaired by judges. These were of two types. On the one hand, there were those which investigated some controversial incident or event, such as a Bloody Sunday. On the other, there were those which reviewed the appropriateness of particular policies, for example the Diplock Commission's review of the 'legal procedures to deal with terrorist activities'. The role of judges in part stemmed from the nature of the investigations, but it also reflected the extent to which the authorities hoped to diffuse a difficult political situation or to distance themselves from recommendations which were likely to be controversial. As Harvey has pointed out:

> The fiction of the doctrine of the constitutional separation of power has never been more clearly exposed than by these attempts to assure the public that British judges can provide solutions to the political problems of Northern Ireland.[33]

1975–1982: Reconstituting the Problem of Political Violence

Following the Labour government's victory in 1974, it began to reconsider the strategy of dealing with violence in Northern Ireland. It subsequently initiated a totally different strategy. The central aim was to deny totally the political dimensions of the conflict and to reconstitute the problem in terms of law and order. To this end, the government initiated three related policies. First, it began to restore full responsibility for law and order to the RUC. This policy has since been described as Ulsterization. Second, it stopped the use of internment in February 1975 and began to rely upon the courts as the sole method of dealing with those suspected of violence. Third, it announced that special category status would be withdrawn for any prisoner sentenced for crimes commited after 1 March 1976. The latter two policies have been widely referred to as a policy of criminalization.

Ulsterization

The first indication of the Ulsterization policy came in April 1974 when the new Secretary of State for Northern Ireland, Merlyn Rees, announced that he intended to restore 'the full responsibility of law and order to the police'. Later in the year he announced a five-point plan for the further extension of policing. The plan consisted of setting up a series of new local police centres in selected communities to act as focal points for policing. They were to be mainly staffed by RUC reserves working in their own areas.

The impact of the policy of Ulsterization can be best illustrated by considering the numbers in the security forces. In 1973, there were 31,000 security personnel of whom 14,500 were in the UDR, RUC and RUC Reserve. In 1986, the total numbers were roughly similar, but the numbers in the UDR, RUC and RUC Reserve had expanded to 19,500. As the vast majority of personnel in these forces are Protestant, one effect of the policy of Ulsterization has been to replace British security personnel by Ulster Protestants. The policy of Ulsterization has also been characterized by an expansion in the weaponry for the force. The RUC is now armed with pistols and Sterling sub-machine-guns, MI carbines and SLRs. In this respect, the RUC has therefore returned to being a military force rather than the civilian force which the Hunt Committee had recommended.

Perhaps the most important development since the start of the Ulsterization policy has been the strengthening of the intelligence capacity of the RUC. This has taken a number of different forms: an expansion in the number of confidential telephones, the use of police informers and various surveillance techniques and the use of arrest and detention powers to interrogate at length all those whom the police consider may provide them with information. The use of these powers for interrogation has been a major feature of the strategy and it appears that the widespread screening and trawling which the army carried out in the previous period is now being carried out by the RUC.

The police, as has been noted, have very extensive powers of arrest and detention under the Northern Ireland (Emergency Provisions) Act and the Prevention of Terrorism Act. In addition, they have ordinary powers of arrest under the criminal law. The most frequently used power is Section 11 of the Northern Ireland (Emergency Provisions) Act which allows the police to arrest anyone they suspect of being a terrorist. The use of this power is not surprising as this power is broadest in scope in terms of the degree of suspicion required and allows detention for a longer period than all the other provisions except the 7-day power under the Prevention of Terrorism Act. The almost exclusive use of Section 11 rather than ordinary powers of arrest illustrates very clearly the way in which emergency powers become the norm. More importantly, the effect of mainly using this particular power has been to shift the basis of arrest from suspicion of a particular act to suspicion of the status of the individual.[34]

No figures are regularly published for the number of arrests and prosecutions under the Northern Ireland (Emergency Provisions) Act in contrast to the practice for arrests under the Prevention of Terrorism Act. However, two sets of arrest figures have been published which illustrate not only the extent to which arrest and detention powers are used only for intelligence-gathering, but also how the practice is on the increase.

The Bennett Committee[35] noted that 2,970 persons were arrested under the Northern Ireland (Emergency Provisions) Act and Prevention of

Terrorism Act and detained for more than 4 hours between 1 September 1977 and 31 August 1978. But only 35% were subsequently charged with an offence. In other words, over 1,900 people were arrested, interrogated and subsequently released. The other set of arrest figures was published in reply to a parliamentary question in Hansard on 7 December.[36] These figures show that between 1 January and 30 October 1980, 3,868 persons were arrested under the Northern Ireland (Emergency Provisions) Act and Prevention of Terrorism Act and detained for more than 4 hours. Yet only 11% were charged. When the actual numbers of persons arrested, interrogated and released are compared and adjusted so that the figures refer to periods of the same length, they show that the number of persons involved more than doubled from 1,900 in 1978 to 4,131 in 1980.

Even those who were subsequently charged are often extensively questioned about 'other matters' not associated with the offence in question. In the most recent survey of the Diplock Courts it was found that in over 80% of all cases the suspect made a confession within the first 6 hours of detention. Yet the vast majority of these people were interrogated for substantial periods after the confession.[37]

The evidence is therefore unequivocal. The powers of arrest and interrogation are being primarily used by the police to collect information on individuals and communities rather than to charge and prosecute. Policing in Northern Ireland has therefore moved from a retroactive form, where those suspected of illegal activities are arrested and processed through the courts on evidence obtained after the event, to a pre-emptive form, where large sections of those communities which are perceived as being a distinct threat to the existing status quo are regularly and systematically monitored and surveilled.

Monitoring and surveillance of problem groups is being extended in other directions. In January 1979, a committee was set up under the chairpersonship of Sir Harold Black to review legislation and services relating to the care and treatment of children and young persons. It recommended a comprehensive and integrated approach to provide help for children, emphasizing the important roles of the family, school and community.[38] More specifically, it proposed a dual system of co-ordinating teams in schools and at district level. The school-based care teams are to be made up of the appropriate counsellor, the education welfare officer, the educational psychologist, the social worker familiar with the catchment area, as well as representatives from the police and probation service. At the district level, it was suggested that representatives of statutory agencies concerned with the interests of children should meet together to discuss the best policies to deal with identified problems. In December 1979, the government endorsed the strategy proposed by the report and accepted its recommendations in principle.

The report appears to be remarkably progressive. It begins with an analysis of the social and economic problems of Northern Ireland. Throughout, it emphasizes that the needs of children are paramount. Furthermore, it argues that it is imperative to avoid as far as possible segregating children from their families, schools and communities, or labelling them as deviant, abnormal, troublesome or delinquent. The report, however, is totally uncritical of its own assumptions. In particular, it assumes that the task of identifying children in need is unproblematic and that professionals and parents will agree. But how many working-class parents in West or East Belfast would view 'the lack of attainment at school, apathy, persistent behaviour, truancy, or involvement in delinquent or criminal activity' as 'the outward manifestation of complex, personal or family problems'[39] rather than the result of their children's position in the broader cultural and political environment in which they are brought up?

If the strategy of a co-ordinated approach through school-based and district care teams is implemented in full, it will extend the monitoring and surveillance of particular populations. It is clear from the report that this is the principal aim of the approach. It states:

> There should be a free exchange of information among the agencies involved in the multi-disciplinary team. Problems manifesting themselves in the school, in the home or in the community, whether they first come to the attention of the education authorities, the social services or the police should be referred to the School-based Care Team for discussion and consideration of what help, if any, each of the agencies might provide for the child and his family to help solve the problem.[40]

The more efficient control of particular populations has been attempted at other levels. There is now some evidence to suggest that both the RUC and the army are playing a significant role in the physical planning of Belfast. An article in the *Guardian* in 1982[41] claimed that the Belfast Development Office, to which the Housing Executive forwards all its proposed building plans for clearance, has representatives from the security forces. It was also suggested that the security forces has interfered with a number of planning decisions: they had insisted that a group of houses were removed from a planned development in the Ardoyne; asked for reinforced pavements in the new Poleglass estate to bear the weight of armoured vehicles; and recommended high 'security walls' in new developments in the Lower Falls and at Roden Street in West Belfast.[42]

Other sources have argued that the involvement of the security forces has been more extensive. It is claimed that new housing estates have been built with only two entrances and that factories, warehousing and motorways have been deliberately constructed to form barriers. The aim of these developments, it is suggested, is to prevent residents in Catholic areas from moving from one part of the city to another through safe areas and to force people out on to the main roads, which are more easily policed. If all these developments have occurred then the authorities would appear to be making strenuous attempts to confine the problem of violence within particular areas. In other words, they seem to be deliberately creating ghettoes in which dissident populations may be easily contained.

The role of the army in the period from 1975 has changed considerably. Its method of intelligence-gathering has altered substantially with the rise of the RUC's work in this respect. There has been a very sharp decline in the number of houses searched by the army and the large-scale screening operations have been curtailed. However, there is evidence to suggest that the army still carries out undercover and substantial surveillance operations. In addition, the army is responsible for all the bomb disposal work.

The strategy of Ulsterization has not been without its problems. The army has resented the curtailment of its operations and has developed its own strategies on occasions to deal with those involved in political violence. In a series of incidents, a number of alleged terrorists have been shot dead. While the strains between the RUC and the army have been in existence for a long time, they appear to have deteriorated since the RUC took the dominant role. In August 1979 following the assassination of Lord Mountbatten and the killing of 18 soldiers at Warrenpoint, the Prime Minister visited Ulster and was told that the strategy of Ulsterization had failed and that the army should once again take the dominant role. A few weeks later Sir Morris Oldfield was appointed as Security Co-ordinator. The appointment clearly was an attempt to deal with the differences of approach between the two forces.

The Diplock Court Process

The strategy of relying upon the courts was made possible by the radical modifications in the ordinary criminal process which the Diplock Commission recommended in 1972 and which were enacted in the Emergency Provisions (Northern Ireland) Act 1973. These changes, how-ever, did not become significant until the courts were relied upon as a sole method of dealing with those involved in political violence from the end of 1975 onwards.

It was abundantly clear from the Diplock Commission's report that interrogation was considered to be an essential element for the successful prosecution and conviction of those involved. The commission was critical of what it described as 'technical rules and practice' concerning the admissibility of statements. It drew attention to the 'considerable rigidity' with which the judges' rules had been interpreted in Northern Ireland. It noted a decision of the Court of Appeal in which it had been ruled that the mere creation by the authorities of any 'set-up which makes it more likely that those who did not wish to speak will eventually do so' renders any confession involuntary and inadmissible. It clearly disagreed with judge-ments such as these and it pointed out the whole technique of skilled interrogation is to build up an atmosphere in which the 'initial desire to remain silent is replaced by an urge to confide in the questioner'.[43]

It recommended that all statements in breach of the common law should be admitted provided that they could not be shown to have been produced by subjecting the accused to torture or to inhuman or degrading treatment. The recommendation was enacted in the Emergency Provisions (Northern

Ireland) Act 1973. The provision not only eliminated any retrospective control over the way interrogation was conducted but also legalized, in combination with the power to detain a person up to 72 hours under the Emergency Provisions Act or 7 days under the Prevention of Terrorism Act, prolonged interrogation.

The commission, however, was not only responsible for legalizing prolonged interrogation. In not supporting the Court of Appeal position concerning 'set-ups' which were designed to make it 'more likely that those who did not wish to speak will eventually do so', it gave the green light to the authorities to create special interrogation centres. Two were built, one at Castlereagh and the other at Gough Barracks, and were designed to create the most conducive environment for the interrogation process. Castlereagh was opened in early 1977 and Gough later in the same year.

The subsequent history of these centres is now well known.[44] From early 1977 the number of complaints against the police in respect of ill-treatment during interrogation began to increase. The Association of Forensic Medical Officers made representations to the police authority as early as April 1977. In November 1977 Amnesty International carried out an investigation and called for a public inquiry into the allegations.[45] The government, shortly after receiving Amnesty International's report, established the Bennett Committee, not however to investigate the allegations themselves but to consider police interrogation procedures. Notwithstanding its restrictive terms of reference the committee, however, did conclude that: 'Our own examination of medical evidence reveals cases in which injuries, whatever their precise cause, were not self-inflicted and were sustained in police custody.'[45]

Apart from the evidence of ill-treatment, the other aspect of the interrogation process which gave rise to concern during this period, and subsequently, has been the extent to which the outcome of the trial was in fact determined in the police interrogation centres. In an analysis of all cases dealt with in the Diplock Courts between January and April 1979, it was found that 86% of all defendants had made a confession.[47] Of these, 56% of prosecutions relied solely upon evidence of admission, and in another 30% this was supplemented by additional forensic or identification evidence which pointed to the guilt of the accused, although this additional evidence would often not have been sufficient to justify a conviction on its own. In a more recent study, a very similar pattern has been found.[48] What these figures show is the extent to which the forum for determining guilt or innocence is only very occasionally the courtroom.

The Bennett Committee made a large number of recommendations to prevent abuse of the suspect during interrogation. The most important of these was perhaps the recommendation that all interviews should be monitored by members of the uniformed branch on close-circuit televisions. Most of the Bennett Committee's proposals have now been implemented. It should be emphasized, however, that all the recommendations were designed to prevent physical abuse during interrogation. The safeguards do little to curtail the extreme psychological pressures which are at the heart of the interrogation process.

Since the introduction of the Bennett Committee's suggestions there have been far fewer complaints against the police in respect of ill-treatment during interrogation. It is however hard to ascertain whether this is simply due to Bennett. The underlying assumption was that the pressure to break rules and physically assault suspects stems from the individual policemen themselves. It was assumed that they are either over-zealous or in some circumstances deviant. A similar assumption can be found in the deliberations of the Royal Commission on Criminal Procedure.[49] It is a highly questionable assumption, however. There is a considerable body of evidence which suggests that the pressure on the police to break the rules does not stem from the personality characteristics of the policeman but is located within the organization of policing. The pressures generating physical assaults during questioning tend to be developed in response to the perceived seriousness of the problem and often decisions concerning particular responses are taken at a very high level. Taylor's analysis provides some support for this view. In a chart noting the number of complaints it is clear that there was a tendency for complaints to increase when political pressure was exerted on the police to produce results, as when there was some public outrage, for example, at the La Mon bombings. When there was public concern about police behaviour, complaints tended to decrease.[50]

Apart from the centrality of confessions to the effectiveness of the Diplock Courts, there are a number of other important features of the whole process. To begin with, the Diplock system handles a large proportion of offences which do not appear to be connected with Loyalist or Republican paramilitary activity or with sectarianism. It is estimated that 40% of all cases processed through the Diplock Courts have nothing to do with the Troubles.[51] In other words, a system which was widely regarded as a temporary measure to deal with the particular problems of political violence is now becoming the normal process for all offences.

A second feature of the Diplock Court system is the extent to which judges appear to have become case-hardened.[52] Since the introduction of juryless trials, the acquittal rate has been declining. There are a number of possible explanations for this. One widely stated explanation is that the prosecuting authorities are now taking greater care in the selection and preparation of cases. But when the trends for jury trials, for which the same prosecuting authorities have responsibility, are considered, no similar decline in the acquittal rate is observable. On the contrary, jury acquittals have been increasing. These very different trends provide strong support that the declining acquittal rate is principally a result of judges becoming case-hardened.

A third feature of the Diplock Court system is the extent of bargaining. This may occur in connection with either the charges, where the defence enters into negotiations to secure the withdrawal of the more serious charge or charges, or the plea, where the defendant pleads guilty to lesser charges in the expectation of a lower sentence in return for the subsequent saving of time and costs. No research has been carried out to ascertain the extent of plea bargaining, but Boyle, Hadden and Hillyard[53] in their study of the cases which were dealt with in the Diplock Courts between January and April 1979 found specific evidence of charge bargaining. In about 20% of all cases the prosecution withdrew or substituted a number of charges which were already on the indictment sheet and in which the defence pleaded to the remaining or substituted charge.

Charge and plea bargaining are, of course, features of other criminal justice systems. What is important about the phenomenon of bargaining in Northern Ireland is that the pressure to bargain is likely to be much more intensive than in other systems. The number and seriousness of cases in Northern Ireland are of a different magnitude and this will tend to place certain organizational demands upon the prosecuting and court authorities to encourage bargaining. In addition, the Bar in Northern Ireland is very small. The importance of this has been well expressed by Harvey:

> Defence lawyers, both solictors and barristers, are under their own pro-
> fessional, institutional and financial pressures to co-operate with the
> prosecuting authorities and avoid judicial disapproval. The smaller the bar the
> greater the pressure on its members to avoid a reputation for contesting cases
> with little likely chance of success.[54]

The study of the Diplock Courts in 1979 could not establish that any specific sentence had been reduced as a result of bargaining.[55] But what did emerge from the data was that the severest of sentences were imposed on defendants refusing to recognize the court, while the lowest sentences were imposed on those who pleaded guilty at the very start. In between were sentences on those who pleaded not guilty and seriously contested the case against them. The evidence suggests that the differential in terms of length and severity of sentences as between Loyalist and Republican defendants is not to be explained, as is often suggested[56] in terms of simple religious or political bias, but rather in terms of the defendant's choice whether to co-operate or not to co-operate with the system. This important point emphasizes the need to consider decision-making in this or any other criminal process not as a series of sequential phases which can be dealt with in isolation but rather as a process involving a complex series of interacting stages in which decisions taken cumulatively contribute to outcomes. Thus, the much discussed argument of whether judge or jury is superior for normal offences should not be conducted without emphasizing that decisions as to guilt or innocence are in fact an outcome of this complex bureaucratic process where the principles of criminal law and its procedure interact with the demands of the administration. The context in which judge or jury operates is much more important than whether the final decisions are left to judge and jury or solely to a judge.

The fourth feature of the Diplock Court system which needs to be mentioned is that a higher standard of proof appears to be required in the case of charges laid against the security forces than against civilians. The Bennett Committee[57] notes that, between 1972 and the end of 1978, 19 officers were prosecuted for alleged offences against prisoners in custody or during the course of interrogation. Of these, only 2 were convicted but the convictions were set aside on appeal. Another case was *nolle prosequi* and the rest were acquitted. The 1979 study of cases dealt with in the Diplock Courts between January and April 1979 found an acquittal rate of 100% for members of the security forces.[58]

Special Category Status

The other strand in the Labour government's criminalization policy was to phase out special category status. This, as has been noted above, was granted in 1972 to members of paramilitary organizations who had been convicted in the courts and who had claimed to have been politically motivated. The Gardiner Committee had considered that its introduction had been 'a serious mistake' and argued that it should be abolished.[59] One argument was that the compound system in which the special category prisoners were held made it more likely that prisoners would emerge with an increased commitment to terrorism. The other argument was that it could see no justification in granting privileges 'to a large number of criminals convicted of very serious crimes, in many cases, murder, merely because they claimed political motivation.'[60] The government concurred with these arguments and announced that no prisoner sentenced for crimes committed after 1 March 1976 could be granted special category status. In March 1980 it announced that this would apply to any prisoner charged after 1 April, 1980 for crimes wherever committed. In practice, this meant that all those convicted would be put into a conventional cellular prison and denied the special privileges which had been granted in 1972. To accommodate the prisoners the government built 800 cells in the form of an H, hence the H-Block protest, at the cost of £19,000 per cell.

There have been many previous struggles in British prisons over special or political status.[61] But the decision to phase out special category status in Northern Ireland was to lead to the longest ever collective struggle over this issue.[62] The protest started in September 1976, when Kieran Nugent was sentenced to the new cellular prison at the Maze. He refused to wear the prison clothes issued to him. The authorities reacted with considerable severity. He was kept in solitary confinement, denied exercise and all 'privileges', visits, letters, parcels. In addition, he lost a day's remission for every day of his protest. He was soon joined by other prisoners. The Blanket Protest, as it became known, as the prisoners had only blankets to wear, had begun. The protest soon escalated. In early 1978, after what appeared to be considerable intransigence by the authorities combined with a desire to make life as uncomfortable as possible for the prisoners, the prisoners extended the protest by smearing their cells with their own excreta. In 1980 the women in Armagh prison joined the dirty protest.[63] On 10 October

1980 it was announced that prisoners were starting a hunger strike on 27 October, four-and-a-half years after the initial protest had begun.

Hunger strikes have a long tradition in Irish history. They had been used in previous prison struggles and under early Irish Brehon law of the sixth and eighth centuries an offended person fasted on the doorstep of an offender to embarrass them into resolving the dispute. On 27 October, seven men went on hunger strike. This strike was called off on 18 December mainly because one of the seven was about to die and there was, at that time, a widely held view in the prison that the British government would make a number of important concessions. When the concessions were revealed, they failed to meet the prisoners' expectations. It was their understanding that they were to receive their own clothes and then be issued with civilian prison clothing. The British government statement, however, issued on 19 December announcing the concessions, reversed the sequence. Civilian prison clothing had to be accepted before the prisoners could be moved to clean cells.[64]

Inevitably, another hunger strike was organized but on this occasion it was decided that volunteers should begin their fasts at intervals. Sands was the first volunteer and began his hunger strike on 1 March 1981. He died on 5 May. Nine others died before the hunger strike was ended on 5 October 1981, after the government made a number of concessions. Prisoners were granted the right to wear their own clothes, and new facilities to improve association between prisoners were promised. In addition, a proportion of the loss of remission arising out of the protest was to be restored. In terms of penal reform, these concessions were trivial, but in the face of the government's intransigence over the five-and-a-half years of prison protest, they were considerable.

Throughout the length of the protest numerous attempts were made by various individuals and organizations to seek a solution to the problems. In 1978, a number of protesting prisoners initiated procedures before the European Commission of Human Rights. They claimed that the regime under which they lived amounted to inhuman and degrading treatment and punishment in breach of Article 3 of the European Convention. They also claimed that their right to freedom of conscience and belief under Article 9 of the Convention was denied to them because the prison authorities sought to apply to them the normal prison regimes. The British government's case was that the conditions were essentially self-inflicted and that the Convention afforded no preferential status for certain categories of prisoners.

In June 1980, the European Commission declared that the major part of the case was inadmissible. It concurred with the British government's view that these conditions were self-inflicted. It also agreed that the right to preferential status for certain category of prisoners was not guaranteed by the Convention. The commission, however, was critical of the authorities:

The Commission must express its concern at the inflexible approach of the

state authorities which has been concerned more to punish offenders against
prison discipline than to explore ways of resolving such a serious deadlock.
Furthermore, the Commission is of the view that for humanitarian reasons,
efforts should have been made by the authorities to ensure that the applicants
could avail of certain facilities such as taking regular exercise in the open air
and with some form of clothing [other than prison clothing] and making
greater use of the prison amenities under similar conditions.[65]

The decision, however, did nothing to end the protest. As the confrontation between the authorities and the protesting prisoners intensified,
Provisional Sinn Fein began a political campaign in support of the prisoners'
claim to political status. An H-Block information centre was established to
supply local and foreign journalists with information. The authorities on
their part increased their efforts to emphasize the criminality of the
activities of the IRA. They issued numerous press releases as well as glossy
brochures entitled 'H-Blocks: The Reality', 'Day to Day Life in Northern
Ireland Prisons', and 'H-Blocks: What the Papers Say'. In August 1981, they
began to issue 'fact files' on each of the hunger strikers. These included a
brief description of the activities leading to conviction and a montage of
selected newspaper reports on the case.

All these activities emphasized the extent to which the authorities were
prepared to go to maintain its policy of criminalization. They were largely
successful in convincing the British media of its case as almost without
exception all newspapers and the media accepted the government's
position.[66]

The policy of eliminating special category status, however, was fraught
with contradiction. To begin with, those involved in political violence are
dealt with in a very different way from the ordinary person who gets
involved in crime. They are arrested under emergency powers and
convicted in radically modified courts. Secondly, the motivations for their
activities are very different from those of 'ordinary' criminals. They carry
out their activities for deliberate political purposes. They do not regard
themselves as 'ordinary' criminals, nor are they seen as such by the
communities from which they are drawn. Neither does the law under which
they are convicted define them as 'ordinary' criminals. Most were arrested
under suspicion of being a 'terrorist'. 'Terrorism' is defined as 'the use of
violence for political ends'. As Tomlinson points out, 'they are considered as
political in the courtroom but criminal for the purposes of punishment.'[67]

Third, the abolition of special category status created the anomalous
situation in which hundreds of prisoners who had committed similar
offences, but at different times, were serving their sentences with special
category status in compounds in the very same prison.

Fourth, the penological justifications for the elimination of special
category status, namely that the compound system made it more likely that
prisoners would 'emerge with an increased commitment to terrorism', was
not supported by any empirical evidence. All the evidence which now exists
tends to support the opposite conclusion. The 1979 Diplock Court study

found that only 11% of all those who came before the courts had previous convictions for scheduled offences.[68] In other words, very few people who had been released from the Maze were subsequently reconvicted. Further support for the view that the compound system does not encourage 'terrorism' is presented in the only sociological study of the Maze, carried out by Crawford. He found that of a cohort of prisoners leaving the compound between 1976 and 1979 only 12% had been reconvicted for either political or non-political offences.[69]

Fifth, the claim that the prison system in Northern Ireland is the best in the world is only part of the truth. Certainly the facilities are better than most but the regime within the prisons, particularly the Maze, is repressive.

When the first hunger strike began, it received widespread support. There were huge demonstrations in Belfast and Dublin. In the North there were 1,205 demonstrations requiring 2½ million hours of police duty. The total cost of policing these parades and ensuring order was over £12 million.[70] During the period 100,000 rounds of rubber bullets were fired, 16,000 in one month alone. The hunger strikes and the authorities' response did more to unite Catholic opinion than any other single event since internment in 1971 or Bloody Sunday in 1972.

One very significant feature of the rioting and marches which took place during this time was the extent to which they were confined to the Catholic areas and away from the centres of Belfast and other towns. Any attempt to march to the Belfast city centre was strenuously resisted. The Troubles and the protests have now become ghettoized. The barriers across certain roads and the huge security gates on the roads leading out of the city centre to the Catholic areas are physical reminders of the extent to which this process has taken place. It shows how possible it is for the authorities to confine the problem of street violence to specific areas while life goes on 'normally' elsewhere.

The struggle which developed out of the authorities' attempt to deny the political nature of the conflict in order to curtail support for the para-militaries had considerable unintended consequences. Ironically the policy had the effect of depoliticizing the IRA campaign to the extent that it pushed the central aim of the IRA's struggle, its object of achieving Irish unity, into the background. But in its place it provided a powerful humanitarian issue around which to mobilize support. The H-Block issue to the Catholic community was yet another example of a long line of injustices which had been inflicted upon them by Unionist and British administrations.

1982–1986: Supergrasses and 'Shoot to Kill'

There were further radical changes in the security strategy at the end of 1981 and the beginning of 1982. First, the authorities began to rely extensively upon the use of supergrasses as the principal method of securing convictions. Second, there appears to have been a deliberate policy to 'shoot to kill'. Although the use of supergrasses has a long history in Ireland,[71] and there were at least four paramilitary supergrasses in the 10-year period before 1981,[72] the start of the supergrass policy began with the arrest of Christopher Black in November 1981. Just over a year later 38 people appeared on trial accused of 184 separate charges arising out of 45 alleged separate incidents and Black was the principal witness. Thirty-five were subsequently convicted mainly on the uncorroborated evidence of Black. Since then there have been other trials based on the evidence of supergrasses. Greer has calculated that between 1983 and the end of 1985 there were three loyalist and seven Republican supergrasses who were responsible for 223 people being charged with offences connected with paramilitary activities. Of these, 120 were subsequently convicted, over half on the uncorroborated evidence of the accomplice.[73]

The most obvious reason for the introduction of the supergrass policy was the public outcry and adverse publicity over the methods used by the police at Castlereagh and Gough interrogation centres. But other factors were also important. It is known that Sir John Hermon, who succeeded Sir Kenneth Newman as Chief Constable of the RUC in 1981, was very much opposed to rough treatment during interrogation and he certainly would have had an influence in developing the new policy. An equally important factor, however, was what may be called 'the European connection'. In 1978, following the kidnapping of Mr Aldo Moro, the Italian government introduced a new measure which provided for a substantial reduction in the punishment where accomplices dissociate themselves from others and endeavour to release the victim. Subsequent legislation extended the notion of dissociation and collaboration still further. The British authorities would have been aware of these developments through the regular meetings of the Ministers of Justice under the auspices of the Council of Europe and it is probable that the success of the measures in dealing with political violence in Italy influenced the development of the supergrass strategy in Northern Ireland.

Two particular points add support to this contention. First, at the heart of the Italian legislation was the notion of the 'repentant' terrorist and Sir John Hermon used a similar term 'converted' terrorist to refer to a supergrass.[74] Second, only a year after the introduction of the supergrass policy in Northern Ireland in 1982, the Ministers of Justice held a meeting at which it was proposed that the Italian strategy should be adopted by all European countries.[75]

The opposition to the supergrass system has been considerable. It has been opposed by both Republican and Loyalist communities, large sections of the legal profession, civil liberty organizations and various other groups. The criticisms have covered all aspects of the system: the methods of recruitment, the type of people recruited, the extensive preparation of the supergrasses for trial, the inducements and offers of a new life elsewhere and, above all, the preparedness of the judiciary to accept the uncorroborated evidence of supergrasses even in the face of credible alibis – on one occasion the judge described the evidence as 'contradictory and bizarre and in some respects incredible', yet he still convicted on the basis of it.[76]

The apparent 'shoot-to-kill' policy of the RUC emerged at about the same time as the supergrass system. In 1980 the RUC set up a Special Branch unit called E4A with about 30 to 40 members. It is intended as a deep surveillance unit and is apparently trained by the Special Air Services unit of the army. The emphasis in training is upon, as a senior RUC officer has expressed it, 'firepower, speed and aggression'.[77] Sometime a little later the RUC established a number of Headquarter Mobile Support Units (HQMSUs). These are composed of 30 members, split into quick-reaction squads under a sergeant, and each unit having its own small surveillance team. It is thought that there are now 12 such units and all of them are trained under simulated fire and in tactics which abandon the concept of minimum force.

Both units have been involved in a number of disputed killings and six of these, which occurred over a 5-week period in 1982, have now been investigated by the Stalker inquiry. This was begun in 1985 following widespread concern about the shootings and the failure of an internal RUC inquiry to satisfy the Director of Public Prosecutions in Northern Ireland, Sir Barry Shaw, who brought further pressure on the RUC. In the end, Sir John Hermon consulted the Chief Inspector of Constabulary for the North-west area of England whose responsibility also includes Northern Ireland. He in turn consulted the Chief Constable of Manchester and Mr Stalker was appointed to head an inquiry.

The killings which Mr Stalker investigated began in November 1982 when an E4A unit opened fire on a car, killing all three unarmed occupants.[78] Three RUC officers were brought to trial for the killings but were acquitted by the judge. In his remarks he said that he considered the three were absolutely blameless in the matter and he commended their courage and determination 'in bringing the three deceased men to justice, in this case, the final court of justice'.[79] These comments were widely condemned by elected representatives of the Nationalist community, the Irish government and many others. The case was significant in another respect. It was admitted that there had been an attempt to cover up the undercover nature of the operation and that the officers involved had told detectives who investigated the killings that they were on a normal RUC patrol.[80]

Two weeks later another person was shot dead in a hay shed. An HQMSU claimed it came across two men pointing rifles at them. It subsequently emerged that neither man had any paramilitary connections, the rifles found in the shed were more than 50 years old and had no firing bolts and, most significantly, the hay shed had been staked out for a number of days. At the trial of the survivor, who was charged with possession, it was revealed that officers had lied in statements.[81]

The third incident took place a few weeks later when two members of the illegal Irish National Liberation Army were stopped by an unmarked police surveillance vehicle from an HQMSU. A police officer went to the passenger side of the car and shot dead one occupant and then went round the other side and shot dead the driver. Both men were unarmed. At the trial of the officer another attempted cover-up was revealed.[82]

Mr Stalker submitted an interim report to RUC Headquarters in September 1985 dealing mainly with the first killings. It is believed that the report was highly critical of the way the force was structured and operated and recommended several prosecutions including charges of conspiracy to pervert the course of justice and conspiracy to murder.[83] In May 1985 Mr Stalker was removed from the investigation and suspended from duty while an investigation was conducted into a number of allegations against him, including allegations of his associations with known criminals.

His suspension received widespread press and media coverage and many aspects of his own personal life and the cases which he was investigating were widely reported. There were suggestions that his suspension was part of a broader conspiracy to undermine his work and prevent the public knowing about the way the covert security forces operated in Northern Ireland. Because of the blanket secrecy which surround the Special Branch and the secret services, the public are never likely to know whether there is any truth in these suggestions. But it is known that Mr Stalker had a difficult time with the RUC and it is reported that it was made clear to him that it had more than a passing interest in his personal life.[84] In addition, if prosecutions were brought for conspiracy to pervert the course of justice and conspiracy to murder, considerable details about the way a number of specialized forces — HQMSUs, E4As, the police Special Branch and army intelligence — operate, would be revealed.

It would not be the first time that some section within the state attempted to cover up the illegal activities of the security forces in Northern Ireland by attempting to discredit people involved in disclosure. In 1979 the *Daily Telegraph* was fed a story by a confidential source in Whitehall concerning Dr Irwin's wife shortly after he had appeared on LWT's *Weekend World* reporting that he had seen over a 3-year period between 150 and 160 people who had been injured by the police during interrogation. The paper was informed that his wife had been raped in 1976 and that he harboured a grudge against the RUC for failing to find the offender. The aim of the story was clearly to undermine the credibility of Dr Irwin's information and to question his motives.[85]

Whatever the outcome of the investigation now being conducted by the Chief Constable of West Yorkshire, the investigation into the shoot-to-kill policy has been irrevocably damaged. As Dr Ian Paisley has pointed out, the final report had to be coloured after the removal from duty, however temporary, of the principal author. According to Dr Paisley, there is no way natural justice can now be done.[86] It is also most unlikely that the public will ever be informed whether there was a shoot-to-kill policy from 1982 onwards.

In any event, it is clear that the law governing the use of deadly force is totally inadequate. It has been calculated that over 270 civilians have been killed by the security forces in Northern Ireland since 1969 and at least 155 of these were people with no known connection to paramilitary organizations or activities.[87] Included in the total are 13 deaths caused by plastic bullets. Overall, little or no attempt has been made by the authorities to curb these deaths and the attitude of some judges amounts virtually to the endorsement of martial laws.[88]

The Anglo-Irish Agreement and beyond

In November 1985 the British and Irish governments signed the Anglo-Irish Agreement. It was a product of growing fears in the South of Ireland to the threat which the Provisional IRA and its political wing Sinn Fein, poses to the stability of the whole of Ireland. Pressure was put on the British government by the Irish government and the SDLP in the North to recognize this threat and to take some action to deal with the political impasse. How far it will assist in changing the form of law in Northern Ireland is a matter of some conjecture.

When it was first introduced it was argued that the agreement would be of benefit to both the Unionists, because it would lead to greater co-operation on security matters between the North and the South, and to Nationalists because it would lead eventually to the reform of the administration of justice. In practice the reality has been very different. There has certainly been greater co-operation on security matters between the two governments over border security. The most visible feature of this co-operation is a whole series of hill forts along the border. In addition the government in the Republic has now become a signature to the European Convention on the Suppression of Terrorism, which will now allow the extradition from the South to the North of those claiming political motivation for their activities.[89] But by the beginning of December 1986 no reforms had been announced by the government to the administration of justice in Northern Ireland. It was, however, widely rumoured that only slight modifications would be introduced and that the reforms would fall far short of a return to jury trial. In any event there are certainly no plans to deal with other aspects of the security system from which the Catholic community has suffered, such as the emphasis upon 'policing people', the normalization and bureaucratization of emergency legislation and the 'Protestant' character of the whole law enforcement process.

From a broader perspective the agreement is likely only to exacerbate the present situation in Northern Ireland. It has already united the many fractions within Unionism and led to considerable opposition shown in mass marches, rallies, withdrawal from local government, organized campaigns of intimidation against the RUC and RUC Reserve and sectarian attacks on Catholics. The present situation has much in common with that which gave rise to the establishment of the Northern Ireland state itself. Once again the unique combination of British involvement and indigenous class forces in Northern Ireland has produced a unified Protestant bloc which cuts across class lines and whose attitude to the rule of law is highly conditional. At the same time the British government through its policies of Ulsterization has created a local security force which is solidly Protestant and extensively armed.

The difficulties of confronting the Unionist opposition head-on are obvious. The authorities would be forced to use the same sorts of methods and strategies which they have used for years against the Catholic community. Moreover, the policing would have to be carried out by the almost exclusively Protestant security forces. The possibility of mutiny by some sections must be very real. The most likely policy is to back-pedal on the agreement particularly in relation to any reforms of the more overtly repressive apparatus. Although the cost of having to deal with years of internal political dissent is high, as yet it is not an electoral issue in Great Britain. In the meantime, the methods and strategies for dealing with the high level of political violence in Northern Ireland are increasingly being introduced into policing and the administration of justice in the rest of the United Kingdom.

Policing Northern Ireland and Policing Britain

At the outset, two points need to be emphasized to avoid misunderstanding. First, it is not being argued that the developments have been identical, only that there are many similarities despite the cast differences in the context in which the law and order policies and practices are being pursued. Second, it is not being suggested that Northern Ireland has been used as some sort of social laboratory for testing various styles and methods of policing dissent and dealing with political violence. Such a view implies that there has been some deliberate policy to experiment using Ireland as the laboratory. On the contrary, the explanation for the incorporation of many of the policies and practices developed in Northern Ireland is less sinister but perhaps more insidious. It has occurred mainly by default principally because those responsible for developing policies in Northern Ireland have been the people who have also had responsibility for developing the same policies in Britain. For any real understanding of the impact that Northern Ireland is having on British domestic policies it is essential to study the careers of the personnel who have been involved. There has been a constant interchange between all sections of the Civil Service in Britain and Northern Ireland, but particularly between the Northern Ireland Office, the Home Office and the Ministry of Defence. The police in Northern Ireland and Britain have also had a close relationship. Senior offices have visited Northern Ireland and studied policing tactics at first hand and many officers from the RUC have attended courses in England. Of particular importance, Sir Kenneth Newman, the present Commissioner of the Metropolitan Police, spent over 8 years in Northern Ireland, first a Deputy Chief Constable and then as Chief Constable.

The first and most important area of similarity has been in the *form* of policing. There are two dimensions to this. First, the British police, like their North of Ireland contemporaries have become increasingly militarized both in thinking and in practice. While there are still important differences between the two, for example the RUC is permanently armed and the British police are armed only occasionally or for special duties, nevertheless there are other important similarities. British police forces now have at their disposal extensive armouries which not only include lethal weapons ranging from pistols to sub-machine-guns but many forces now possess guns to fire plastic bullets and CS gas – two crowd-control weapons which have been used extensively in Northern Ireland. Much of the equipment – flak jackets, steel helmets and plastic visors, leg-guards, plastic shields and batons – which is now available to police in England and Wales is similar to that used for many years in Northern Ireland. In 1986 the Metropolitan Police took its militarization still further and ordered a number of armour-plated Land Rovers, similar to the ones used by the RUC.

Increasingly, British police forces are adopting military styles of policing. As early as 1972 Sir Robert Mark had his 200-strong SPG trained in methods used by the RUC, including the snatch-squad method of making arrests, flying wedges to break up crowds and random stop-and-search and road-block techniques.[90] The 1984–85 coal dispute provided the majority of police forces in Britain with the opportunity to develop military methods of policing. Every weekday morning the police organized what amounted to a military campaign against the striking miners. Every day huge convoys of police Transit vans, horse-boxes, smaller vans with dogs and their handlers, and Land Rovers with arc-lights moved into position to confront the pickets. Police tactics ranging from the extensive use of road-blocks to the specific methods of crowd control clearly owed much to the experiences of policing in Northern Ireland. All the police documents which have become available since the strike reflect military thinking and tactics. They talk of targets, drawing fire, missiles and decoys.

This military style of policing was not some aberration during the coal dispute. As in Northern Ireland, it is now the dominant style of policing and is visible almost daily from policing inner-city incidents to industrial disputes. It also characterized the policing of the Peace Convoy travellers in the West Country during the summers of 1985 and 1986.[91]

The other dimension concerning the *form* of policing which has parallels to Northern Ireland has been the way in which the focus of police work has increasingly been upon policing people rather than policing crime. It has been shown earlier how since the foundation of the Northern Ireland state the principal concern of authorities has been to police, in the broadest meaning of the term, the Nationalist population. Since 1969 this has involved a number of strands: the gathering of intelligence, monitoring and control of people in and out of Nationalist areas and the incorporation of other agencies in what has been called multi-agency policing. In Britain a similar emphasis on policing people has been emerging in recent years, particularly in relation to the black community. But it is not only the black community; many different sections of the population ranging from those who take part in industrial disputes to the travellers have been treated as suspect and subjected to surveillance and techniques of control, many of which are of dubious legality.

The second area in which the Northern Ireland experience appears to be having an impact in Britain is in relation to the organization of policing. From the setting-up of the state in Northern Ireland the police have been organized as a centralized national force. While the tradition in Britain has long been for local police forces, recent developments have been steadily eroding this principle. Two factors have been important in these developments: first the introduction of the police national computer supplying a service to all police forces and, second, the common practice of police forces supplying 'mutual aid', which is increasingly becoming centralized through the use of the National Reporting Centre. The use and operation of the centre was particularly visible during the coal dispute and illustrated the ease with which the police in England and Wales could be nationally co-ordinated.

The third area in which there are similarities between Northern Ireland and Britain has been in relation to the form of the criminal justice system. The radical changes made to the administration of justice in Northern Ireland in the early 1970s involved four components: the vast expansion of the police powers of arrest, search and detention; fundamental changes in the rules of evidence particularly in the admissibility rule; the abolition of trial by jury; and the introduction of a public prosecutor system.

Many similar changes have now been introduced into England and Wales. The Police and Criminal Evidence Act 1984 (PACE) increases the powers of arrest and search and allows a person to be detained for up to 4 days. This period goes beyond the 3 days allowed under the emergency legislation in Northern Ireland. PACE also changed the rules of evidence concerning the admissibility of evidence. Although it does not go as far as the emergency legislation in Northern Ireland which allows all statements to be admitted in court provided that they were not produced as a result of degrading or inhuman treatment or torture, nevertheless, as in Northern Ireland, the old voluntary rule that a statement can only be admitted provided that it was obtained voluntarily, has been replaced by a less stringent rule, reducing the amount of control which the court may exert over police interrogation practices. Trial by jury has not yet been abolished in England and Wales. However, it has been under threat. There have been a number of changes which have restricted the range of cases which may go for trial and the number of challenges the defence may make has altered. In addition, there have been examples of the authorities vetting the jury before important trials.[92] Finally, the introduction of a public prosecutor system in 1985 adds further support to the view that the form of the British criminal system has increasingly become similar to the form introduced into Northern Ireland in the early 1970s.

Conclusions

From a broader perspective a number of points may be stressed about the characteristics of law and order strategies and policies adopted in Northern Ireland and similarities between developments there and in Great Britain. The first point to note is the extent to which emergency laws in all parts of the United Kingdom have become normalized. The 1973 Northern Ireland (Emergency Provisions) Act, with only minor amendments, is still on the statute book. Similarly the Prevention of Terrorism Act, initially described as a temporary provision, has been extended to deal with all types of political violence, not only that connected with Ireland. The normalization, however, goes beyond the mere continuation of exceptional measures: it is now treated as permanent and all discussions of ordinary legislation assume that the exceptional measures will continue. At the same time, the exceptional measures are increasingly used in circumstances for which they were never intended. In Northern Ireland powers under the Northern Ireland (Temporary Provisions) Act are used to arrest people involved in 'non-political' crime.

The second feature of the use of the strategies in Northern Ireland has been the scant respect paid to the notion of the rule of law. Throughout all the strategies law has been used as 'an instrument of the state's security rather than justice'.[93] From the introduction of internment through to the supergrass and shoot-to-kill policies, the rule of law has been systematically abused. Legal arbitrariness has been a permanent characteristic.

The third feature has been the increased bureaucratization and professionalization of the response. Instead of a relatively informal system of the administration of the criminal law, there are a number of separate and relatively autonomous agencies with responsibilities for different aspects of the process, ranging from the police through to the judiciary. The decision about guilt or innocence is the product of a complex bureaucratic process where the principles of criminal law interact with the various demands of the separate administrative agencies which are themselves influenced by the broader political context in which the decisions are taken. The idea that the court is the forum for the determination of guilt or innocence bears little resemblance to the reality.

The fourth feature has been the decline in the power of the legislature in the development of law and order policies. The policies are increasingly being developed by the executive in conjunction with the higher echelons of the police and army. They are frequently helped in this task by judges who redefine traditional problems in technical and operational terms. Most of the strategies, as has been shown, have been developed through internal reviews. The public are never consulted and Members of Parliament are simply presented with the formulated policies. They have little or no impact on them. The role of key administrators appears to have been crucial and warrants further study.

Many of these features are also characteristic of the modern British state. Although neither the army nor a paramilitary police regularly patrol the streets, the movement towards a new form of repressive apparatus which shares much in common with that which was evolved in Northern Ireland at the beginning of the 1970s is unmistakable.

Despite the clear parallels and the obvious impact which Northern Ireland has had on developments in Britain, Northern Ireland has been largely ignored by British academics interested in issues of policing, criminal justice and the state. It appears to have been assumed that both the social divisions in Northern Ireland and the response to them are too complex and too exceptional to provide any lessons for the study of law and order in Great Britain. This is far from the case. Although the nature of the social divisions are certainly unique and have long roots stretching over a number of centuries, the study of policing in and the administration of justice in Northern Ireland adds much to any analysis of policing and administering justice in the context of any multiracial society.

An analysis of Northern Ireland throws a very different perspective on many of the current British ideas and debates. Would the new realist's[94] concept of a state in which it is considered possible to make the police accountable to a marginal section of the working class have survived if a rigorous examination of the police in Northern Ireland had been included in their analysis? Similarly, would the new realists have been so prepared to believe in the possibility of achieving radical reform under a Labour government if they had carefully analysed previous Labour governments' record on law and order in Northern Ireland? It was under a Labour administration that some of the worst abuses occurred and a Labour government was principally responsible for the Ulsterization and criminalization policies. Similarly, would the many recent analyses of the police in Britain have reached the same conclusions if an analysis of policing in Northern Ireland had been included?[95] While the answers can only be guessed, the problem of Northern Ireland is clearly crucial to an accurate conceptualization of contemporary issues in the rest of the UK.

The final point to make in conclusion is that it is wrong to see either Northern Ireland or Britain as exceptional in terms of their evolving repressive apparatus. Many other European countries are developing systems with very similar characteristics.[96] Poulantzas identified this trend as early as 1978 when he wrote:

> In western capitalist societies, the State is undergoing considerable modification. A new form of State is currently being imposed – we would have to be blind not to notice (and passion always blinds, even if it springs from the noblest of motives). For want of a better term, I shall refer to this state form as authoritarian statism. This will perhaps indicate the general direction of change: namely, intensified state control over every sphere of socio-economic life combined with radical decline of the institutions of political democracy and with draconian and multiform curtailment of so-called 'formal' liberties, whose reality is being discovered now that they are going overboard.[97]

Acknowledgements

This is an updated and extended version of a paper published in Darby, J. Northern Ireland. The Background to Conflict, Appletree Press, 1982. My thanks to John Darby for permission to reproduce parts of the original chapter.

I would also like to thank Margaret Ward for her comments and suggestions and to Fintan for providing occasional space and time to write.

Notes

1 Patrick Buckland, *The Factory of Grievances: Devolved Government in Northern Ireland 1921–1939*, Dublin, Gill & Macmillan, 1979, pp. 179–205.
2 M. Farrell, 'The establishment of the Ulster Constabulary', in A. Morgan and B. Purdie, *Ireland: Divided Nation Divided Class*, London, Irish Links, 1980, p. 126.
3 M. Farrell, *Arming the Protestants: the formation of the Ulster Special Constabulary 1920–27*, London, Pluto, 1983.
4 Farrell, 1980, op. cit. p. 127.
5 Farrell, 1980, op. cit. p. 134.
6 P. Bew, P. Gibbon and H. Patterson, *The State in Northern Ireland*, Manchester, Manchester University Press, 1979.
7 Cameron Commission, *Disturbances in Northern Ireland*, Cmd 532, Belfast, HMSO, 1969, pp. 62–3.
8 Hunt Committee, *Report of the Advisory Committee on Police in Northern Ireland*, Cmd 535, Belfast, HMSO, 1969.
9 MacDermott Working Party, *Report of the Working Party on Public Prosecutions*, Cmd 554, Belfast, HMSO, 1971.
10 K. Boyle, 'The Minimum Sentences Act', *Northern Ireland Legal Quarterly*, vol. 21, no. 4, 1970, pp. 425–41.
11 See L. O'Dowd, B. Rolston and B. Tomlinson, *Northern Ireland: Between Civil Rights and Civil War*, London, CSE Books, 1980; and D. Birrell and A. Murie, *Policy and Government in Northern Ireland: Lessons of Devolution*, Dublin, Gill & Macmillan, 1980.
12 S. O'Fearghail, *Law (?) and Orders: The Belfast Curfew of 3rd–5th July, 1970*, Belfast Central Citizens' Defence Committee, 1970.
13 F. Kitson, *Low Intensity Operations: Subversion, Insurgency and Peace-keeping*, London, Faber, 1971.
14 See, for example, J. McGuffin, *Internment*, Tralee, Co. Kerry, Anvil Press, 1973; and D. Faul and R. Murray, *Flames of Long Kesh*, Belfast, 1974.
15 Widgery Tribunal, *Report of the Tribunal Appointed to inquire into the events on Sunday 30 January 1972 which led to loss of life in connection with the procession in Londonderry on that day*, HC. 220, London, HMSO, 1972. For critical commentaries see S. Dash, *Justice Denied: A Challenge to Lord Widgery's Report on Bloody Sunday*, London, NCCL, 1972; and B.M.E. McMahon, 'The impaired asset: a legal commentary on the Report of the Widgery Tribunal'. *The Human Context*, vol. VI, no. 3, 1974, pp. 681–99.
16 K. Boyle, T. Hadden and P. Hillyard, *Law and the State: The Case of Northern Ireland*, London, Martin Robertson, 1975 pp. 58–77.
17 See, for example, D. Faul and F. Murray, *Whitelaw's Tribunals: Long Kesh Internment*

Camp, November 1972–January 1973, Dungannon, Co. Tyrone, 1973.

18 Gardiner Committee, *Report of a Committee to Consider, in the Context of Civil Liberties and Human Rights, Measures to Deal with Terrorism in Northern Ireland*, Cmnd 5847, London, 1975.

19 Diplock Commission, *Report of the Commission to Consider Legal Procedures to Deal with Terrorist Activities in Northern Ireland*, Cmnd 5185, London, HMSO, 1972.

20 Criminal Law Revision Committee, Eleventh Report, Cmnd 4991, London, HMSO, 1972.

21 F. Burton and P. Carlen, *Official Discourse*, London, Routledge & Kegan Paul, 1978.

22 F. Kitson, op. cit., p. 97.

23 See for details J. McGuffin, *The Guineapigs*, Harmondsworth, Middx, Penguin, 1974; Amnesty International, *Report of an Inquiry into Allegations of Ill-treatment in Northern Ireland*, London, Amnesty International, 1975; and D. Faul and R. Murray, *British Army and Special Branch RUC Brutalities*, December 1971–72, Cavan, 1972.

24 T. Shallice, 'The Ulster depth interrogation techniques', *Cognition*, vol. 1, no. 4, 1973.

25 Compton Committee, *Report of the Enquiry into Allegations against the Security Forces of Physical Brutality in Northern Ireland Arising out of Events on 9 August 1971*, Cmnd 4823, London, HMSO, 1971.

26 Parker Committee, *Report of the Committee of Privy Counsellors Appointed to Consider Authorised Procedures for the Interrogation of Persons Suspected of Terrorism*, Cmnd 4901, HMSO, 1972.

27 European Commission of Human Rights, *Ireland against the United Kingdom*, Application No 5310/71, Report of the Commission (adopted 25 January, 1976) Strasbourg, 1976.

28 K. Boyle, T. Hadden and P. Hillyard, op. cit. pp. 41–53.

29 Northern Ireland Information Office, Statistics on Security, 27 February, 1986.

30 C. Scorer, S. Spencer and P. Hewitt, *The New Prevention of Terrorism Act: The Case for Repeal*, London, NCCL, 1985.

31 See, for example, K. Lindsay, *The British Intelligence Service in Action*, Dundalk, Co. Louth, Dundrod, 1980; B. Brady, D. Faul and R. Murray, *British Army Terror Tactics*, West Belfast, September–October 1976, Dungannon, Co. Tyrone, 1977; and T. Geraghty, *Who Dares Wins: The Story of the SAS 1950–1980*, London, Fontana, 1980.

32 See C. Ackroyd, K. Margolis, J. Rosenhead and T. Shallice, *The Technology of Political Control*, Harmondsworth, Middx, Penguin, 1977; S. Wright 'An assessment of the new technologies of repression', in M. Hoefnagels (ed.), *Repression and Repressive Violence*, Amsterdam, Swets & Zeitlinger, 1977; and S. Wright, 'New police technologies: an exploration of the social implications and unforeseen impacts of some recent developments', *Journal of Peace Research*, vol. XV, no. 4, 1978, pp. 305–22.

33 R. Harvey, *Diplock and the Assault on Civil Liberties*, London, Haldane Society, 1981, p. 6.

34 P. Hillyard and K. Boyle, 'The Diplock Court strategy: some reflections on law and the politics of law', in *Power and Conflict*, M. Kelly, L. O'Dowd and J. Wickham (eds.), Dublin, Truroe Press, 1982, p. 8.

35 Bennett Committee, *Report of the Committee of Inquiry into Police Interrogation Procedures in Northern Ireland*, Cmnd 7497, London, HMSO, 1979.

36 Hansard, 7 December 1980.
37 D. Walsh, *The Use and Abuse of Emergency Legislation in Northern Ireland,* London, Cobden Trust, 1983, pp. 70–1.
38 Black Review Group, *Report of the Children and Young Persons Review Group,* Belfast, HMSO, 1979.
39 Ibid. p. 6.
40 Ibid. p. 9.
41 *The Guardian,* 13 March 1982.
42 D. Alcorn, 'Who Plans Belfast?', *Scope,* 52, 4–6, 1982.
43 Diplock Commission, op. cit. p. 30.
44 P. Taylor, *Beating the Terrorists? Interrogation in Omagh, Gough and Castlereagh,* Harmondsworth, Middx, Penguin, 1980.
45 Amnesty International, *Report of an Amnesty International Mission to Northern Ireland,* London, Amnesty International, 1978.
46 Bennett Committee, op. cit. p. 136.
47 K. Boyle, T. Hadden and P. Hillyard, *Ten Years on in Northern Ireland: The Legal Control of Political Violence,* London, Cobden Trust, 1980, p. 44.
48 D. Walsh, op. cit. p. 92.
49 P. Hillyard, 'From Belfast to Britain: The Royal Commission on Criminal Procedure', in *Law, Politics and Justice,* London, Routledge & Kegan Paul, 1981, pp. 86–7.
50 P. Taylor, op. cit. p. 323.
51 D. Walsh, op. cit. pp. 81–2.
52 K. Boyle, T. Hadden and P. Hillyard, 1980, op. cit. pp. 60–62.
53 Ibid. p. 72.
54 R. Harvey, op. cit. p. 32.
55 K. Boyle, T. Hadden and P. Hillyard, 1980, op. cit. p. 73.
56 Workers Research Unit, *The Law in Northern Ireland,* Bulletin No. 10, Belfast, 1982.
57 Bennett Committee, op. cit. p. 82.
58 K. Boyle, T. Hadden and P. Hillyard, op. cit. p. 79.
59 Gardiner Committee, op. cit. p. 34.
60 Ibid. p. 34.
61 L. Radzinowicz and R. Hood, 'The status of political prisoners in England: the struggle for recognition', *Virginia Law Review Association,* vol. 65, no. 8, 1979, pp. 1421–81.
62 T.P. Coogan, *On the Blanket: The H-Block Story,* Dublin, Ward River Press, 1980.
63 N. McCafferty, *The Armagh Women,* Dublin, Co-op Books, 1981.
64 V. Browne, 'H-Block crisis: courage, lies and confusion', Magill, August 1981.
65 European Commission on Human Rights, *McFeely v United Kingdom* Application No. 8317/78 (Partial Decision, adopted 15 May 1980), Strasbourg, 1980, p. 86.
66 See P. Hillyard, 'The media coverage of crime and justice in Northern Ireland', Cropwood Conference Paper, 1982; P. Elliott, 'Reporting Northern Ireland' in J. O'Halloran *et al.* (eds), *Ethnicity and the Media,* Paris, UNESCO, 1977; P. Schlesinger, G. Murdock and P. Elliot, *Televising 'Terrorism': Political Violence in Popular Culture,* London, Comedia, 1983; and Information on Ireland, *The British Media and Ireland,* London, Information on Ireland, 1980.
67 L. O'Dowd, B. Rolston and B. Tomlinson, op. cit. p. 193.
68 K. Boyle, T. Hadden and P. Hillyard, 1980, op. cit. p. 22.
69 C. Crawford *'Long Kesh: an alternative perspective',* MSc thesis, Cranfield Institute of

Technology, 1979.

70 Royal Ulster Constabulary, Chief Constable's Report, Belfast, RUC, Annual, 1982, p. xii.

71 See P. Hillyard and J. Percy-Smith, 'Converting terrorists: the use of super-grasses in Northern Ireland', *Journal of Law and Society*, 1984, 11; and P. Hillyard, 'Popular justice in Northern Ireland: continuities and change', in S. Spitzer and A. Scull (eds), *Research in Law, Deviance and Social Control, 7*, Greenwich, Conn., JAI Press, 1985, pp. 247–67.

72 S. Greer and T. Hadden, 'Supergrasses on trial', *New Society*, 24 November 1983.

73 Personal communication from Steven Greer.

74 Royal Ulster Constabulary, op. cit. p. xi.

75 P. Hillyard and J. Percy-Smith, op. cit. p. 342.

76 Ibid. p. 350.

77 K. Asmal, *Shoot to Kill: International Lawyers' Inquiry into the Lethal Use of Firearms by the Security Forces in Northern Ireland*, Dublin, Mercier Press, 1983, p. 41.

78 Ibid. p. 41.

79 Ibid. p. 41.

80 Ibid. p. 41.

81 *The Guardian*, 16 June 1986.

82 Asmal, op. cit. p. 81.

83 *The Guardian*, op. cit.

84 Ibid.

85 Taylor, op. cit. p. 319.

86 *The Guardian*, op. cit.

87 Asmal, op. cit. p. 87.

88 Ibid.

89 The Act ratifying the Convention was passed at the beginning of 1987 and its date of introduction was December 1987. For a full account of Irish extradition see M. Farrell, *Sheltering the Fugitive*, Dublin, Mercier Press, 1985.

90 T. Bunyan, 'The police against the people', *Race and Class*, vol. XXII, no. 2/3 1981/82, p. 165.

91 National Council for Civil Liberties, *Stonehenge*, London, NCCL, 1986.

92 See H. Harman and J. Griffith, *Justice Denied*, NCCL, 1979.

93 P.J. McCory, *Law and the Constitution: Present Discontents*, A Field Day Pamphlet, no. 12, Derry, 1986, p. 16.

94 For example, J. Lea and J. Young, *What Is to Be Done about Law and Order?* Harmondsworth, Middx, Penguin, 1984; and R. Kinsey, J. Lea and J. Young, *Losing the Fight against Crime*, Oxford, Basil Blackwell, 1986.

95 For example, R. Reiner, *The Politics of the Police*, Brighton, Wheatsheaf, 1985.

96 See European Group for the Study of Deviance and Social Control, The Expansion of European Prison systems, Working Paper No. 7, 1986.

97 N. Pulantzas, *State, Power and Socialism*, London, New Left Books, 1978, pp. 203–4.

Index

Figures in bold type indicate the main reference for each subject.